Adoption Law and Human Rights

In recent decades, there have been many changes to adoption law and practice, such as a sharp decline in the voluntary relinquishment of children, an increase in the number consigned to public care, and an abrupt decrease in those made available on an intercountry basis. Additionally, human rights are becoming more prominent, particularly in relation to issues such as: non-consensual adoption; the ethics of intercountry adoption; the eligibility of LGBT adopters; the impact of commercial surrogacy; and the sometimes conflicting rights of birth parents and adoptees when accessing agency birth records.

In this book, O'Halloran presents a comparative analysis of the interaction between adoption law and human rights in common law (England and the US), civil law (France and Germany) and Asiatic traditions (Japan and China), while also developing a matrix of legal functions to assist in identifying and analysing areas of tension between human rights and adoption.

This book is intended for a lawyer readership, whether professional, student or academic: researchers and postgraduate students in subjects such as social work, social policy and politics may also find it helpful.

Kerry O'Halloran is an academic with extensive adoption experience, due to having worked as both a social worker and a lawyer. He has also served for 11 years on a UK adoption panel, and has contributed quarterly for the past 17 years to the BAAF *Adoption & Fostering* journal.

Human Rights and International Law

Series Editor: Professor Surya P. Subedi, OBE, QC (Hon)

This series will explore human right law's place within the international legal order, offering much-needed interdisciplinary and global perspectives on human rights' increasingly central role in the development and implementation of international law and policy.

Human Rights and International Law is committed to providing critical and contextual accounts of human rights' relationship with international law theory and practice. To achieve this, volumes in the series will take a thematic approach that focuses on major debates in the field, looking at how human rights impacts on areas as diverse and divisive as security, terrorism, climate change, refugee law, migration, bioethics, natural resources and international trade.

Exploring the interaction, interrelationship and potential conflicts between human rights and other branches of international law, books in the series will address both historical development and contemporary contexts, before outlining the most urgent questions facing scholars and policy makers today

Available titles:

The Effectiveness of the UN Human Rights System
Reform and the Judicialisation of Human Rights
Surya P. Subedi

Socio-Economic Human Rights in Essential Public Services Provision
Marlies Hesselman, Antenor Hallo de Wolf and Brigit Toebes

Forthcoming titles:

The Right to Truth in International Law
Victims' Rights in Human Rights and International Criminal Law
Melanie Klinkner and Howard Davis

About the Series Editor
Professor Surya P. Subedi, OBE, QC (Hon) is Professor of International Law, University of Leeds, member of the Institut de Droit International and former UN Special Rapporteur for human rights in Cambodia.

https://www.routledge.com/Human-Rights-and-International-Law/book-series/HRIL

Adoption Law and Human Rights

International Perspectives

Kerry O'Halloran

Routledge
Taylor & Francis Group
LONDON AND NEW YORK

First published 2018
by Routledge

2 Park Square, Milton Park, Abingdon, Oxfordshire OX14 4RN
52 Vanderbilt Avenue, New York, NY 10017

Routledge is an imprint of the Taylor & Francis Group, an informa business

First issued in paperback 2019

British Library Cataloguing in Publication Data
A catalogue record for this book is available from the British Library

Library of Congress Cataloging in Publication Data
Names: O'Halloran, Kerry, author.
Title: Adoption law and human rights : international perspectives / Kerry O'Halloran.
Description: Abingdon, Oxon [UK] ; New York, NY : Routledge, 2018. | Series: Human rights and international law | Includes bibliographical references and index.
Identifiers: LCCN 2017052852 | ISBN 9781138121072 (hbk) | ISBN 9781317309550 (web pdf) | ISBN 9781317309543 (epub) | ISBN 9781317309536 (mobipocket)
Subjects: LCSH: Adoption--Law and legislation. | Intercountry adoption--Law and legislation. | Human rights. | European Court of Human Rights.
Classification: LCC K704 .O33 2018 | DDC 346.01/78--dc23
LC record available at https://lccn.loc.gov/2017052852

ISBN: 978-1-138-12107-2 (hbk)
ISBN: 978-0-367-89365-1 (pbk)

Typeset in Galliard
by Taylor & Francis Books

This is dedicated to Elizabeth with thanks for her patience during what has been, for her, a very stressful period.

Contents

Acknowledgements

This book necessarily overlaps to a degree with others completed during my 13-year tenure as Adjunct Professor at the Australian Centre for Philanthropy and Nonprofit Studies, QUT, Brisbane. I am thankful to the Centre for the support it has always provided and to the publishers concerned, particularly to Springer,[1] for their understanding in respect of any material that may have first seen life under their imprint.

Thanks are also due to those who offered comment on draft chapters. In particular, I greatly appreciate the very valuable helpful feedback received from: Julie Doughty[2] (England); Jean-François Mignot[3] (France); Andreas Botthof[4] (Germany); Anne Estin[5] (the US); Margaret Ryznar[6] (China); and Satoshi Minamikata (Japan).[7]

It is a privilege to make this second contribution to the series *Human Rights and International Law*, edited by Professor Surya P. Subedi, and I am grateful to Routledge for the opportunity to do so. Responsibility for any mistakes, inconsistencies or other faults, as for all views expressed, must rest exclusively with me.

1 O'Halloran, K., *The Politics of Adoption* (3rd edn), Dordrecht, Springer, 2015.
2 Lecturer in law, Cardiff University, UK.
3 Faculty member, French National Centre for Scientific Research, GEMASS.
4 Judge (district court), Offenburg, Germany.
5 Professor of law, University of Iowa, US.
6 Associate Professor of law, Indiana University McKinney School of Law, US.
7 Professor of law, Faculty of Law, Niigata 950-218, Japan.

Introduction

There is now an unmistakable fault line, clearly discernible in adoption law, which rests on the right of the State to authorise the non-consensual adoption of children failed by parental care. Other factors, also emerging as indicators of change in international adoption law and practice, include: the plummeting rate of intercountry adoptions; the adoption of older children and of those with complex health and social care issues; its use as an adjunct to divorce proceedings and to surrogacy arrangements; the increasing numbers of LGBT adopters; the availability of State finance for adopters; post-adoption contact; and access to identifying information. These have become familiar if sometimes contested features of contemporary adoption in all countries. Others, however, are culture specific: some are long-standing, such as the adoption of adults in Japan for inheritance and tax purposes and the Islamic prohibition on adoption; while some are recent but quite singular, like the practice of 'rehoming' adopted children no longer wanted by their adopters in the US and the weight restrictions imposed by China on prospective adopters. In the twenty-first century, adoption is no longer – if it ever was – a purely private care arrangement undertaken by an altruistic but childless couple wishing to provide a loving home for a parentless child. The State now has a much greater say, domestically and internationally, in how and why adoption is used.

As the international human rights framework becomes steadily more refined and extensive, so its network of standards is tightening around adoption as it is around other fields of law and practice. While concern tends to naturally focus mostly on the more obviously endangered human rights of those children and birth parents caught up in the links between international adoption and trafficking or surrogacy arrangements, there is also good reason to be worried about human rights violations in a domestic context. The interface between the public child protection system and adoption is one such problematic area: particularly as public service cuts translate into less preventative family support services but more funding for childcare adopters. As the UN Committee on the Rights of the Child pointed out in its 2016 UK report, the State removal of children "from their biological families owing to the family's economic situation or because a foster family may provide a more beneficial environment for the child"[1] is to be deplored, not least because once in foster care the next step can be towards non-consensual adoption. This book examines these and the many other points at which international human rights and national adoption law intersect.

Human Rights and Adoption Law: International Perspectives consists of 11 chapters and loosely follows the format of its predecessor which dealt with charity law.

Part I deals with the background to the book, and consists of four chapters. Chapter 1: 'Human Rights and the Concepts, Principles and Social Construct of Adoption', deals with basic concepts, the legal definition of adoption and related human rights; Chapter 2: 'The Domestic Legal Framework', from a UK perspective, provides a historical overview of the developing relationship between adoption and human rights and identifies the key functions in each body of law; Chapter 3: 'The International Legal Framework and Intercountry Adoption', considers the social phenomenon of intercountry adoption and outlines the related international framework of treaties, conventions, protocols, etc. and the associated regulatory bodies; while Chapter 4: 'The Adoption Process, Human Rights and the ECtHR' essentially outlines each stage of the adoption process, identifies the interplay between legal function and human rights, as illustrated by reference to ECtHR case law.

Parts II–IV which together constitute the bulk of the book, deal with contemporary international perspectives. Parts II–IV, in six chapters, focus on contemporary law, policy and practice: in a common law context, viz. England and the US; in a civil law context, viz. France and Germany; and in an Asian context, viz. Japan and China. These jurisdiction-specific chapters closely follow the same format. Beginning with on overview of some human rights issues that have characterised the evolving law, policy and practice relating to adoption, each chapter then identifies the principles and significant statistical trends in modern adoption practice before outlining the contemporary legislative and regulatory frameworks. Each then examines the sequential stages of the domestic adoption process: the thresholds for entry; the hearing and the grounds for making an adoption order; and the thresholds for exiting. Each considers the effects of an adoption order on the parties concerned and ends with a brief summary of post-adoption information rights, tracing and reunification services. At each stage, the chapters identify and reflect upon the related human rights considerations.

Part V, the final part of the book, consists of Chapter 11, entitled 'Adoption and Human Rights: National Tensions and International Standards', and concludes the book by drawing material from Parts II–IV to examine current tensions in national adoption law and consider how they relate to specific international

1 UN Committee on the Rights of the Child, Concluding observations on the fifth periodic report of the United Kingdom of Great Britain and Northern Ireland (CRC/C/GBR/CO/5), 2016, para. 52(b).

human rights. It summarises and compares jurisdictional performance in relation to key human rights indicators at each stage of the adoption process and then considers whether jurisdictional differences align with a differentiation between common law, civil law and Asian law. It reflects on the significance of cultural context for human rights.

Part I

Background

1 Human rights and the concepts, principles and social construct of adoption

Introduction

This chapter begins by identifying those human rights that would seem to have a particular relevance for adoption. By way of a broad introduction it discusses the challenges and conflicts involved in the relationship between these two bodies of law. To that extent it prepares the ground for the more functional analysis that follows in Chapter 4. It then turns to focus on the social role of adoption and does so by tracing its genesis in the law, policy and practice of England. It considers the concept and its culture-specific determinants. It considers values and taboos, the 'blood link' and boundaries. It examines the purposes served by adoption: dealing with inheritance, kinship, welfare, step-parents and the needs of childless couples. It distinguishes adoption from other legally authorised forms of alternative parenting (e.g. guardianship and *kafala*): giving particular attention to the concept of 'permanency' and the relative merits of adoption or long-term foster care.

The chapter then explains and differentiates each of the three main types of modern adoption as experienced in England and elsewhere – family, childcare and intercountry. It identifies the different permutations that constitute each type, assesses their relative strengths and weaknesses, taking into account the related governing principles. It notes the extent to which adoption has, in England as in many other countries, become a discretionary adjunct to matrimonial and child-care proceedings. In particular, it considers childcare and intercountry adoptions (ICAs) and the controversies they generate.

Human rights and adoption

While many of the 30 rights enumerated in the Universal Declaration of Human Rights (UDHR) and endorsed by the United Nations General Assembly in 1948 have relevance for adoption, a few are of particular importance. This cluster of core rights has long since been amplified and added to by subsequent international treaties, conventions, protocols, etc. (see further Chapter 3) and extended by rulings of the European Court of Human Rights (ECtHR) (see Chapter 4). As is readily apparent, the list contains different groupings of rights and freedoms: some with implications for the adoption process and the legal system it operates within;

others with direct implications for the child concerned; others for the parties and countries involved; and finally some have a relevance for adoption outcomes.

The legal system and regulatory procedures

The UDHR provisions that seem most relevant in this context are those relating to: equality; legal protection, representation and access to a fair legal system; and to freedoms of association and assembly.

Independent forum

For the rights of the parties concerned to be protected, issues resolved and for an adoption application to be determined, an independent forum with powers to scrutinise all aspects of a proposed adoption, and with discretion to make an order other than the one sought, is a fundamental necessity. This requires that such a forum has access to the professional expertise needed to provide reports and assessments on the circumstances of all parties.

Representation

While equal representation for the parties involved in any legal proceedings is always at least desirable, it is arguably essential when such proceedings concern lifelong changes for a vulnerable child.

Due process

Again, a process designed to permanently and irrevocably change the legal status of the parties is one that requires clear and transparent grounds for initiating proceedings, for decision-making and for appeal. The procedures, grounds, rules governing participation, the orders that may be made and their effects must be statutorily stated and enforced.

Discretion and choice in decision-making

Adoption should never be a rubber-stamping administrative exercise. Unless the grounds for issuing an adoption order can be fully satisfied, and such an order would be in the best interests of the child concerned, then other disposal options must be available.

Adoption agencies

The right to freedom of association is as important in the context of adoption as in other fields. Independent adoption societies or agencies established to improve practice, advocate on behalf of the interests of the parties, raise issues and lobby for changes in legislation have historically played a significant role in developing the adoption process. The presence or absence of such organisations can be a revealing indicator of the prevailing policy governing State intervention in family affairs.

Circumstances giving rise to adoption

In this context the most relevant UDHR provisions are those relating to: life, security and freedom from inhuman treatment; protection for the mother and child relationship, whether marital or not; family life, an adequate standard of living, recreation and education; freedom of movement; and the freedoms of expression, religious belief and culture.

Welfare interests of the child

In circumstances where a child has been orphaned, abandoned or voluntarily relinquished, is a disaster victim, or has become the subject of grievous parental abuse or neglect – and no kinship care arrangements are possible – then it is readily apparent that adoption would be an appropriate means of ensuring life, security and freedom from inhuman treatment for that child. In all other circumstances, justification for adoption remains to be proven. Moreover, adoption cannot be viewed solely in an immediate time frame, it is important that it can be justified by projecting the welfare test into the future to show that it will continue to be satisfied on a lifelong basis.

Parental rights

Studies in developmental psychology show that, absent any untoward factors, the bonding relationship provided by a birth parent is an intrinsic element of the welfare interests of a child and affords the best means of safeguarding and promoting those interests. While the concept of 'parental rights' no longer has validity in law, having been displaced by 'parental responsibilities', it still requires a convincing weight of evidence to divest a parent of the rights/responsibilities inherent to that role and there is a presumption that a birth parent would be best placed to continue as holder of such rights/responsibilities following a divorce. Whether parenting arrangements have been disputed in public or private family law proceedings, there is also a presumption that if parental rights/responsibilities have to be transferred then it would be most conducive to facilitating the development of a child's identity if that transfer were conducted on a kinship basis.

State intervention

The grounds justifying State intervention, to exclusively and permanently transfer the care of a child from the birth parent/s to others, is a matter of crucial importance in any democratic society. Whether in the context of private family law or public childcare law, this issue is of profound significance for the human rights of all concerned.

Adoption outcomes

Following completion of an adoption process the most relevant UDHR rights are those that address the changed legal status of the parties involved, namely: the recognition due to an individual; to privacy; and the right to nationality.

Change to the legal status of the parties

The absolute, exclusive and permanent nature of adoption – and its wider and intergenerational implications for the families involved – means that if successful the outcome of proceedings have a very real and lasting significance. Essentially the importance of adoption lies in the fact that it alters the legal status of the parties relative to each other. Most importantly, it provides a legal framework within which the adoptee will have the opportunity to acquire a new identity with accompanying rights to citizenship and inheritance. The privacy rights of the parties involved may be safeguarded by laws regulating the disclosure of identifying information.

At the heart of adoption, and represented in the new legal arrangements that come into effect on the granting of an adoption order, is the right of a child to a family rather than any reverse right of a person or couple to a child. The adoption process – and this book – is basically about how the checks and balances in the laws of different jurisdictions, as measured against human rights indicators, play out amid the conflicts and complexities involved in ensuring that for the children concerned the prospect of family life with adopters is a justifiable alternative to family life with their birth parents. The above classification of human rights offers a guide for exploring such matters.

Adoption and cultural context

Adoption has been acclaimed as the chosen means of providing homes for children in need.[1] However, while this may have become one of its current social functions, it was acquired relatively recently.

In agricultural societies the modern problem of unwanted children did not seem to arise, as an extra pair of hands was always useful in societies tied to the land, but when society changed from being land based to industrial, wage earning and mobile, then the nuclear family unit became more independent and children often simply represented more mouths to feed. Abandoning children to the workhouse was the only option available to the many poverty-stricken parents who had not benefited from the Industrial Revolution and this was the fate of very many children. Neither in this society nor in others has adoption necessarily always related to the needs of children: in some societies, adults were the preferred adoptees; in others it was designed specifically to serve the interests of adults in need of children. The tension between altruism and self-interest has been a constant feature.

1 Houghton Committee, *Report of the Departmental Committee on the Adoption of* Children (Cmnd 5107), London, HMSO, 1972.

The reasons for recourse to adoption depend on the significance attached to 'family', which in turn have always been determined by cultural context, reflecting the nature of different societies and the changes in the same society over time.

Inheritance

Adoption has its legal origins in the law relating to the ownership and inheritance of property.[2] The concern of those with land but without children to legally acquire heirs and so consolidate and perpetuate their family's property rights for successive generations, is one which is common to all settled, organised or tribal societies. In China, India and Africa adoption has long served this purpose.[3] This function transferred in time to western societies to accommodate the inheritance of estates, other assets and social status.

Roman law

It was the tradition established over the several hundreds of years and throughout the extent of the Roman Empire which laid the European foundations for this social role. A Roman, for example, could adopt only if he did not have an heir, was aged at least 60 and the adopted was no longer a minor.[4] Heir adoption, therefore, owed its origins to an 'inheritance' motive and all other factors being favourable found early acknowledgment in law.

Community solidarity

Closely linked to this property based social role is the practice of kinship adoption.[5] For some agricultural societies, such as those of India and China, these were synonymous as a relative was the preferred adoptee. Ethnic groups such as Native Americans and the Indigenous People in Australia have long practiced kinship fostering and adoption as a means of strengthening the extended family, and their society as a whole, by weakening the exclusive bond between parents and children.[6] The importance of this social function is illustrated by the fact that for the Hindus of India adoption outside the caste is prohibited[7] while for the Polynesians

2 See, for example, Benet, M. K., *The Character of Adoption*, London, Johnathan Cape, 1976.
3 Ibid., p. 22; see also Goody, E., *Contexts of Kinship*, Cambridge University Press, 1973.
4 As Benet explains: 'Full adoption, *adrogatio*, was only possible for a person who was himself *sui iuris* – that is, a member of no family but his own. A minor could not be *adrogated* because a minor *sui iuris* had *tutores* or guardians . . .The adopter "must be 60 or from some cause unlikely to have children"' (*Character of Adoption*, p. 30).
5 Ibid., p. 14.
6 Ibid., p. 17.
7 Ibid., p. 35.

the adoption of anyone other than a relative is an insult to the extended family.[8] Kinship adoption in such a cultural context seems to rest on an 'exchange' motive, whereby the donor nuclear family acquires a stronger affiliation with the wider social group, in exchange for relinquishing parental rights.

Social advancement

In some cases, the purpose of adoption is to secure social advancement for the adopted.[9] This is not unlike the Roman practice of non-kinship adoption for the purpose of allying the fortunes of two families. A Roman patrician, or even an emperor, would adopt, for example, a successful general as his successor.[10] In Japan, also, the adoption of non-relatives was traditionally seen as a means of allying with the fortunes of the ruling family.[11] In Ireland under the Brehon laws much the same ends were achieved by reciprocal placements of children between clans as a demonstration of mutual allegiance.[12] It bears a strong resemblance to the feudal practice in England of paying fealty and showing allegiance to a lord by placing a child for court service.

Concepts and constructs

The concept of 'adoption' addresses the act of the adopter, an act which sets in motion a chain of events that changes the status and relationships of the adoptee and many others. As a social construct, adoption reveals that its usefulness at various times and places has rested on a capacity to meet the needs of adopters and their range of quite different motives.

Concepts

The modern practice of adoption rests on the voluntary acceptance of responsibility by an adult or adults for the care and protection of the child of another, and for the promotion of his or her development, at least until that child attains adulthood. It is an act which brings that child into the adopter's family with all the implications for sharing in the family name, home, assets and kinship relationships which are thereby entailed. As a corollary, it is an act which also implies a severance by the adopter of those same links between the child and his or her family of origin.

8 Ibid., pp. 35 and 48–50.
9 As Gibbons explains, at the time of the Roman Empire a returning successful adventurer might seek to ingratiate himself 'by the custom of adopting the name of their patron' and thereby hope to secure his position in society (R. Gibbons, *The Decline and Fall of the Roman Empire*, London, Harrap, 1949, p. 131).
10 Ibid., p. 30. Marcus Aurelius being a good example.
11 Ibid.
12 See Gilligan, R., *Irish Child Care Services: Policy, Practice and Provision*, Dublin, Institute of Public Administration, 1991.

Blood-link

In common law jurisdictions the 'blood-link' or *jus sanguinis* has long been accepted as signifying an entitlement to rights by virtue of the circumstances of birth. The feudal preoccupation with the importance of 'blood lines' survived in Victorian England, and elsewhere, into the late nineteenth century. Maintaining established family lines, and the estates that had survived intact for generations, was viewed as dependent to some degree upon protecting the status quo and with it the ability for families to continue discreetly managing opportunities for marriage and eventual succession rights. There were many who considered that adoption would introduce an unknown element into the rules governing inheritance and succession with potential to undermine established rights and thereby threaten the orderly devolution of family property. This was accompanied by the taboo of 'bad blood': a fear of the unknown; once evident in the belief that the adoption of a 'foundling' could introduce an unknown element that would dilute the authenticity of lineage; and can now sometimes be found in biased perceptions applied to unfairly discriminate against adopted persons.

In more recent years the blood-link has come to ground a presumption that care provided by a child's parent or relative is in the best interests of that child. It can also be detected in the prohibited degrees of relationship rule, in the resistance to third party childcare adoptions and in the professional encouragement of family adoptions.

Attachment or bonding

The act of the adopter essentially displaces birth relationships with an alternative legal relationship and leaves to time the possibility that a bonding relationship will achieve the attachment between adopter and child necessary to fulfil the needs of both for a family.[13]

Social construct

'Adoption' acquired a common currency definition throughout most modern western societies. It had been shaped to have a specific meaning: imprinted with considerable consistency by the legislatures of common law nations on a range of different cultural traditions, in order to address much the same social problems; and varies accordingly to fit with the norms of other cultures such as those of Japan, Islam and of indigenous communities. In acquiring its identity, adoption became differentiated from alternative childcare arrangements within such societies (e.g. long-term foster care, in *loco parentis* care, etc.) and from comparable arrangements in other societies. For example, 'simple' adoption is still common in many African nations and elsewhere, while in Islamic countries, under sharia law, adoption is prohibited but the practice of *kafala*, a form of long-term foster care, has long been used.

13 See, for example, Bowlby, J., *Attachment*, London, Penguin, 1969.

Legitimation

At a time when the marital family unit was upheld as the essential building block of society, particularly a Christian society where marital status conferred respectability, then non-marital births were a matter of considerable disgrace – as much for a child as for the mother. Adoption was socially very important as it provided a means for the 'legitimation' of such a child: enclosing the child within a properly constituted marital family; reinforcing the 'sanctity' of marriage and expunging the 'sin' of an illicit relationship.

Artificial relationship

As a social construct, adoption is an artificial parent–child relationship that normally acquires its validity by means of a legal process; though some countries and religions provide for forms of de facto adoption. It remains fundamentally a legal relationship. It fails to wholly displace all incidences of the child's pre-adoption legal relationships and fails also to legally subsume him or her fully into the adopter's family. From the outset, the courts had some difficulty in accommodating the piece of legal fiction that purported to place a child in exactly the same relationship to 'strangers' as he or she would otherwise have stood in relation to their birth parents. Judicial resistance to the legislative intent was evident in relation to matters such as inheritance and succession rights, while legislation continued the exemption extended to an adopted brother and sister from the laws relating to incest and, more recently, it has been illustrated by the practice of issuing contact orders in conjunction with some adoption orders.

Children and the Poor Laws: a human rights perspective

While it is clearly wrong to ascribe modern values to an era in which they did not pertain, it is nonetheless salutary to reflect on the social context which gave rise to adoption as we now know it.

Parental rights

By the middle of the nineteenth century, in all common law countries, the doctrine of paternal rights was firmly established. The prima facie right of a father to the control and custody of the children of his marriage, subject to an absence of abuse,[14] was virtually impregnable. It was absolute as against the mother.[15] The approach of the common law was reflected clearly in the judgment delivered by James LJ in *Re Agar – Ellis*[16] when, on giving the decision of the Court of Appeal, he added:

14 *Re Thomasset* [1894] 300.
15 See *ex parte Skinner*, 9 Moo 278; *Simpson on Infants* (2nd edn), 1908, p. 115.
16 (1883) 23 Ch D 317, 71–2.

> The right of the father to the custody and control of his children is one of the most sacred rights.

This paternal right[17] applied only to marital children. Until 1839 the custody of a legitimate child vested automatically and exclusively in the father. As head of the family, he had the right to administer reasonable chastisement to his child.[18] Such was the stringent judicial approach to the legal standing of the father that the courts would not allow a father to avoid his parental responsibilities by voluntarily giving up his right to custody and control.[19] The common law prohibited any attempt by a parent to irrevocably transfer all rights and duties in respect of a child to another. As was stated in *In re O'Hara*:

> English law does not permit a parent to relieve himself of the responsibility or to deprive himself of the comfort of his position.[20]

And:

> English law does not recognise the power of blindingly abdicating either parental right or parental duty.[21]

Parental rights were regarded as inalienable. Parental culpability alone set the threshold for State intervention on behalf of child welfare.

Parental duty was also firmly recognised in the common law. As Sir W. Blackstone stated:[22]

> The duty of parents to provide for the maintenance of their children is a principle of natural law; an obligation . . . laid on them not only by nature herself, but by their own proper act, in bringing them into the world.

This duty was underpinned by the criminal law. The common law evolved a number of criminal offences particular to children and their parents. They were focused not on the welfare of a child but on the abuse of a parental right; child welfare was incidental, legally recognised only in an obverse relationship to parental right.

17 *De Mannerville* v. *De Mannerville.*
18 *Gardner* v. *Bygrave* [1889] 6 TLR 23 DC, *Mansell* v. *Griffin* [1908] 1 KB, 160, *obiter*, *R* v. *Hopley* [1860] 2F and F 160.
19 *St John* v. *St John* (1805) 11 Vessey 530 and *Vansittart* v. *Vansittart* (1858) 2 De Gex & Jones 249, p. 256; *Hamilton* v. *Hector* (1872) LR 13 Equity 511.
20 [1900] 2 IR 232, per Holmes LJ, p. 253; (1899) 34 ILTR 17 CA; see also *Humphrys* v. *Polak* [1901] 2 KB 385, CA and *Brooks* v. *Brooks* [1923] 1 KB 257.
21 Ibid., per Fitzgibbon LJ.
22 *Commentaries on the Laws of England*, Oxford, Clarendon Press, 1765.

Illegitimacy

The status of the patriarchal marital family in Victorian England was policed by the common law approach to 'illegitimacy'. This term served both to reinforce the 'legitimate' family while simultaneously disenfranchising the non-marital child and father and singling out the child's mother (though not the father) for social opprobrium. All three were firmly and publicly placed outside the law as it then related to the family. Adoption, in that context, was viewed as an important legal device for rectifying some of the social consequences of illegitimacy.

The consequences for those tainted by 'illegitimacy' involved serious status constraints not least in regard to rights of inheritance. It also meant that as such a child was designated *sui juris* (outside the law) – being legally construed as a child of no one and receiving no recognition in law – parental responsibilities could be transferred without any breach of paternal rights. This, in effect, confined the practice of adoption as a common law process to the relinquishment of illegitimate children by their unmarried mothers who, given the weight of public approbation and lack of any legal means of securing financial support, were left with little option. This distinction between 'legitimate' and 'illegitimate' children and between the social standing of their respective sets of parents had a value for many which carried through into the mid-twentieth century. Status considerations extended to include matters such as family name, property, religion, residence, domicile, etc.

In relation to illegitimate children, the courts took the pragmatic view that, in the circumstances, the decision to terminate parenting was itself a responsible parental act.[23] Where the responsibility for an illegitimate, abandoned or orphaned child could be assumed within the care arrangements of a private family, instead of becoming an additional burden on public rates, then the courts did not interfere.

Child welfare

The concept of 'child welfare', accompanied by an assumption that the State should have a role in child protection, is a relatively modern innovation.

Right to life

For centuries the criminal law in England, as in other countries, made little distinction between children and adults. While those below the age of 10 were held to be *doli incapax*, or lacking the necessary intent to be fully accountable, children of that age and older were frequently found guilty of crimes and duly flogged, imprisoned, transported overseas or hanged.[24] The civil law, as administered by

23 *In re O'Hara* [1900] 2 IR 233 per Fitz-Gibbon LJ, p. 244.

24 Not until the Children Act 1908 were the executions of children aged under 16 banned.

the Poor Law authorities, provided a rudimentary care system for children in the insanitary conditions of workhouses which were not improved until the introduction of the Infant Life Protection Act 1872.

The workhouse

By the mid-nineteenth century, abandonment of children to the Poor Law authorities was the only option available to the many poverty-stricken parents who had not benefited from the Industrial Revolution. In the UK before the First World War at any one time there were some 80,000 children in care under the Poor Laws.

Governing principles

Adoption has always been a value-laden social practice.

Secrecy

The traditional 'closed' model of adoption was rooted in an approach to child development that maintained the importance of allowing a child to form attachments within a clear and consistent set of relationships free from any ambiguity. Any proposed ongoing involvement of members of the child's family of origin was viewed as introducing complicating and confusing factors that might threaten the new and vulnerable family unit. It was also considered likely to impose unnecessary stress on birth parent/s, who needed to come to terms with their loss, and on the adopters who very often wanted to close the door on the facts and relationships associated with the birth history of 'their' child. A clean break and a new start were seen as being in the best interests of all parties and secrecy regarding the disclosure of identifying information was a means to that end. This reliance on a cloak of secrecy was also prompted by taboos which were then associated with adoption: the perception of disgrace and inadequacy accompanying the role of relinquishing birth parent/s; the 'bad blood' risk accepted by adopters; and the personal identity issues arising for an adoptee. Ultimately, in England and Wales as mentioned above, s. 51 of the 1975 Act marked an important break with the traditional veil of secrecy by facilitating adopters' rights of access to personal identity information.

The welfare principle

Adoption has always required that every application be subject to the 'welfare test', meaning that any decision must be taken only after consideration has been given to ensure its compatibility with the welfare interests of the child concerned. The part to be played by this imprecise term in adoption proceedings has for many years generated much controversy. Three aspects of 'welfare interests' are relevant in the context of adoption proceedings:

- how is the term's content or meaning defined in statute and case law?
- what role does the law assign to the welfare test, i.e. when and to what is it to be applied and over what period?
- and crucially, what weighting is to be attached to the welfare component relative to the withholding of parental consent at the time of placement and when determining an application?

Paramountcy

While adoption law traditionally made many references to 'welfare interests' for decades no statute made any attempt to define or indicate the meaning or weighting to be attached to this term. Not until 1954 were the first steps taken to rectify this omission when the Hurst Committee[25] suggested that the 'primary object . . . in the arrangement of adoptions is the welfare of the child' and subsequently the Houghton Committee in 1972[26] recommended that 'the long-term welfare of the child should be the first and paramount consideration'. Traditionally, an adoption order was required to be at least compatible with the child's welfare interests which could comprise 'material and financial prospects, education, general surroundings, happiness, stability of home and the like'.[27] Not until the 1989 Act, however, was the paramountcy principle statutorily introduced which required all other factors to be subordinated to the overriding principle that the child's welfare be given priority. This was reinforced by the 'welfare checklist' which specified the component parts of 'welfare' (see Chapter 5).

Permanency

Attachment theory brought with it an acceptance that this could only be realistically achieved if a child was retained within a fixed set of relationships and a familiar social context. It was and is accepted that there may well be a range of permanency options for a child in need of long-term care away from their family of origin. A child leaving the public care system for private family care has, for example, always been able to do so under the authority of a private law order such as guardianship. However, adoption has become the exit strategy favoured by local authority social workers for children in public care. 'Permanence' is understood as 'a framework of emotional, physical and legal conditions that gives a child a sense of security, continuity, commitment and identity'[28] while 'permanency planning' has been defined as:[29]

25 *Report of the Departmental Committee on Adoption Societies and Agencies* (Cmnd 5499), London, HMSO, 1937, p. 4.
26 *Report of the Departmental Committee on the Adoption of Children*, para. 17.
27 *Re B* [1971] 1 QB 437, per Davies LJ, p. 443.
28 Department of Education and Skills, Draft Regulations and Guidance for Consultation (Care Planning, Special Guardianship), London, HMSO, 2004, p. 20.
29 Maluccio, A. and Fein, E., 'Permanency planning: a redefinition', *Child Welfare* 62(3) (1983): 195–201.

> the systematic process of carrying out within a limited period a set of goal-directed activities designed to help children and youths live with families that offer continuity of relationships with nurturing parents or caretakers, and the opportunity to offer lifetime relationships.

The age of the child, their wishes and the quality of his or her relationship with parents may well indicate adoption as the preferred means of securing permanency, whether or not parental consent is available. UK local authorities will always apply permanency planning to identify the best option for a child in care, most often this will be either adoption or long-term fostering or by way of such private law measures as a residence order and special guardianship.

Openness

The practice of openness was initially associated with family adoptions, where access to information relating to origins and identity was most likely to be readily facilitated. In childcare adoptions, however, which often involve older children, it has been embraced as an unavoidable necessity unless there is good reason for secrecy such as a background of child abuse or domestic violence.[30] More recently, with a growing awareness of 'attachment theory', there has been a willingness to allow adoption orders to coexist alongside contact orders which permitted arrangements to be made between an adopted child and members of their family of origin with whom a significant relationship had been established. Moreover, as childcare adoption increased so too did the frequency of public service commitments to sustaining adoptions through the provision of ongoing professional and other resources. Increasingly, an adoption that allows for such degree of 'openness' as is compatible with the comfort levels of all parties came to be viewed as being in the long-term perhaps healthier and more honest than the traditional closed approach. That arrangements between the parties should be made and maintained in secrecy, and information disclosure relating to identity kept to a minimum, was seen as contravening basic human rights principles: in particular, it compromised the right of an adoptee to develop an authentic identity. As has been observed, adoption practice reflects social, political, economic and moral changes and the move towards openness in adoption reflects a general trend towards more openness in society.[31]

The adoption process gradually became much more 'open' than could ever have been foreseen and, arguably, brings with it the challenge that perhaps the traditional interpretation of adoption should also be broadened to rebalance the human rights of the parties. Is the complete and permanent severing of birth

30 See, for example, *Gunn – Russo* v. *Nugent Care Society and Secretary of State for Health* [2001] EWHC Admin. 566 [2002] 1 FLR 1 [2001] UKHRR 1320 [2002] Fam. Law 92, QBD.

31 Grotevant, H. and McRoy, R., *Openness in Adoption*, Sage, Thousand Oaks, CA, 1998, p. 196.

parents' rights and duties in relation to their child, coupled with the equally exclusive vesting of such responsibilities in the adopters, now strictly necessary?

Social change and the role of adoption

As the structured homogeneity of late Victorian England gave way to a more fluid, multicultural society with permeable boundaries so family life became much less likely to be based on marriage, more impermanent, with serial parenting and shared care arrangements increasingly common. The modern self-reliant fairly mobile nuclear unit was less likely to be reinforced by an extended kinship network or by community links and became more transient as families relocated in pursuit of employment opportunities. Moreover, these changes were accompanied by improvements in family planning, in welfare benefits and in perceptions of stigma that transformed the social circumstances of unmarried mothers.

Against this background the welfare interests and indeed the rights of the child steadily acquired a more defined salience. This was partly a consequence of increased knowledge of child development, particularly in relation to theories of attachment and bonding. It is also attributable to the general withdrawal throughout family law from a defence of the status determined obligations of adults (e.g. marriage) to upholding the principle that the welfare interests of children must prevail in any set of circumstances.

Advances in medical science

Such advances have allowed parenting to become more a matter of choice, mostly to be exercised by women. The availability and continuing improvements in the efficiency of methods of birth control and abortion services have clearly affected the number of unwanted births and therefore the number of birth parent/s wishing to voluntarily relinquish their babies. Improved techniques for assisting conception (artificial insemination by donor (AID) and gamete intrafallopian transfer (GIFT), etc.) have had profound implications for the adoption process. As mentioned above, medical science has also greatly improved the survival rate for babies born with complex health and social care needs resulting in more such children becoming available for adoption.

Surrogacy

In recent years surrogacy in particular has had a significant impact upon adoption. It enables very many single persons and childless couples – homosexual or heterosexual – to make the arrangements necessary to ensure that they will be in a position to consensually adopt a healthy baby. Consequently, there are now increasing concerns about a new form of 'baby-farming' and worries regarding the human rights of birth mothers who may be vulnerable to exploitation by prospective adopters and others.

Welfare benefits

Birth parents who choose to provide ongoing care for their child, unlike their predecessors, now have access to the range of welfare benefits and public services necessary to undertake and sustain that parental role. This – together with the fading of the social stigma previously associated with that role, access to contraceptives and the growth in equality of employment opportunities – has transformed the relationship between unmarried mothers and the adoption process.

Failed parenting

Failed family life is becoming more evident as illustrated by media reports of child abuse, the growing childcare population, the number of child abuse inquiries, paedophilia scandals and related government policy initiatives. There is now a recognition that new measures need to be taken to provide both a better level of child protection[32] and also safe and permanent alternative care arrangements for children failed by parental care.

Child development knowledge

The importance of 'nurture', physical and emotional, of 'bonding' between child and a significant carer, in contributing towards a child's well-balanced psychosocial development have been extensively researched and are now accepted as key concepts in child-rearing practice.[33]

'Attachment theory'

It was 'attachment theory'[34] more than any other aspect of modern child development knowledge, impacting upon childcare policy and practice that in turn caused a strategic change in professional attitudes towards the adoption process. Attachment theory suggests that the future psychological well-being of every child is dependent upon their experiencing an intimate one-to-one relationship with a caring adult for a crucial period during their formative early years.

32 Department of Health, *The Victoria Climbie Inquiry* ('the Laming Report'), London, HMSO, 2003; Ward, H., Brown, R. and Westlake, D., *Safeguarding Babies and Very Young Children from Abuse and Neglect*, London, Jessica Kingsley, 2012.

33 See, for example, Goldstein, J., Freud, A. and Solnit, A. J., *Beyond the Best Interests of the Child*, New York, Free Press, 1973.

34 See, for example, Bowlby, J., *Attachment and Loss*, London, Hogarth Press, 1969; Howe, D. et al., *Attachment Theory: Social, Developmental and Clinical Perspectives*, New Jersey, Analytical Press, 1999; Harris, G., 'The human life cycle: infancy', in Davies, M. (ed.), *The Blackwell Companion to Social Work* (2nd edn), Oxford, Blackwell, 2003.

Failed State care

The failings of State care have been only too apparent and are well documented.[35] The effect of public care scandals, combined with the expense of State care and the influence of the principle that family care is best, led to a period of intense research focused on evidence-based practice to clarify which option was most satisfactory. The outcomes research,[36] for example, together with attachment theory, suggested that once rehabilitation had been found to be impracticable then a local authority should institute permanency planning and that adoption rather than foster care was more likely to produce long-term beneficial outcomes for the children concerned.

Long-term foster care and adoption

Given the virtual disappearance of residential care provided by voluntary organisations and the influence of the principle that family care is most conducive to promoting the welfare of a child, permanency planning in practice meant a choice between two forms of placement, long-term foster care and adoption. Generally speaking, long-term foster care is most often the placement of choice in circumstances where the probability of successful bonding, the crucial component in any attempt to replicate in adoption the dynamics of a 'normal' nuclear family, is reduced by some added complication. This may be the case where the children concerned are older, have been repeatedly fostered, comprise a multiple sibling group, have complex health or special needs or are children from a minority culture background. Quite often the choice is made because a child has close relationships with his or her family of origin which the local authority wants to maintain, and a placement with foster parents rather than adopters is more conducive to facilitating open-ended contact arrangements. Also, there are times

35 A number of official inquiries reported on the capacity of the care system itself to permit and sustain a culture of child abuse. See, for example, Waterhouse, Sir R., *Lost in Care: Report of the Tribunal of Inquiry into the Abuse of Children in Care in the Former County Council Areas of Gwynedd and Clwyd since 1974*, London, HMSO, 2000.

36 The 'outcomes research', analysing and evaluating the care careers of looked-after children, comprises many different reports compiled in the main from within the social work and allied professions. These include: Triseliotis, J. and Hill, M., *Hard to Place – the Outcome of Adoption and Residential Care*, London, Gower, 1984; Thoburn, J., *Captive Clients*, London, Routledge, 1980; Millham, S. et al., *Lost in Care*, Gower, London, 1986; Rowe, J., Hundleby, M., and Garnett, L., *Child Care Now – A Survey of Placement Patterns*, London, BAAF, 1989; Farmer, E. and Parker, R., *Trials and Tribulations*, London, HMSO, 1991; Parker, R., Ward, H., and Jackson, S. et al. (eds), *Looking After Children: Assessing Outcomes in Child Care*, London, HMSO, 1991; Bullock, R. et al., *Going Home*, Aldershot, Ashgate, 1993; Department of Health, *Caring for Children Away from Home: Messages from Research*, London, HMSO, 1998; Rushton, A., *Adoption as a Placement Choice: Argument and Evidence*, Maudsley Discussion Paper No. 9 (1999); Broad, R. et al., *Kith and Kin: Kinship Care for Vulnerable Young People*, National Children's Bureau, 2001.

when an intended short-term placement has been so successful that any change would threaten the welfare interests of the child concerned. The disadvantages of long-term foster care are that:

- There is intrusion.
- Drift can happen with the child moving from one place to another. It is more likely to lead to breakdown.
- It reinforces impermanence.
- Matters such as surname can be important. Self-image is important as children get older.
- The existence of other children in foster care can increase the insecurity as they come and go.
- Children frequently act out with the other foster children the abuse they have suffered.
- Placements in long-term foster care are more likely to fail than adoption placements.

The advantages of adoption, on the other hand, have been stated as follows:[37]

> The importance of family life to a child cannot be overstated. It is the fundamental right of every child to belong to a family and this principle underpins the United Nations Convention on the Rights of the Child which United Kingdom ratified in 1991. Where, for whatever reason, children cannot live with their families, society has a duty to provide them with a fresh start and, where appropriate, a permanent alternative home. Adoption is the means of giving children an opportunity to experience positive family relationships. Adoption continues to provide an important service for children, offering a positive and beneficial outcome. Research shows that adopted children generally make very good progress compared with similar children who are brought up by their parents. Adopted children do considerably better than children who have remained in the care system throughout most of their childhood. Adoption provides children with a unique opportunity to become permanent members of new families enjoying a sense of security and well-being previously denied to them.

The government has since firmed up on this approach with an unequivocal policy commitment to prioritising adoption in preference to long-term foster care (Chapter 5). In every instance, however, the court will be guided not by government policy but by evidence that this is the best option for a particular child.

37 Local Authority Circular (20) Departmental Guidance: *Permanency Planning for Children: Adoption – Achieving the Right Balance*, 1998; government's Green Paper, *Every Child Matters*, 2003; Biehal, N. et al., *Belonging and Permanence: Outcomes in Long-Term Foster Care and Adoption*, London, BAAF, 2010.

Children's rights

An important modern development in the law relating to children has been the relatively recent paradigm shift from a central concern for the protection of welfare interests to one of asserting children's rights. This is largely due to the weight of case law precedents established under Convention provisions (see further Chapter 3). One effect of this development is that in certain issues, such as disputes regarding contact or parental responsibility, judicial determination will proceed from the premise that the child has a right to whatever arrangement is most conducive to securing and promoting their welfare. A more general effect has been to centre-stage children's interests in all family proceedings; the law is now much more for children than about them.

The voice of the child

Independent representation for the interests of any child the subject of adoption proceedings is a central principle in the English judicial process. Whereas this was formerly the responsibility of a *guardian ad litem*, it has now passed to CAFCASS officials. The duty to represent is accompanied by a duty to ascertain and take into account the wishes of any child of an age to give an informed view.

Contemporary adoption

In more recent times, adoption had come to be seen as a provident answer to a matching set of needs characteristic of most developed societies: the burden of costs required to maintain children for whom the adequate care of a birth parent was unavailable; and the wishes of settled, married but childless couples able and willing to provide care for such children. This equation was dramatically affected by the introduction of readily available means of birth control, by general demographic trends and then by the rising incidences of family breakdown and numbers of children in care. Moreover, in keeping with broader changes in cultural context and the impact of globalisation, the role of adoption now reflects the complexities of modern society. It has also been affected by human rights considerations, as established by rulings of the ECtHR, and by improved regulatory controls in respect of the adoption process (see Chapters 3 and 4 and Part II).

Types of adoption

There are essentially three main types of adoption – family, childcare and inter-country – the purposes of which can be clearly differentiated from each other and from the traditional form of third party adoption. The children, their needs and the relative bearing of the welfare principle are also quite different in each context, as are the motives of adopters and the reasons governing the availability of children. The extent to which each type attracts professional and public service intervention differs considerably.

Third party adoption

Adoption, as known to the law in the UK and similar western societies, initially conformed to a single generic type: the third party assumption of all responsibilities in respect of a healthy white Caucasian baby by a married couple, unrelated and unknown to the birth mother; who were permanently and irrevocably vested with full parental rights and responsibilities in respect of her child. Such was the legacy of nineteenth-century 'baby-farming' scandals that the legislative intent from the outset was directed towards putting in place the legal functions necessary to test the bona fides of would be third party adopters. Ultimately, this led to third party placements made by a birth mother or some person acting at her direction, being prohibited (unless made directly with a relative) because this test was judged more likely to be applied objectively if entrusted exclusively to professionals. The law was concerned to replicate for the child the type of family unit conforming most closely to the approved model prevailing in society at that time. Traditionally, conformity with that model required an archetypal childless marital couple of sound health and morals, in secure material circumstances and resident within the jurisdiction; it extended to matching the child – including physical characteristics and aptitudes where feasible – to those of applicant adopters.

As society became less homogeneous, marriage less popular and less permanent, while the population of working age became more accustomed to transient home, employment and relationship ties, so the profile of third party adopters changed. From a position whereby they initially comprised the vast majority of adopters, they steadily declined both numerically and as a proportion of total annual applicants. Third party or 'stranger' adoptions, where the adopters are unrelated in every respect to the child voluntarily relinquished or otherwise consensually available, is the model that has consistently been the subject of legislative intent in the UK but is also the one that has been consistently in decline since the 1970s.

That single generic type faded as adoption evolved and permutated to accommodate changed needs. These included: providing for orphaned, abandoned and older children, and for those with health issues children, both within the jurisdiction and internationally; responding to the plight of childless heterosexual individuals and to the parenting needs of same-gender couples; reducing the number of children being maintained in public childcare facilities; and enabling parents to secure the legal cohesion of their re-formed families. Consequently, all modern western societies have had to readjust their laws relating to adoption.

Childcare adoption

This subspecies of third party adoption, also known as 'agency adoption', has become prominent in many western countries as governments introduce legislative measures to divert the interest of potential adopters from the few non-marital babies to the needs of the many disadvantaged older, disabled children, or those in public care, in respect of whom full parental rights have been obtained. However, the flow of children from the public childcare sector into the private law adoption process has been a relatively modern development. For many generations, when care in the family of origin failed, whether due to criminal abuse perpetrated by a culpable parent or neglect by a well-meaning but inadequate parent, children have entered the public care system. This seldom resulted in their becoming available for adoption.[38]

However, by the beginning of the twenty-first century, the imbalance between type/volume of childcare resources and the needs of children requiring alternative long-term care arrangements had become a matter of acute concern to all local authorities. Residential accommodation for children subject to care orders, where desirable, was difficult to secure. Foster parents were a scarce resource and serial placements for a child in care was the norm. These problems were unfolding in the context of a dramatic decline in the availability of freely relinquished healthy babies and a continued increase in the number of childless couples wishing to adopt. Moreover, research findings on the outcomes for looked-after children together with the results of evidence-based practice utilising attachment theory and implementing the permanency planning policy indicated that traditional approaches to securing care arrangements for looked-after children were unsustainable. It seemed that an assertive policy to expedite non-consensual adoption for older and often abused or impaired children might be timely.

The childcare adoption policy was one driven partly by government need to cut back on the expensive costs of institutional care and partly in response to research findings that the positive outcomes for adopted children greatly exceeds that of those who linger in long-term public care. Nonetheless, despite legislative synchronisation of grounds for care orders and grounds for dispensing with parental consent so as to permit adoption, judicial resistance to the welfare test as a bridge between childcare and adoption succeeded for many decades in preventing ready access to the process for children in care. In the UK, the unfortunate consequences of this state of affairs were graphically highlighted by Rowe and Lambert in *Children Who Wait*[39] and by an accompanying body of research which convincingly demonstrated that the life chances of a child who had grown up in the public care system compared very badly, across a number of indicators (including employment, mental health, relationships, etc.), with one who had matured in a safe family environment. This variant of adoption, with its reliance upon ongoing post-adoption professional services and the necessity to protect welfare interests by facilitating the continuation of any significant relationships between an adopted child and members of their family of origin, has contributed greatly to the 'openness' that has come to replace secrecy as a characteristic of modern adoption.

38 In the UK, this was despite recommendations in the Curtis Report, *The Care of Children* (Cmnd 6922), London, HMSO, 1946, where adoption was advocated for older children in care and subsequently those of the Houghton Committee, *Report of the Departmental Committee on the Adoption of Children* (Cmnd 5107), London, HMSO, 1972 which pressed for adoption to be made available to children in public care where this was in the best interests of a particular child.

39 Rowe, J. and Lambert, L., *Children Who Wait*, London, ABAA, 1973.

ICA

Again, this can be seen largely as a subspecies of third party adoption. For some decades, the number of babies available for adoption had been declining in all modern western societies as family planning became more prevalent following the introduction of readily available means of birth control, coupled with greatly improved welfare benefits and a falling fertility rate, which combined to induce prospective adopters to look overseas for available children. At the same time, circumstances of war and natural disaster have induced other countries to permit the adoption of orphaned or abandoned children by couples in western societies. The welfare interests of such children can usually only be improved by this modern 'child rescue' approach and by those first party adopters who, having successfully emigrated, then seek to adopt and bring to their new home child relatives from their country of origin.

However, ICA is replete with human rights issues. In the main these arise in relation to the eligibility of the children involved and most concern matters such as unauthorised payments, unauthorised placements and proof of consents. The first two represent the traditional legal abhorrence of 'trafficking' in children: improper payments (e.g. direct or indirect payments to the child's mother) may, if proven, prevent the court from making an adoption order, though much will depend on the circumstances and whether the child's welfare interests are otherwise impaired; while unauthorised placements tend to be viewed more seriously and have generally resulted in the refusal of an adoption order. The problems in relation to proof of consents refers to the difficulty in establishing, across geographical, cultural and language barriers, the legal status of parent and child and confirming that any consent given was done so freely and with full understanding of the consequences. Any one or combination of these issues may well complicate the court's ultimate application of the welfare test to a particular ICA application. Although the Hague Convention has contributed greatly to raising the standards of practice, not all countries involved in ICA subscribe to it and some signatory States also simultaneously pursue bilateral agreements with non-Hague-compliant countries, an approach that would seem to cynically detract from Hague objectives. Moreover, as this Convention lacks any regulatory authority it can only issue guidance and is relatively powerless to enforce the standards it seeks to uphold.

Even if an ICA is successfully concluded, there may still be grounds for misgivings. The availability of many children is conditioned by the social economy of their country of origin and the dislocation to their sense of family, culture and authentic identity resulting from being adopted elsewhere could, in the long run, prove inconducive to promoting their welfare interests. Arguably, ICA will only be compliant with the human rights of the child concerned when neither rehabilitation in their family of origin nor adoption within the country of origin is possible.

Kinship adoption

Kinship or family adoption, whereby a child is adopted by a relative such as an uncle, aunt or grandparent, though traditionally of little numerical significance is now increasing as a proportion of total annual applications, as also are adoptions by foster carers. Such adoptions are regarded by some as problematic because: a new and lesser legal status is being substituted for an existing legal and actual relationship; purpose and motive can be open to question; kinship adopters are usually older than others; it can obscure the nature of the actual relationship between child and adopter and be confusing for other children in the family; and it can have a divisive effect by alienating other relatives. On the other hand, they may be viewed positively because:[40] it often retains the child in their home and social environment; it always maintains the child within their actual network of relationships (though in some circumstances this can be problematic); it facilitates an honest sharing of information between all parties; and by retaining the child within their culture of origin it minimises the possibility of long-term identity problems. The latter reasoning accounts for kinship adoptions being often the preferred option for children in care.

The applicants in this type of adoption are often a birth parent of the child concerned and the former's spouse, motivated by a joint wish to legally secure exclusive parental rights and responsibilities. Pre-application professional assessment is generally not required and counselling is usually not wanted. The child will probably be older than the average and their wishes, or their consent if old enough, is likely to be sought and the order may well be compromised by a contact arrangements in favour of the child's other parent. Post-adoption public support services are not provided. Grandparents may also be kinship adopters although this has generally been viewed as undesirable.[41] Reservations have rested on the significance of age differentials between adopter and adopted and echoed the warning given by Vaisey J that they should be regarded as exceptional and made with great caution. Nonetheless, such adoptions are now becoming fairly common in the UK and in the US.

Step-parent adoption

The post-divorce adoption of 'legitimate' children accounts for the rise in step-parent adoptions and this in turn has inflated the number of family adoptions relative to all other types. The attraction of a means whereby a second partner, who has all the day-to-day care responsibilities but none of the rights in respect of their spouse's child from a previous relationship, may acquire with the latter exclusive parental rights, has been and continues to be a frequent motive for adoption. A wish to ensure inheritance rights can also be a factor. As marriage becomes less popular and less durable and parenting arrangements more fluid so an adoption order has come to be regarded as a useful authority for bolting the

40 For further arguments in support of kinship care, see, for example, Broad, B. (ed.), *Kinship Care: The Placement Choice for Children and Young People*, Lyme Regis, Russell House, 2001; Greef, R. (ed.), *Fostering Kinship: An International Perspective on Kinship Foster Care*, Aldershot, Ashgate, 1999; Hegar, R. L. and Scannapieco, M., *Kinship Foster Care: Policy, Practice and Research*, Oxford University Press, 1999.

41 Houghton Report, paras 111–14.

door behind a re-formed family unit to the exclusion of previous and now inconvenient relationships.[12] It may also, of course, signify to the child concerned that both birth parent and spouse are wholly committed to making him or her as much a part of the new family unit as is legally possible.

Variants in adoption practice

In the UK, as elsewhere, the traditional form of adoption is dying out. The third party adoption of healthy babies, voluntarily relinquished by birth parents resident and domiciled within the jurisdiction, by heterosexual married couples, most probably has no future. This has given way to new variants which have brought with them possibilities for reinterpreting the process and clarifying its functions.

Adoption of children with 'special needs'

In all western societies, the reduction in the number of healthy babies available for adoption has led to adopters broadening their outlook. This has been matched by a commensurate change in the factors governing the availability of children, particularly babies. Previously, the few children with complex healthcare or special needs, unwanted or inadequately cared for by their birth parents, would have been consigned to long-term institutional care. Due to the advances made in medical sciences, many more vulnerable children are surviving, and some need an intensity of care well beyond the abilities of 'average' parents. Many such children are now successfully placed for adoption; most often with ongoing professional and financial support.

Transracial adoption

ICAs are often transracial, some of the rationale and many of the same tensions prevail in both,[43] and can give rise to identity issues for children removed from contexts of family, kinship, language and culture to be reared in a foreign ethnic environment. The controversy surrounding such adoptions has tended to centre on a practice by some adoption agencies and local authorities to make and break placements on the basis of a racial match between child and prospective adopters. The emerging consensus would seem to be that where possible placement arrangements should reflect a child's ethnic background and cultural identity – in so far as such considerations are compatible with the welfare interests of that child, which must always have priority. In particular, there is no doubting the value of preserving established relationships as a key component of welfare interests in

42 Utting, D., *Family and Parenthood*, London, Rowntree Foundation, 1995 noted that 40 per cent of marriages end in divorce, 20 per cent of families are headed by a lone parent and 8 per cent of dependent children live in stepfamilies.

43 Murphy, J., 'Child welfare in transracial adoptions: colour-blind children and colour-blind law', in Murphy, J. (ed.), *Ethnic Minorities – Their Families and the Law*, Oxford, Hart, 2000.

transracial as in all other kinds of placements; the duration of current care arrangements and age of the child being of crucial importance.

Single adoption

Adoption has naturally reflected the traditional archetypal family model by catering almost exclusively for applications from married couples. In recent years, again in keeping with prevailing family models, there has been a noticeable increase in the number of single adopters. Such applicants may well offer the best chance of furthering the welfare interests of a child in care: perhaps, in particular, a child who requires a one-to-one relationship due to attachment or health issues.

Gay adoption

Traditionally, the prospect of adoption by a same-sex couple was simply not within the ambit of legislative intent. Indeed, not until very recently would a household consisting of a same-sex couple be construed as coming within the legal definition of 'family'.[44] The possibility of adoption by a single person, however, was and is provided for; the earlier statutory prohibition on adoption of a female child by a single adult male having been removed. An adoption application by a single homosexual male or lesbian, where the applicant is living with a partner of the same gender, has therefore for some time been legally possible,[45] but not until recently has it become professionally and socially acceptable; an acceptance that is still far from universal.

Surrogacy and adoption

The introduction of techniques of artificial insemination and the practice of surrogate motherhood have resulted in many children becoming available for adoption by private arrangement. This new form of 'adoption to order' is not without its problems and many court cases have been generated by the withdrawal of consents freely given before birth of the children concerned.[46] The gravity of concerns regarding the legal and ethical issues involved has resulted, according to a 2010 EU report, in altruistic surrogacy being banned in France, Austria, Switzerland, Sweden, Norway, Italy and Bulgaria. It also gives rise to concern for the child's long-term sense of identity and rights of access to information.

44 See *Fitzpatrick* v. *Sterling Housing Association Ltd* [2001] 11 FLR 271 where the House of Lords ruled that a settled homosexual relationship did constitute a 'family' for the purposes of the law relating to landlord and tenant.

45 In *Re E (Adoption: Freeing Order)* [1995] 1 FLR 382 the Court of Appeal, albeit reluctantly, approved the placement of a girl with a single lesbian adopter.

46 In *Re MW (Adoption: Surrogacy)* [1995] 2 FLR 789 the court dismissed a surrogate mother's opposition to an adoption application by commissioning parents in respect of a child who by then had been in the applicants care for two-and-a-half years.

Conclusion

Adoption is the most radical of all family law orders. No other order so fundamentally changes the legal status of its subject on a lifetime basis. Its effect is to rewrite the relationships between three sets of legal interests with implications for the wider family circles of those involved, the consequences of which will be felt by subsequent generations. Many different societies and the same society at different times, led by the changing motivations of adopters, have shaped adoption to fit the needs of its particular cultural context.

The traditional form of adoption has now largely been displaced by new variants, some of which are wholly driven by private interests (e.g. family adoptions, surrogacy associated adoption) and others by the public interest (e.g. childcare adoptions). Sustained adopter demand in the face of the shrinking consensual availability of healthy white babies has broadened the adoption 'market'. Intercountry and transracial adoptions, once rare occurrences, are now very common. Adoption by same-sex couples is increasing, while many more children with 'special needs' are now being adopted than would ever have been thought possible. All this has given rise to changes in governing principles.

2 The domestic legal framework

Introduction

From a UK perspective, this chapter explores the legal boundaries that frame the terms of reference for 'adoption' and differentiate it from other care arrangements. It considers the historical background: the evolving legislative framework; the interface between the laws governing adoption and those relating to divorce and childcare; and the growing professional input to the adoption process. It introduces the core legal definitional matters in the adoption process – 'child', 'family', consent, adopters, etc. – and explains the 'contract', the parties, the governing principles and the roles played by mediating statutory and voluntary bodies. It deals with: legally defined eligibility to adopt and to be adopted; the rights/duties of the parties; the existence of statutory regulatory bodies and their responsibilities. It identifies the different stages of an adoption process, outlines the outcomes and notes the emergence of associated human rights issues.

Towards modern adoption

In England, when family care was not possible – in circumstances of parental death, absence or criminal abuse – then Parliament used the Poor Laws to place responsibility on public authorities to provide alternative arrangements in residential child-care facilities or, in due course, through boarding-out provision and for a few possibly even adoption. The legal status of a non-marital child in such circumstances was somewhat different from their marital counterpart: such a child was outside the legal definition of 'family' and thus a transfer of care did not require legal intervention.

The Poor Laws

This legislation significantly extended State interest in parenting standards by making the fact of child need itself, rather than its cause, a sufficient threshold for voluntary State intervention. Parental death or absence was no longer a necessary prerequisite for the transfer of responsibility for a child from the private to the public domain. Parents unable or unwilling to continue caring could voluntarily place their children with the Poor Law guardians who could then assume parental rights and place the child in the workhouse, make boarding-out arrangements or place for adoption. However, when children reached an age to be useful or earn a wage, members of their families of origin often reappeared to demand a child's return.

The legacy of non-kinship adoption from the Poor Law period established the principle that the State as ultimate guardian should assume responsibility for those children whose parents were unavailable, unable or unwilling to care for them and it then could legally arrange for that responsibility to be vested in approved adopters (see below).

Adoption and other care arrangements

Traditionally, adoption in England was founded as an expedient legal means of addressing what was then seen as the scandal of unmarried mothers. As such it depended upon the voluntary consent of a young woman, often destitute and rejected by her own family, who had little option other than to relinquish her child for adoption. Indeed, the courts were prepared to interpret such a relinquishment as the act of a responsible parent. As Fitz-Gibbon LJ commented in *In re O'Hara:*[1]

> the surrender of a child to an adopted parent, as an act of prudence or of necessity, under the pressure of present inability to maintain it, being an act done in the interests of the child, cannot be regarded as abandonment or desertion, or even as unmindfullness of parental duty within the meaning of the Act.

Initially, however, while adoption offered the prospect of sparing some children, mainly babies, from the few grim alternative care arrangements available, it was dependent upon the timely intervention of voluntary societies and did little to affect the lives of older abandoned children.

Boarding out

Schemes to 'board-out' abandoned or neglected children for a fee with non-kinship families were first introduced by the Poor Law authorities in the nineteenth century. By the end of that century, following effective campaigning by voluntary organisations concerned for the welfare of children, there had been a general change in the attitude towards workhouses as suitable environments. By giving preference to family based rather than institutional care, the boarded-out schemes paved the way for the modern policy of State-sponsored foster care and adoption arrangements for abandoned children.

1 [1900] 2 IR 233, p. 244.

Residential care

While residential care for children in England had been traditionally provided by charities, churches and other voluntary bodies, it was not until the introduction of the Poor Law in 1834 that State provision commenced for children who were orphaned, neglected or impoverished. From the middle of the nineteenth century, a national network of residential care homes and schools was gradually established, including large institutions run by charities like Barnardo's which were subsidised by Poor Law fees.

Transportation overseas

The practice of transporting children to the British colonies continued throughout the latter half of the nineteenth and the first half of the twentieth centuries. During that period many thousands, perhaps hundreds of thousands, of children were exported by philanthropic societies from the UK and Ireland to the US, Australia and Canada[2] and elsewhere. There, it was felt, they would have opportunities to lead useful lives;[3] it was also candidly admitted that this would ease the burden on English ratepayers. This precursor to the contemporary pernicious evil of 'trafficking' is, arguably if retrospectively, open to criticism on the same human rights grounds.

Policy development

By the end of the nineteenth century, following the effective campaigning of voluntary organisations concerned for the welfare of children, there had been a general change in the attitude towards workhouses as suitable environments. The better survival rates of children who were boarded-out compared to those consigned to the workhouse, and the consequent saving in public expenditure, provided convincing evidence that the welfare of children was best assured by transferring responsibility to those who wanted to adopt a child to complete their family life and in due course this became recognised by legislators. As Cretney has pointed out:[4]

> 'Adoption' first appeared in the statute book in the context of the Poor Law: the Poor Law Act 1899 provided that the Guardians could in certain circumstances assume by resolution all the parents' rights and powers until the child reached the age of eighteen; and the Guardians were then empowered to arrange for the child to be 'adopted'.

2 Bean and Melville, *Lost Children of the Empire*, London, Unwin Hyman, 1989.
3 See, for example, Tizard, B., *Adoption: A Second Chance*, London, Open Books, 1977.
4 Cretney, S., 'Adoption – contract to status?', in *Law, Law Reform and the Family*, Clarendon Press, Oxford, 1998, p. 186.

Child protection

In England, the Custody of Children Act 1891 was introduced to provide a civil remedy for third party carers whose provision for destitute children was opposed by fathers demanding restitution of their custody rights. The rationale for the 1891 Act was explained in the course of the preceding House of Commons debates:

> the Bill is intended to deal with... children who have been thrown helpless on the streets, and wickedly deserted by their parents, and who are taken by the hand by benevolent persons or by charitable institutions.

Its purpose was to provide a civil remedy to protect abandoned children from their neglectful parents by not enforcing parental rights. As such it was the first piece of legislation to offer protection for children from their parents and to others acting in *loco parentis*. Not until the report of the Tomlin Committee in 1925 did policy begin to entertain the possibility of dispensing with parental consent[5] and even then it preferred to restrict such a power to cases of parental abandonment or desertion, where the parent could not be found or was incapable of giving consent or 'being a person unable to contribute to the support of the minor has persistently neglected or refused to contribute to such support'.[6] The point being that whereas the State would step in and take responsibility for a child when a parent did not have or was unable to exercise their inherent parental rights, only in the most extreme circumstances would it do so when a married parent – in effect a father – abused their child (see Chapter 1).

Philanthropic voluntary societies

The role played by various philanthropic societies during the period governed by the Poor Laws was crucially important in effecting policy development. By the end of the nineteenth century, child welfare voluntary organisations such as Barnardo's and the NSPCC began their current specialist services for children by developing a 'child rescue' approach to those abandoned, impoverished or ill-treated. These charitable organisations, providing care in hostels and through boarding-out arrangements, also proved to be effective lobbyists for legislative change. Arguably, the groundwork for recognition of the human rights of unmarried mothers and the welfare interests of children was done by these voluntary societies; their care initiatives were eventually taken up by the State.

Public childcare services

An adoption policy was initially opposed by many who believed that this would serve only to condone the actions of feckless parents seeking to avoid their legal,

5 Lowe, N., 'English adoption law: past, present and future', in Katz, S., Eekelaar, J. and Maclean, M. (eds), *Cross-Currents: Family Law and Policy in the United States and England*, Oxford University Press, 2000, p. 311.

6 Clause 2(3) of the draft Bill prepared by the Tomlin Committee.

moral and financial duties to provide for the upbringing of their children. At a time when family law was governed by paternal rights and duties, rather than child welfare considerations, adoption was viewed by some with scepticism as a potential licence for continued permissiveness. As the Tomlin Committee reported, adoption was not the answer to the problem of unwanted children because 'the people wishing to get rid of children are far more numerous than those wishing to receive them'.[7] However, there were a number of specific public concerns which steadily added to the pressure for change.

Baby farming

The practice of 'baby farming', whereby unmarried mothers would entrust the care of their children to childminders who would then often neglect, abuse, murder or arrange for the informal adoption of their children, caused growing public disquiet.[8] The Infant Life Protection Act 1872 had sought to extend legal protection not only to the vulnerable young residents of workhouses but also to all those whose care was entrusted by their unmarried mothers to such childminders. This was a period when charitable organisations were very active in rescuing children from abuse situations.[9]

De facto *adoptions*

Those who undertook responsibility for children, abandoned by parents when they were young and needing care and maintenance, were often faced with parental demands for the return of their children when the latter were old enough to be useful and earn a wage. In an era when the courts were steadfastly upholding the principle that parental rights were inalienable, such demands were difficult to lawfully resist. Consequently, by the latter half of the nineteenth century, Parliament was under growing pressure to provide legal protection for persons who cared for the children of others.

War orphans

In the aftermath of the First World War, adoption became a matter of general public concern as families informally undertook the care of very many orphaned children but without any guarantee of legal security for their voluntarily assumed care arrangements. Some of these caring families, like the children concerned, were from influential social backgrounds and were not prepared to passively accept the legal insecurity that accompanied informal adoption arrangements. It should

7 McWhinnie, A., *Adopted Children: How They Grew Up*, London, Routledge & Keagan Paul, 1967.

8 Report by Select Committee on the Protection of Infant Life. This 'baby-farming' scandal resonated with similar experiences in Australia and Ireland.

9 Thomas Coram Hospital for Foundling Children, for example, and the Infant Life Protection Society were very active at this time.

also be remembered that this was a period when adoption law had already been successfully introduced in some former British colonies[10] to which there was an established practice of sending children for the purposes of their adoption.[11] The issue as to why England should continue to resist introducing legislation to regulate a practice that was good enough for its former colonies, and good enough to send its children to, would not go away.[12]

Legislating for adoption

Following publication of the Tomlin Report[13] and further failed Bills,[14] the government introduced the Adoption Act 1926, permitting, for the first time in these islands, a formal legal procedure for adoption of children. The subsequent developments in legislation and governing principles were not untypical of those that evolved in other common law jurisdictions.

Adoption within a family law legislative context

From the outset there has been some difficulty in disentangling UK adoption from the body of essentially private family law in which it had always been subsumed: largely due to the more pronounced interest in the public law justification for a change in legal status; the corresponding issue in other areas, such as divorce, was accepted more readily as being fundamentally a private matter resting on grounds limited to reciprocal spousal obligations. In particular, managing the interface between adoption and the law governing both childcare and marital status proved difficult.

Childcare law

As the doctrine of parental, or paternal rights, faded under the pressure of lobbying from voluntary societies concerned for the welfare of increasing numbers of marital and non-marital children abandoned to workhouses, exploited for cheap labour, or subject to parental abuse, so the law relating to children began to emphasise parental care responsibilities and place a duty on public authorities to take the steps necessary to ensure their protection and, where necessary, to wholly assume all parental rights. The emergence of 'the State as carer of last resort' was unproblematic in a Poor Law context – when a child of unmarried or unknown parents was abandoned to public care – he or she could then be placed for adoption. However, the latter step proved more difficult to take in relation to a child in

10 For example: in Massachusetts, US in 1873; in New Brunswick, Canada in 1881; in New Zealand in 1881; and in Western Australia in 1896.
11 Bean and Melville, *Lost Children of the Empire.*
12 See, for example, the report of the Royal Commission on the Poor Law (Cmnd 4499), 1909.
13 *Report of the Child Adoption Committee* 1924–5 (Cmnd 2401).
14 A total of six adoption Bills were introduced during 1924 to 1925.

public care due to the neglect or abuse of parents who might later demand the return of their child or, for fear of social stigma, would allow the State to continue alternative care arrangements but veto any suggestion of adoption. The history of the relationship between the laws of child protection and adoption is one in which the principle of the welfare of the child gradually acquired more traction until it became the paramount factor with the capacity to passport an abused or neglected child into the adoption process. This slow evolution – not completed in the UK until the end of the twentieth century – illustrates the crucial importance of human rights in an adoption context and has done much to define the contemporary social role of adoption – a matter to be pursued in the jurisdiction-specific chapters of Part II.

Marital law

As serial parenting with or without marital status became an accepted social norm, so also did the practice of step-parent adoptions, i.e. the joint use of adoption by a birth parent and new partner to legally seal the boundaries of their newly formed family unit. This use of adoption, as a post-divorce quick fix to establish a nuclear family unit enclosing a set of relationships that were clearly severed from those of the former spouse grew to become its main social function in the latter half of the twentieth century in the UK. Adoption became an almost routine adjunct to divorce proceedings. Such a reductionist approach to a legal process, previously viewed as probably the most grave and far-reaching of all family law orders, was repeatedly challenged by legislative initiatives that sought to prohibit step-parent adoptions except in special circumstances. That these initiatives were unsuccessful was largely due to judicial intransigence: in the light of precedents, and in the absence of any reasonable alternative, the courts were prepared to hold that such adoptions were usually compatible with the best interests of the children involved.

Evolving adoption legislation

Although launched much later in England than in other common law countries, adoption legislation began with the 1926 Act and set in train a sequence of statutes that ultimately concluded with the present legal framework (see Chapter 5).

Adoption Act 1926

This legislation was introduced not to facilitate birth parents nor, particularly, to advance the welfare interests of children, instead it was primarily intended to provide protection for those third parties who had assumed care responsibility for children. In the aftermath of world war, when very many orphans were receiving such care, this legislative initiative was welcomed. It avoided dealing with the thorny issues of: inheritance and succession; dispensing with parental consent; and the possible rights of an older child to give or withhold consent to his or her adoption[15] and to maintain contact with their birth parent. The 1926 Act did, however, incorporate three basic principles: all parental responsibilities would irrevocably and exclusively vest in the adopter/s; the welfare interests of the child were to be independently assessed; and the informed consent of birth parent/s would be required unless they were dead, or had abandoned the child, or their whereabouts were unknown or they were incapacitated. It also embedded a singular and enduring feature of adoption in these islands and one of great significance for human rights: it was to be a process that would have judicial scrutiny and authority at its heart. As Cretney pointed out, the role of the court has been the 'only constant in the development of the adoption process over the past 70 years'.[16]

Adoption of Children (Regulation) Act 1939

The recommendations of the Horsburgh Committee[17] were given effect by this legislation which provided for the registration of all adoption societies or agencies and prohibited the making of adoption arrangements by any other body. As Lowe notes, this legislation established the rudiments of today's adoption service, and outlined the remit of the modern Adoption Panel, by empowering the secretary of state to make regulations to:[18]

a ensure that parents wishing to place their children for adoption were given a written explanation of their legal position;
b prescribe the inquiries to be made and reports to be obtained to ensure the suitability of the child and adopter; and
c secure that no child would be delivered to an adopter until the adopter had been interviewed by a case committee.

Adoption Act 1949

This statute rectified an omission in earlier legislation by establishing the principle that adoption changed the child's status and vested him or her with certain succession rights in relation to their adopter's estate,[19] though not to any title, while also empowering local authorities to make and participate in adoption arrangements. Subsequently, both the Hurst Committee[20] and the Houghton

15 In Scotland this right has been available to children aged 12 or older from the introduction of the first adoption legislation (the Adoption of Children (Scotland) Act 1930, s. 2(3)).
16 Cretney, S., *Family Law in the Twentieth Century: A History*, Oxford University Press, 2003, p. 268.
17 *Report of the Departmental Committee on the Adoption of Children* (Cmnd 9248), London, HMSO, 1954.
18 Lowe, 'English adoption law', p. 322.
19 Such succession rights were further extended in the Children Act 1975.
20 *Report of the Departmental Committee on the Adoption of Children* (Cmnd 9248), para. 24.

Committee[21] recommended strengthening the role ascribed to local authorities and eventually in 1988 a provision was inserted into the 1976 Act making it mandatory for all local authorities to ensure the provision of an adoption service in their areas.

Children Act 1975

This legislation introduced a new part for welfare to play in the adoption process. Section 3 stated:

> In reaching any decision relating to the adoption of a child, a court or adoption agency shall have regard to all the circumstances, first considerations being given to the need to safeguard and promote the welfare of the child through his childhood; and shall so far as practicable ascertain the wishes and feelings of the child regarding the decision and give due consideration to them, having regard to his age and understanding.

It indicated that the public interest in adoption was to be represented by the welfare principle which was to be applied in all decisions, not just in the decision to make an adoption order. Following recommendations made in the Houghton Report, the 1975 Act also introduced custodianship orders[22] which were intended to provide an alternative to adoption for applicants whose circumstances did not warrant the absolute and exclusive effects of adoption.

Adoption Act 1976

Although not coming into effect until 1988, this statute implemented most of the recommendations made by the Houghton Committee. These provisions provided an improved framework for the judiciary to meet contemporary practice demands. The freeing procedures, for example, together with case law principles which stressed the weighting to be given to child welfare concerns relative to parental unreasonableness, facilitated an increase in non-consensual childcare adoptions. The scope provided by s. 12(6) for the court to make a supplementary order in conjunction with one for adoption, allowed the judiciary to moderate the more extreme effects of adoption by issuing an accompanying order permitting an adopted child's continued contact with members of their family of origin. Also, the introduction in s. 51 of an adopted person's right to obtain a copy of their original birth certificate prepared the ground for more openness in adoption. These were important steps in the path towards recognising and giving effect to the separate human rights of an adopted child.

21 *Report of the Departmental Committee on the Adoption of Children* (Cmnd 5107), London, HMSO, 1972, paras 33 and 34 and recommendation 2.

22 Ibid., para. 121. Custodianship became available in 1985.

Children Act 1989

The 1989 Act affected adoption law and practice in a number of ways. It made available a menu of family proceedings orders some of which like residence orders and parental responsibility orders reduced the need for adoption while others such as contact orders could be used in conjunction with adoption orders. It accelerated the general movement towards accommodating more openness in adoption. It also introduced the paramountcy principle to govern judicial decision-making and by doing so sparked off a long period of debate as to why the principle should not be extended to adoption proceedings. More broadly, the flexibility provided by the 1989 Act revealed the absence of this approach in the 1976 Act (see, further, Chapter 5).

Adoption (Intercountry Aspects) Act 1999

This Act amended the Adoption Act 1976 in respect of intercountry adoption (ICA) and enabled the UK to ratify the Hague Convention on Protection of Children and Co-operation in Respect of Intercountry Adoption.

Adoption and Children Act 2002

This statute, an important milestone in adoption legislation, came fully into effect in December 2005.

It was accompanied by the introduction of National Standards, followed by the Children Act 2004 and the Children and Adoption Act 2006. Together this body of legislative provisions created a new platform for adoption law and practice in England (see Chapter 5).

Adoption within a family planning context

Against the background of an evolving legislative framework for adoption, advances were also being made in family planning options and in associated regulatory controls. As with adoption, it was not so much the practice as the legislative recognition and the introduction of designated processes that ushered in a new era of socially acceptable and agency-supported choices in relation to the prospect of becoming a parent.

Abortion and contraception

Legal abortion was introduced in the UK under the Abortion Act 1967, which continues to be the governing legislation. The ensuing annual increase in abortions has been accompanied by a rapid decline in the number of children available for adoption, an inverse correlation that shows no sign of changing. This, in conjunction with the fact that most types of contraception are free, and have become significantly more efficient, has added to well-established trends.

Assisted reproduction technology

The development of fertility treatment (AID, GIFT, etc.) continues to grow in ways that have come to fundamentally challenge our understanding of parenthood by introducing new concepts of 'parent' that include genetic/biological, gestational, legal and extend to accommodate the notion of three parents for a child. This technology, as well as greatly complicating family law, has been important in reducing reliance on adoption. In the UK, the Human Fertilisation and Embryology Act 1990 and the consequent improvement in treatment methods have offered an alternative route for childless couples hoping to start a family.

Surrogacy agreements, though generally not legally enforceable, have become a popular means of achieving parenthood. They are legislatively defined and largely confined to serve altruistic intentions. For those seeking a healthy baby, rather than the older child with perhaps healthcare issues most usually available through domestic adoption, surrogacy is a feasible if expensive way of doing so. It has proved a particularly popular option for single persons and for gay couples. Surrogacy arrangements generally conclude with the child being adopted by the commissioning parent/s (see Chapter 3).

Adoption: evolving practice and principles

By the turn of the twenty-first century, the UK government was faced with the needs of large numbers of children failed by parental care, a judiciary concerned to protect established precedents in the law of adoption from being undermined by the paramountcy principle and practice developments that threatened to entirely privatise the future use of adoption.

The birth mother

Arguably, in the UK as elsewhere in the western world, the needs of the birth mother had by the final decades of the twentieth century become the principal bargaining position around which the needs of the child and those of the adopters had to be configured. The dominance of the patriarchal model of the autonomous marital family unit had long gone. The legislative and judicial hesitancy to accommodate the paramountcy principle in adoption law had constrained opportunities to give priority to the needs of the child. The needs of adopters, as always the driving force in this dynamic, remained totally dependent upon children being available and all traditional sources were rapidly drying up. But the weighting given to the legal interests of birth mothers had grown to have a powerful impact upon adoption: it could be said that while the law had brought to an end the long era of paternal rights it had allowed the exercise of maternal rights to become the governing factor in the adoption process. Always of pivotal importance in the triangle of adoption relationships, by the end of the twentieth century the decisions of a birth mother had become wholly dominant. Not only did improved welfare benefits, access to contraception and abortion, and the disappearance of associated social stigma, enable her to choose to avoid what had previously been the forced option of adoption but, should she decide to opt for her traditional role in that process, she could still claim the protection of confidentiality and anonymity that accompanied it. Moreover, as adoption came to be used as an almost routine adjunct to divorce processes, she was increasingly likely to be engaged in an adoption process as applicant rather than as respondent.

These trends inevitably meant that domestic sources for the kind of children traditionally adopted were rapidly drying up. This in turn led to growing numbers of prospective adopters being unable to satisfy their needs from such sources and many turned towards ICA – particularly as a source for consensually available healthy babies. By the closing decades of the twentieth century the 'adoption market' was rapidly changing.

The direction of change was largely driven by the numbers of children in public care, the well-documented evidence of the consequent harm to their welfare interests and the associated cost to the public purse. The numbers of children compulsorily removed had not only vigorously outgrown the number voluntarily relinquished from parental care but were most often accompanied by a parental veto preventing adoption. It was an effective veto: in 1952 of all children adopted only 3.2 per cent were from public care,[23] rising to 8.7 per cent in 1968; by the end of the 1980s, only a very small proportion of children in care were subsequently adopted.[24] This was due mainly to the number of childcare adoptions remaining fairly constant in a context where overall annual adoptions were falling while the childcare population continued to increase. Parental consent continued to be the essential legal passport for a child to pass from public care to private family care via adoption. In order to overcome the parental veto and make the opportunity of adoption available to more children, a new legislative initiative was needed.

Paramountcy principle

The introduction of the paramountcy principle, to overcome the parental veto and thereby bridge the gap between childcare law and adoption law, constituted a landmark change in UK adoption law and practice. It was inserted as the overriding consideration in the adoption and children statutes of 2002, 2006 and 2014.

The adoption contract

Adoption was initially conceived as, and has remained, essentially a contractual process dealing separately with the legal interests of each of the parties and the

23 Lowe, N., 'English Adoption Law: Past, Present and Future' in Katz, S., Eekelaar, J., and Maclean, M., *Cross Currents: Family Law and Policy in the United States and England*, Oxford University Press, 2000, p. 315.

24 A survey of six local authorities in England revealed that only 0.8 per cent were eventually placed for adoption (see Rowe, J., Hundleby, M. and Garnett, L., *Child Care Now – A Survey of Placement Patterns*, London, BAAF, 1989).

welfare interests of the child concerned. While the law has always rigorously protected the rights of the parties, providing for their representations, etc., it has also been clear that there is no right as such to adopt.

The 'contract'

Adoption is a process which, at its most basic, redistributes the legal interests of the three main participants and, unlike any other orders relating to children, does so on a permanent, irrevocable and on an unqualified basis. Some of these customary hallmarks have been steadily eroded as the process has adapted to fit the contemporary needs of the parties. Like all contracts, the commitments entered into by the parties must be evidenced by their informed consent; though in the UK this requirement has, in relation to older children, been given statutory recognition only in Scotland. The courts have also stressed the importance of ensuring the propriety of the contract by, for example, prohibiting any element of financial reward for the parties involved and any improper practice such as the unauthorised removal of a child from their jurisdiction of origin.[25] In recent years, the contractual standing of the parties to an adoption has been affected not only by a transformation in the legal weighting ascribed to the role of the birth mother and that of an unmarried father; more recently the legal interests of the child concerned have also undergone a radical change. From being confined to a legal role as merely the object of adoption proceedings, the child and their welfare have now become fully the subject and purpose of such. In England and Wales, the incorporation of the paramountcy principle in the 2002 Act considerably altered the balance struck between the parties to an adoption contract (see Chapter 5).

Private and confidential

From the outset, the statutory process of adoption was viewed and treated as essentially a matter of private family law; in fact, the most private of all family proceedings. The contractual arrangements reflected this in the guarantees of anonymity given to adopters and birth parent/s, in the court use of serial numbers to hide the identity of children, and in the subsequent lack of access to agency files, etc. While this continues to be largely true, it is also the case that adoption in recent years has gradually become increasingly a matter of public law, ushered in by a new era of 'openness' in which processes are now available to facilitate information sharing and contact arrangements, with the agreement of the parties concerned.

25 Both practices, associated with the traditional abhorrence of 'trafficking' in children, were criminal offences under s. 57 and s. 11, respectively, of the 1976 Act.

Permanent and irrevocable

The absolute nature of adoption, relative to other family orders, was apparent from the fact that once made, it retained its binding effect on all parties at least until the child concerned reached maturity. A valid order was not open to challenge by any of the parties, nor by anyone else. Throughout the history of this statutory process, and unlike any other family order, it was not amenable to appeal nor to revocation: in particular, it could not be refuted by the adopters. This characteristic has remained immutable.

Exclusive

An adoption order was intended to extinguish all parental rights and duties of the birth parents and vest the full complement of parental responsibilities in the named adopter/s to the exclusion of all others. However, the legal fiction that purported to place an adopter in the shoes of the birth parent was for many years qualified in relation to matters such as inheritance and succession rights while legislation continued the exemption extended to an adopted brother and sister from the laws relating to incest. Moreover, with an increasing awareness of the importance of 'attachments' for a child's psychological development has come a willingness to allow a contact order to be made in conjunction with adoption so as to permit ongoing contact between a child and members of their family of origin with whom a significant relationship has been established.

Consensual

The principle that adoption should rest on the full, free and informed consent of the birth parent/s, or the absence of dissent, was the starting point for statutorily regulating the process in the UK. For most of its history, it has in the main been a consensual process resting on the freely given consent of the birth parent/s or on the absence of any need for it due to the child being orphaned or abandoned. In recent years the law has extended the principle to afford recognition to the interests of the birth father, particularly if he has acquired parental responsibilities. The further extension, providing grounds for dispensing with the need for parental consent to facilitate the adoption of children in public care, has been a significant but controversial milestone in the evolving social role of adoption in the developed western nations.

As the non-consensual proportion of annual applications has slowly grown, mainly due to an increase in childcare adoptions, so too has contention as to the proper balance to be struck between the grounds on which a birth parent may withhold consent and the welfare interests of their child. When should welfare interests prevail over the wishes of a non-consenting parent? What, if any, rights could a non-consenting or indeed a consenting parent retain?

The parties

Traditionally, the legal process of adoption has rested on a triangular relationship: the unmarried birth parent/s, their lovingly relinquished healthy baby and the unrelated, married but childless heterosexual couple. Full party status has usually been confined to two of these participants: the relinquishing birth parent/parents or guardian and the person or couple wishing to undertake responsibility; though normally not to the child, the subject of the proceedings. Others may mediate, such as statutory and voluntary agencies, in arranging or supervising care arrangements, but the legal framework is concerned exclusively with the redistribution of legal responsibilities within this triangle of relationships. The judiciary and a range of professionals have also always been involved in a process that affects an extensive network of family relationships.

While this framework remains essentially intact, it has broadened in recent years to cater for parties who are no longer restricted by traditional legal definitions and to accommodate a wider range of carers and professionals.

The child

Children – their needs, availability and ultimately their acquisition – have always been and remain central to adoption in the UK. When children were orphaned or abandoned, when their 'illegitimate' status could be transformed to 'legitimate', where parental consent was available or not withheld and where it was judged to be compatible with the child's welfare interests, then adoption was judicially viewed as wholly appropriate. Most usually, such children were babies. However, when complications arose, especially in relation to the child in care whose married parents refused consent, then the courts were a great deal more circumspect.

The profile of today's typical adopted child is very different from the one traditionally placed for adoption. Then the process largely catered for healthy, indigenous, 'illegitimate', white Caucasian babies.[26] Now, while there are far fewer babies,[27] and of those many are likely to be from a different country and quite possibly from a different race than that of their adopters, the children adopted

26 In 1968, the peak year for adoptions in the UK and Ireland, one in five of all 'illegitimate' children were adopted in the former jurisdiction compared with four in every five in the latter. See also Bridge, C. and Swindells, H., *Adoption: The Modern Law*, Family Law, Bristol, 2003, where it is stated that by 1951, baby adoptions comprised 52 per cent of all adoptions. By 1968 this proportion was even greater – amounting to 76 per cent of all adoptions – and in the same year, 91 per cent of all adoptions were of illegitimate children. Adoption of illegitimate babies had become the primary focus of adoption law (p. 6).

27 In 1975, the proportion of children adopted aged 10 or more was 19 per cent whereas by 1987 it had grown to 27 per cent, but has since continued a downward trend falling from 21 per cent in 1998 to 8.4 per cent in 2012. Adoptions of children aged under 1 decreased overall from 4.6 per cent of all adoptions in 1998 to 1.6 per cent in 2011 before rising slightly to 2.2 per cent in 2012. In contrast, the percentage of adopted children aged 1–4 has increased steadily since 1998 when they constituted 34 per cent of the total to reach 63 per cent in 2012. See further at: www.ons.gov.uk/ons/rel/vsob1/adoptions-in-england-and-wales/2012/stb-adoptions-in-england-and-wales–2012-.html#tab-Adoptions-by-age-and-sex

continue to be very largely from unmarried parents.[28] The preponderance of family adoptions naturally raised the average age of children being adopted as did the increase in children adopted by their long-term foster carers. Childcare adoptions – often accompanied by very necessary long-term financial, professional and other forms of support – have introduced many children to the adoption process with needs that would not have been within the contemplation of initial legislators. Most contemporary agency adoptions involve children that are the subject of care orders, have some degree of 'special needs', whether suffering from a physical or learning disability, from a behavioural disorder or from 'foetal alcohol syndrome' and may be placed in sibling groups; none of which was envisaged by initial legislators. In this context it is worth noting that under the Children and Young Persons Act 1933, a child is defined as a person under the age of 16 for the purpose of the criminal law on child abuse and neglect; an anomaly that was of concern to the Committee on the Rights of the Child in its 2016 report.[29]

In the UK there would seem to have always been an imbalance in the number of children available relative to prospective adopters. For the earliest and longest part of its history as a statutory process that imbalance was evident in an excess of children; resulting in their transportation for adoption overseas. In recent decades this imbalance has been reversed. While the courts have always required an independent assessment of a child's welfare interests, only in recent years have they been prepared to grant party full party status and rights of representation to older children in adoption proceedings.

The birth parent/s

The birth parent and/or legal guardian of the child, vested with parental responsibility, has always had full party status in any proceedings for the adoption of that child: the birth mother being inherently vested with such responsibility; the birth father, if unmarried to the mother, having to legally acquire it. Traditionally 'birth parent' has been interpreted as referring to the mother of a non-marital child whose involvement with the adoption process was solely for the purpose of voluntarily relinquishing all parental responsibility. In recent years, however, as a direct consequence of human rights rulings by the ECtHR, the *locus standi* of an unmarried father has gradually acquired greater salience.

In the past, the forced option of adoption was often unavoidable for an unmarried mother facing social censure, financial hardship and without the means to seek recourse to the courts. Of the three parties, only she held a legal right in relation to adoption; the right to relinquish all future rights. She could consent to the adoption of her child and, until the Adoption Act 1976, could directly place

28 The percentage of adopted children, born outside of marriage, increased slightly to 85 per cent in 2012, up from 82 per cent in 2011.

29 UN Committee on the Rights of the Child, Concluding observations on the fifth periodic report of the United Kingdom of Great Britain and Northern Ireland (CRC/C/GBR/CO/5), 2016, para. 42(b).

him or her for adoption with whomsoever she chose. However, improved welfare benefits, contraceptives and access to abortion facilities gave unmarried mothers more freedom of choice. Also, the increased use of adoption by remarried parents in respect of legitimate children transformed the traditional role of the birth parent. Adoption had become the recourse of birth parents for reasons exactly the opposite of those initially intended: to reassert rather than relinquish legal responsibilities. The role reversal was also apparent in childcare adoptions where, unlike formerly, this is now likely to be on a non-consensual basis to resist the enforced adoption of their child. Finally, access to information rights has meant that the birth parent/s cannot step forever out of the life of their adopted child. The latter will always have access to the information necessary to identify, trace and possibly contact their birth mother if not both parents.

The traditional and rather dismissive approach of the law towards unmarried fathers without parental responsibility, which clearly constituted a refutation of his human rights, has gradually given way to a more accommodating attitude. Undoubtedly this change in judicial attitude has been influenced by the European Convention on Fundamental Freedoms and Human Rights. In *Keagan* v. *Ireland*,[30] for example, the European Court of Human Rights established the principle that where an unmarried father had previously enjoyed a settled cohabiting relationship with a mother who had decided to place their child for adoption then that father should be informed and consulted because the protection given to 'family life' provided by Article 8 extended to include such a relationship (see Chapter 4).

The adopter/s

In the UK, as elsewhere, while the number of adopters has fallen dramatically it had become apparent that the legal functions of adoption were being driven mostly by their needs: most obviously in relation to intercountry, surrogacy arrangements and 'step-adoptions'.

By the early years of the twenty-first century, more mothers were resorting to adoption, with their new partner, as a means of jointly acquiring rather than relinquishing absolute and irrevocable rights in respect of a natural child.[31] Ironically, birth parents had come to constitute the largest group of annual adoption applicants: an irony with a very real human rights dimension – how did it come to pass that the law was such that a birth parent was required to adopt their own child as the best means of securing their family life? A birth parent acting, jointly with their new spouse to adopt the former's child, marital or non-marital, emerged as the most pronounced characteristic in the modern use of adoption.

There were other changes which had altered the status of adopters. Traditionally adoption applicants were required to be a married couple whose age, health and social circumstances were such that they could be reasonably expected to

30 (1994) 18 EHRR 342.
31 Bridge and Swindells, *Adoption*, p. 217.

provide as normal and secure a home life for an adopted child as would any average middle-class couple. Single applicants were usually viewed with suspicion. The profile of the typical adopter is now very different: they may well be single, older, not necessarily married and perhaps be financially assisted and professionally supported; they may be of the same gender; and may be of a different nationality and perhaps different race to the child they propose to adopt. Today's adopters may be seen in the main as comprising three distinct groups. First, there are those who adopt children from a childcare context. These are likely to be foster parents, or agency-approved adopters with similar abilities, who will adopt older children or those with special needs and who may well rely upon and welcome ongoing and intrusive public service support. Second, there are those with the motivation, determination and resources to adopt babies from another country. These are more likely to be from a professional or upper middle-class background and are unlikely to want any post-adoption public service intrusion. Finally, there are those who adopt children to whom they are related, usually as birth parent or as spouse of the latter. This group is again unlikely to want or welcome any post-adoption public service intrusion. Adoption in the first two groups will be as a result of agency placements involving professional assessments; the first group will be selected not because they conform to an average middle-class profile but because they have the particular strengths and attributes that will be required to cope with the challenging needs of the typical child now in the public care system. A majority of adopters are now likely to have ongoing contact, direct or indirect, with members of the adopted child's family of origin.

The adoption process

Traditionally, the adoption parties – typically the relinquishing birth parent/s, the child orphaned, abandoned, unwanted or inadequately cared for, and the applicant couple – engaged in a legal process that in practice was mediated by various bodies before being finalised by the court. While this remains essentially the same, the modern adoption process no longer necessarily begins with an application for, nor ends with the making of, an adoption order. Pre adoption counselling services are now available to all parties and local authorities are required to ensure the provision of an adoption service including post-adoption support services. Moreover, the process is increasingly likely to be complicated by contested proceedings, particularly in non-consensual childcare adoptions, or by the fact that the child has ongoing healthcare needs, is the subject of a surrogacy arrangement or of an ICA. Mostly the modern adoption process differs from the traditional version in that it has come to serve a purpose contrary to the premise on which it was statutorily established: birth mothers are more likely to be asserting rather than relinquishing parental responsibility; and the process has become increasingly non-consensual. One singular traditional characteristic it has retained is the lack of any specific central regulating body. The UK, unlike for example Ireland, has never established a body with responsibility for coordinating all agencies, monitoring standards of practice, maintaining archives of adoption files and determining adoption applications, etc. Although the judicial role has always and continues to serve many of these functions, its role is not activated until proceedings are lodged in court.

Voluntary bodies

Until the 1970s, the business of matching prospective adopters with the child of relinquishing birth parents continued to be conducted in the UK very largely by the same voluntary adoption societies[32] that had pioneered adoption practice.[33] However, there are now far fewer such societies involved in an adoption process and many more professional checks and balances.[34] The role of voluntary bodies has become restricted in recent years to the provision of services such as pre-adoption counselling and post-adoption support and information and tracing.

Adoption society

Arrangements were formerly made on the basis of consent for adoption being available and placements conducted in a confidential manner so as to ensure that all identifying information was held by the society and not shared between the birth parent/s, child and adopters. Record-keeping by adoption societies was a matter for their discretion; many were destroyed in the belief that this was in keeping with the confidential relationship between the society and the three parties. The consequences of this process were intended to be essentially private, absolute and irrevocable.

By the closing decades of the twentieth century, the involvement of voluntary adoption societies had faded as the process became dominated by family applicants, for whom there is no need to provide a placement service, and by childcare placements which being usually non-consensual were required to be authorised and managed by local authorities.

Public authorities

Provision for post-adoption support, information rights and reunification services has led to local authorities having a more intrusive and ongoing role as adoption becomes more 'open' and less absolute, anonymous, taboo tainted and exclusive. It now often accommodates ongoing contact arrangements which are sometimes

32 Such as Dr Barnardo's.

33 In 1966, for example, of all agency adoptions, 73 per cent were arranged by voluntary societies; by 1971 this had fallen to 60 per cent.

34 The transformation of adoption practice from a patchwork of activities provided largely by voluntary societies to a comprehensive and professionalised adoption service provided in the main by local authorities dates from the recommendations of the Houghton Committee in *Report of the Departmental Committee on the Adoption of Children* (Cmnd 5107), para. 38.

permitted by contact orders issued in conjunction with adoption orders.[35] It may also require years of post-adoption support from health and social care professionals in respect of the many adopted children with physical or mental health issues or with complicated relationships with members of their families of origin.

Social workers

The assessment of prospective adopters and the matching of successful applicants with an appropriate child selected on the basis of the latter's particular profile of needs are tasks that fall to professionally qualified and registered social workers. In the majority of cases, the child concerned will be a child in care and the social workers will be employed by the local authority. In other cases – in a kinship or intercountry context – the assessing social worker may well be employed by a voluntary adoption society. Where a parental rehabilitation programme has concluded unsuccessfully in respect of a child in care, then again the key social workers involved will have been from the local authority (see Chapter 5).

Adoption allowances

The payment of adoption allowances by local authorities in respect of childcare adoptions has broadened the pool of prospective adopters as foster parents and other carers have opted for financially supported adoption as the preferred means of securing long-term care arrangements. This policy, which has been likened to 'paying people to adopt children', proved controversial[36] and arguably has a human rights dimension. It represented a significant shift in the approach of government to what had been regarded as a private area of family law where the motivation of adopters was expected to be altruistic, above reproach and untainted by considerations of personal benefit.

The courts

The fact that the judiciary have always been at the heart of the UK adoption process does indeed provide the best possible guarantee that the process will be human rights compliant. Arguably, however, the judicial role has in recent years

35 Under s. 12(6) of the Adoption Act 1976, the court was given such a discretionary power.

36 British Association of Social Workers, *Analysis of the Children Bill*, 1975, which states it would be an intolerable situation if financial resources were made available to subsidise adoption when an allocation of similar resources to the natural parents may have prevented the break-up of the family in the first place (p. 22). In support of this approach, it has to be noted that childcare adoption is virtually non-existent in Denmark where the State heavily invests in the family support services necessary to keep vulnerable children at home.

become functionally marginalised: the operative decisions in respect of most UK adoptions – childcare and intercountry – are now taken well before matters come before the court; the judicial power to affect the outcome of an adoption process has usually been pre-empted by events.

Court officers

In adoption proceedings the courts have always been able to call upon, or direct the appointment of, social workers who would undertake an assessment of: the circumstances giving rise to the application; the home, relationships and social setting of the prospective adopters; and on anything having a bearing upon the welfare of the child. Formerly, in the UK, such responsibilities fell to a guardian *ad litem* who was required to report to the court on all such matters.

Contested proceedings

The adoption process has come to accommodate a growing number of contested applications. A process, very largely consensual until the 1980s, has since become increasingly non-consensual as childcare adoptions are contested and occasionally so also are family adoptions. This has led to a range of professional involvement that would previously have been thought incongruous; psychologists, psychiatrists and child development specialists are now frequently called as expert witnesses.

The hearing

All successful adoption applications in the UK, unlike in other jurisdictions, conclude with a court order as this has always been a judicial proceeding thereby ensuring that it conformed to the highest standards of 'due process'. However, while they would traditionally have been a mere legal formality, held in a judge's chambers and conducted in a discreet and solicitous manner, increasingly they have become the final step of a heavily litigated process which will have involved social workers, legal representation for the parties, expert witnesses and possibly the cross-examination of witnesses. Moreover, the views of the child concerned, age and understanding permitting, will now be sought in relation to their proposed adoption.

The outcome

Adoption proceedings have had the singular characteristic that they have always concluded simply on the basis of the desired order being granted or rejected, and almost always it was granted as the grounds for approval were invariably established before the matter came before the court. By nature, an absolute and unequivocal order, it has never been possible to add conditions or otherwise qualify an adoption order, though in recent years this effect can be achieved by coupling it with a contact order.

Conclusion

Adoption proceedings have remained essentially the same as when they were first statutorily established. Those recognised as parties, the main governing principles, the elements of their contractual relationship and the effect of an adoption order on their status are all essentially as initially defined. However, the balance then struck between the public and private interests has since undergone significant change. The key component in this rebalancing has been the welfare interests of the child.

In recent years the triangular relationship of legal interests had become very lopsided. The number of children compulsorily removed from abusing parents had not only vigorously outgrown the number voluntarily relinquished from parental care but their admission to the public childcare system was most often accompanied by a parental veto preventing adoption and consigning the children to institutional care or to the revolving door of foster care. Ironically, the number of prospective adopters unable to achieve family life by adopting a child within the jurisdiction had also grown but for many years the parental veto prevented any legal bridging between both sets of needs. Moreover, the prevailing social context had become one where birth control, serial parenting and transient family relationships had radically altered the previously prevailing marital, monogamous and nuclear family unit which in turn had transformed adoption into an expedient adjunct to marriage or remarriage. Not until the welfare interests of the child was statutorily established as the paramount principle governing the use of adoption did it become possible to realign the interests of all parties and clarify the functions of adoption proceedings (see Chapter 4).

3 The international legal framework and intercountry adoption

Introduction

This chapter begins by considering the social phenomenon of intercountry adoption (ICA), it briefly reflects on its history, examines some key definitional matters and summarises the current trends in its use. It then identifies the supranational framework of bodies and outlines the human rights provisions that have a bearing, direct or otherwise, on national or transnational adoption law and practice. It notes the key principles as stated in various Conventions, particular attention being given to the United Nations Convention on the Rights of the Child (UNCROC) and the European Convention for the Protection of Human Rights and Fundamental Freedoms (ECHR). It considers the relevance of the United Nations Declaration on Social and Legal Principles relating to the Protection and Welfare of Children with Special Reference to Foster Placement and Adoption Nationally and Internationally and to the Convention on Protection of Children and Co-operation in Respect of Intercountry Adoption.

Having sketched the international framework of adoption-related law in general terms, this chapter then turns to examine contemporary ICA practice in particular, with a special focus on those adoptions governed by the Hague Convention on Intercountry Adoption. It states the main provisions of that Convention (as amended in 2008), identifies its related administrative bodies and concludes by outlining the associated adoption process and its outcomes.

ICA: background and definitions

This phenomenon has existed for a long time. It was evident, for example, in the practice of sending many tens of thousands of orphaned, abandoned and/or neglected children from the UK[1] and Ireland[2] to Australia,[3] Canada[4] and other

1 Bean, P. and Melville, J., *Lost Children of the Empire*, London, Unwin Hyman, 1989.
2 Robbins, J., *The Lost Children: A Study of Charity Children in Ireland 1700–1900*, Dublin, Institute of Public Administration, 1980.
3 Humphreys, M., *Empty Cradles*, London, Random House, 2009.
4 Parker, R., *Uprooted: The Shipment of Poor Children to Canada, 1867–1919*, Bristol, Policy Press, 2008.

British colonial and postcolonial countries in the late nineteenth and early twentieth centuries.[5] Indeed, it has been estimated that Canada alone received some 80,000 in the space of 50 years to be informally adopted into Canadian families.[6] Now, as then, political expediency in allowing citizens of other countries to bear the cost of rearing surplus children continues to play a prominent role.

Human rights, politics and ICA

To the extent that ICA can be seen in child rescue terms, an unavoidable corollary is that it must also be viewed as a consequence of the flawed domestic politics of sending countries. This is most often due to the failure of the latter to provide the domestic services necessary to retain children within their country and culture of origin, a failure further complicated by the political complicity of receiving nations in choosing to facilitate such removal rather than resourcing the means for their retention.

Social disruption

The modern manifestation of ICA, signifying the movement of children from institutional care in impoverished or conflict ravaged countries into the middle-class homes of adopters in western society, most probably dates from the aftermath of the Second World War. This 'child rescue' approach has its origins in a very practical and necessary humanitarian response to the plight of refugee children abandoned or orphaned in the many theatres of war. Then, from about the mid 1970s, stimulated in part by the social dislocation in South-East Asia following the Vietnam War, ICA became a global phenomenon. By that time, it also embraced sending countries in South America and such receiving countries as Canada, Australia, the US and most of Western Europe. From the 1990s, it extended to include sending countries in Eastern Europe, most notably Romania. Since then recourse to ICA has been heavily influenced by social context factors that determine the domestic availability of surplus children. In countries such as the UK, where there is a relatively high incidence of adoption from the public childcare route and methods of assisting conception (e.g. AID, GIFT, etc.) and surrogacy are legally available and accessible through the National Health Service, the ICA rate is low. In countries such as Ireland the opposite is the case.

Natural disaster

The 'child rescue' dimension to ICA is most obviously apparent, and most likely to be altruistic, when it occurs in the aftermath of one of nature's recurring devastating events such as an earthquake. Even then, however, as illustrated by the

5 Milotte, M., *Banished Babies: The Secret History of Ireland's Baby Export Business*, New Island Books, 1997.
6 Parker, *Uprooted.*

controversy generated by the very many unprocessed adoptions that followed immediately after the Haitian disaster, there will be adopters and agencies that put opportunism before altruism.

Contemporary trends

Until the mid 2000s, ICA had grown into a popular and accepted practice whereby those in the developed western societies assumed care responsibilities for children abandoned in the poorer undeveloped nations of Eastern Europe and Asia. This transaction was one that rose from a level of some 2,500 children in the 1950s, involved approximately 40,000 by the early years of the twentieth century, but within a brief decade that number had shrunk by two-thirds. By 2013, in global terms, ICAs had returned to the level recorded in the early 1980s.[7] However, the socio-economic divide between countries of origin (the 'sending' countries) and countries of destination (the 'receiving' countries) for the children involved has remained unchanged. The flow of children has invariably been from the more undeveloped countries of the southern hemisphere to the more affluent western societies; a reversal of the direction first established in the latter part of the nineteenth century and continuing until the middle of the twentieth.

Sending countries

The political reality driving a national policy of sending children overseas has always been rooted in poverty. Invariably it is the poor children, whose parents are unavailable or unable to care for them, that are exported by under-resourced State authorities to meet the needs of adopters elsewhere.

Many formerly high-volume sending countries, including Korea, Romania, Bulgaria and Guatemala, have stopped ICAs altogether. In 2003, 70 per cent of intercountry adoptees came from one of the ten main countries of origin, mainly China, Russia, Guatemala, Ukraine and South Korea. Between 2004 and 2013, China and Russia continued to be the two main countries of origin, but the number of internationally adopted children fell by three-quarters in both countries (from 13,415 to 3,400 in China, and from 7,737 to 1,767 in Russia). In particular, the availability of healthy babies has tailed off markedly: for example, Chinese adoptees have changed from 95 per cent healthy, 'normal' girls in 2005 to more than 90 per cent special needs children in 2015. By way of contrast, adoptions from Africa rose from 5 per cent of all ICAs in 2003 to 28 per cent in 2014. But even on that continent the trend in now in reverse for many countries, including Ethiopia which has been by far the largest African sending country.

7 Mignot, J.-F., 'Why is intercountry adoption declining worldwide?', *Population & Societies*, 519 (February 2015), 1.

Receiving countries

'Intercountry adoptions' as the Special Rapporteur has succinctly noted, 'have been fuelled by a demand from prospective adoptive parents in higher-income countries for children from lower-income countries'.[8]

In 2003, 90 per cent of international adoptees went to one of the ten main receiving countries mainly to the US, France, Spain, Italy and Germany. By 2014, all major receiving countries reported a 70 per cent drop in the number of adoptees over a ten-year period; dropping by 64 per cent, from 42,194 to 15,188, between 2004 and 2013 in the top ten adopting countries; a steep trend which continued in 2015. The US continues to be the world's largest intercountry adopting State, but while 23,000 children were adopted in 2004, this figure had fallen to 5,000 in 2015. By way of contrast, Portugal and the UK and Japan are at the other end of the scale and collectively account for less than 2 per cent of all ICAs. The national variation is interesting: at one extreme, 95 per cent of adoptions in Belgium, 94 per cent in Luxembourg and 90 per cent in France are intercountry; compared with 1 per cent in Portugal and 5 per cent in the UK.

Reasons for current trend

According to Selman, the initial sharp but sustained downward trend has been for two main reasons: fewer children being abandoned and a rise in domestic adoption.[9] A contributory factor to the latter may be the existence of a government policy permitting the adoption of children in the long-term care of the State due to parental fault or default. Some, however, point to the rising complexities and costs of international adoptions as regulated by the Hague Convention: for example, both Guatemala and Vietnam have been aligning their laws and processes since ratification in 2009 and 2011 respectively. Other causes include: more widespread recourse to contraception and abortion; the reduced stigma associated with nonmarital births; and, undoubtedly, rising prosperity in the traditional sending countries is encouraging governments to renounce policies now associated with failed States and dependency upon western society. The more restrictive policies introduced by the main sending countries are also a constraint: China, for example, since 2006 has limited applications to married heterosexual couples, who hold a high-school diploma, are in employment and are not morbidly obese. Moreover, the particular attraction of ICA lay in the probability of obtaining the baby or young child unavailable domestically but, as by far the majority of children

8 Report of the Special Rapporteur on the Sale of Children, Child Prostitution and Child Pornography (27 February–24 March 2017), A/HRC/34/55, para. 43; at: https://documents-dds-ny.un.org/doc/UNDOC/GEN/G16/440/24/PDF/G1644024.pdf?OpenElement

9 Selman, P., 'The rise and fall of intercountry adoption in the 21st century: global trends from 2001 to 2010', in Gibbons, J. and Rotabi, K. (eds), *Intercountry Adoption: Policies, Practices, and Outcomes*, Farnham, Ashgate, 2012.

now available are older and with 'special needs', many prospective adopters are instead turning towards international commercial surrogacy.[10]

Commercial surrogacy

This practice, prohibited in most western nations and outsourced to developing countries, which has grown exponentially in recent years with an undoubted impact upon ICA, is one which, of course, brings the added bonus of a genetic link. It is also a practice that endangers the human rights of the children involved, and indeed those of the birth parents. The Special Rapporteur has drawn attention to this escalating international problem:[11]

> The international regulatory vacuum that persists in relation to international commercial surrogacy arrangements leaves children born through this method vulnerable to breaches of their rights, and the practice often amounts to the sale of children and may lead to illegal adoption. Indeed, several countries do not recognize such arrangements and, in order to establish a parent–child relationship, national laws often require parents to legally adopt the child born through international commercial surrogacy. However, if the international commercial surrogacy arrangement is found to amount to the sale of a child, the adoption too will consequently be illegal under international standards. Such a situation underscores the need for States to ensure that they are not inadvertently legitimizing the sale of children born through international commercial surrogacy by granting adoption orders.

The legalities of adopting children from another country

Although the Hague Convention now provides an international framework of standards and guiding principles, its capacity to raise levels of practice has been limited by the fact that a number of participant nations have been slow to become signatories. While ICA is now generally required to function within Hague parameters, there are many examples in Europe and North America of the courts being faced with issues relating to children 'adopted' outside that process.

Full and simple adoptions

'Adoption' in law may be either 'full' or 'simple': in the former the legal relationship between the birth parent/s and their child is terminated; in the latter it is not completely severed. The legal systems of countries such as the UK, the US,

10 As commercial surrogacy is illegal in many developed countries (e.g. France, Sweden, Norway, Italy, Spain, Switzerland and Canada) the 'providers' are largely the developing nations in the East and Asia (e.g. India and Thailand, though recently prohibited in both).

11 Special Rapporteur report, A/HRC/34/55, para. 52.

Australia and the Scandinavian countries restrict recognition to full adoptions while such others as France, Romania, Japan together with many countries in South America and Africa also recognise simple adoptions. Article 26 of The Hague Convention gives recognition to both forms and Article 27 empowers a receiving country to convert a simple adoption into a full adoption if the law of that country permits such a conversion and if the appropriate consents are available.

Kafala

This is a form of simple adoption, widely used in Islamic countries or by Muslims living elsewhere, which circumvents the Quran prohibition[12] on legally mixing bloodlines by facilitating the raising of another's child as the carer's own while providing safeguards to prevent full legal assimilation into the carer's family: the birth parent/s can never be replaced by adopters, the former retain important rights. As Duncan has explained, *kafala*:[13]

> does not have the effect of integrating the child into the new family. The child remains in name a member of the birth family and there are no inheritance rights in respect of the new family. However, kafala may if necessary involve delegation of guardianship in respect of the person and property of the child and in an intercountry situation it may result in a change in the child's nationality.

The gap between statutory adoption and *kafala* is one which continues to jeopardise the human rights of those involved: particularly the children, many of whom have been taken into public care due to the concern of authorities about their uncertain legal status and the absence of a parent within the jurisdiction. Not only are some children denied the opportunity of 'full' domestic adoption but some 20 Islamic states also prohibit ICA. On the other hand, 'the conversion of a *kafala* guardianship arrangement into a domestic adoption, once the child has been brought back to the receiving country, has also been used to circumvent ICA procedures under the 1993 Hague Convention'.[14] The Islamic interpretation of 'adoption' is a matter of growing relevance to the legal systems of western countries following the 2015–17 migrant crisis (see Chapter 4).

ICA

The Hague Convention on Intercountry Adoption defines such an adoption as occurring when:

12 Quran, verse 33 and the Sura, verses 4 and 5.
13 Duncan, W., 'Children's rights, cultural diversity and private international law', in Douglas, G. and Sebba, L. (eds), *Children's Rights and Traditional Values*, Aldershot, Ashgate, 1998, p. 32.
14 Special Rapporteur report, A/HRC/34/55, para. 49.

> a child habitually resident in one Contracting State ('the State of origin') has been, is being, or is to be moved to another Contracting State ('the receiving State') either after his or her adoption in the State of Origin by spouses or a person habitually resident in the receiving State, or for the purposes of such an adoption in the receiving State or in the State of origin.

According to the UNCROC, Article 21, ICA may be considered as an alternative means of childcare, if the child cannot be placed in a foster or an adoptive family or cannot in any suitable manner be cared for in the child's country of origin. It can occur in one of three ways:

- adoption of a child from a Hague Convention State in accordance with the national legislation endorsing or incorporating the Hague Convention;
- adoption of a child in a country with 'compatible' legislation; and
- adoption of a child from a non-Hague Convention State using other non-Hague Convention-related national legislation and procedures.

In the UK, for example, adoption is defined as including a Convention adoption thereby giving automatic effect to the first while allowing for the possibility of granting recognition to adoptions arising by either of the other two methods.[15] The Convention requires ICAs to be managed by an 'accredited body' or privately but, in either case, to be subject to oversight by relevant national government departments and the 'Central Authorities'. However, in some countries prospective adoptive parents are free to proceed outside the Hague framework and instead of working with an accredited body agency specialising in ICA they may choose to arrange an adoptive placement with the assistance of licensed or unlicensed intermediaries many of which are unregulated by any public body and elude sanctions or penalties.

Overseas adoption

An 'overseas adoption' is one that has taken place in another country but falls outside the definition of a Convention adoption. The term refers to the associated legal difficulties in determining whether and to what effect such an adoption may be recognised by the court in the country where the issue of recognition has arisen. Most often it was an issue that occurred when immigrants sought recognition for an adoption order, issued in their country of origin, so that they could satisfy immigration/citizenship requirements in respect of their child. Essentially, 'overseas adoption' signifies national rules and procedures for managing a conflict of laws and was of particular importance in the years prior to the unrolling of Hague. Nations independently legislated for the recognition of overseas adoption that occurred in a designated list of countries where adoption law and practice conformed to certain standards. In England and Wales there is legislative provision for overseas adoptions to be included within the definition of 'adoption' and

15 Adoption and Children Act 2002, s. 66.

provision for arrangements to be made for their recognition.[16] As Bridge and Swindells point out, the criteria for such recognition are likely to include:[17]

a confirming that the law in the overseas country ensures that the child has been freely given up for adoption and that this has not been induced by payment or compensation of any kind;
b confirming that the overseas country has made attempts to place the child in a family in that country;
c confirming that ICA is in the child's best interests;
d requiring that the domestic and ICA arrangements are the same; and
e ensuring that profit is not made from the process.

Currently, in many nations, the challenge in relation to overseas adoption is to ensure that it is used appropriately to supplement Hague Convention procedures. In some, however, adopters are using overseas adoption rules to circumvent Convention constraints by adopting children in non-Convention-compliant countries. On the other hand, it is also argued that leading adopting nations, such as the US, are using the Convention to freeze adoptions altogether from non-compliant countries such as Guatemala. Whatever the analytical perspective, the inescapable fact remains that two decades after Hague came into effect (1 May 1995), and despite almost 100 States having contracted to abide by it, the majority of ICAs still take place outside the protective legal framework it provides.

Adoption of children from another country and human rights

As has been rightly said, 'for most of the homeless children of the world, international adoption represents the only realistic opportunity for permanent families of their own'.[18] However, many present-day adopters are often most interested in babies, preferably healthy and voluntarily relinquished, rather than children simply in need of a home.

Recourse to ICA presents issues with human rights implications for all parties involved.[19]

Human rights issues concerning the sending countries

- it removes the most adoptable children from their own country, culture and kin and thereby exposes them to possible future difficulties in relation to matters of identity, racism and language;

16 Ibid., sections 66 and 87, respectively.
17 Bridge, C. and Swindells, H., *Adoption – The Modern Law*, Bristol, Family Law, 2003, p. 314.
18 Bartholet, E., 'International adoption: current status and future prospects', *Adoption*, 3(1) (1993): 90; see also, generally, Doek, van Loon and Vlaardingerbroek, P. (eds), *Children on the Move*, Dordrecht, Martinus Nijhoff, 1996.
19 Fenton-Glynn, C., *Children's Rights in Intercountry Adoption*, Antwerp, Intersentia, 2014.

- it pre-empts any possibility of meeting the needs of that country's own adopters;
- it leaves behind those children who are statistically less likely to be adopted and who will therefore probably be consigned to institutional care; and
- because the ICA market now places a higher value on young healthy babies, there is a correspondingly greater likelihood of market forces introducing profit motivated persons and agencies with potential to compromise the legality of the process.

There is also the possible inequity of restrictions placed upon prospective adopters. As Mignot points out:[20]

> The conditions to be satisfied by potential adopters vary from one country to another. For example, 100 countries allow single people to adopt while 15 only authorize married couples to do so; 81 countries set a minimum age for adopting and 15 a maximum age. Intercountry adoption is prohibited in 30 countries.

Human rights issues concerning birth parents in sending countries

In some cases, the benefit to poverty stricken birth parents in places such as South America and Africa derives not only from the ending of care responsibility and the comfort of knowing that their child will be better cared for by others, but from the direct or indirect payments made by intermediaries seeking to arrange adoption placements. To some this equation presents as just another instance of the west 'outsourcing' its production requirements to third world countries: another form of international trade in which children are the 'goods' to be traded; a 'commodification' of children.[21] For birth parents ICA can present certain difficulties:

- circumstances of poverty and hardship can make them vulnerable to exploitation – possibly relinquishing a child for financial gain – which may raise issues of 'trafficking';
- the post-adoption opportunities for contact, access or for practicing 'open' adoption are seriously restricted; and
- whether or not financial gain is involved, they can be exposed to subsequent discriminatory attitudes from within their local communities.

Human rights issues concerning adopters in receiving countries

Adopter choice is a factor in the growth of ICA. In countries where the source of children for third party adoptions is very largely via the public childcare system the

20 'Why is intercountry adoption declining worldwide?', p. 1.
21 Triseliotis, J., 'Intercountry adoption: global trade or global gift?', *Adoption & Fostering*, 24(2) (2000): 45–54.

fact is that the majority of those available have problems of some sort, if only in forming attachments, but for many their exposure to abuse and transient relationships has left them seriously impaired – psychologically if not also physically. Adopters seeking a child more in need of love and nurture than long-term emotional rehabilitation will be tempted to look overseas. Moreover, as contemporary domestic adoption embraces the principle of 'openness' – and with it the probability of some degree of contact with a parent and/or other members of the adopted child's family of origin – the prospect of adopting a child born in a foreign land many thousands of miles away may carry with it the attraction of privacy, anonymity and escape from any ongoing complicating entanglements. Then there is the little discussed matter of race. Some adopters opt for racial congruity through their choice of 'sending' country with white Caucasians in Ireland, for example, looking more towards Russia, Romania, and Eastern Europe (approx. 65 per cent of all registered foreign adoptions in the period 1991–2006).[22] One consequence of adoption being led more by choice than altruism is that those children in receiving countries who are most in need of family care are least likely to get it; recourse to ICA has left more children in the long term public childcare systems of western society.

For adopters ICA presents certain difficulties:

- achieving an appropriate and satisfactory match between home circumstances and the needs of a child from a different socio-economic context – that respects and maintains the latter's cultural identity – will be difficult to achieve;
- accessing verifiable information regarding parental consents, health and genetic background of the child, etc. – sufficient to ensure that their removal was not unlawful and to permit the development of an authentic personal identity – can be problematic;
- while the costs will always be considerable, it may be impossible to monitor all payments – to prevent those that are improper – which could constitute 'trafficking' and vitiate the validity of the adoption process; and
- as they are often older than the average adopter, they may be ill equipped to further the welfare interests of the child – likely to have complex health and care needs – that is now typically available.

Human rights issues concerning the children adopted

For modern western nations and their value systems – the legal structures of which are highly sensitised to issues of equality and non-discrimination as played out in matters of race, class, religion, etc. – the ICA phenomenon carries considerable baggage. For third world countries, coming to terms with the legacy of

22 Adoption Board, *Annual Report 2006*, Dublin, p. 43, table 14. Note the contrast with Sweden where in 2005, for example, of the 1,083 foreign children between the ages of 0–10 years adopted in Sweden, 773 were from Asia.

colonialism, this phenomenon resonates with earlier experiences of exploitation. For some observers such as Hubinette, ICA carries 'ugly parallels to contemporary trafficking of women and the historic transatlantic slave trade'.[23] As Silberman puts it: 'while critics of intercountry adoption view transnational and transracial placement of children as forms of imperialism and genocide, others argue that intercountry adoption offers the only viable opportunity for many of these children'.[24]

For the child involved, ICA can present certain difficulties:

- shedding the culture of their family of origin and substituting that of their adopters involves being stripped of name, language, religion and culture which greatly compounds the usual problems for an adoptee who wishes to trace their roots;
- the children involved now tended to be older and therefore are likely to have formed relationships and to have begun to develop a sense of 'belonging' which will make it difficult for them to settle in a wholly different environment;
- denial and assimilation may occur despite any commitment from adopters that they will endeavour to instil and nurture in the adoptee a sense of their culture of origin and not restrict the latter to their own mono-cultural environment;
- the fact of abandonment can be hard for any adopted child to come to terms with, but this will the case for many if not most ICA children; and
- discovering the facts relating to families of origin can be most difficult for an ICA subject as in many cases the information is missing, misleading or false which makes accessing their culture of origin, so that it may contribute towards creating an authentic identity, a considerable challenge.

The Special Rapporteur has rightly deplored the fact that 'there are no strategies aimed at tackling the systemic issues that give rise to an enabling environment for illegal adoptions and at ensuring that adoptions take place solely in the best interests of the child and in conformity with international norms and standards'.[25]

International bodies with a brief for adoption

Adoption, domestic and intercountry, is primarily a matter of concern for The Hague Conference Permanent Bureau but other international bodies also have an interest which from time to time can call for their direct involvement.

23 Hubinette, T., 'Adopted Koreans and the development of identity in the "third space"', *Adoption & Fostering*, 28(1) (2004): 16–24, 19.
24 Silberman, L., 'The Hague Children's Conventions: the internationalization of child law', in Katz, S., Eekelaar, J. and Maclean, M. (eds), *Cross Currents: Family Law and Policy in the United States and England*, Oxford University Press.
25 Special Rapporteur report (A/HRC/34/55), para. 69.

European Parliament

In February 2017 this institution passed a resolution calling upon the EU Commission to require all 28 Member States to provide a European Certificate of Adoption as the means for ensuring the automatic recognition of each other's adoption orders. It also called for 'common minimum standards' to be drawn up for adoption by the Commission to define 'best practice' guidelines. This initiative was prompted by concerns that the existing disparity in national rules could compromise human rights: of some adoptees, including their right to family life, to non-discrimination, to inheritance rights and right to nationality; and of some adopters by impacting on their ability and willingness to exercise their rights of free movement. It is anticipated that such certification, harmonising legal provisions, may well encounter opposition from countries where gay marriage and gay adoption have yet to be legalised.

Council of Europe

The Council of Europe, among other things, works to promote consistency in the various domestic adoption laws of its 47 member States. It is known primarily for producing the 1950 Convention for the Protection of Human Rights and Fundamental Freedoms which, although not containing any specific reference to adoption, provides safeguards for private and family life (Art. 8) and guarantees the right to marry and found a family (Art. 12).

Commissioner for Human Rights

Established in 1999, this is an independent and non-judicial office which functions in an ambassadorial capacity on behalf of the Council of Europe by engaging with member States to raise awareness about human rights issues and to promote the development of national human rights structures. Adoption and other family-related issues are among the matters pursued by the Commissioner. For example, a 2011 study by the Council of Europe Commissioner for Human Rights explains that:[26]

> LGBT [lesbian, gay, bisexual and transgender persons] can adopt a child by one of three procedures. A single lesbian woman or gay man may apply to become an adoptive parent (single-parent adoption). Alternatively, a same-sex couple can adopt their partner's biological or adopted children without terminating the first parent's legal rights. These are so called 'second-parent adoptions' and give the child two legal guardians. Second-parent adoptions also protect the parents by giving both of them legally recognised parental status. The lack of second-parent adoption deprives the child and the non-biological parent of

26 Council of Europe Commissioner for Human Rights, 'Discrimination on Grounds of Sexual Orientation and Gender Identity in Europe', Council of Europe Publishing, June 2011.

> rights if the biological parent dies or in the case of divorce, separation, or other circumstances that would bar the parent from carrying out parental responsibilities. The child also has no right to inherit from the non-biological parent. Moreover, at an everyday level, the lack of second-parent adoption rules out parental leave, which can be harmful financially for LGBT families. The third procedure is joint adoption of a child by a same sex couple.

It then lists those few countries which provided for same sex adoption and notes the very many which, at that time, did not.

The United Nations

Founded in 1945 to promote international co-operation and prevent further wars, the UN is now the world's largest and most powerful human rights organisation. It works on behalf of its almost 200 member States to maintain international peace and security, conciliate disputes, promote human rights, foster social and economic development, protect the environment, and provide humanitarian aid in cases of famine, natural disaster, and armed conflict. It has been responsible for formulating such foundational human rights instruments as the Universal Declaration of Human Rights 1945, the 1966 International Covenant on Civil and Political Rights (ICCPR) together with the International Covenant on Economic, Social and Cultural Rights, the UNCROC 1989 and the Declaration on the Rights of Indigenous People 2006.

UN Human Rights Council

This body was established in 2006 when it replaced the UN Commission on Human Rights, which was formed in 1946. This subsidiary of the General Assembly works with the High Commissioner on behalf of its 47 member States to oversee human rights issues for the UN. Among the many human rights themes addressed by the Council are those relating to women's rights, LGBT rights and the rights of racial and ethnic minorities; areas which at times interface with domestic and ICA.

UN Special Rapporteur

The remit of this official – examining the sale of children, child prostitution and child pornography – has been extended to include illegal adoptions.[27] A report on this matter was submitted to the UN Human Rights Council in 2017 recommending new measures to combat illegal adoptions, including proposals for

27 Such activity clearly violates Article 3(1) of the Optional Protocol to the Convention on the Rights of the Child on the Sale of Children, Child Prostitution and Child Pornography.

tackling the systems in which such practices occur.[28] It noted that 'it is high time that all parties concerned put the best interests of the child at the centre of adoptions'.

International conventions with a brief for adoption

As with most other fundamental human rights, international recognition of the need to protect children probably has its roots in the Universal Declaration of Human Rights 1948. Following the UN Declaration of the Rights of the Child 1959 – which built upon principles established in the League of Nations Declaration 1924 – the range of international instruments giving recognition to the needs and rights of children has been steadily growing. All such treaties, declarations, conventions and protocols, etc. contribute to the building of an international human rights context for the adoption of children. They also further the growing international harmonisation of principles and processes in family law.

Universal Declaration of Human Rights 1948

The ever-growing international body of human rights is underpinned by this foundation document.

Article 2 – Rights to equality and non-discrimination

Enlarged in Article 14 of the ECHR and supported by Article 2 of the International Covenant on Civil and Political Rights (ICCPR), this provides for the right not to be discriminated against. It requires any difference in treatment to be objectively and reasonably justified.

Article 12 – Protection of individuals from arbitrary action by public authorities

This places an obligation on the court to ensure that the rights of an individual are properly secured and protected against infringements and requires public authorities to exercise fairness in their procedures.

Article 25(2) – Right to protection for mother and child

This provision states that 'motherhood and childhood are entitled to special care and assistance. All children, whether born in or out of wedlock, shall enjoy the same social protection'. It is supported by the proclamation regarding the importance of the family, the right of adults to marry and form such a unit and the duty of the State to protect it, as expressed in Article 16.

28 http://wunrn.com/2017/04/illegal-adoptions-un-special-rapporteur-report-2017

European Convention for the Protection of Human Rights and Fundamental Freedoms 1950

The ECHR is, of course, the Convention that is of fundamental importance for adoption law and practice throughout Europe; it provides a framework of human rights that are constantly evoked and the related rulings by the ECtHR have grown to form a considerable body of ever evolving governing principles. However, the attendant difficulties in setting common benchmarks for human rights across so many different national cultures has been very apparent. This is evident from even the most cursory analysis of contemporary differences between the UK and continental Europe in their approach to adoption: in the former, the non-consensual use of adoption in relation to children in the public care system has become a distinguishing feature; while in the latter, public childcare institutions have a high investment in the family support and long-term foster care services which reduce the need to have recourse to such adoptions.

The 'margin of appreciation' rule

Nationally, the experience of adoption has been somewhat disparate giving rise to a range of legal issues with which the ECtHR copes by applying the doctrine of a 'margin of appreciation'. This doctrine declares that countries are entitled to act with a level of discretion in accordance with their particular legal and cultural traditions. However, as stated in *Saviny* v. *Ukraine*:[29]

> notwithstanding a margin of appreciation enjoyed by the domestic authorities in deciding on placing a child into public care, severing family ties means cutting a child off from its roots, which can only be justified in very exceptional circumstances. . .A relevant decision must therefore be supported by sufficiently sound and weighty considerations in the interests of the child, and it is for the respondent State to establish that a careful assessment of the impact of the proposed care measure on the parents and the child has been made.

As illustrated in the case law below, the exercise of discretion is only permissible within the judicial parameters established by principles such as 'necessity' and 'proportionality'.

All the following articles have a general relevance for family proceedings, and therefore also for adoption, some specifically so. Indeed, for present purposes, this Convention is particularly significant because it was the first international instrument to declare the principles that should govern adoption. The judiciary have cautioned against any inclination to simply refer to these articles *en passant* in a

29 No. 39948/06 (18 December 2008), para. 49; see also *Kutzner* v. *Germany* No. 46544/99 (26 February 2002), at paras 67 and 81; *Moser* v. *Austria* no. 12643/02 (21 September 2006); *Kurochkin* v. *Ukraine* No. 42276/08 (20 May 2010); *Schalk and Kopf* v. *Austria*, No. 30141/04 (24 June 2010); and *Burden* v. *the United Kingdom* [GC], No. 13378/05 (60, ECHR 2008).

routine or ritualistic fashion.[30] In fact, contemporary case law contains constant references to such rights which are treated as essential benchmarks of good practice.

Article 6 – Everyone is entitled to a fair and public hearing within a reasonable time by an independent and impartial tribunal established by law

A majority of applications to the ECtHR have been generated by alleged breaches of Article 6, though it is of lesser direct importance to adoption than Article 8.

Article 8 – Right to respect for private and family life

This Article requires respect for a person's private and family life, their home and correspondence. According to the ECtHR, it necessitates parental involvement in the decision-making process to a degree sufficient to provide them with the requisite protection of their interests.[31] If they are not so involved, there will have been a failure to respect their family life. Parents are entitled to be involved in the decision-making process relating to the religious education of their children. Essentially this right aims to provide protection for an individual against arbitrary action by public authorities, for example a local authority.[32] It places an obligation on the court to ensure that the rights of an individual are properly secured and are protected against infringements by other individuals.[33] It also inherently requires procedural fairness. However, the prohibition on public authority interference is made subject to the exception that where to do so is: (a) in accordance with the law; and (b) is necessary in a democratic society[34] (i) in the interests of national security, public safety or the economic well-being of the country, (ii) for the prevention of crime and disorder, (iii) for the protection of health or morals or (iv) for the protection of the rights and freedom of others.

Article 12 – Right to marry and found a family

Article 12 provides that men and women of a marriageable age have the right to marry and to found a family, according to national law. The right to found a family is absolute and the State cannot interfere with the exercise of this right,

30 *Daniels* v. *Walker (Practice Note)* [2000] 1 WLR 1382, p. 1387.
31 *W* v. *United Kingdom* (1987) 10 EHRR 29.
32 *Re M (Care: Challenging Decisions by Local Authority)* [2001] 2 FLR 1300 and *C* v. *Bury Metropolitan Borough Council* [2002] 2 FLR 868.
33 *Airey* v. *Ireland* (1979) Series A No. 32, 2 EHRR 305.
34 *Olson* v. *Sweden (No. 1)* (1988) 11 EHRR 299, where it is explained that to be justifiable such interference must be 'relevant and sufficient; it must meet a pressing social need; and it must be proportionate to the need'. Advice subsequently echoed in *Johansen* v. *Norway* (1997) 23 EHRR 33 where it was observed, that 'the notion of necessity implies that the interference corresponds to a pressing social need and, in particular, that it is proportional to the legitimate aim pursued'.

though it has no legal obligation to provide the services that may be necessary for the right to be exercised. However, the fact that there is no legal right to adopt or to access artificial reproduction treatment was emphasised in *X* v. *Belgium and The Netherlands*[35] where it was held that unmarried persons cannot claim a right to adopt. The absence of such a right was also considered in *Pini and Others* v. *Romania*.[36]

Article 14 – Prohibition of discrimination

Article 14 provides that the rights enumerated in the Convention shall be assured without discrimination on grounds such as sex, race, colour, language, religion, political or other opinion, national or social origin, association with a national minority, property, birth[37] or other status. It must be shown that an applicant is: subject to a difference in treatment from others in a similar situation; in the enjoyment of one of the rights protected by the Convention; which difference cannot be objectively and reasonably justified, having regard to the concepts of legitimate aim, proportionality and margin of appreciation. There is no definitive list of matters susceptible to discriminatory treatment.

Optional Protocol on the Sale of Children, Child Prostitution, and Child Pornography 2000 (Sex Trafficking Protocol) 2000

This Protocol, appended to the UNCROC, addressed the many purposes for which children are bought and sold, including adoption. It defined and prohibited the sale of children and, in that context, established the principle that improperly inducing consent, as a means of procuring the adoption of a child, violates human rights and is to be treated as a criminal offence.

European Convention on the Adoption of Children 1967

This Convention – preceded by the Hague Convention on Jurisdiction, etc., Relating to Adoptions 1965 and the European Convention on the Adoption of Children 1967 – sought to identify some common principles and standards of practice to serve as international benchmarks for the parties involved in adoption. For example, it established the principle that adoption should be in the interests of the child (Art. 8, para. 1) and should provide the child with a stable and harmonious home (Art. 8, para. 2). It gave protection to adopter's rights by emphasising the need for anonymity (Art. 20) and to birth parent's rights by establishing that any consent given by a mother to the adoption of her child is invalid if given

35 Application No. 6482/147 (1975) 7 DR 75.
36 [2004] EHRR 275.
37 A marital child cannot be accorded prior legal rights over a non-marital child: *Inze* v. *Austria* (1988) Series A No. 126, 10 EHRR 394; see also *Marckx* v. *Belgium* (1979) Series A No. 31, 2 EHRR 330.

within six weeks of that child's birth (Art. 52, para. 3); but she can give a valid consent to placement within that period. Some principles, however, proved contentious. One such was the requirement stated in Article 6(1) that national adoption laws 'shall not permit a child to be adopted except by either two persons married to each other, whether they adopt simultaneously or successively, or by one person'.[38]

A Working Party on Adoption, composed of experts from member States (the 'Committee of Experts in Family Law'), was established to revise the 1967 European Convention.

Declaration on Social and Legal Principles relating to the Protection and Welfare of Children, with special reference to Foster Placement and Adoption Nationally and Internationally 1986

The General Assembly of the United Nations adopted this Declaration in 1986. Article 13 states that the primary aim of adoption should be to provide a permanent family for a child who cannot be cared for by its own parents. Article 17 recognises that ICA is a childcare mechanism of last resort and states that:

> If a child cannot be placed in a foster or an adoptive family or cannot in any suitable manner be cared for in the country of origin, intercountry adoption may be considered as an alternative means of providing the child with a family.

This UN Convention states that the best interests of a child should be paramount including the right to affection, security and continuing care.

Article 3 – Care outside the family of origin

Article 3 provides that 'the first priority for a child is to be cared for by his or her own parents' but, failing that '. . .care by relatives of the child's parents, by another substitute – foster or adoptive – family or, if necessary, by an appropriate institution should be considered'.[39]

Article 8 – Right to name, etc.

Article 8 provides for a child's right to name, nationality and legal representation. It also requires signatory States to provide for the supervision of placements.

38 In July 2002 Sweden withdrew from the Convention following changes in its national adoption laws allowing for adoption by homosexual couples in a registered partnership, as it determined that this aspect of its new national adoption laws conflicted with Article 6(1).

39 Article 4.

Article 24 – Intercountry adoption

Article 24 requires due weight to be given to both the law of the State to which the child is the national and the law of the respective adoptive parents. In that context it requires due regard to be given to 'the child's cultural and religious background and interests'.

UNCROC 1989

This Convention, signed by nearly 200 countries, was ratified by the UK on 16 December 1991. It has now been ratified by all UN member States except for Somalia and the US.[40] It lists 42 substantive rights that comprehensively address the needs of children – including Articles 18, 20, 21, and 35 with direct relevance to adoption – and requires national courts to ensure that decisions broadly comply with the general and specific obligations set out in the Convention. While the Convention has no specifically designated means of enforcement, the UN Committee on the Rights of the Child (CRC) does make recommendations to States, on the basis of reports filed with it under Article 44, for improvements in national law and practice.[41] This audit mechanism provides a useful tool for promoting transparency and accountability and for benchmarking developments in national law while also facilitating international comparative assessments.

The following are some of the more significant provisions of the UN Convention with relevance for contemporary national adoption law and practice.

Article 2 – Non-discrimination principle

Article 2 directs that all Convention rights are to apply to children without exception and without discrimination of any kind. This applies irrespective of the child's – or his or her parent's or guardian's – race, colour, sex, language, religion, political or other opinion, national, ethnic or social origin, property, disability, birth or other status. In the latter respect, it therefore prohibits discrimination on the basis of parental marital status. All appropriate measures must be taken to ensure that the child is protected against all forms of discrimination or punishment on the basis of the status, activities, expressed opinions, or beliefs of the child's parents, legal guardians, or family members.

40 The US has signed the Convention but has not yet ratified it (O'Connor, D., 'Children's rights and youth justice in the USA', *International Family Law Journal* (2006): 183).

41 The UK government made its first report to the Committee on the Rights of the Child in January 1995 and submitted its consolidated third and fourth report on 15 July 2007. The UK entered reservations when it ratified the Convention and has not ratified the optional protocol on the sale of children, child prostitution and child pornography.

Article 3 – Best interests of the child is a primary consideration

Article 3 states the most important principle in the Convention. This article requires that in all actions concerning children, whether undertaken by public or private social welfare institutions, courts of law, administrative authorities or legislative bodies, the best interests of the child shall be the primary consideration.

Article 7 – Right of the child to know their identity

Article 7 recognises the right of a child to information relating to his or her parents as the means of establishing their own identity. This is a powerful legal acknowledgement that an adopted person has a right of access to information, in the form of agency records, etc., that could potentially contribute to their sense of identity.

Article 9 – Right of the child not to be separated from his or her parents

Article 9 requires the State to ensure that a child shall not be separated from his or her parents against their will, except when competent authorities subject to judicial review determine, in accordance with applicable law and procedures, that such separation is necessary for the best interests of the child.

Article 12 – Right of the child to express an opinion in administrative and judicial proceedings

Article 12 states that the child has the right to express his or her opinion freely and the right to have that opinion taken into account in any matter or procedure affecting the child. This is subject to the caveat that the child concerned must be capable of forming his or her own views. Due weight, in accordance with the age and maturity of the child, must be given to those views.

Articles 13 and 14 – Right of the child to self-determination, dignity, respect, non-interference and the right to make informed decisions

Articles 13 and 14 require the State to ensure that the child has the right to freedom of expression and the right to express his or her own views.

Article 18 – Primary responsibility for the upbringing of a child rests with the parent/s

Article 18 requires the State to render appropriate assistance to parents and legal guardians to facilitate the upbringing and development of their children. It requires the State to ensure that children of working parents have the right to benefit from those childcare services and facilities for which they are eligible.

Article 20 – State duty to protect child without family

Article 20. 3 suggests that:

> Such care could include, *inter alia*, foster placement, *kafala* of Islamic law, adoption, or if necessary placement in suitable institutions for the care of children. When considering solutions, due regard shall be paid to the desirability of continuity in a child's upbringing and to the child's ethnic, religious, cultural and linguistic background.

Article 20 requires the State to provide care for a child deprived of a family environment and in doing so must have due regard to the child's cultural background.

Article 21 – Adoption shall ensure that the best interests of the child shall be the paramount consideration

Article 21 is of particular significance for adoption as it requires those State Parties that recognise and/or permit adoption to give paramount consideration to the welfare interests of the children concerned when doing so. It requires State Parties to:

a ensure that the adoption of a child is authorised only by competent authorities who determine, in accordance with applicable law and procedures and on the basis of all pertinent and reliable information, that the adoption is permissible in view of the child's status concerning parents, relatives and legal guardians and that, if required, the persons concerned have given their informed consent to the adoption on the basis of such counselling as may be necessary;
b recognise that intercountry adoption may be considered as an alternative means of a child's care, if the child cannot be placed in a foster or an adoptive family or cannot in any suitable manner be cared for in the child's country of origin;
c ensure that the child concerned by intercountry adoption enjoys safeguards and standards equivalent to those existing in the case of national adoption;
d take all appropriate measures to ensure that, in intercountry adoption, the placement does not result in improper financial gain for those involved in it; and
e promote, where appropriate, the objectives of this article by concluding bilateral or multilateral arrangements or agreements, and endeavour, within this framework, to ensure that the placement of the child in another country is carried out by competent authorities or organs.

Article 21(d), in conjunction with Articles 8 and 32 of the Hague Convention, requires a State Party to take all appropriate measures to ensure that adoption placements do not result in any improper financial gain for any of the parties involved.

Article 25 – Adoption placements must be subject to periodic review

Article 25 requires periodic review of placements of all types, including foster care and residential units, to ensure that no child in State care is overlooked.

Article 27 – Every child is entitled to a reasonable standard of living

Article 27 requires the State to recognise the right of every child to a standard of living adequate for that child's physical, mental, spiritual, moral and social development.

Article 35 – Prevention of trafficking in children

Article 35 requires State Parties to:

> take all appropriate national, bilateral and multilateral measures to prevent the abduction, the sale of or traffic in children for any purpose or in any form.

Articles 44 and 45 – Every State is required to audit, progress and publish a report

Articles 44 and 45 require a State Party to report on the measures it has adopted which give effect to the rights recognised in the Convention and on the progress made on enjoyment of those rights.

Hague Convention on Protection of Children and Co-operation in Respect of Intercountry Adoption 1993

Of the four Hague Conventions on matters relating to children[42] this one has the distinction of being truly international due to the near global reach of its provisions; by 2015 it had been signed by some 90 States.[43] However it is constrained: implementation of its provisions depends upon the voluntary cooperation of signatory States; there is no regulatory body or governing authority. The Preamble explicitly states that this Convention is to be read in conjunction with the UNCROC.[44] It is underpinned by the following principles, sometimes explicitly stated sometimes not, that are intended to guide international practice.

42 Those being: the Convention on the Civil Aspects of International Child Abduction 1980; the Hague Convention on Intercountry Adoption 1993; the Convention on the International Recovery of Child Support and Other Forms of Family Maintenance 2007; and the Convention on Jurisdiction, Applicable Law, Recognition, Enforcement and Co-operation in Respect of Parental Responsibility and Measures for the Protection of Children 1996.

43 www.hcch.net/e/status/adoshtc.html

44 The Preamble also refers to its links with the 1986 UN Declaration.

Welfare interests of the child are paramount in adoption law and practice (see also UNCROC)

This clear statement, intended to guide the decisions of all bodies involved in the adoption process, usefully reinforces the firming-up of the paramountcy principle in recent ECHR case law.

ICA is only justified after in-country placement options have been eliminated

This principle is expressed in the Preamble and in Article 4(b).

Adoption is a service for children, rather than for an adult seeking to acquire a child (see also UNCROC)

This principle recognises that no person has an automatic right to adopt a child.

Children requiring adoptive placements are entitled to know and have access to information about their family background and cultural heritage and maintain or develop cultural identity (see also UNCROC)

This recognises that due regard must be given to a child's ethnic, religious, cultural and linguistic background when considering adoption. It also recognises that ICA must respect the child's fundamental rights which include the foregoing.

Birth parent/s have an entitlement to make decisions about their child's future care (see also UNCROC)

Both parents are recognised as entitled to make decisions about their child, including consenting to the child's adoption and participating in the selection of approved prospective adopters. Article 4(b) provides that a Convention adoption 'shall only take place if the competent authorities of the State of origin have determined, after the possibilities of placement within the State of origin have been given due consideration, that intercountry adoption is in the child's best interests'.

The child is entitled to be involved in decision-making (see also UNCROC, Art. 12)

On issues relating to his or her upbringing, the child's views must be sought, must be taken into consideration and may be determinative depending upon their maturity.

Parties are entitled to negotiate mutually agreed adoption arrangements (not explicitly stated)

This recognises that parties to an adoption are, with mutual agreement, entitled to participate in ongoing information exchange and/or contact after an adoption order is made. The child's views must be sought and must be taken into account.

Adoption should safeguard and promote the welfare interests of the child throughout his or her life (not explicitly stated)

The lifelong nature of adoption is recognised as is the need to ensure that the interests of the adopted person are always given priority over those of other parties.

An adoption authority should 'promote the development of adoption counselling and post-adoption services' (Art. 9)

This requires, under Article 9C, the accreditation of bodies established to provide adoption services. The responsibilities in relation to such bodies are addressed in subsequent Articles.

ARTICLE 10

Accreditation shall be granted to and properly maintained by bodies demonstrating their competence to carry out the tasks with which they may be entrusted.

ARTICLE 11

An accredited body shall –

a pursue only non-profit objectives according to such conditions and within such limits as may be established by the competent authorities of the State accreditation;
b be directed and staffed by persons qualified by their ethical standards and by training or experience to work in the field of intercountry adoption; and
c be subject to supervision by competent authorities of that State as to its composition, operation and financial situation.

ARTICLE 12

A body accredited in one Contracting State may act in another Contracting State only if the competent authorities of both States have authorised it to do so.

ARTICLE 22

1 The functions of a Central Authority under this Chapter may be performed by public authorities or by bodies accredited under Chapter III, to the extent permitted by the law of its State.
2 Any Contracting State may declare to the depositary of the Convention that the functions of the Central Authority under Articles 15–21 may be performed in that State, to the extent permitted by the law and subject to the supervision of the competent authorities of that State, also by bodies or persons
3 who –

4 meet the requirements of integrity, professional competence, experience and accountability of that State; and
5 are qualified by their ethical standards and by training or experience to work in the field of intercountry adoption.

European Convention on the Adoption of Children 2008

The provisions introduced by this Convention include:

- a requirement that the father's consent be obtained in all cases, even when the child is born out of wedlock;
- a requirement that the child's consent be obtained if the child has sufficient understanding to give it;
- a requirement that adoption be available to heterosexual unmarried couples who have entered into a registered partnership in States which recognise that institution, and to single applicants;
- it also leaves States free to extend adoptions to homosexual couples and same sex-couples living together in a stable relationship;
- a requirement that a better balance be struck between adopted children's right to know their identity and the right of the biological parents to remain anonymous; and
- a requirement that the minimum age of an adopter must be between 18 and 30, and the age difference between adopter and child should preferably be at least 16 years.

United Nations Guidelines for the Alternative Care of Children 2009

These Guidelines were intended to enhance UNCROC implementation 'regarding the protection and well-being of children deprived of parental care or who are at risk of being so' (para. 3). They start from the general principle that efforts should primarily be directed towards enabling children to remain in or return to the care of their parents.

Removal from family of origin

Removing a child from the care of the family should be seen as a measure of last resort and should, whenever possible, be temporary and for the shortest duration possible (para. 14). Children temporarily or permanently deprived of their family environment, or in whose best interests cannot be allowed to remain in that environment, are entitled to special government protection and assistance (UNCROC, Art. 20(1)).

Alternative care

Such alternative care can include 'foster placement . . . adoption or, if necessary, placements in suitable institutions for the care of children' (UNCROC, Art. 20

(3)). Decisions regarding children in alternative care should have due regard for the importance of ensuring children a stable home and meeting their basic need for safe and continuous attachment to their care givers, with permanency generally being a key goal (para. 12).

Family-based care

In accordance with the predominant opinion of experts, alternative care for young children, especially those under the age of 3 years, should be provided in family based settings (para. 22). 'Where such arrangements are not possible or are not in the best interests of the child, efforts should be made to find a permanent family placement within a reasonable period' (para. 44).

Committee of Ministers Recommendation CM/Rec 5, 2010

This recommendation on measures to combat discrimination on grounds of sexual orientation or gender identity was adopted by member States on 31 March 2010. It covers a wide range of areas where LGBT persons may encounter discrimination. In the chapter entitled 'Right to respect for private and family life' it provides:

- 27. Taking into account that the child's best interests should be the primary consideration in decisions regarding adoption of a child, member States whose national legislation permits single individuals to adopt children should ensure that the law is applied without discrimination based on sexual orientation or gender identity.

Brussels II

This is a regulation in relation to family law cases with cross-border elements, which came into effect on 1 August 2004. Its application to childcare cases, custody and abduction – particularly as regards implementation of Articles 15, 55 and 56 – can make it relevant to international adoption.

Other relevant instruments

An ever-growing list of international treaties, conventions, protocols, etc. are constantly enlarging the number of bodies and themes which interface with domestic and ICA. These include the International Covenant on Economic, Social and Cultural Rights 1966 and the ICCPR 1966, the latter being of particular significance as its periodic review process requires signatory States to submit a review of progress on human rights issues which can include matters relating to adoption. This procedure has a uniform application to all 193 UN member States. It provides an opportunity for each State to make a periodic declaration to the Human Rights Council regarding the actions taken to improve human rights in its country, to receive comment from its peer signatory States and to agree goals for the next review. This process operates in conjunction with the Principles relating to the Status of National Institutions (the Paris Principles), adopted by the UN General Assembly in 1993,[33] which set out the minimum standards required from national human rights institutions if they are to operate effectively and to be considered credible.

Also of importance is the Convention on the Elimination of all Forms of Discrimination against Women 1979 (CEDAW) which refers to the interests of children being paramount in relation to the common responsibility of men and women for their children's upbringing and development (Art. 5(b)) as well as in regard to States Parties' ensuring the same rights and responsibilities between men and women as parents in matters relating to their children and in matters of guardianship, wardship, trusteeship, and adoption of children (Art. 16 (1)(d) and (f)). The Convention on the Civil Aspects of International Child Abduction, the Convention on Jurisdiction, Applicable Law, Recognition, Enforcement and Cooperation in Respect of Parental Responsibility and Measures for the Protection of Children, the Charter of Fundamental Rights of the European Union 2000, the European Convention on the Exercise of Children's Rights 1996 and the Declaration on the Rights of Indigenous People 2006 have a varying relevance, the latter of which makes specific reference to the special features of adoption in an indigenous cultural context.

Hague Convention framework and contemporary ICA

The Hague Convention applies whenever a child habitually resident in a Convention-compliant sending country has been, is being, or is to be moved for the purposes of adoption to another Convention-compliant receiving country; it does not matter in which of the two countries the adoption takes place. It applies to both full and simple adoptions and provides for the automatic recognition of all adoptions made in accordance with Convention requirements in any Contracting State.

Hague Convention administrative bodies

This Convention aims to raise standards of practice but cannot be said to have a strictly regulatory function. It stops short of prohibiting non-agency adoptions: prospective adopters remain free to make their own private independent adoption arrangements; though these are not encouraged and are restricted.[45] Its administrative bodies are, therefore, advisory in nature.

45 The Report of The Hague's Special Commission on the Practical Operation of the Convention in 2005 recommended that member countries actively discourage direct contacts between prospective adoptive parents and authorities in the child's country of origin until authorised to do so by those authorities.

Hague Conference Permanent Bureau

The Bureau provides a supervisory function for the Hague Convention. It gives effect to its role by monitoring practice and issuing extensive guidance on ICA issues.[46] So, for example, in its *Good Practice Guide* it pointed out a need for stricter accreditation and authorisation of agencies involved in ICA, with special attention to the professional quality and scope of the services they provide and to restricting their numbers to no more than necessary. In an important policy statement, the *Guide* also explains the role to be played by the subsidiarity principle:[47]

> The subsidiarity principle is central to the success of the Convention. It implies that efforts should be made to . . . ensure that a child has the opportunity to be adopted or cared for nationally. It implies also that intercountry adoption procedures should be set within an integrated child protection and care system which maintains these priorities. However, States should also ensure that efforts to achieve this goal do not unintentionally harm children by delaying unduly a permanent solution through intercountry adoption. States should guarantee permanency planning in the shortest time possible for each child deprived of his/her parents. Policies should work to promote family preservation and national solutions, rather than to hinder intercountry adoption.

Hague Conference Special Commission

The 80 member States that now constitute this body, meet every five years to review national progress on relevant issues. It has taken steps to improve the operation of the Convention by publishing a guide to implementation and initiating the Intercountry Adoption Technical Assistance Programme (ICATAP) to provide support and training to those new signatory nations, such as Guatemala, that are struggling to meet Convention standards. As Estin notes:[48]

> the Conference has also encouraged receiving States to accept more responsibility for improving the situation in States of origin by providing development aid for child protection that is not directly linked to intercountry adoption, by

46 Permanent Bureau, 'The implementation and operation of the 1993 Hague International Adoption Convention: a guide to good practice', 2008. See also publications by the Permanent Bureau in 2012: by the Working Group established to develop a common approach to preventing and addressing illicit practices in intercountry adoption cases; and by the Expert Group on the Financial Aspects of Intercountry Adoption.

47 Permanent Bureau, 'The implementation and operation of the 1993 Hague International Adoption Convention', p. 22.

48 Estin, A., 'Families across borders: the Hague Children's conventions and the case for international family law in the United States', p. 90. See further at: www.law.uiowa.edu/documents/Estin_BOOK.pdf

controlling the numbers of applications from adoptive parents and the amount of money that flows into the system, and by applying the standards of the Convention to adoptions from non-Convention countries.

The main European grouping of accredited agencies, Euradopt, has also developed ethical guidelines to which its membership commits.

Hague Convention: promoting childcare in country of origin

The Hague Convention recognises and addresses the obligation to promote measures that enable children to remain in their country and, further, in its Preamble it urges every country to 'take, as a matter of priority, appropriate measures to enable the child to remain in the care of his or her family of origin'. This message is reinforced by Article 4(b) which promotes the development of professional adoption services in 'donor' countries i.e. countries which for reasons of poverty and/or social instability are allowing children to be adopted by non-nationals. This constitutes a significant stand for the human rights of children and their birth parent/s.

The 'child rescue' approach, with its attendant dislocation for human relationships and cultural identity, is not to be the preferred means of safeguarding welfare interests either domestically or internationally. Priority is to be given to retaining a child in need within his or her family and social context of origin. Where consensually based retention is not feasible then foster care services should be provided which would permit a child to be placed as close as possible, in terms of geography and relationships, to his or her family/culture/ community of origin. Resort to adoption should occur only when these options are not possible and then preference should again be given to maintaining the child within the cultural norms of his or her family of origin. When such circumstances arise, it has been argued, this should trigger 'a reversal in the flow of files' meaning that adoption applications should only be sent to the authorities of a country of origin in response to a request made for prospective adoptive parents appropriate for a specific child in need of adoption.[49]

The Convention views ICA as the final step in a continuum, to be taken when all others have been tried, when all the professional filters are in place and the adoption process is regulated to ensure that welfare interests are safeguarded. This approach very much echoes that embodied in Article 21(b) of the UN Convention.

Hague Convention adoption process

By operating through a system of national Central Authorities, the Hague Convention reinforces the UNCROC (Art. 21) and seeks to ensure that the adoption

49 Special Rapporteur report (A/HRC/34/55), para. 78.

process functions in the best interests of the child, with respect for his or her fundamental rights.

Role of a central authority

The Hague Convention requires a Central Authority to be established to serve as a country's primary contact in any adoption process. This body must conduct several checks to ensure that a child eligible for adoption, including: verifying the propriety of the adoption under the laws of both countries; making a reasonable effort to facilitate a domestic adoption instead; and agreeing to use only certified adoption agencies.

An 'accredited body'

The Convention requires ICAs to be managed by an 'accredited body' or privately but, in either case, to be subject to oversight by relevant national government departments and the Central Authorities. For most purposes the term refers to a registered adoption agency. The report of the Special Rapporteur is particularly critical of the lax supervision of the role played by adoption agencies, whether or not accredited, and of the dangers that arise when such agencies compete to identify and secure adoptable children.[50] It emphasises that 'it is the joint responsibility of countries of origin and receiving countries to regulate the number of adoption accredited bodies wanting to engage in intercountry adoptions, as a means of limiting the number of adoptions to the number of legally adoptable children'.[51]

The prospective adopter/s

The person/s wishing to adopt must make application to the designated authority in the country where they are habitually resident. In the UK the 'authority', a registered adoption agency, will assign a professional social worker to undertake an assessment of the applicant/s eligibility and suitability to adopt and to compile a 'home study' report on their family background and a personal history for submission to the agency's Adoption Panel. The approved report will then be forwarded to the relevant authority in the chosen country with children available.

The sending country

On receipt of the 'home study' report and other documentation attesting to the eligibility and suitability of the applicants, the appropriate authorities in the sending country will then make a preliminary determination as to whether or not the proposed placement is in the best interests of a particular child. In so doing the authorities are required, under Article 29 of the Convention, to give due

50 Ibid., paras 74–7.
51 Ibid., para. 76.

consideration to the child's ethnic, religious and cultural background. A report on the child is then sent to the authorities in the receiving country together with evidence that all necessary consents have been obtained and the reasons for its 'best interests' determination in respect of that child. Article 16(2) provides for the withholding of identifying information regarding the child's birth parent/s where the authorities deem this to be necessary.

Transfer of child

When all administrative requirements have been satisfied, Article 17 of the Convention allows the child to be 'entrusted' (rather than placed) by the authorities in the sending country into the care of the prospective adopters. The responsibility for ensuring that the prospective adopters accept the transfer of the child rests with the authorities of the sending rather than the receiving country. Both sets of authorities, however, must agree to the proposed adoption and under Article 17(c) either may withhold consent if not satisfied that all legal requirements have been met.

Hague Convention adoption process: outcomes

Article 4(b) provides that a Convention adoption 'shall only take place if the competent authorities of the State of origin have determined after the possibilities for placement within the State of origin have been given due consideration that intercountry adoption is in the child's best interests'.

Adoption order

The adoption order may be made in either the sending or receiving country. The sending country bears responsibility for producing in court evidence that:

- ICA is in the child's best interests;
- all necessary consents have been obtained;
- the prospective adopters satisfy eligibility and suitability criteria; and
- the child is or will be authorised to enter and remain in the receiving country.

The Convention mandates that an adoption order made in a signatory State: must be one that creates a permanent and full parent/child relationship; must normally be given full recognition in all other signatory States; but may be repudiated by any signatory State if in breach of its public policy. In some Hague-compliant sending countries, such as China, the practice is to finalise the adoption order before the child leaves the jurisdiction.

Interim adoption order

Increasingly, some Hague-compliant countries such as Russia (which has signed but not yet ratified the Convention) are choosing to proceed by allowing the adopters to return home with their child under the authority of an interim adoption order. Thereafter, on return of six satisfactory consecutive monthly reports by the appropriate authority in the receiving country, the adoption order is automatically finalised.

Hague Convention adoption process: legal effects

Article 26(1) of Hague states that a Convention-compliant adoption order will terminate pre-adoption legal relationships (if permitted under the law of the sending country), vest parental responsibility in the adopter/s, establish a permanent legal parental relationship between adopter/s and the child and be recognised by the law of the receiving country and that of all other Convention countries.

Full and simple adoptions

The subsequent legal standing of the birth parent/s in relation to the child will depend on whether the order made in the sending country is a 'full' or a 'simple' adoption order. In the former case the adoption order will then operate to wholly and permanently terminate the rights of the birth parent/s, whereas in the latter these rights are not completely extinguished. The statutory processes of some countries, such as the UK, have only ever provided for full adoption and while it provides automatic recognition for that form it also allows for conversion of simple adoptions. Article 26(2) of the Convention provides that, in the case of full adoptions, a Convention-compliant adoption order will have a legal effect equivalent to an order made under the statute law of the receiving country.

Access to identifying information

Under Article 30(1) of the Convention, the sending countries are required to preserve information relating to the identity of birth parent/s and in particular to the child's personal and family history; this is to include information regarding the family's medical history. However, Article 30(2) leaves the issue of access to that information to be determined by the laws of the receiving country. From the perspective of the rights of the child, this raises human rights questions – e.g. what about information that is not recorded? Where does the obligation (to protect the child's right to identity) lie?

Conclusion

Article 1 of the Hague Convention declares that it provides 'safeguards to ensure that intercountry adoptions take place in the best interests of the child and with respect for his or her fundamental rights as recognised in international law'. Unfortunately, this remains largely aspirational: many such adoptions still take place outside the Convention framework; an increasing number, for example, are falling between the gap defined by statutory and sharia laws; and the Convention lacks the international regulatory powers necessary to enforce its 'safeguards'.

ICA, like its domestic third party counterpart, would seem to be in steep decline. However, surrogacy tourism would seem set to become a booming industry. This is likely to bring further complications to ICA which, together with the consequences of mass migration from Islamic countries, may well require the excellent principles of the Hague Convention to be reinforced by regulatory authority if the human rights of those involved are to be adequately protected.

4 The adoption process, human rights and the ECtHR

Introduction

This chapter studies the interaction between human rights and adoption in contemporary law. It considers the nature, role and effect of the human rights engaged in adoption. It identifies the points at which the human rights of the parties intersect with the main legal functions that constitute a typical adoption process in contemporary modern western jurisdictions. This functional analysis of the bearing of human rights on adoption – the rights engaged or not and their effectiveness or otherwise – provides a schematic for assessing the relationship between these two bodies of law in each of the six jurisdictions examined in the following chapters.

Recognising that the existence and operational efficiency of an independent regulatory body, together with proceedings that provide access and appropriate representation for the parties involved, are essential for safeguarding human rights, the chapter begins by examining their roles in relation to adoption. It then, at each stage of the adoption process, considers the interplay between legal function and human rights – with reference to ECtHR case law principles – in order to establish the evolving effect of human rights on the parties. It notes that entry to the process is controlled through the application of threshold criteria to all parties. Placement of the child is subject to an authorised consent. Supervision of the child, after placement and until determination of proceedings, is usually a statutorily ascribed responsibility. The outcome of an adoption application is determined with regard to the rights of the parties but in accordance with the principle of the welfare of the child and may result in the issue of an accompanying contact order or in an order other than the one sought. Finally, the effects of an adoption order, the possible availability of post-adoption support and of long-term services relating to information disclosure, tracing and possible reunification and the responsibilities of the parties concerned are usually set by statute.

Attention is given to recent changes in emphasis in ECtHR rulings and to the rebalancing of the human rights of the child relative to those of other parties in the adoption process. Basically, this chapter applies a human rights perspective to adoption by considering in turn:

- the regulatory framework;
- the roles of determining bodies
- the roles of other administrative agencies;
- the sequential stages of the adoption process and the nature and the weighting of different legal functions at each stage;
- the legal criteria governing entry to and exit from the process;
- the legal effects of an adoption order; and
- the outcomes of the process for the parties concerned.

Regulating the adoption process

In the UK jurisdictions, both the local authority and the court undertake a regulatory role, unlike Ireland where it falls to an adoption board.

Adoption proceedings

The existence of proceedings necessary to give effect to a recognised cause of action is a basic human right. However, while Article 12 provides that men and women of a marriageable age have the right to marry and to found a family, according to national law, the fact that there is no legal right to do so by adoption or by accessing artificial reproduction treatment was emphasised in *X* v. *Belgium and the Netherlands*.[1] The absence of such a right was also considered in *Pini and Others* v. *Romania*.[2] The following is thus subject to this one overriding omission.

Kafala

Much litigation has been generated in western countries by difficulties arising from the distinction between statutory adoption and *kafala* (see Chapter 3).

In *Harroudj* v. *France*[3] the ECtHR considered the refusal of permission for a French national to adopt an abandoned Algerian baby girl, in her care since 2004 under the terms of a *kafala* agreement endorsed by an Algerian court. The French court had noted that *kafala* gave the applicant parental authority, enabling her to take all decisions in the child's interest, and gave the child the protection to which all children are entitled under the international treaties, but had also pointed out that under the French Civil Code a child could not be adopted if the law of his or her country prohibited adoption, which it did as Algerian family law authorised *kafala* not adoption. The ECtHR accepted that for the purposes of Article 8 there existed a state of family life between Mrs Harroudj and the child, but upheld the ruling of the French court which denied that the refusal to let the applicant adopt amounted to an 'interference' with the applicant's family life. It found that there

1 Application No. 6482/147 (1975) 7 DR 75.
2 [2004] EHRR 275.
3 Application No. 43631/09, 2012.

had been no breach of the applicant's human rights. Again, *Chbihi Loudoudi and Others* v. *Belgium*[1] concerned the applicants' 'adoption' of their Moroccan niece, who had been entrusted to their care by *kafala*. The applicants complained in particular of the Belgian authorities' refusal to recognise the *kafala* agreement and approve the adoption of their niece, to the detriment of the child's best interests, and the consequent uncertain nature of her residence status. The ECtHR held that neither the refusal to grant the adoption nor the child's residence status violated Article 8. It found in particular that the refusal to grant adoption was based on a law which sought to ensure, in accordance with the Hague Convention, that international adoptions took place in the best interests of the child and with respect for the child's private and family life, and that the Belgian authorities could legitimately consider that such a refusal was in the child's best interests as in this way they could ensure that the parent–child relationship in Morocco and Belgium was maintained.

Reciprocal recognition of orders

In addition to determining domestic applications, a regulatory body is obliged to formally recognise adoption orders lawfully issued in other jurisdictions. In *Wagner and JMWL* v. *Luxembourg*[5] the ECtHR found that the Luxembourg courts had breached the applicant's Article 8 rights when it declined to recognise an adoption, completed in Peru, on the grounds that the Civil Code of Luxembourg made no provision for full adoption by a single woman.

Right to due process

Article 6 of the ECHR declares that everyone is entitled to a fair and public hearing within a reasonable time by an independent and impartial tribunal established by law. Its significance may be measured by the fact that a majority of applications to the ECtHR have been generated by alleged breaches of Article 6. It was found to be breached, for example, in *Negrepontis-Giannisis* v. *Greece*[6] when a Greek court refused to recognise a monk's adoption of his nephew, which was valid in the US where an order to that effect had been issued. In *Moretti and Benedetti* v. *Italy*,[7] the ECtHR, found serious shortcomings in the proceedings followed by Italian authorities when they prevented an adoption application in respect of a child placed in the applicants care by the authorities. The court found it regrettable that their request to adopt had not been examined before the authorities declared the child to be available for adoption and that it had been dismissed with no reasons being stated. Again, in *Mizzi* v. *Malta*,[8] the ECtHR

4 Application No. 60125/11, 2017.
5 Application No. 76240/01, 2007.
6 Application No. 56759/08, 2011.
7 Application No. 16318/07, 2010.
8 Application No. 26111/02, 2006.

found that the inability of the applicant to bring civil proceedings to repudiate his paternity of the child constituted a violation of Article 6.

Undue delay

Delay in legal processes can clearly compromise the human rights of the parties involved and can be especially harmful to the welfare interests of children. *KAB* v. *Spain*,[9] for example, concerned the adoption – despite the father's opposition – of a child who had been declared abandoned after his mother's deportation. The applicant complained that he had been deprived of all contact with his son and that neither he nor the child's mother had been informed of the proposal to adopt the child. The ECtHR held that there had been a violation of Article 8: in particular, that the passage of time resulting from the authorities' inaction, the deportation of the child's mother without the necessary prior verification, the failure to assist the applicant when his social and financial situation was most fragile at the earlier stage, together with the failure of the courts to give weight to any other responsibility for the child's abandonment and the finding that the applicant had lost interest in his son's welfare, had decisively contributed to preventing the possibility of reunion between father and son.

According to the ECtHR the following factors should be taken into account when considering whether there has been undue delay in determining a case:

- the complexity of the case;[10]
- the conduct of the applicant and the other parties;[11]
- the conduct of the relevant authorities;[12] and
- what is at stake for the applicant in the litigation.[13]

9 Application No. 59819/08, 2012.

10 See *Glasser* v. *United Kingdom* [2001] 1 FLR 153 where the court recognised that the complexities arising from the case being transferred between jurisdictions required additional reports to ensure that the eventual decision affecting the welfare interests of the child was based on a thorough investigation.

11 Ibid.; see also *Hokkanen* v. *Finland* [1944] 19 EHRR 139 [1996] 1 FLR 289, where, in both cases, the delay was attributable to the party awarded custody refusing to comply with the terms of contact orders. More recently, in *Pini and Others* v. *Romania* [2004] EHRR 275, the ECtHR found that the Romanian authorities, by failing for more than three years to take effective measures to comply with final and enforceable judicial decisions, had rendered nugatory the provisions of Article 6.

12 See *Bock* v. *Germany* [1990] 12 EHRR 247, where the court held that there had been a breach of Article 6 by the delay resulting from domestic courts seeking an unnecessary number of reports.

13 See *H* v. *United Kingdom* [1988] 10 EHRR 95, where the court noted that the irreversibility of adoption proceedings was a factor in the adopters' failure to apply promptly. See also *Mikulic* v. *Croatia*, Application No. 53176/99, ECtHR, 07.02.02 where the court ruled that, given what was at stake for the applicant, the four-year delay before hearing did not satisfy the obligation to act with particular diligence to progress the proceedings.

In *H* v. *United Kingdom*[14] the parent complained of the 'deplorable delay' of almost two years in court proceedings concerning a contact application in respect of her child in local authority care. By the time the matter was brought before the court almost three and a half years had elapsed since she had last seen her child who was by then well settled with prospective adopters. The court stressed that:

> In cases of this kind the authorities are under a duty to exercise exceptional diligence since . . . there is always the danger that any procedural delay will result in the *de facto* determination of the issue submitted to the court before it has held the hearing.

The ECtHR held that the time it had taken the parent to pursue a claim for contact with her daughter constituted 'excessive delay' and thus breached Article 6(1).

An essential element of a 'fair hearing' is the provision of appropriate legal representation.[15] For example, in *P, C and S* v. *UK*[16] the court was clear that the failure to provide parents with legal representation was in breach of their rights under Article 6 because:

> the complexity of the case, along with the importance of what was at stake and the highly emotive nature of the subject matter, lead this Court to conclude that the principles of effective access to court and fairness required that P receive the assistance of a lawyer.

The parents had a right to legal representation in adoption proceedings, including at the administrative stage. This is an aspect of the 'equality of arms' principle whereby to ensure human rights compliance both parties to proceedings must be placed in a position where they have equal knowledge of and be permitted to comment on evidence held by the other.[17] A capacity to participate effectively in decision-making is dependent upon access to all relevant information and a parent must be able to obtain access to information relied upon by the authorities. The right is also relevant to the issues of disclosure of documents and other evidence to the court and may have a relevance for the availability or otherwise of legal aid. The ECtHR has made a number of rulings in which it has emphasised the importance of ensuring that defendants are not disadvantaged by a non-disclosure of documents that may have a material bearing on the outcome of their case.[18] Alleged breaches of a parent's right of access to their child in care have also been defined as procedural matters and heard under Article 6.[19]

14 Ibid; see also *Paulsen-Medalen and Svenson* v. *Sweden* (1998) 26 EHRR 260 and *ZM and KP* v. *Slovakia*, Application No. 50232/99, 11.05.2005.
15 See, for example, *Airey* v. *Ireland* (1979) 2 EHRR 305.
16 (2002) 35 EHRR 31; [2002] 2 FLR 631.
17 *P, C and S* v. *United Kingdom.*
18 See, for example, *TP and KM* v. *United Kingdom* [2001] 2 FLR 549.
19 *O* v. *United Kingdom, B* v. *United Kingdom, H* v. *United Kingdom, R* v. *United Kingdom and W* v. *United Kingdom* (1987) 10 EHRR 29.

Adoption process

In recent years, instead of the traditional all or nothing, private or public resolution of adoption proceedings, the law in many jurisdictions has developed to provide a longer, broader and more balanced response to adoption applications. At its fullest extent, an adoption process will now most usually consist of the following stages:

- pre-placement counselling;
- legal procedures regarding availability of child, status of parties, consents, identification of any residual post-adoption rights, etc.;
- placement of child;
- pre-application supervision of placement;
- legal procedures relating to application;
- the hearing and issue of orders, with or without attached conditions;
- post-adoption support services; and
- information disclosure, tracing and possibly reunification services.

This sequence of stages may be more compressed in some jurisdictions, with consequent shortcomings in human rights, and is now governed by a mix of some prescriptive rules and large areas of professional discretion but otherwise the continuum itself has not undergone any substantive change. What has changed most significantly in some jurisdictions is the nature of the process. This has developed from being almost exclusively consensual to becoming increasingly coercive with regard to authorising the availability of children; and agency controlled, in terms of determining adopter suitability, selection of children and matching of child and adopter.

Role of the judiciary or other determining body

The consequences of adoption for the legal status of all concerned have always been viewed in the UK, unlike some other jurisdictions such as Ireland, as of such significance as to necessitate the exercise of judicial rather than administrative authority. This is often also a matter of practical necessity; as the non-consensual proportion of adoption applications grows, so too does the need to involve the court to adjudicate on contentious legal issues. The role of the court or other determining body is to:

- ensure that criteria of eligibility/suitability and status are fulfilled by all parties;
- ascertain consent or adjudicate on consent issues where necessary;
- check adherence to law, procedures and propriety;
- ensure the welfare of the child; and
- then make such order as may be appropriate.

This role is usually supplemented by the responsibilities of other officials, such as social workers and/or court officers.

Role of administrative agencies

Adoption legislation generally contains few objective criteria; control over the adoption process has effectively been delegated to adoption agencies. In recent years that process has, in most modern western jurisdictions, become greatly contracted in terms of the numbers of applicants and babies involved while also becoming increasingly professionalised. The fewer children now being adopted, many in the course of contested proceedings and bringing with them complicated legal problems, receive attention from an increasing range of bodies and officials; their bearing on the process differing according to whether an application is 'family', 'agency' or 'intercountry'.

An adoption society or agency is the key professional reference point in the adoption process; in many jurisdictions they are required to register with a designated government body and such registration is dependent upon ability to satisfy prescriptive standards. The key professional functions of an adoption agency are likely to include:

- assessing prospective adopters;
- providing pre-placement counselling for birth parents and where appropriate, for the children concerned;
- providing information to adopters on health, social care and well-being of children to be placed;
- arranging adoption placements;
- assessing and where appropriate meeting any need for post-adoption support services; and
- providing post-adoption counselling, information disclosure and tracing services.

The local authority

This State body, or its equivalent in other jurisdictions, plays an additional and important role in relation to the adoption process. The statutory powers available to it for registering and supervising adoption agencies are again indicative of the public dimension of that process. Coupled with this is the extent to which it acts as a feeder channel to the adoption process. In some jurisdictions it will manage the child protection context for permanency planning on behalf of children in need of long-term foster care but otherwise be positioned alongside and carefully distanced from the adoption process. In others such a body will ensure that the adoption process is firmly embedded and integrated within a public child protection context.

The Registrar General

This official, or their equivalent in other jurisdictions, has duties with a bearing on the adoption process, though in effect they are tied to a post-adoption role. At a minimum, these will allow for the collection of information sufficient to identify child, adopters, the date and place in respect of every adoption order issued.

Illegal adoptions

Defined as an adoption resulting from abuses – such as abduction, the sale of, traffic in and other illegal illicit activities against children[20] – illegal adoptions have been condemned by the Special Rapporteur because they 'violate multiple child rights norms and principles, including the best interests of the child. That principle is breached when the purpose of an adoption is to find a child for adoptive parents rather than a family for the child.'[21]

The Rapporteur goes on to explain that an overarching enabling factor for illegal adoptions is weak or inexistent child protection systems at the national and local levels. Most commonly an illegal adoption occurs when a baby has been abducted, or when parental consent has been improperly acquired by, for example, payments or other inducements made to the birth mother or to intermediaries. The lack of professional counselling procedures for birth parents is singled out as a deficiency often strongly associated with illegal adoptions and which may be a factor in a domestic or intercountry context. Similarly so associated are private and independent adoptions operating in parallel to State adoptions. Because these offer prospective adopters a speedy and less bureaucratic means of securing a placement they can attract improper payments, generate market conditions, produce illegal adoptions and therefore should be prohibited.

In relation to intercountry adoption (ICA), the Rapporteur notes that a lack of transparency regarding the purpose and use of 'adoption-related payments' can blur the line between legitimate and unjustified costs, the latter of which may also create a dependency (e.g. among 'orphanages' and intermediaries) that can further fuel illegal adoptions. She warns that:[22]

> The current system not only facilitates and encourages illegal adoptions but also accepts measures that foster them. A major factor enabling illegal adoptions is the level of financial advantage that can be obtained from the procurement of children for intercountry adoption. As long as adoption fees and costs are not reasonable and not made transparent and as long as contributions and donations are involved, there will continue to be a substantial incentive for illegal adoptions to take place.

20 Hague Conference on Private International Law, at: https://assets.hcch.net/upload/adoguide_e.pdf

21 Report of the Special Rapporteur on the Sale of Children, Child Prostitution and Child Pornography (27 February–24 March 2017) (A/HRC/34/55), paras 28, 53 and 64.

22 Ibid., para 93.

Thresholds for entering the adoption process: eligibility and suitability criteria

Access to the adoption process is clearly crucial for all concerned. Eligibility and suitability criteria – applied to birth parents, the child and to the adopters – provides the gateway which, in the UK, is manned by: adoption agency staff in relation to all applications including 'family' adoptions; by Adoption Panels in respect of all third party adoptions whether childcare, intercountry or arranged by a voluntary adoption agency; and is subject to judicial oversight.

The child

Determining the adoptability of a child is a fundamental first step. For a child to enter an adoption process, most contemporary western jurisdictions require the following criteria to be satisfied:

- the child must be a 'person' known to the law, i.e. he or she must have been born;
- the availability of the child must be appropriately authorised;
- the child must also usually satisfy minimum and maximum age limits;
- conditions relating to residence/domicile, etc. must be satisfied;
- a professional assessment must indicate that adoption would be at least compatible with the specific needs and welfare interests of the child; and
- the consent of the child, or their views, depending on whether he or she is of sufficient age and discernment, must be obtained.

The birth parent/s

In most western jurisdictions the appearance of a birth parent in adoption proceedings will be as either donor parent or respondent. In both instances there is usually a statutory requirement that the parent/s be professionally assessed by a registered adoption agency and have access to a counselling service. Also, there must be no evidence of illegal practices; in some jurisdictions this means that the selling or smuggling of children for adoption purposes is specifically prohibited.[23] Whether married or not, in most jurisdictions any parent with full parental responsibility is entitled to voluntarily relinquish a child for adoption; though the consent of the other parent must be obtained or the need for it dispensed with. In some jurisdictions, such as Northern Ireland, the birth parent/s may determine the religious upbringing of their child. In others, such as New Zealand they have the right to choose the adopters. In summary, the role of the birth parent/s at

23 The 'trafficking' of children for any purpose is prohibited by various international instruments including the United Nations Convention on the Rights of the Child 1989, the ILO Worst Forms of Child Labour Convention 1999, and the United Nations Protocol to Prevent, Suppress and Punish Trafficking in Persons, especially Women and Children 2000.

point of entry to the adoption process will, in most contemporary western jurisdictions, require the following criteria to be satisfied:

- ascertaining legal status regarding marriage, domicile, residence, parental responsibilities, etc.;
- post-counselling consent of birth mother;
- notice served upon or consent of birth father;
- consent for disclosure of health information on child; and
- ascertaining any preconditions for adoption.

The adopters

Adopters, in particular, must meet the full rigour of threshold requirements; though the onus falls unevenly on applicants according to whether they are first or third party adopters.

Generally, third party applicants, with in the eyes of the law no inherent reason to offer love care and protection to a child to whom they are unrelated, are required to satisfy both eligibility and suitability criteria. Eligibility criteria usually require adopters to satisfy statutory conditions relating to:

- stable relationship status;
- residence/domicile;
- income or financial means;
- no evidence of having procured child by illegal means;
- character, or lack of serious criminal convictions; and
- minimum age.

Suitability criteria are additionally required by adoption agencies and although varying to some degree depending on according to whether they are being approved for a specific child or more generally, these will include matters such as:

- maximum age;
- religious and racial compatibility;
- good health;
- appropriate motivation;
- quality of relationships; and
- cultural background and lifestyle.

Formerly adopters were required to fit a stereotypical model of ideal parents: stable loving heterosexual marriage; house owners with secure careers and income; and with an extended family and social network. In recent years adoption law has been challenged and expanded by human rights considerations.

Central to adoption is the human right of a child to 'family life'. This is proclaimed in the Convention on the Rights of the Child, Article 20.3, and a number of ECtHR rulings on what constitutes 'family life' and 'parenting' have made a significant impact upon the threshold criteria applied to adopters. In particular it has held that the definition of 'family' is not restricted to one based on marriage and therefore adoption applicants can include unmarried couples and those in lesbian or homosexual relationships. As the ECtHR has pointed out:[24]

> the notion of 'the family' . . . is not confined solely to marriage based relationships and may encompass other *de facto* 'family' where the parties are living together outside of marriage. A child born out of such a relationship is *ipso iure* part of that 'family' unit from the moment of his birth and by the very fact of it.

Article 8 of the ECHR makes no distinction between the 'legitimate' and 'illegitimate' family:[25]

> 'family life' within the meaning of Article 8 includes at least the ties between near relatives, for instance, those between grandparents and grandchildren, since such relatives may play a considerable part in family life.

In all cases, as the ECtHR recently explained, the existence of 'family life' is a precondition for the operation of Article 8:[26]

> The right to respect for 'family life' does not safeguard the mere desire to found a family; it presupposes the existence of a family (see *Marckx* v. *Belgium*, judgment of 13 June 1979, Series A no. 31, §31), or at the very least the potential relationship between, for example, a child born out of wedlock and his or her natural father (see *Nylund* v. *Finland* (dec.), no. 27110/95, ECHR 1999-VI), or the relationship that arises from a genuine marriage, even if family life has not yet been fully established (see *Abdulaziz, Cabales and Balkandali* v. *the United Kingdom*, judgment of 28 May 1985, Series A no. 94, §62), or the relationship that arises from a lawful and genuine adoption (see *Pini and Others* v. *Romania*, nos 78028/01 and 78030/01, §148, ECtHR 2004 V).

In *X, Y and Z* v. *United Kingdom*[27] it was held that in determining whether a relationship can be defined as 'family life' the following factors are relevant:

> including whether the couple live together, the length of their relationship and whether they have demonstrated their commitment to each other by having children together or by other means.

24 *Keegan* v. *Ireland*: Application No. 16969/90 (1994) Series A No. 290, 18 EHRR 342, para. 44.
25 *Marckx* v. *Belgium* (1979) Series A No. 31, 2 EHRR 330, para. 31.
26 *E. B.* v. *France*, p. 18.
27 [1997] 2 FLR 892.

This approach was taken a step further in *Lebbink* v. *the Netherlands*[28] where the ECtHR accepted that cohabitation was not an essential ingredient of 'family life' but, exceptionally, other factors may serve to demonstrate the required constancy of relationships. In this case the father's position as auxiliary guardian and his established pattern of contact, were sufficient to establish family life with the child. The Commission/court has also found, in the words of Kilkelly,[29] that 'family life may exist between children and their grandparents,[30] between siblings,[31] between an uncle and his nephew[32] and between parents and children born into second relationships'.[33]

The relationship of a cohabiting same-sex couple living in a stable de facto relationship falls within the notion of 'family life' just as the relationship of a different-sex couple in the same situation would.[34] Further, in *Gas and Dubois* v. *France*[35] the ECtHR held that the relationship between two women who were living together and had entered into a civil partnership, and the child conceived by one of them by means of assisted reproduction but being brought up by both of them, constituted 'family life' within the meaning of Article 8 of the Convention. In *Salgueiro da Silva Mouta* v. *Portugal*,[36] the ECtHR held there had been a breach of Article 8 when a court awarded the mother custody on the grounds that the father's homosexuality was an abnormality and the children should not have to grow up in its shadow. This decision is a strong statement that discrimination on the grounds of sexual orientation will not be tolerated. There is an obvious tension between this right and the right to non-discriminatory treatment guaranteed by Article 14 (see below).

The decision in *Frette* v. *France*[37] is difficult to reconcile with the trend developing in the above case law. In that case it was found to be compatible with the Convention to exclude the single, gay, male applicant from the adoption assessment process on the grounds that his sexuality rendered him ineligible. This was notwithstanding his clear suitability as an adoptive parent, and the fact that the eligibility process was only the first of two steps to adopting a child under French law. However, in *E. B.* v. *France*[38] the court reverted to established principles when it ruled that exclusion of individuals from the application process for adoption of children simply because of their sexual orientation was discriminatory and not

28 Application No. 35582/99, ECtHR, 01.06.2004.
29 Kilkelly, U., 'Child and family law', in Kilkelly (ed.), *ECHR and Irish Law*, Bristol, Jordan, p. 113.
30 *Marckx* v. *Belgium*, para. 45.
31 *Olsson* v. *Sweden*, Application No. 10465/83, Series A No. 130, 11 EHRR 259; see also *Boughanemi* v. *France*, Application No. 22070/93, Reports 1996-II, No. 8, p. 593, 22 EHRR 228.
32 *Boyle* v. *UK*, Application No. 16580/90, Comm. Rep., 9.2.93.
33 *Jolie & Lebrun* v. *Belgium*, No. 11418/85, Dec. 14.5.86, DR 47, p. 243.
34 *Schalk and Kopf* v. *Austria* (Application No. 30141/04) 2010.
35 (Application No. 2595/07), 31 August 2010.
36 [2001] 1 FCR 653.
37 Application No. 10828/97, [2003] 2 FLR 9.
38 Application No. 43546/02, 22 January 2008.

Convention compliant. The court returned to this matter in *X and Others* v. *Austria*[39] which concerned an appeal by applicants who alleged they had been discriminated against in comparison with different-sex couples, as under Austrian law, second-parent adoption was possible for unmarried heterosexual couples, but not for unmarried same-sex couples.[40] The first and third applicants were two women living in a stable relationship. The second was the third applicant's son, born outside marriage: his father had paternity rights and did not consent to the adoption; his mother had sole custody of him. The three applicants had been living in a common household and the first and third applicants provided joint care for the second. In 2005 the first and second applicants agreed to commence adoption proceedings in the Austrian District Court so as to create a legal relationship between the first and second applicants without severing the relationship with the second and third. This would enable them to obtain legal recognition of their de facto family unit. However, as the Austrian court pointed out, the relationship with the biological father and his relatives under family law would then cease to exist while the relationship with the biological mother would remain fully intact. It refused the application reasoning that the issue whether a member State provides the possibility for two persons of the same sex to establish a legal relationship with a child on an equal footing is a matter for the State itself to decide and no such possibility existed under Austrian law. On appeal to the Regional Court, the case was dismissed without a hearing, the court noting that from the provisions of Austrian family law as a whole it was clear that the legislature intended that a parental couple should consist, as a matter of principle, of two persons of opposite sex. Subsequently, the Supreme Court upheld the earlier rulings and similarly dismissed the case. The ECtHR considered that the issue was not the general question of same-sex couples' access to second-parent adoption, but the difference in treatment between unmarried different-sex couples and same-sex couples in respect of this type of adoption. Finding that: a de facto family life existed between the applicants; it was important to have the possibility of obtaining legal recognition for that status; the government had not adduced any evidence to show that it would be detrimental to the child to be brought up by a same-sex couple or to have two mothers and two fathers for legal purposes; and that the government had admitted that same-sex couples may be as suited for second-parent adoption as different-sex couples – the Court considered that the Austrian prohibition on second-parent adoption in same-sex couples lacked proportionality. It ruled that the distinction was incompatible with the Convention: there had been a violation of Article 14 of the Convention taken in conjunction with Article 8 when the applicants' situation is compared with that of an unmarried different-sex couple in which one partner wishes to adopt the other partner's child.[41]

39 Application No. 19010/07, 19 February 2013.

40 Borzova, O., *Social Services in Europe: legislation and practice of the removal of children from their families in Council of Europe Member States*, Council of Europe (Committee on Social Affairs, Health and Sustainable Development), Russian Federation, 2015, ch. 3.

41 Ibid., para. 153.

Pre-placement counselling

It is a requirement of the law in general – and of human rights in particular – that any consent must be informed and given freely with a full appreciation of the consequences. In the context of the adoption 'contract' this often requires a counselling service to be made available to all parties at least for that purpose but most usually also for the purpose of assessing any needs, support or service requirements they may have as they prepare to enter the adoption process.

The birth parent/s

Pre-placement counselling services are most usually arranged, if not provided, by adoption agencies and directed towards the birth parent/s of children the agency is considering placing for adoption; traditionally a service associated with the needs of unmarried mothers. In most jurisdictions the provision of this service is now a statutory requirement to be offered to both parents regardless of their marital status; although in relation to fathers, the duty is sometimes restricted to the provision of counselling services to those with legal parental responsibilities. At a minimum the service entails advising the parent/s as to the legal consequences of any adoption decision taken in respect of their child, providing the information necessary and ensuring that this has all been fully understood. It also entails exploring with them all feasible alternative options and, in so far as the law of the jurisdiction permits, establishing whether the parent/s wish to exercise any residual rights in relation to their child such as to maintain a level of contact or determine nature of religious upbringing.

The child

Where the child concerned is of an appropriate age and level of understanding, then there is usually a statutory requirement that the adoption agency at least seeks their views and ensures that a counselling service is provided appropriate to meet their needs. Again, the service is directed as a minimum towards ensuring that appropriate information is made available, that all feasible options are explored, and that the child has an understanding of the consequences that will follow from the making of an adoption order. The counselling will take into account any issues arising from the child's age, gender, religion, ethnic or cultural background and any special health or social care needs. In relation to a 'mature minor' the duty may be to establish whether he or she fully consents to the proposed adoption in addition to the obligation to provide a counselling service.

The adopters

Again, most jurisdictions impose a statutory obligation upon adoption agencies to provide such counselling as is necessary to ensure that prospective adopters fully understand and accept the legal consequences that will follow from the making of an adoption order. This will usually require the agency to satisfy itself that the prospective adopters appreciate the effects of an adoption order on their rights and responsibilities in relation to matters such as care and protection, inheritance and citizenship. It will entail ensuring that they understand and are willing to comply with any possible conditions that may represent the ongoing legal rights of others in relation to matters such as contact and religious upbringing. It will explore their knowledge of and entitlement to any available professional support services, adoption allowances, etc. The counselling may also address issues of willingness to share information with the child as to his or her family and perhaps culture of origin and their acceptance of the child's eventual right to access information held in agency files.

Adoption placement: rights and responsibilities

In practice, a child enters the adoption process when he or she is placed with prospective adopters. The placement decision must be taken by a person or body with the requisite authority; an initial consent is a legal necessity.

Placement decision

The placement decision is the most crucial component of an adoption process: who takes it and subject to what conditions, will largely determine the outcome. For the child concerned, it can have lifelong human rights implications, not just in terms of whether the placement was chosen on the basis of being the one most conducive to furthering his or her particular welfare interests but also as regards their subsequent ability to access the information necessary to form an authentic personal identity.

Traditionally, this decision was private and consensual, taken by birth parent/s or guardian in the belief that it offered the best way of serving the child's welfare interests. It was sometimes implemented by a direct placement, or by placement through the good offices of an intermediary, most often in favour of a third party or stranger, but not infrequently a relative such as an uncle or grandparent, and almost always in conditions of secrecy. In the UK and in most other modern western nations, this traditional right has been statutorily removed and replaced by a requirement that the placement decision is taken by a registered adoption agency. Nowadays, in many jurisdictions, a considerable proportion of such decisions are still taken privately, by birth mothers supported by their spouses, but these are decisions to adopt rather than to relinquish the children concerned.

In the UK, following a policy developed in the US, specific statutory grounds for dispensing with parental consent and authorising an adoption placement against parental wishes have been in place for some years. Decisions taken by the courts – subsequent to childcare proceedings initiated by public authorities on the grounds of parental abuse, neglect or inadequacy – are now determining the placements of many children. The grounds justifying a non-consensual adoption placement by the State of a child subject to parental neglect or abuse generate human rights controversy in many jurisdictions[42] and constitute a particular theme in this book.

As illustrated by *Zhou* v. *Italy*,[43] however, it is clear that any such progression from intervention in respect of a vulnerable parent–child relationship to a non-consensual adoption placement will only be human rights compliant if the intervening authorities have first offered appropriate supportive services and, when this has clearly failed, have then proceeded in a manner that gives the parent every opportunity to engage in decision-making and legally challenge the authorities' course of action. That case concerned a Chinese national, who in 2004 was placed in a welfare housing facility with her son, then aged 1 month. In agreement with the social services, her son was placed with a foster family during the day. Three months later, however, this family was no longer prepared to accept the child. The applicant decided to entrust the child to a neighbouring couple while she went to work. The social services, which did not accept her choice of caregiver, informed the public prosecutor at the children's court about the applicant's situation. At the end of 2007 the prosecutor asked the court to open adoption proceedings in respect of the child, as the mother was not in a position to look after him. The applicant complained in particular that her child had been placed in a foster family with a view to adoption. The ECtHR held that there had been a violation of Article 8 of the ECHR as the Italian authorities had not fulfilled their obligations before envisaging the severing of family ties, and had not made appropriate or sufficient efforts to ensure respect for the applicant's right to live with her child. In particular, the paramount need to preserve, in so far as possible, the family ties between the applicant, who was in a vulnerable situation, and her son, had not been duly considered. The difficulties could have been overcome through targeted support from the social welfare services. Furthermore, the Italian government had provided no convincing explanation to justify the severing of the maternal affiliation between the applicant and her son. Again, in *Soares de Melo* v. *Portugal*,[44] the ECtHR held that there had been a similar violation of Article 8 in respect of an order issued for seven of the applicant's children to be taken into care with a view to their adoption, and its enforcement in respect of six of them. The applicant complained about the implementation of the placement order and the prohibition of her access to the children following the judgment of the Family Court. In that connection she submitted that she had lodged various unsuccessful applications and appeals and complained that the courts had based their decisions on the fact that she had not honoured her family planning undertakings. The ECtHR found in particular that the measures taken by the domestic courts in ordering the placement of the applicant's children with a view to their adoption had not struck a fair balance between the interests at stake, given that the applicant had been deprived of parental rights and all contact with her children; her refusal to undergo

42 Borzova, *Social Services in Europe*; Fenton-Glynn, C., *Adoption without Consent*, Study for the Peti Committee, Brussels, 2015.

43 Application No. 33773/11, 2014; see also *Akinnibosun* v. *Italy* [2015] ECHR 697.

44 Application No. 72850/14, 2016.

sterilisation had formed one of the grounds for that decision; and she had had no effective involvement in the decision-making process. The Court therefore considered that the placement order had not been appropriate to the legitimate aim pursued or necessary in a democratic society, bearing in mind the absence of any violent conduct, the existence of strong emotional ties and the failure of social services to address the applicant's material deprivation as a mother having to raise a large number of children almost unaided.

Unmarried father

The issue of whether an unmarried father should be involved in the decision to place his child for adoption is one that is now recognised as engaging his human rights. In *Keegan* v. *Ireland*[45] the ECtHR held that placing a child for adoption without first informing or seeking the consent of the birth father was an infringement of both his right to respect for his family life under Article 8 and his right to a fair trial under Article 6 of the Convention. It has also acknowledged, however, that the fact that the law disadvantages an unmarried father, unlike either an unmarried mother or a married father, in relation to parental responsibility will not itself constitute a breach of his rights under Article 8. The difference in treatment for married fathers was justified in *McMichael* v. *United Kingdom*[46] on the basis that it was intended to thereby provide a means of identifying 'meritorious' fathers.

In *Elsholz* v. *Germany*[47] the ECtHR ruled that an unjustified violation of an unmarried father's Article 8 rights had occurred when a court had refused to grant him contact, without requesting a report from an expert witness, because of the strength of joint objections from mother and child. He was entitled to greater involvement and to have had his interests presented more fully before the court. Again, in *Zaunegger* v. *Germany*[48] and *Sporer* v. *Austria*,[49] the ECtHR found a violation of Article 14 taken in conjunction with Article 8 when the father of a child born outside marriage was unable to obtain a judicial ruling by the domestic courts on whether the award of joint custody to both parents or sole custody to him was in the child's interests.

Right to family life

There have been many important ECtHR rulings in respect of the Article 8 right to family life; of necessity, such rulings also carry direct implications for the human rights of the parties in an adoption process.

45 *Keegan* v. *Ireland*: Application No. 16969/90 (1994) Series A No. 290, 18 EHRR 342, para. 44.
46 (1995) Fam. Law. 478; see also *B* v. *United Kingdom* [2000] 1 FLR 1.
47 [2000] 2 FLR 486; but see also *Sahin* v. *Germany; Sommerfeld* v. *Germany; Hoffman* v. *Germany*, [2002] 1 FLR 119.
48 Application No. 22028/04, §§61–63, 3 December 2009.
49 Application No. 35637/03 §§88–90, 3 February 2011.

In *K A* v. *Finland*[50] and *Kutzner* v. *Germany*[51] it was made clear that the essential object of Article 8 is to protect the right to respect for family life and that any interference with this right violates Article 8 unless the requirements of Article 8(2) can be satisfied. Draconian intervention, such as the removal of a newborn baby from maternal care in a hospital (an act which is often a precursor to an adoption placement), has been held to be a disproportionate response to the level of risk presented by the mother and breached the latter's rights under Article 8. As the ECtHR explained in *K and T* v. *Finland*:[52]

> when such a drastic measure for the mother, depriving her absolutely of her new-born child immediately on birth, was contemplated, it was incumbent on the competent national authorities to examine whether some less intrusive interference into family life, at such a critical point in the lives of the parents and child, was not possible.

The court must first look at what additional measures of support can be put into place or what alternatives might exist that would obviate the need to make such an extreme intervention. Article 8(1) also provides a guarantee for a right to respect for home and correspondence.

The necessity for limits on an applicant's right to private life was demonstrated in *X* v. *the Netherlands*[53] where the Commission dismissed the protest of a 14-year-old girl who objected to being summarily returned by the authorities to her parents. The court held that such action was justified under Article 8(2) in order to protect her health and morals.

Surrogacy

Surrogacy arrangements, which often conclude with the adoption of the child by the commissioning parents, are fraught with legal issues and have given rise to litigation in many countries. *Mennesson and Others* v. *France* and *Labassee* v. *France*,[54] for example, concerned the refusal to grant legal recognition in France to parent–child relationships that had been legally established in the US between children born as a result of surrogacy. In both cases the ECtHR held that while there had been no violation of Article 8 in respect of the applicants right to 'family life' that there had been such a violation concerning the children's right to respect for their 'private life'. The Court observed that the French authorities, despite being aware that the children had been identified in the US as the children of

50 (2003) 1 FCR 201.
51 (2003) 1 FCR 249; see also, *Haase* v. *Germany* [2004] 2 FLR 39, paras 95ff.
52 (2003) 36 EHRR 255, para. 168.
53 (1974) (Application No. 6753/74) (1975–6) 1–3 DR 118.
54 Application Nos 65192/11 and 65941/11, 2014; see also *Foulon and Bouvet* v. *France*, Application Nos 9063/14 and 10410/14, 2016; *Laborie* v. *France*, Application No. 44024/13, 2017; and *D. and Others* v. *Belgium*, Application No. 29176/13, 2014.

Mr and Mrs Mennesson and Mr and Mrs Labassee, had nevertheless denied them that status under French law. It considered that this contradiction undermined the children's identity within French society. It further noted that the case law completely precluded the establishment of a legal relationship between children born as a result of lawful surrogacy treatment abroad and their biological father which overstepped the wide margin of appreciation left to States regarding decisions relating to surrogacy. In *Paradiso and Campanelli* v. *Italy*[55] the issue concerned the placement in public care of a 9-month-old child who had been born in Russia following a surrogacy contract entered into with a Russian woman by an Italian couple; it subsequently transpired that the latter had no biological relationship with the child. The Grand Chamber found that there had been no violation of Article 8. Having regard to the absence of any biological tie between the child and the applicants, the short duration of their relationship with the child and the uncertainty of the ties between them from a legal perspective, and in spite of the existence of a parental project and the quality of the emotional bonds, the Grand Chamber held that 'family life' did not exist between the applicants and the child. It regarded as legitimate the Italian authorities' wish to reaffirm the State's exclusive competence to recognise a legal parent–child relationship – and this solely in the case of a biological tie or lawful adoption – with a view to protecting children.

Family reunification

Articles 7–9 of the Convention on the Rights of the Child declare that children have, as far as possible, the right to know and be cared for by their parents, the right to preserve their identity, including family relations and the right not to be separated from their parents against their will unless to do so is in their best interests. An admission to the public childcare system, therefore, should be time limited and conclude with a return to parental care as soon as the problems that gave rise to the admission have been resolved: there is an onus, assumed or statutory, on the public authorities to be proactive in working towards a speedy family reunification; an onus which necessitates nurturing the parent–child relationship, while the latter remains in care, in preparation for their return home. The role of the authorities at this stage is critical for the human rights of child and the birth parent/s and the support provided can determine whether or not a child is placed for adoption.[56] The Special Rapporteur has warned against the practice, at this stage, of 'child protection services using the placement of children in alternative care, which may involve adoption, as an option of first resort, rather than providing the required support to families'.[57]

In *Johansen* v. *Norway*,[58] for example, the ECtHR considered the decision of a Norwegian court which had directed that a child be taken into care, placed in a

55 [2017] ECHR 96.
56 UN General Assembly, Guidelines for the Alternative Care of Children (24 February 2010), A/RES/64/142, paras 155–6.
57 Special Rapporteur report, A/HRC/34/55, para. 42.
58 (1996) 23 EHRR 33.

foster placement with a view to adoption and refused contact between the child and her applicant mother. The ECtHR viewed these measures as 'particularly far reaching in that they totally deprived the applicant of her family life with the child and were inconsistent with the aim of reuniting them'. It stressed the importance to be attached to the continuing interest of birth parents in the future upbringing of their child. As was subsequently noted in the House of Lords:[59]

> The leading case of *Johansen* v. *Norway* makes clear that deprivation of parental rights and access should only occur in exceptional circumstances. It would be justified if motivated by an overriding requirement pertaining to the child's best interests . . . The opposite of a trivial test.

This approach was reaffirmed by the ECtHR in the above-mentioned *K and T* v. *Finland*[60] when it drew attention to:

> the guiding principle whereby a care order should in principle be regarded as a temporary measure, to be discontinued as soon as circumstances permit, and that any measures implementing temporary care should be consistent with the ultimate aim of reuniting the natural parents and the child. The positive duty to take measures to facilitate family reunification as soon as reasonably feasible will begin to weigh on the responsible authorities with progressively increasing force as from the commencement of the period of care, subject always to its being balanced against the duty to consider the best interests of the child.

Again, in *R* v. *Finland*,[61] the court was concerned that the evidence showed a lack of will on the part of State authorities to facilitate family reunification where a child had been placed in a children's home as a consequence of parental incapacity and maternal violence. For three years the father had maintained regular contact and had repeatedly but unsuccessfully sought either the child's return or increased access. Instead access was reduced and the child was moved to a substitute family. The ECtHR found that no serious and sustained effort had been made by the social welfare authority to further reunification.[62] In ruling that there had been a breach of Article 8, the court stated:

> a fair balance has to be struck between the interests of the child in remaining in public care and those of the parent in being reunited with the child. In carrying out this balancing exercise, the Court will attach particular importance to the best interests of the child, which may override those of the parent. In particular, the parent cannot be entitled under Article 8 of the

59 Hansard, Lords, 16.10.02, col. 929.
60 [2000] 2 FLR 79, para. 178.
61 Application No. 3414/96, 30 May 2006; see also, *HK* v. *Finland*, Application No. 36065/97, 2006.
62 See also *Neulinger and Shuruk* v. *Switzerland* [GC], No. 41615/07, §134 (6 July 2010).

> Convention to have such measures taken as would harm the child's health and development.

The court returned to this theme in *YC* v. *United Kingdom*[63] when it warned that:[64]

> family ties may only be severed in very exceptional circumstances and … everything must be done to preserve personal relations and, where appropriate, to 'rebuild' the family. It is not enough to show that a child could be placed in a more beneficial environment for his upbringing.

Placement supervision

The placement period is of pivotal significance in an adoption process. The longer it lasts, the stronger the growth in bonds between child and prospective adopter/s with a consequently stronger prejudice against any possibility of a resumption of a relationship with the birth parent/s or for the child forming attachments in any other care arrangement. In order to avoid the passage of time becoming prejudicial to the human rights of the child and, possibly, the birth parent/s, it is therefore necessary that: close professional supervision is maintained to ensure that safe, loving relationships are developing appropriately; and that lodging an adoption application is not unduly delayed.

In most jurisdictions there is a legal requirement to ensure that an adoption placement is safeguarded until such time as a court or other body determines whether or not an adoption order is to be made in respect of the child concerned. Most usually, once made the placement cannot be terminated without prior approval of the placing agency or court.

The hearing and issue of order/s

In most jurisdictions, although not in Ireland, the hearing of an adoption application is a judicial process. Whether judicial or administrative, satisfying the statutory grounds relating to eligibility, suitability and consent will itself be insufficient to allow the process to conclude with a granting of the order sought. Whereas any contested application will fail because the statutory grounds have not been met, no contested or uncontested application (even where the grounds have been met) will succeed unless the court is assured that the welfare test is also fully satisfied. Applying the test may result in the issue of an altogether different order or no order at all.

Where consent is available

Adoption in the UK and elsewhere was traditionally a largely consensual process. Where the necessary consents were available or could be dispensed with and all

63 (2012) 55 EHRR 967.
64 Ibid., para. 134.

statutory criteria were met, then no obstacle existed to prevent a court or similar body from concluding the adoption process by granting the order sought. In many jurisdictions, the availability of all required consents will not necessarily prevent consideration of whether an order other than the one sought would not offer a more appropriate means of ensuring the welfare of the child concerned.

Consent of unmarried father

The presumption, that the role of an unmarried father can constitute 'family life',[65] may be rebutted. In *Soderback* v. *Sweden*,[66] for example, the applicant unmarried father had never cohabited with the mother and had a tenuous relationship with his daughter whom the mother and her spouse were proposing to adopt. The ECtHR ruled that the granting of an adoption order did not breach the father's Article 8 rights.

Consent of a minor

Nowadays, in most jurisdictions, the fact that the informed consent of an older child is a necessary prerequisite for decisions affecting his or her welfare interests has come to be regarded as a basic human right. However, in adoption proceedings, although the wishes and/or consent of the child will be sought, the result is not always regarded as determinative.

Paradoxically, the consent of a minor may be held to be valid even if that person lacks the capacity to give an informed consent. *V. S.* v. *Germany*,[67] for example, concerned a minor who had consented to the adoption of her child, but the ECtHR found that the German authorities had not overstepped their margin of appreciation in finding that under German law a valid consent had been given.

Where consent is not available

In recent decades, non-consensual adoption applications have become a prominent feature of the law in some countries. Adoption law in modern western jurisdictions will now often provide specific statutory grounds for dispensing with parental consent on grounds of child neglect or abuse as well as on the traditional grounds of parental absence, incapacity or death. Provision is also generally made for contested family adoptions.

65 *Johansen* v. *Norway* (1996) 23 EHRR 33 and *Rieme* v. *Sweden* (1993) 16 EHRR 155. Note that in *B.* v. *United Kingdom* [2000] 1 FLR 1 the court found against an unmarried father without parental responsibility and held that the UK court had been justifiably discriminatory between his standing and that of a married father as he had no custody rights in respect of the child.
66 [1999] 1 FLR 250.
67 Application No. 4261/02, ECHR, 22.05.07.

Incapacity

Mental incapacity nullifies the validity of consent. This was the conclusion in *A. K. and L.* v. *Croatia*[68] where a mother with mild mental disability had been divested of her parental rights and her son placed for adoption without her knowledge, consent or participation in the adoption proceedings. The ECtHR held that there had been a violation of Article 8 and found that, by not informing the applicant about the adoption proceedings, the national authorities had deprived her of the opportunity to seek restoration of her parental rights before the ties between her and her son had been finally severed by his adoption.

Childcare adoption: the grounds

In the context of third party adoptions, the specific synchronising of some grounds for dispensing with parental consent with those of childcare legislation is a very significant development in modern family law and highly contentious in human rights terms. The effect of introducing grounds, closely aligned to those already established in childcare legislation, as justifying an application for freeing a child for adoption, has finally bridged the gap between the public and private sectors of this law in the UK. The rights of an abusing parent who falls foul of statutory care proceedings may now not only be qualified by the issue of a care order but may also be abrogated by an adoption order. From statutory origins based on serving the private parental interests of a closed nuclear family unit, the legal functions of adoption in some jurisdictions have now been strategically repositioned to openly serve a public interest in rescuing a child from parental abuse and providing permanent alternative family care.

Contested family adoption: the grounds

In the context of first party adoptions, non-consensual applications also pose a fundamental dilemma for human rights in modern western jurisdictions. As parenting becomes less marriage based and features looser ties with extended family networks, transient home and locality links and serial care arrangements, the circumstances in which it can be safely predicted that the permanence and exclusive nature of an adoption order will be an appropriate legal intervention in family relationships are decreasing. The use of adoption as an expedient form of parental custody order, with extreme consequences for parent–child relationships and for other relationships associated with a previous spouse/partner, is becoming a serious human rights issue in many jurisdictions.

Thresholds for exiting the adoption process

As mentioned above, there is no general right to adopt or to be adopted. In all modern western jurisdictions, the legal function applied by the court or similar

68 Application No. 37956/11, 2013.

body in concluding adoption proceedings – being assured that all other criteria and grounds are satisfied – is that of making a determination which is at least compatible with the best interests of the particular child.

The welfare interests of the child

Whether an adoption order can be made is determined in accordance with the statutory criteria relating to eligibility, suitability and consent. Whether it will be made is determined by the welfare test. In adoption proceedings this test has three functions:

- it identifies the 'substance' of welfare in relation to the child concerned;
- it indicates the professionals required/permitted to bring welfare related matters before the court/body; and
- it defines the weighting to be given to such matters in deciding whether or not to make an adoption order.

In such proceedings, the weighting given to welfare has always been contentious: reflecting the balance struck in any jurisdiction between public–private interests and parent–child rights in this area of family law. Traditionally in the UK, both legislative intent and judicial practice have painstakingly differentiated between the paramount weighting given to welfare interests in childcare proceedings and a lesser weighting ascribed to such interests in adoption proceedings. This distinction has now been statutorily erased following a government policy initiative to expedite childcare adoptions: in effect the welfare interests of a child have been repositioned to act as a threshold test for entry to the adoption process. Moreover, in some jurisdictions, a characteristic of the adoption process is that the absolute and exclusive effect of an adoption order may be qualified by other orders – representing an increasing public commitment to acknowledge and promote the independent interests of a child, over and above the interests of birth and adoptive parents, before and after the issue of an adoption order – to further the lifelong welfare of such a child. In that sense, the capacity to further lifelong welfare interests has, for prospective adopter/s, become a threshold test for exiting the adoption process.

The ECtHR has played a critical but evolving role in relation to welfare interests. Where there is a conflict between the rights and interests of the child and those of a parent, which can only be resolved to the disadvantage of one of them (as in *Hendricks* v. *the Netherlands*),[69] then it has ruled that Article 8(2) requires the interests of the child to prevail. For example, in *Sahin* v. *Germany, Sommerfield* v. *Germany, Hoffmann* v. *Germany*,[70] it stressed the crucial importance of the best

69 (1982) 5 EHRR 223. See also *Kroon* v. *the Netherlands* (1994) Series A No.297-C, 19 EHRR 263 where the court commented that it was a principle of good law to hold that the interests of the child were paramount.

70 [2002] 1 FLR 119; see also *Scott* v. *UK* [2000] 1 FLR 958, where the ECtHR upheld the decision of the court at first instance to dispense with the consent of an alcoholic mother and free her child for adoption.

interests of the child. Moreover, the fact that adoption severs parental ties can be construed as compatible with Article 8.[71] In *Neulinger and Shuruk* v. *Switzerland*,[72] it emphasised that there are two considerations that must be balanced when determining the child's welfare interests: first, the maintenance of family ties, except in cases where the family has proved particularly unfit; and, second, the development of the child in a safe and secure environment. In other words, the benefits the child gains from maintaining a connection with his or her biological family must be balanced against the need to be provided with a secure and permanent home and family life; even if that family is adoptive rather than biological.

Paramountcy

While Article 21 of UNCROC establishes that the best interests of the child are to be the paramount consideration in all matters related to adoption,[73] this does not mean that the rights of the birth parent/s under Article 8 of the ECHR can be ignored; given that in general a child's welfare is best assured by parental care. Arguably, there is a danger that practice developments in some nations are pushing the boundaries established by ECtHR case law and by the requirements of Articles 3 and 21 of the Convention on the Rights of the Child.

It was in *Yousef* v. *the Netherlands*,[74] that the ECtHR first referred to 'paramountcy of welfare' when comparing the interests of a child with those of the parent:[75]

> The Court reiterates that in judicial decisions where the rights under Article 8 of parents and those of a child are at stake, the child's rights must be the paramount consideration. If any balancing of interests is necessary, the interests of the child must prevail.

Consent/views of child and welfare interests

In *Pini and Others* v. *Romania*,[76] the ECtHR had an opportunity to consider a child's rights to consent/object to their adoption. This case concerned two Romanian children, Florentina and Mariana, judicially declared to have been abandoned at the ages of 3 and 7, and who had been in the care of the Poiana Soarelui Educational Centre in Braşov (the CEPSB) for some years when they

71 *Emonet and Others* v. *Switzerland* (No. 39051/03, 13 December 2007); *Eski* v. *Austria* (No. 21949/03, 25 January 2007).
72 [2010] ECHR 1053.
73 Also established by Article 24 of the African Charter on the Rights and Welfare of the Child and Article 4 of the European Convention on the Adoption of Children (Revised).
74 [2003] 1 FLR 210.
75 Ibid., para 73; see also *R and H* v. *United Kingdom* (2012) 54 EHRR 2 [2011] 2 FLR 1236.
76 [2004] EHRR 275.

were made the subjects of adoption orders issued in favour of two Italian couples. The adopters had sought to enforce the adoption orders, but the CEPSB refused to cooperate and Florentina and Mariana issued proceedings to have the adoption orders revoked on the ground that they did not know their adoptive parents and did not wish to leave Romania and the CEPSB. The action brought by Florentina was dismissed, inter alia, on the ground that it was not in her interests for the adoption order to be revoked. However, the Braşov District Court granted Mariana's application and revoked the adoption order after noting that she was receiving a sound education and living in good conditions at the CEPSB and had not formed any emotional ties with her adoptive parents. The adopters complained to the ECtHR that the Romanian authorities' failure to enforce final judicial decisions was in breach of Article 8 as this had deprived them of all contact with their adopted children.

The ECtHR noted the conflict between: the children's interest in not having imposed upon them against their will new emotional relations with people with whom they had no biological ties and whom they perceived as strangers; and the applicants' interest in creating a new family relationship with their adopted daughters. It took the view that in adoption cases, it was even more important to give the child's interests precedence over those of its parents, as adoption meant 'giving a family to a child and not the child to a family'. The children's interest meant that their opinions had to be taken into account once they had the necessary maturity to express them and their opposition to adoption would make their harmonious integration in their new adoptive family unlikely. Consequently, the ECtHR found that the Romanian authorities could legitimately and reasonably have considered that the applicants' right to create ties with the adopted children could not take priority over the children's interest, notwithstanding the applicants' legitimate aspirations to found a family.

The orders available

For the applicant/s, an adoption order is of course the desired outcome and its issue is the intended threshold for exiting this process. As family life becomes more impermanent, however, with serial parenting arrangements and consequent extra-familial child attachments being commonly a part of a child's upbringing, it is questionable whether this most absolute of all family orders is as necessary as formerly.

Alternative orders

The availability of alternative statutory orders to be issued, as indicated by the particular welfare interests of the child concerned, is an interesting indicator of jurisdictional sensitivity to the increasing need for flexibility if the human rights of all parties are to be respected. Some jurisdictions provide such orders to be used in circumstances where the grounds for adoption have not been satisfied or can be satisfied but long-term complications can be foreseen which would make adoption inappropriate.

The effect of an adoption order

In most if not all jurisdictions the traditional outcome of the adoption process for many generations was either no order or a full order with its characteristic permanent, exclusive and absolute legal effects on all parties. This has been dramatically changed in all modern western jurisdictions by the recognition now given to a child's human rights.

Effect on the parties

As human rights law developed, bringing with it the statutory introduction of information rights, contact registers, schemes for payment and support, etc., so the traditional legal effects of an adoption order on the parties have changed. These changes have had variable consequences for the parties and their legal status across jurisdictions.

The child

Generally, the law in most jurisdictions states the primary effects of an adoption order to be that thereafter the child's legal status cannot be anything other than 'legitimate', he or she will bear the surname of the adopters and in all respects is to be treated in law as their child. Because the child's status is thereafter defined by that of the adopters so also, for the duration of childhood, are all matters of residence, domicile and nationality. The succession rights of an adopted child are usually expressly addressed by legislation and provide that for most purposes there should be no distinction between the inheritance rights of a parent's natural and adopted children. Usually, also, such legislation provides that adoption does not affect the law relating to marriage and incest (i.e. an adopted person may not marry anyone he or she would have been prohibited from marrying if the adoption had not occurred).

The birth parent/s

Again, in most jurisdictions the law states the primary effects of adoption on the birth parent/s to be the abrupt, permanent and absolute termination of their rights and responsibilities in respect of their child. It will also operate to extinguish any court order relating to the child and any agency directive requiring payments for the child's maintenance or upbringing. The law is not always as certain regarding the right of the child to inherit from the birth parent/s; in some jurisdictions the adopted child will retain the right to benefit from the estate of the birth parent/s unless specifically excluded. However, for most purposes the birth parent/s will be treated in law as if the child had never been born to them.

The adopters

The law in most jurisdictions states the primary effect of an adoption order on the adopters to be the vesting in them of all parental rights and responsibilities in respect of the adopted child. There is usually a specific legislative provision declaring that in any will, testament or in the event of intestacy, in the absence of any statement to the contrary, the estate of the adopters will devolve to the adopted child as though the latter was their birth child. For most purposes the adopter/s will be treated in law as if the child had been born to them though in some jurisdictions exceptions are made to the rules relating to consanguinity so as to permit marriage within degrees of blood relationship that would otherwise be prohibited.

Revocation of an adoption order

In the UK, the absolute and permanent legal characteristics of an adoption order have been judicially treated as immutable. This is not always the case in other jurisdictions. In Russia, for example, the authorities removed two adopted children and revoked the adoption orders following an incident when one was burnt at home and required hospital treatment. Subsequently, the ECtHR found that these actions had breached the applicant's Article 8 rights.[77]

Entitlement to post-adoption support services

Traditionally, in keeping with the essentially private nature of adoption, once an order was made then the door was closed on the newly formed family unit, professional intrusion in its affairs ended and no further contact with public service agencies was anticipated. However, in recent years there has been a growing recognition that such families should be entitled to call upon the State for ongoing support services as required. In particular, as many jurisdictions began to accommodate and give effect to a policy of increased use of adoption as a resource for public care bodies, it has become customary for the latter to facilitate this by providing such short or long-term support services as are likely to sustain the child within that care arrangement. Currently, these support services are usually confined to third party rather than first party adopters and are not always extended to benefit the birth parent/s. The jurisdictional variation in availability of post-adoption support services is most usually tied to childcare adoption and may therefore be conditioned by jurisdictional recognition of the human rights of a child in public care to family life.

Childcare adoptions

In a public childcare context, the making of an adoption order marks a double change in the status of the child concerned. He or she is legally transplanted not only from one family to another but also from public to private care. In modern western jurisdictions there is now a much greater willingness on the part of adoption agencies, courts and the families concerned to facilitate a carry-over of

77 *Ageyevy* v. *Russia* [2013] ECHR 346.

any relationships, services and professional input deemed important for the welfare of such a child in their post-adoption life. Adoption allowances are the most common form of service and are particularly important to secure and support adoption placements for those requiring particularly high levels of attention, such as disabled children, sibling groups or those with complex healthcare or special needs. The introduction of public finance to what has always been regarded as a private area of family law breaches a long-established taboo and legal prohibition relating to payments made to facilitate adoption and for that reason has proven contentious in some jurisdictions.

Information rights: disclosure, tracing and reunification

The traditional guarantee of absolute and permanent confidentiality, given by an adoption agency to a mother voluntarily relinquishing her baby for adoption, has become steadily diluted in all modern jurisdictions in recent years. Case law, particularly under Articles 7 and 8 of UNCROC, has established that individuals have a basic human right to the information necessary to form a personal and cultural identity. Consequently, an adopted person now generally has the right to information about the fact and circumstances of their adoption, the means for accessing that information and an entitlement to related counselling services.

Information rights

Legislative provisions and procedures enabling an adopted person to acquire by right information relating to the circumstances of the adoption have now been introduced in many countries. This right is one which challenges the traditional veto of birth parents and/or adopters by giving precedence to the identity interests of an adopted person relative to the right of others to private family life. So, for example, in *Godelli* v. *Italy*[78] the ECtHR held that the applicant's Article 8 rights had been violated by Italian legislation which, in cases where the mother had opted not to disclose her identity, did not allow a child – who had not been formally recognised at birth and was subsequently adopted – to request either non-identifying information about his or her origins or the disclosure of the birth mother's identity with the latter's consent.

Information disclosure duties

In addition to the statutory duties of the Registrar General, or similar government body, it is now also customary to have similar information disclosure obligations placed upon such other relevant bodies as the courts and public healthcare agencies. However, as it is the adoption agencies that are central to an adoption process and serve as the primary repository for all adoption information, the critical issue is whether or not they are legally obliged to disclose information given to them in

78 Application No. 33783/09, 2012.

confidence. The usefulness of any disclosure procedures will be wholly dependent upon the amount and quality of information recorded and held on file by adoption agencies which in turn depends upon the existence of legislative provisions requiring them to maintain their records for a specified minimum period.

Tracing and reunification

While not strictly a matter of human rights, many jurisdictions have introduced 'contact registers' as a means of coordinating information relating to desired contact between adopted persons and members of their family of origin. Again, the crucial issue is whether or not the existence of such a register, its contents and rights of access to it are prescribed in legislation. Finally, most jurisdictions now have a procedure whereby the relevant adoption agency will undertake to trace and contact the relative and relay the request for a meeting. Clearly, whether this is available as a statutory right or left to agency discretion is a matter affecting the human rights of all parties to an adoption.

Conclusion

The social functions of adoption reflect the society of which it is a part and are adjusted by it in response to emerging pressures. The legal functions of adoption, being internally referenced and remaining relatively fixed, retain their basic characteristics. If human rights law is to be effective it must, directly or indirectly, impact upon those legal functions.

This chapter has identified the sequence of stages that constitute the modern adoption process and the range of essential and possible legal functions that are available to give effect to the legislatively determined purposes of each stage. It then considered how human rights law – as evidenced in ECtHR rulings – interacted with those functions to affect the interests of the parties involved. In so doing it has provided a thematic structure that will be applied in later chapters to identify and explore possible similar patterns of interaction in the adoption process of other jurisdictions.

Part II

Contemporary law, policy and practice in a common law context

5 England

Introduction

This, the first of the jurisdiction-specific chapters, begins with on overview of the human rights issues that have characterised the evolving law, policy and practice relating to adoption in England.[1] It identifies the principles and significant statistical trends in modern adoption practice, before outlining the contemporary legislative and regulatory frameworks. It then examines each stage of the domestic adoption process: the thresholds for entry; the hearing and the grounds for making an adoption order; and the thresholds for exiting (for an outline of the equivalent intercountry adoption (ICA) process, see Chapter 3). It considers the effects of an adoption order on the parties concerned and ends with a brief summary of post-adoption information rights, tracing and reunification services. At each stage it identifies and reflects upon the related human rights considerations.

Background

As has been pointed out, the traditional function of adoption has simply been 'a way of making a child legally part of a new family and severing any legal relationship with the birth family'.[2]

Adoption and human rights: the early challenges

From its late statutory inception in 1926 through to the middle of the twentieth century, adoption in this jurisdiction was very much a private matter and treated as such under family law. Not until the report of the Houghton Committee[3] did

1 Since the devolution of powers to the four jurisdictions that comprise the UK, in the interests of accuracy it has become customary to differentiate between them when referencing contemporary legislation and associated case law.

2 Waterhouse Inquiry, *Lost in Care: Report of the Tribunal of Inquiry into the Abuse of Children in Care in the former County Council Areas of Gwynedd and Clwyd since 1974*, London, HMSO, 2000, para. 3.6.

3 *Report of the Departmental Committee on the Adoption of Children* (Cmnd 5107), London, HMSO, 1972.

adoption become a regulated public service with placements undertaken by registered adoption agencies instead of being arranged privately (see Chapter 2). By the end of the twentieth century the principles and case law of the Human Rights Act 1998 were beginning to make their influence felt. This became apparent, for example: in the switch from defending parental rights to an emphasis upon parental responsibilities;[4] in a central focus on the welfare interests of the child; and in a changed approach to unmarried fathers without parental responsibility whose involvement in decision-making was now to be sought.[5]

Poverty

Regardless of cultural context, poverty has always been a driving force in determining the flow of children entering the adoption process; except when the latter is used as an expedient adjunct to marital proceedings or to surrogacy arrangements. A considerable body of research testifies to both the enduring level of poverty in the UK[6] and the strength of the correlation between it and family breakdown.[7] In so doing it also highlights government inability to satisfy its obligation to safeguard the welfare of children in need and promote their upbringing by their families through a range of support services: under the Children Act 1989, s. 17(1); and under Article 27 of the Convention on the Rights of the Child (UNCROC). There can be little doubt that there would be fewer children coming into public care, and then being moved on into adoption, if the coping capacity of vulnerable families was reinforced by State provision of adequate family support services.[8]

Shaping modern adoption policy

As the twentieth century drew to a close, it was apparent that the traditional functions of adoption were no longer aligned with contemporary family law pressures: its primary use had become one of repairing boundaries in the aftermath of family breakdown; while the principles governing childcare and adoption had become increasingly conflicted since the introduction of the Children Act 1989, which established the paramountcy principle as the governing benchmark for

4 Baroness Hale '[t]here is no question of a parental right', in *Re G (Children)* [2006] UKHL 43, para. 30.
5 See, for example, *Re B (Adoption Order)* [2001] EWCA Civ. 347 [2001] 2 FLR 26.
6 UN Committee on the Rights of the Child, *Concluding Observations on the Fifth Periodic Report of the United Kingdom of Great Britain and Northern Ireland* (CRC/C/GBR/CO/5), 2016, para. 70; see also Unicef 2017 report which found that one in three British children were in 'multi-dimensional poverty' at: www.theguardian.com/society/2017/jun/15/levels-of-child-hunger-and-deprivation-in-uk-among-highest-of-rich-nations
7 See, for example, the HBAI (Households Below Average Income) report which concluded that 3.8 million children – one in three – are currently living in poverty in the UK, one of the highest rates in western Europe.
8 Bywaters, P., 'Inequalities in child welfare: towards a new policy, research and action agenda', *British Journal of Social Work*, 45(1) (2015): 6–23.

decisions affecting a child in care but without application to decisions relating to adoption. Moreover, this was a time when the failings of State care were becoming only too apparent. The effect of public childcare scandals, combined with the expense of that care and the influence of the principle that family care is best, led to the outcomes research[9] for looked-after children which, together with attachment theory,[10] suggested that once rehabilitation had been found to be impracticable then a local authority should institute permanency planning and that adoption rather than foster care was more likely to produce long-term beneficial outcomes for the children concerned.

The 1992 review of adoption law, conducted jointly by the Department of Health and the Law Commission,[11] resulted in the *Consultation Document*[12] which recommended that: adoption should continue to be restricted to married applicants; extended to single persons only in exceptional circumstances; that the consent of unmarried fathers without parental responsibility should remain unnecessary; and that post-adoption contact and greater openness[13] in accessing information should have a part to play in adoption in the future. It also addressed the long-standing concern that step-adoptions had the effect of legally guillotining the interests of all members of one side of the child's family in maintaining relationships with that child[14] and suggested that other less extreme orders, such as a residence order, would be more appropriate. This led in turn to the publication of the government's White Paper *Adoption – The Future*[15] and its sequel the *Adoption – A Service for Children.*[16] However, despite a gestation period of 13 years, it was not until the pressure generated by childcare scandals became acute that the government was finally prompted to consider new legislation.[17]

Preparations for new legislation began with the White Paper, *Adoption: A New Approach* in December 2000 which proposed that childcare and adoption legislation should be brought into alignment to make the welfare interests of the child, interpreted in the light of the welfare checklist, the matter of paramount

9 The 'outcomes research', analysing and evaluating the care careers of looked-after children, is comprised of many different reports compiled in the main from within the social work and allied professions.

10 Bowlby, J., *Attachment and Loss*, London, Hogarth Press, 1973.

11 The working party, drawn from the two agencies, was established in 1989. Constituted as the Interdepartmental Review of Adoption Law, it published four preliminary discussion papers: *The Nature and Effect of Adoption* (1990), *Agreement and Freeing, The Adoption Process*, and *Intercountry Adoption*; and three background papers: *International Perspectives* (1990), *Review of Research Relating to Adoption* (1990), followed by *Intercountry Adoption* (1991–2).

12 Department of Health, *Adoption Law Review: Consultation Document*, London, HMSO, 1992.

13 *Review of Adoption Law*, para. 4.2.

14 Ibid., para. 19.2.

15 (Cmnd 2288), 1993.

16 *Adoption – A Service for Children*, London, HMSO, 1996. Note also the Green Paper, *Every Child Matters* (2003) and *Every Child Matters: Next Steps*, Department of Skills and Education, London, HMSO, 2004.

17 See, in particular, the Waterhouse Inquiry.

importance in all decisions throughout the adoption process. It set out the government's expectation that there would be a 40 per cent increase in adoption orders over the next five years in respect of looked-after children. It also prepared the ground for the introduction of National Standards to govern matters such as the length of time such a child should expect to wait before a decision is taken regarding his or her eligibility for adoption and before a placement is found. It noted that post-adoption contact and 'openness' in general had become an established part of modern adoption policy and practice, acknowledging that 'links with birth families are very important to children',[18] but refrained from including any provisions to address this matter. It did focus on the issue of information disclosure to adopted persons, proposing that new legislation should include the right of both birth parents and adopted persons to register a wish for 'no contact' in the Adoption Contact Register,[19] declaring that 'all adopted people should be able to discover their family history if and when they wished to do so'.[20] The preparations were accelerated with the launch of the prime minister's policy initiative stating that 'adoption from care is not about providing couples with trouble-free babies. It is about finding families for children of all ages, with challenging backgrounds and complex needs.'[21] This process concluded with the Adoption and Children Act 2002.

Transracial

Transracial adoption has always been controversial in this jurisdiction. A policy in its favour, implemented in the 1960s and 1970s, was replaced in the following decades by one giving priority to ethnic matching. The Children and Families Act 2014 reversed the latter policy by removing a statutory requirement to take ethnicity into account when making adoption placements in order to expedite the adoption of the many children of ethnic minority background in public care for whom matching prospective adopters were unavailable.

Principles

Aligning the principles of the 1989 and 2002 Acts succeeded in mainstreaming adoption into childcare and protection policy and created a new platform for addressing the needs of children failed by their parents.

Adult adoption

Neither adult adoption nor simple adoption are legally permissible.

18 Ibid., para. 2.6.
19 Ibid., para. 4.22.
20 Ibid., para. 6.44.
21 Department of Health, Consultation Report by the Performance and Innovation Unit, *Adoption: Prime Minister's Review*, Cabinet Office, London, HMSO, 2000, p. 14.

The paramountcy principle

As embedded in s. 1(2) of the 2002 Act, this principle provided for the first time a statutory mechanism to bridge both childcare and adoption proceedings. Although held to govern all decisions taken in respect of a child's upbringing – whether by local authority or court – including dispensing with consent of the birth parent/s, the UN Committee on the Rights of the Child (CRC) nonetheless had 'regrets that the right of the child to have his or her best interests taken as a primary consideration is still not reflected in all legislative and policy matters and judicial decisions affecting children, especially in the area of alternative care'.[22]

Permanency planning

As implied, this principle requires the provision of a secure and consistent framework of care relationships sufficient to allow a child in care to optimise their potential for emotional, psychological and physical growth. Adoption is viewed by childcare professionals as the gold standard of the permanency planning options available.

Concurrent placements

This is a practice whereby a local authority, in order to reduce the number of placement changes, will commit to a rehabilitation programme designed to return a child to safe parental care, while also putting in place a parallel permanent placement plan.[23] It relies upon foster parents chosen for their capacity to engage directly with the birth parents and facilitate the rehabilitation plan but who, in the event of that plan failing, are also approved and willing to adopt the children concerned. These two options will then be played out in tandem with emphasis given to rehabilitation but the fallback position of adoption is kept alive and preparations for utilising it are attended to constantly. In very many cases, where the rehabilitation option has demonstrably failed, children have then been successfully and relatively swiftly adopted by their carers.[24] This approach avoids the traditional care career of serial placements and 'drift' in long-term foster care. Arguably, however, there is cause for some concern as to whether such a practice is wholly Convention compliant: specifically, there are grounds for considering that, by allowing alternative attachments to form over a considerable period, concurrent placements may in effect prejudice the welfare principle, reduce the likelihood of a return to parental care and pre-empt the court's decision-making, thereby possibly compromising Articles 6 and 8.

22 UN CRC, *Concluding Observations*, para. 26.
23 See, for example, Wolfson, R., 'Concurrent planning: a route to earlier permanence for young children', *Seen and Heard*, 23(2) (2012): 46–58.
24 *Re M'P-P (Children)* [2015] EWCA Civ. 584. Accelerated by provisions of the 2014 Act.

Openness

The probability of an adopted child retaining some degree of contact with his or her birth family has increased considerably in recent years. As has been officially noted:[25]

> All adoption agencies involved birth families in ongoing contact arrangements to promote and maintain the child's identity. For birth parents, this contact was usually through periodic exchanges of letters and photos.

The principle of 'openness' is now standard practice in this jurisdiction and extends to facilitating post-adoption access to identifying information.

Contemporary adoption trends

Adoption in this jurisdiction has changed from being in the main a form of private family law proceedings to instead being more of a public service. The proportion of children entering the adoption process whose parents are married and/or whose availability has been determined by coercive intervention of the State has grown to become a particularly distinctive characteristic. Other such characteristics include the consistently high proportion (though perhaps not as high as it has been) of parental applications and the growing proportion of foster parent applicants.

Childcare adoption

The broad upward trajectory of childcare adoptions has been maintained since at least 1994. However, the phase of annual increases that commenced in 2011 ended in 2016 when 4,690 were adopted, representing a decrease of 12 per cent on the high of 5,360 reached in 2015.[26] This has to be seen in the context of a rising childcare population which, by March 2016, consisted of: 70,440 children, of whom 62 per cent were aged 10 years or older; and 4,210 were unaccompanied asylum seekers.[27]

Foster care

In 2015 of the 69,540 children in the public care system some 52,050 were in foster care: an increase of 8 per cent since 2011.[28] By far the majority of those admitted to the public care system remain in foster care.

25 Commission for Social Care Inspection, *Adoption: Messages from Inspections of Adoption Agencies*, London, HMSO, 2006, para. 2.8.

26 www.gov.uk/government/uploads/system/uploads/attachment_data/file/556331/SFR41_2016_Text.pdf

27 The CRC has expressed its concern regarding this 'increase in the number of children in care' (UN CRC, *Concluding Observations*, para. 52(a)).

28 Department of Education at: www.gov.uk/government/statistics/children-looked-after-in-england-including-adoption-2015-to-2016

Foster parent adoption

The percentage of children exiting the care system by way of adoption increased from 11 per cent in 2011 to 17 per cent in 2015. In the year ending March 2016: 51,850 children were placed in foster care but only 320 (1 per cent) were in placements where the carer was an approved adopter; 4,690 exited the care system by way of adoption.

Family adoption

Adoptions by a grandparent, brother, sister, uncle or aunt – whether of full-blood or half-blood – have increased in recent years. This is probably due to local authority policy of looking first to family members as potential adopters for a child in public care.

Step-parent adoptions

For many years these constituted the largest category of adopters, but they are now decreasing both in number and as a proportion of annual orders. In 1998, when they were achieved by way of a joint application by both birth parent and spouse, they accounted for more than 50 per cent of all orders made. This changed following implementation of the Adoption and Children Act 2002 as joint applications were thereafter no longer necessary.[29] During 2005, of the 3,867 adoption orders made, 20 per cent (800) were made to step-parents, 3 per cent less than in 2004 (when 1,040 of the 4,539 orders were to step-parents).[30]

Intercountry adoption

The consistently low reliance on ICA in this jurisdiction, relative to all other western nations, is fading further. Between 2004 and 2014, the record shows a total of 2,484 ICAs but it also reveals a sharp drop in annual numbers from a high of 369 in 2005 to a low of 68 in 2014 and sinking yet lower to 57 in 2015.[31] This is partly due to a government policy of channelling prospective adopters towards children in the domestic public care system.

Adoption-related issues in human rights reports

In 2016 the CRC regretted, as mentioned above, that the best interests of the child were given inadequate priority and recommended that 'this right is appropriately integrated and consistently interpreted and applied in all legislative,

29 Adoption and Children Act 2002, s. 52(2).

30 Department for Constitutional Affairs, *Judicial Statistics Annual Report 2005*, London, HMSO, May 2006, p. 71.

31 Selman, P., *Global Statistics for Intercountry Adoption: Receiving States and States of Origin 2004–2015* (2016), at: https://assets.hcch.net/docs/3bead31e-6234-44ae-9f4e-2352b190ca21.pdf

administrative and judicial proceedings and decisions and in all policies, programmes and projects that are relevant to and have an impact on children'.[32]

A recent report, *Suffer the Little Children*,[33] found that: the number of children currently in care in England is greater than it has been since 1985 and childcare adoptions, more numerous than in any other European country, now stand at the highest level since data was first collected; 90 per cent of adoptions occur without parental consent; from 2001 to 2016 the number leaving care to live with adopted parents or special guardians increased from 87,090 to 143,440 – a rise of 65 per cent. It suggests that the continued increase in the childcare population, despite increased recourse to adoption and guardianship, indicates that the primary change agent has been a lowering of the threshold for State intervention in parental care. This interpretation is reinforced by the research of Featherstone et al. that draws attention to the current emphasis placed on managing risk and risk aversion in child protection.[34] Such research findings raise a question as to whether professional practice is in danger of treating somewhat lightly the principle, stated in Article 9 of UNCROC, that children should not be separated from their parents against their will, except when it is in their best interests.

The current legislative framework

For at least the last decade, the central planks of the domestic legislative framework for adoption have been provided by the Adoption Act 2002 and the Children Act 1989. However, a number of other statutes, supplemented by the provisions of international treaties, conventions and protocols combine to form a sophisticated platform of adoption law. For information on the corresponding ICA legislative framework, see Chapter 3.

The legislation: adoption-related law

This has become a complex and overlapping area of statutory provision which includes much secondary legislation.

Children and Social Work Act 2017

This statute, particularly ss. 8 and 9, introduced some changes to the factors considered by courts and practitioners when making decisions on adoption.

Education and Adoption Act 2016,

This Act intends to create regional, instead of local, adoption registers, to ensure that the widest range of adoptive parents is available for children.

32 UN CRC, *Concluding Observations*, paras 26–7.
33 Bilson, A., *Suffer the Little Children*, London, Legal Action for Women, 2017.
34 Featherstone, B. et al., *The Future of Child Protection: A Social Model*, Bristol, Policy Press, 2017.

Children and Families Act 2014

This statute amended the 2002 Act to allow a contact order to be issued, at the making of the adoption order or at any time afterwards – and also to prohibit any contact – between a child and member/s of their birth family. Before granting an adoption order, the court must consider whether there should be arrangements for allowing any person contact with the child, must consider any existing or proposed arrangements and must take account of the views of the parties; such contact may be direct or indirect.

Children and Young Persons Act 2008

This statute intended to reform the statutory framework for the care system in England and Wales, and made provision in relation to the well-being of children and young people and as regards private fostering.

Children and Adoption Act 2006

By way of amendments to the 2002 and 1989 Acts, this statute makes provision regarding contact with children, family assistance orders, risk assessments and in relation to ICA where there are concerns about a country's adoption practices. It also introduced a procedure enabling a step-parent to be a sole adoption applicant in respect of their partner's child.

Children Act 2004

Following on from the Victoria Climbié inquiry,[35] this Act supplemented provisions in the 1989 Act and provided for a Children's Commissioner, for better provision and regulation of children's services, for adoption review panels and other matters.

Adoption and Children Act 2002

This formative legislation, introducing a wide range of provisions to update and coordinate childcare and adoption practice, came into effect in December 2005; repealing the Adoption Act 1976 and amending the Children Act 1989. Most importantly, it provided that the paramountcy principle must govern all decisions, whether taken by court or agency, affecting a child's upbringing throughout his or her life including dispensing with parental consent for adoption. Provision was made for the introduction of placement orders and special guardianship orders, for single applicant adopters and for post-adoption information disclosure.

35 Led by Laming LJ, this inquiry into the brutal torture and murder of an 8-year-old girl revealed the 'blinding incompetence' of the professionals from many statutory and voluntary agencies involved with the relatives responsible for her death.

Care Standards Act 2000

As amended by the Health and Social Care (Community Health and Standards) Act 2003, this statute established regulatory bodies for social care, but it also provided authority: for the National Adoption Standards, given the force of statutory guidance from April 2003; and the National Minimum Standards for adoption; and, thereby, the means for assessing the performance of all adoption agencies in inspections undertaken by the Adoption and Permanence Taskforce.

Adoption (Intercountry Aspects) Act 1999

By giving effect to the Hague Convention 1993, the 1999 Act introduced a new framework to govern the adoption of overseas children by UK citizens. It requires prospective adopters to be assessed, approved and authorised in the UK before children are brought into the jurisdiction;[36] reinforced by the Adoption of Children from Overseas Regulations 2001. It also requires all local authorities to include services to intercountry adopters within the general duty to provide an adoption service; a provision reinforced by s. 2(8) of the 2002 Act.

Children Act 1989

This cornerstone of modern childcare law has been subject to considerable amendment and now seems quite dated. By stating the matters held to constitute a checklist of welfare interests, it enabled a new, more uniform and objective application of this inherently subjective concept. By introducing the concept of parental responsibility and requirements on local authorities to provide services for children in need it placed a new emphasis on measures to prevent children entering the public care system. Among its more significant statements of principle are: that the welfare of the child is paramount; children should be brought up and cared for within their own families and services should be provided to families in need; the State should work in partnership with such families; children should be protected by effective intervention if they are at risk of significant harm; and that parental responsibility may need to be shared with the State.

Other relevant provisions

Council Regulation (EC) No. 2201/2003 of 27 November 2003 (Brussels II) is of importance because it requires central authorities in Member States to collect and exchange information on any child of another Member State resident within their jurisdiction in respect of whom significant decisions are to be taken.

36 *Re C* [1998] 2 FCR 641 and the case of 'the internet twins'.

The legislation: human rights law

The Human Rights Act 1998 and the Equality Act 2010 for most purposes comprise the relevant domestic human rights framework for adoption. This is supplemented by certain international conventions, protocols, etc. including the Universal Declaration of Human Rights (UDHR), the European Convention on Human Rights (ECHR), UNCROC and the Hague Convention on Protection of Children and Co-operation in respect of Intercountry Adoption 1993 (see Chapter 3).[37]

Regulating the adoption process

Adoption proceedings are tightly regulated, resting on a body of specific requirements with definite sanctions for non-compliance, and underpinned by court rules. Although the primary regulatory role falls to the judiciary, other bodies have assumed intrusive and extensive responsibilities.

The judiciary

The Adoption and Children Act 2002, in keeping with all previous legislation (see Chapter 2), retains adoption as a judicially regulated process. The court ensures that eligibility/suitability criteria are fulfilled by all parties, ascertains or adjudicates on consent requirements, confirms that the proposed arrangements are compatible with the child's welfare and then issues or refuses the order sought. The 2002 Act amended the judicial role to permit:

- flexibility in relation to marital status of applicants;
- application of the welfare checklist;
- obligation to check whether post-adoption contact arrangements are necessary;
- determine whether a conditional adoption order would be appropriate; and to
- consider the appropriateness of an alternative order.

CAFCASS

The Children and Family Court Advisory and Support Service[38] appoints CAFCASS officers (previously a guardian *ad litem* and a children and family reporter) – though not in all cases – to carry out an exhaustive investigation into all the circumstances of the proposed adoption, interviewing all applicants and respondents

37 Intercountry Adoption (Hague Convention) Regulations and the Adoption (Amendment) Rules incorporated the 1993 Hague Convention which, together with the 2002 Act, s. 83, and the Adoption (Bringing Children into the United Kingdom) Regulations, provide the governing provisions for ICA.

38 Established in April 2000, this non-departmental body provides welfare reports and other support services in family proceedings throughout the three tiers of the court system and is accountable to the Lord Chancellor.

including, where feasible, the child and ensuring that any factor having a bearing on the welfare of the child is brought to the attention of the court. In particular, s. 102 of the 2002 Act requires the CAFCASS officer to advise parents on the implications of giving consent and to witness any consent then given. The court will also receive a report from the adoption agency or local authority in all cases. In the absence of complicating factors, such as a lack of consent from a birth parent, CAFCASS will not normally be involved in family adoptions other than to witness any consents.

Government bodies

Local authorities are required by the 2002 Act to maintain an adoption service for all parties whether they are involved in an agency, intercountry or family adoption.[39] There is also a right to an assessment of needs for adoption support services (but no corresponding duty on a local authority to provide the services assessed as being necessary) for adoptive families and others[40] which can be undertaken on a pre-adoption basis. Adoption support service providers are required to be registered.[41]

Adoption agencies

Defined as a 'local authority or registered adoption society',[42] the latter includes voluntary adoption societies, which unlike local authorities are required to register. Each agency is required to set up at least one Adoption Panel[43] which must take all referrals relating to whether: adoption is in the best interests of a particular child; a prospective adopter should be approved as an adoptive parent and; if the home of a particular approved prospective adopter would provide a suitable placement for a particular child. It does not have a role in relation to family adoptions, but it does screen all assessments of prospective intercountry adopters undertaken by voluntary adoption agencies.[44] Although it makes recommendations rather than decisions for its agency, the latter is prevented from taking decisions in those areas without first inviting recommendations from the Panel and it must make its decisions before the child is placed for adoption. The Adoption Agency Regulations and the Suitability of Adopters Regulations 2004 in the main continue the previous provisions but make some important additional changes to practice. The prospective adopters, for example, are now to be given relevant information relating

39 Section 3(2) (b).
40 Section 4. See the Adoption Support Services Regs. 2005.
41 Under Part II of the Care Standards Act 2000.
42 Section 2(1) of the Adoption and Children Act 2002.
43 Department of Health, *Adopter Preparation and Assessment and the Operation of Adoption Panels: A Fundamental Review*, London, HMSO, 2002.
44 Adoption of Children from Overseas Regulations 2001 require prospective intercountry adopters to submit to the same assessment process as prospective domestic adopters; since reinforced by the provisions of s. 83 of the 2002 Act.

to the child in question before referral to the Panel and this must include any plans relating to post-adoption support services and contact arrangements.

Registration of adoption orders

This duty falls to the Registrar General who is obliged to maintain an Adopted Children Register and keep an index of this in the General Register Office. The duty imposes a further requirement that records are kept which provide a link between an entry in the Register of Births marked 'adopted' and the corresponding entry in the Adopted Children Register (a link not publicly accessible). This allows for the collection of information sufficient to identify child, adopters, the date and place in respect of every adoption order issued. The Registrar General is required to maintain an Adoption Contact Register which enables adopted persons and their birth parents who want to contact each other to do so.

Other

The brief of independent monitoring bodies such as the Equality and Human Rights Commission and the Children's Commissioner extends to the adoption process but as yet there is little evidence of their engagement with it. Given the concerns expressed in the 2016 CRC report regarding local authority use of alternative care arrangements – which can often prove to be points of entry to that process – such engagement may be overdue.

Human rights considerations

Although easily overlooked, perhaps the main consideration in human rights terms is the lack of experienced childcare social workers,[45] the low investment in resources directed towards preventing children coming into the public care system and the poor standard of care provided for those in that system.

Local authority discretion

The Children Act 1989, s. 34, requires a local authority to provide arrangements for reasonable contact between a child in care and their parents and/or other members of the birth family; a level of once or twice a week would not be uncommon. When such a child is placed for adoption then, under the Adoption and Children Act 2002, ss. 26 and 27, those arrangements are terminated. At that point, in the absence of a contact order – and the judiciary often prefer to leave contact arrangements to local authority discretion – the frequency of contact may abruptly drop to once every couple of months, under social work management. In the absence of judicial monitoring, contact arrangements can prove prejudicial to sustaining a parent–child attachment.

45 As noted in UN CRC, *Concluding Observations*, paras 52–3.

The CRC has expressed concern that 'parents have not been provided with adequate family support' and that 'children have reportedly been removed from their biological families owing to the family's economic situation or because a foster family may provide a more beneficial environment for the child'.[46] This point had been made earlier by Munby J in *Re B-S*:[47]

> The local authority cannot press for a more drastic form of order, least of all press for adoption, because it is unable or unwilling to support a less interventionist form of order. Judges must be alert to the point and must be rigorous in exploring and probing local authority thinking in cases where there is any reason to suspect that resource issues may be affecting the local authority's thinking.

This inability of under resourced local authorities to provide sufficient preventative services to satisfy the family support obligations of Article 18 of UNCROC is problematic. Preventing children identified as 'in need' from becoming children at risk of 'significant harm' is ostensibly central to local authority policy but the continued increase in children coming into public care, a minority of whom are then compulsorily adopted, indicates a failure to achieve this in practice.

Adoption Panel functions

Prospective adoption applications from relatives of the child concerned are not subject to scrutiny by the local Adoption Panel (unless the child is in care). This, in effect, means that perhaps the most important quality control mechanism in the adoption process has no relevance for a proportion of UK adoptions. They avoid this forum for professional assessment on the grounds that this is viewed as a matter of private family law.

As regards childcare adoptions, although the Panel is required to make its matching recommendation prior to the agency placement decision, the latter's practice of concurrent placement in fact circumvents the Panel leaving it to rubberstamp a placement already made. This can seriously undermine the Panel's independence.

Adoption proceedings

Decisions regarding adoption applications – as opposed to placement order decisions – are made in private hearings, for very good reason, but this may inhibit robust challenging and hinder transparency in respect of the rationale involved.

Representation

It is to be noted that, contrary to Articles 13 and 14 of UNCROC, the 2002 Act makes no mention of legal aid and thereby continues the practice of not making

46 Ibid., para. 52.
47 (Children) [2013] EWCA Civ. 1146, para. 29.

provision for automatic representation by a solicitor in private family law proceedings: consequently, many birth parents and children do not have independent legal representation throughout the course of an adoption process;[48] and prospective kinship carers, wishing to contest local authority proceedings, are ineligible for legal aid. The CRC, in its 2016 report, expressed concern that 'the reduction of legal aid in all four jurisdictions appear to have a negative impact on the right of children to be heard in judicial and administrative proceedings affecting them'.[49]

Due process

A basic human right is that a person whose interests are at stake in any decision-making process must be afforded every opportunity to fully engage in that process. In *Re C (Care Proceedings: Disclosure of Local Authority's Decision-Making Process)*[50] a mother challenged the local authority for failing to involve her in its decision-making process claiming that she had never been informed that she was required to acknowledge responsibility for the death of her first child as a step towards possible rehabilitation with the second. The court found that by not informing the mother of the contents of the report, in which an expert witness had raised the responsibility issue, the local authority may have failed to respect her 'right to a fair trial' and thereby been in breach of Article 6 of the ECHR. The court held that under Article 6 the mother should have had an opportunity to examine and comment on the documents being considered by the expert and to cross-examine witnesses interviewed by the expert on whose evidence the report was based. This was reiterated in *H* v. *Kingston upon Hull City Council*[51] when the court warned that a child should not be removed from the family 'unless and until there has been due and proper consultation and an opportunity to challenge the proposal'. Such consultation must consist of more than mere information giving; the parent/s must be listened to and their views taken into account. In *Re B-S*,[52] Sir James Munby, the president of the High Court family division, in a ruling that was to restrain childcare adoptions for several years, urged his colleagues in the lower courts to explore all possible options in such cases and stressed the need for proper evidence, warning that current 'sloppy practice must stop. It is simply unacceptable in a forensic context where the issues are so grave and the stakes, for both child and parent, so high.'[53]

48 In childcare adoptions, however, as Julie Doughty has pointed out, the birth parents are provided with legal representation under the Legal Aid Sentencing and Punishment of Offenders Act 2012 (note to author, 22.10.17).
49 UN CRC, *Concluding Observations*, para. 30(b).
50 [2002] 2 FCR 673.
51 [2013] EWHC 388 (Admin.), para. 54.
52 (Children) [2013] EWCA Civ. 1146.
53 Para. 40.

Undue delay

In 2012 the Department for Education noted in *An Action Plan for Adoption*[54] that delays in the adoption system were causing lasting harm for vulnerable children. It advised that local authorities must consider whether adoption or another form of permanent care is best for the child as early as possible, and referred to the statutory guidance requirement that this decision be made within four months of the child entering care. It might be added that undue delay is at times quite deliberate. Local authority social workers can and do plan many placements with a view to foster parents becoming adopters, once sufficient time has passed to allow bonding to occur and make removal of the child non-compliant with the welfare principle, thereby positioning adoption as the best option for securing established attachments.

Thresholds for entering the adoption process: eligibility, suitability and placement

As adoption in this jurisdiction sheds its traditional private and 'closed' characteristics – in response to equality, human rights and transparency requirements – so its social functions have been statutorily adjusted to accommodate a broader range of adoptees and adopters. The same formal statutory criteria apply to all applicants whether the adoption is family, agency or intercountry while the non-statutory suitability criteria may vary to take account of factors such as sensitivity to possible transracial or cultural issues.

Role of adoption agency

The agency must ensure that adoption applicants satisfy eligibility and suitability criteria. It is also required to be satisfied that: the requisite consent, or alternative authority, is available for placement; arrangements are made to monitor the welfare of the child for the duration of the placement; and that such assessment reports are prepared and statutory checks carried out as the court may require.

Pre-placement counselling

The provision of pre-placement counselling to the birth parent/s – to ensure an awareness of options, access to ongoing support services and ability to make an informed decision – and to prepare prospective adopters and child, is now a statutory requirement that rests upon the adoption agency involved.

Eligibility and suitability of the parties

Access to the adoption process is subject to mandatory professional scrutiny to ensure that all parties meet the statutory threshold criteria and that the placement

54 *An Action Plan for Adoption: Tackling Delay*, London, HMSO, 2012.

is at least compatible with the welfare interests of the child. In this jurisdiction that responsibility falls initially to adoption agency staff in relation to all applications including 'family' adoptions and then to Adoption Panels in respect of all third party adoptions whether childcare, intercountry (even the child of a relative overseas) or arranged by a voluntary adoption agency.

The child

The subject must meet the legal definition of 'child': he or she must be born and be less than 18 years of age when the application is lodged; it is not possible to adopt a foetus, though modern surrogacy arrangements often come close to challenging this traditional rule; and it's not possible to adopt an adult, even if aged 19 and with 'special needs'. The legal necessity of obtaining an informed parental consent imposes a minimum requirement in terms of the child's age; usually not until six weeks after the birth is a mother considered capable of making such an important decision. Of necessity there is also a residency requirement: the subject must be amenable to the courts of the jurisdiction in which proceedings are initiated.

The birth parent/s

Married or not, any parent with full parental responsibility is entitled to voluntarily relinquish a child for adoption; though the consent of the other parent must be obtained or the need for it dispensed with. Eligibility to relinquish is evidenced by a signed and witnessed form to that effect. Also there must be no evidence of illegal practices such as involvement in the selling or smuggling of children for adoption purposes.[55] Since the introduction of the 2006 Act, a birth parent is no longer required to be a joint applicant with a step-parent in order to adopt their child of a previous relationship.

The birth parent/s and rehabilitation

Where there are reasonable grounds for optimism, regarding a possible reunification of parent and child, then the local authority should give first preference to pursuing that option. The basic principle underpinning the law remains as stated 30 years ago by Templeman LJ:[56]

> The best person to bring up a child is the natural parent. It matters not whether the parent is wise or foolish, rich or poor, educated or illiterate,

55 The 'trafficking' of children for any purpose is prohibited by various international instruments including UNCROC 1989, the ILO Worst Forms of Child Labour Convention 1999, and the United Nations Protocol to Prevent, Suppress and Punish Trafficking in Persons, especially Women and Children 2000.

56 *Re KD (A Minor: Ward) (Termination of Access)* [1988] 1 AC 806 [1988] 2 FLR 139, 141.

> provided the child's moral and physical health are not in danger. Public authorities cannot improve on nature.

Arguably, as this principle implies, child welfare interests cannot be easily separated from parental welfare: the younger the child, the stronger the assumption that – save in exceptional circumstances – this symbiotic relationship of mutual attachment must be the primary determinant of his or her welfare interests.

In the light of the draconian effect of adoption on such a parent–child relationship, the guidance from the ECtHR[57] is apt – every effort should be made to explore rehabilitation if a subsequent recourse to adoption is to be compliant with Article 8 of the ECHR. As it stressed in the above-mentioned *YC* v. *the United Kingdom*: 'family ties may only be severed in very exceptional circumstances and that everything must be done to preserve personal relations and, where appropriate, to "rebuild" the family. It is not enough to show that a child could be placed in a more beneficial environment for his upbringing.'[58] Accordingly, as was stated in *Re B*,[59] the court must consider that a child's welfare includes the interest of that child in being brought up by his or her family of origin, and must therefore assess the possibility of that family meeting the child's needs with appropriate support services from the State. In particular, *Gorgulu* v. *Germany*[60] provides authority for the view that the child's welfare must be seen in a long-term context and this may even require terminating an adoption placement, however satisfactory, if local authority intervention is to meet the test of 'proportionality'.

The adopters

All prospective adopters must satisfy statutory conditions relating to age, domicile/habitual residence, improper payments and duration of placement—always most stringent in relation to third party prospective adopters – and in relation to ICA, they will also have to satisfy any additional 'sending nation' requirements. Since the introduction of the 2002 Act, unmarried couples will satisfy eligibility criteria if the child concerned has been part of their household for at least the previous six months. For step-parent applicants the minimum care period is six months and one year for foster parents. All other applicants (e.g. a partner of the child's parent) must have had direct care responsibility for the child for at least three years preceding the application. In addition, the suitability criteria consisting of administrative conditions as assessed by adoption agencies and relating to factors such as maximum age, health, quality and duration of relationships, cultural background and lifestyle must also be satisfied but these are now governed by the National Standards and/or the

57 *Haase v. Germany* (2005) (App. No. 11057/02, ECHR).
58 *YC* v. *the United Kingdom*, para. 35.
59 [2013] UKSC 33, paras 26–8.
60 Application No. 74969/01, ECtHR, 26.02.2004; see also *P, C and S* v. *UK* (2002) 35 EHRR 31, *K and T* v. *Finland* [2001] 2 FLR 707 and *Johansen* v. *Norway* (1996) 23 EHRR 33; see Chapter 4.

Regulations.[61] An Adoption and Children Act Register is available to promote the recruitment of adopters and facilitate the matching process.[62]

LGBT adopters

Adoption by gay couples has been possible since the introduction of the 2002 Act.[63]

Placement with consent

An adoption agency placement may be authorised by the consent[64] of birth parents with parental responsibility – including 'advanced consent'[65] which may breach the Hague Convention, Article 4(c), stipulation that the consent of the mother be given only after the birth of the child – after which placement is made with those prospective adopters identified either in the consent form or by the agency.[66] The 2014 Act has deleted the provision in the 2002 Act that required an adoption agency, when placing a child for adoption, to consider religious, racial, cultural and linguistic factors.[67]

Placement by the birth parent/s

In compliance with Article 29 of the Hague Convention, direct adoption placements by the birth parent/s are statutorily prohibited.

Placement without consent

The court may dispense with the need for parental consent for placement but only if satisfied that: (a) the parent or guardian cannot be found or lacks capacity; or (b) the welfare of the child requires the consent to be dispensed with.[68]

Welfare interests

This ground is the one most frequently relied upon and it requires the court to have regard to the following welfare checklist, as stated in the Children Act 1989, s. 1(3), before dispensing with consent of the parent/s:

61 See Suitability of Adopters Regulations 2005.
62 Sections 125–31; see National Standards and Practice Guidance.
63 Section 144(4) (b) of the 2002 Act which permits applications from 'two people (whether of different sexes or the same sex) living as partners in an enduring family relationship'.
64 Section 19 of the 2002 Act.
65 Section 20.
66 Section 19(1) (a) and (b).
67 Section 1(5). There was no equivalent requirement regarding racial considerations in the 1976 Act.
68 Section 52.

a the child's ascertainable wishes and feelings regarding the decision (considered in the light of the child's age and understanding);
b the child's particular needs;
c the likely effect on the child (throughout his life) of having ceased to be a member of the original family and become an adopted person;
d the child's age, sex, background and any of the child's characteristics which the court or agency considers relevant;
e any harm (within the meaning of the Children Act 1989) which the child has suffered or is at risk of suffering;
f the relationship which the child has with relatives, and with any other person in relation to whom the court or agency considers the relationship to be relevant, including:

 i the likelihood of any such relationship continuing and the value to the child of its doing so;
 ii the ability and willingness of any of the child's relatives, or of any such person, to provide the child with a secure environment in which the child can develop, and otherwise to meet the child's needs;
 iii the wishes and feelings of any of the child's relatives, or of any such person, regarding the child.

It must also consider whether making no order would be a preferable means of satisfying this welfare test.

Placement order

An application for a placement order[69] must be by a local authority as voluntary adoption agencies are not permitted to use this procedure. The child concerned will be a party to the application and must be the subject of a care order or the court must be satisfied that the grounds for such can be met[70] and that either parental consent is available (and has not been withdrawn) or can be dispensed with.[71] The Court of Appeal[72] has stressed that the proper test for dispensing with parental agreement to the making of a placement order, under Adoption and Children Act 2002, s. 52(1)(b), is whether the child's welfare requires adoption as opposed to something short of adoption; under s. 1(2) of the 2002 Act the child's welfare throughout his life was the paramount consideration. Before making the order, the court must consider whether contact arrangements are necessary and may make an order for contact when making the placement order. Once made, a placement order vests parental responsibility in the local authority which will then

69 Section 21(1).
70 Section 21(2) (a) and (b).
71 Section 21(3).
72 *SB* v. *A County Council; Re P* [2008] EWCA Civ. 535; see also *Re P (Placement Orders: Parental Consent)* [2008] EWCA Civ. 535 [2008] 2 FLR 625, per Wall LJ, para. 126.

identify an appropriate adoption placement;[73] if it fails to do so, which often happens, then the child will remain in foster care.[74]

In *YC* v. *the United Kingdom*[75] the ECtHR considered the childcare proceedings in respect of the applicant mother's son, born in 2001, which had resulted in an order authorising the child to be placed for adoption because of concerns about the mother's relationship with the child's father. The applicant complained in particular about the court's refusal to order an assessment of her as a sole carer for her son. The ECtHR held that there had been no violation of Article 8 of the ECHR, finding that the decision to make a placement order had not exceeded the State's margin of appreciation and that the reasons for the decision had been relevant and sufficient.

Placement supervision

Parental responsibility is vested in the agency and in the prospective adopters[76] for the duration of the placement. While a placement order is in force the child may not be removed[77] except by the local authority.[78] After an adoption application has been made, removal requires leave of the court.[79]

Once a child is placed for adoption, any existing order for contact made under the Children Act 1989 is extinguished,[80] though the court may at any time during the placement make a contact order[81] subject to such conditions as it sees fit[82] or authorise the agency to refuse contact. A placement order can be revoked[83] but parents may only apply for revocation with the leave of the court, before the child has been placed for adoption with the prospective adoptive parents, and leave will only be granted where the court is satisfied that there has been a change of circumstances since the order was made.[84] Also, while it is true that parental responsibilities rest with a local authority for the duration of a placement order, the birth parent/s may exercise some care responsibility – but only as and when permitted by the local authority.[85] This makes any local authority initiative – by means of a rehabilitation programme, and/or contact arrangements between child and their birth family – critically important as a determinant of outcome.

Parental consent cannot be withdrawn after an application has been lodged.[86]

73 Section 25(2).
74 Author acknowledges advice of Julie Doughty on this matter (note to author, 22.10.17).
75 Application No. 4547/10, 2012.
76 Section 25(3).
77 Section 30.
78 Section 34.
79 Section 37(a).
80 Adoption and Children Act 2002, s. 26(1).
81 Section 27(3).
82 Section 27(5).
83 Section 24.
84 Section 24(3).
85 Section 25(4).
86 Section 52(4).

Human rights considerations

The placement decision – including management of the interests of all parties until the court hearing – is the most crucial phase in the adoption process. Because it effectively determines the outcome, this phase generates most human rights issues.

First party applicants

Adoption is often inappropriate in circumstances where it can obscure the true nature of blood relationships. The 2002 Act, therefore, introduced special guardianship orders[87] as an alternative for relatives and step-parents who constituted a majority of adoption applicants in the closing decades of the twentieth century. Although this alternative has recently been gaining acceptability, and bearing in mind the difficulty in disaggregating adoption statistics, it seems likely that kinship applicants – including step-parents and those family members with whom a child in care has been placed – are still the recipients of a large proportion of all adoption orders. The use of adoption to facilitate step-parents has always been questionable as it legally distorts family relationships which, by marginalising one set of relationships, may well leave an adoptee with a compromised sense of identity as well as potentially depriving one set of grandparents of an opportunity to include that child in their family life. Procedurally, it is flawed as the legal requirement to serve notice on the local authority runs from the date of application to adopt rather than from the date of placement: the child could be in the care of relatives intending to adopt for several years before the application is lodged; making it difficult to then challenge the established care arrangement.

Unmarried father

The fact that for the purposes of parental consent 'parent' is defined as restricted to one with legal responsibility means that an unmarried father will have to first go through the procedure of acquiring that status. Although there is a mandatory requirement for a legal parent to be given notice of the proceedings[88] this, in practice, can be dependent upon the birth mother divulging his name and contact details which are often withheld or not sought by the local authority.

Same-sex adopters

Not until the introduction of the Adoption and Children Act 2002 did adoption by same-sex couples become legal and not until the Equality Act 2010 did it become illegal for adoption agencies to refuse such applicants. Since then some religious organisations with objections to homosexuality have chosen to close rather than conform to the equality provisions. This has resulted in disrupted

87 *Re S (Adoption Order or Special Guardianship Order)* [2007] EWCA Civ. 54.
88 Family Procedure Rules 2010, Rule 12.3.

care arrangements for many children – with implications for their human rights – as they were transferred from agency foster care to the public childcare system.[89]

Significant harm

Article 8(2) of the ECHR declares that a public authority shall not interfere with the right to respect for family life, the existence or otherwise of which can be determined as a matter of fact.

Under the Children Act 1989, s. 31(2), the threshold of State interference in family life is set by the concept of 'significant harm': a child cannot enter the public childcare system and therefore cannot pass through to the adoption process unless he or she is judged to have suffered, or is likely to suffer, significant harm. This has proved problematic because this key threshold concept for entering the process – unlike its the equally subjective counterpart 'the welfare interests of a child' for exiting it – is not legislatively defined; there are no benchmarks, checklist or statutory guidance by which it can be demonstrated that the threshold has been, or may be, breached. The difficulties involved were illustrated in *Re B (A Child)*[90] when the highest court in the land upheld an earlier ruling that the child of currently exemplary parents was correctly made the subject of a care order, despite the absence of any harm to that child, because of the risk that significant harm could befall him given the parental history. A deciding factor for the judge at first instance, endorsed by the Supreme Court, was the finding that the parents had a non-compliant and obstructive attitude to social services; they would have to abide by a programme of monitoring and support with which they would be incapable of complying. In the course of its judgment the Supreme Court supported as a principle that it would not be helpful for the court to explain the meaning of 'significant' harm. Clearly this troubling decision confers considerable power upon local authorities to require compliant cooperation from parents if the latter are not to be viewed as threatening the threshold that justifies State intervention and could lead to non-consensual adoption. It would appear to licence undue latitude on the part of the State to interfere with respect for family life.

Intervention 'necessary in a democratic society'

The necessity for imposing the most absolute order known to family law must be justified: all other options, assessed in accordance with the welfare test, should first be discounted. As has been said:[91]

> what therefore has to be shown is that the child's welfare 'requires' adoption as opposed to something short of adoption. A child's circumstances may

89 *Catholic Care (Diocese of Leeds)* v. *the Charity Commission for England and Wales and the Equality and Human Rights Commission* [2012] Ch 214.

90 [2013] UKSC 33.

91 *Re P (Placement Orders: Parental Consent)* [2008] EWCA Civ. 535, para. 115.

> 'require' statutory intervention, perhaps even 'require' the indefinite or long-term removal of the child from the family and his or her placement with strangers, but that is not to say that the same circumstances will necessarily 'require' that the child be adopted.

This warning, that such a use of draconian judicial power to permanently sever the parent–child relationship needs to be justified by exceptional circumstances, was forcefully reiterated in the leading case of *Re B-S*[92] which proved to be a milestone in childcare adoption in this jurisdiction (see below).

Proportionality

Article 8 of the ECHR requires that any intervention of the State between parents and child should be proportionate to the legitimate aim for the protection of family life.[93] This 'principle of proportionality'[94] has emerged as a key benchmark and has attracted repeated judicial affirmation of its importance in the context of childcare cases[95] as noted, for example, by the late Wall J:[96]

> Inevitably, however, every order made under Section 8 of the Children Order 1989 represents in some measure interference by a public authority (the court) in the right to respect for family life contended in Article 8. The court's interference must, of course, be in accordance with the powers given to that court under the Children Act 1989 and be proportionate. Every application involves a court balancing the rights of the participants to the application (including the children who are the subject of it) and arriving at a result which is in the interest of those children . . . and proportionate to the legitimate aim being pursued.

The significance of this principle was explained by Hale LJ in *Re C and B*[97] as follows:

> one comes back to the principle of proportionality. The principle has to be that the local authority works to support, and eventually to reunite, the family, unless the risks are so high that the child's welfare requires alternative family

92 [2013] EWCA Civ. 1146.
93 *Re O (A Child) (Supervision Order)* [2001] 1 FLR 923.
94 *Johansen* v. *Norway* (1996) 23 EHRR 33; *K and T* v. *Finland* (2001) 36 EHRR 18; *R and H* v. *United Kingdom* (2012) 54 EHRR 2 [2011] 2 FLR 1236; *YC* v. *United Kingdom* (2012) 55 EHRR 33.
95 *Re B (A Child)* [2013] UKSC 33. As Julie Doughty points out, this is currently the leading authority on application of the proportionality principle in a childcare context (note to author, 22.10.17).
96 *Re H (Contact Order)* [2002] 1 FLR 22 at 37; see also *Re O. (Supervision Order)* [2001] 1 FLR 923 paras 24–8.
97 [2001] 1 FLR 611, para. 31.

> care. I cannot except that this was a case for a care order with a care plan of adoption or nothing. There could have been other options. There could have been time taken to explore those other options.

Again, and more recently, in *SB* v. *A County Council; Re P*[98] the Court of Appeal stressed that any placement or adoption order made without parental consent must be proportionate to the legitimate aim of protecting the welfare and interests of the child; only in exceptional circumstances could measures totally depriving a parent of family life with a child be justified. The human rights relevance of this principle has been graphically illustrated in the many cases of peremptory removal of newborn babies from the care of their hospitalised mothers. For example, in *P, C and S* v. *UK*[99] the newborn child of a woman suffering from Munchausen's syndrome by proxy was removed from her care in hospital under an emergency protection order which was followed promptly by the instigation of care and freeing proceedings. The ECtHR ruled that:[100]

> the taking of a new-born baby into public care at the moment of its birth is an extremely harsh measure. There must be extraordinarily compelling reasons before a baby can be physically removed from its mother, against her will, immediately after birth as a consequence of a procedure in which neither she nor her partner has been involved.

Cultural compatibility

Contemporary adoption practice gives rise to two different types of cultural compatibility issues.

The placement of a child of different race or ethnicity to that of their prospective adopters is a common occurrence; arising as a natural consequence of ICA, but also not unusual in multicultural England. There has been much contention on the respective merits of 'colour blind' or racially congruent policies but it is, perhaps, beyond contention that for an older child a placement which provides for a cultural affinity between with adopters and child, in accordance with Article 20(3) of UNCROC, is best for the latter's long-term welfare. The above noted deletion of the previous requirement to consider religious, racial, cultural and linguistic factors when making an adoption placement could, arguably, license a potentially serious infringement of such a child's right to have the opportunity to develop an authentic cultural identity.

Another, and increasingly common occurrence, is the admission of a child of a foreign national into the childcare system and possibly on into the adoption process. There has been considerable legal and political debate accompanying some such cases, focusing on the importance of respecting the nationality of the child

98 [2008] EWCA Civ. 535.

99 See also the similar case of *Venema* v. *the Netherlands*, Application No. 35137/1977, ECtHR, 17.12.2002.

100 Ibid., para. 116.

and their family concerned and preventing their assimilation into a different culture. Complaints from governments of countries such as Latvia, Slovakia and Bulgaria have centred on claims – which are not unreasonable – that if children of their nationals have to pass from the child protection system into the UK adoption process, then perhaps adoptive applicants from within the countries of origin should be considered first. Such issues are now governed by Brussels II.[101] This requires an immediate cross-border exchange of information on the circumstances in order to allow time for the negotiations necessary to explore placement options with the authorities in the relevant country. The need to comply with Brussels II was emphasised in *Re E (A Child)*.[102]

Children with complex health/social needs

As in other jurisdictions, an older child, one with siblings, or one with health or social care needs is comparatively disadvantaged – if not in effect discriminated against contrary to Article 2 of UNCROC – as the opportunity of adoption is much less available for them than for a young, healthy single child.

The hearing and the grounds

The court ensures that eligibility/suitability criteria are fulfilled by all parties, ascertains or adjudicates on consent requirements, confirms that the proposed arrangements are compatible with the child's welfare and then issues or refuses the order sought. The provisions of the 2002 Act, as mentioned earlier, are particularly relevant at this stage.

Specified criteria relating to an applicant's age, marital status and domicile, etc. must be satisfied; though habitual residence (of both applicants in a joint application) is an alternative even if they are not domiciled within the jurisdiction. All prospective adopters must have provided care for the child for a stated minimum period, which must have been subject to professional monitoring,[103] and assessment reports are required in respect of all agency adoption applicants.

Where consent is available

The consent of the parent/s with legal responsibility must be obtained or dispensed with before the making of an adoption order[104] and the paramountcy principle applies to dispensing with parental consent.[105] Even where all necessary consents are available, court and agency are statutorily required to consider whether an alternative order under either the 1989 or 2002 Act would be more

101 Council Regulation (EC) No. 2201/2003 of 27 November 2003.
102 [2014] EWHC 6 (Fam.).
103 Section 42(7).
104 Section 47(2).
105 Section 52(b).

appropriate and/or whether ongoing contact arrangements will be necessary to promote the welfare interests of the child concerned.

Consent of unmarried father

As before the 2002 Act, the consent of an unmarried father without parental responsibility is still not a strict requirement, but all appropriate steps should be taken to serve him with notice of the hearing.

Consent of a minor

The consent of the prospective adoptee is not a legal requirement. However, the 2002 Act, s. 1(4), requires the court to have regard to 'the child's ascertainable wishes and feelings regarding the decision (considered in the light of the child's age and understanding)'. The wishes of an older child regarding his or her proposed adoption have to be ascertained and taken into account and case law indicates that good reason will have to be shown if an order is to be made contrary to those wishes.[106]

Where consent is not available

Leaving aside the possibility that the consent required of the parent/s cannot be obtained due to their incapacity, the ability of a non-consenting parent to challenge the making of an adoption order, where a placement order is in effect, will depend in the first instance on obtaining leave to be heard.[107] This requires evidence of flawed proceedings[108] or of a significant change in birth parent circumstances. In assessing whether to grant leave it has been said that leniency should be exercised because parents 'should not be discouraged from bettering themselves or from seeking to prevent the adoption of their child by the imposition of a test which is unachievable'.[109]

Childcare adoption: the grounds

While State intervention and admission of a child to the public childcare system are governed by the Children Act 1989, with specific reference to the significant harm threshold, the passporting of such a child into the adoption process is governed by the Adoption and Children Act 2002. The link between the two is provided by the welfare test. Under s. 52 of the 2002 Act the need for parental consent may be dispensed with by applying exactly the same test as was applied when authorising the placement: unless concrete evidence can be adduced to show a significant

106 *Re D (Minors) (Adoption by Step-parent)* (1981) 2 FLR 102.
107 *Re P (Adoption: Leave Provisions)* [2007] EWCA Civ. 616.
108 *Re H (A Child)* [2015] EWCA Civ. 1284.
109 *CH* v. *London Borough of Merton* [2014] EWHC 3311 (Fam.), para. 6.

change in circumstances the same outcome is a foregone conclusion. Even when there has been 'an astonishing change in circumstances', as in *Re B-S (Children)*,[110] leave to challenge an adoption application may be refused. In that case, and subsequently in *Re R (Children)*,[111] the judiciary expressed concern regarding the 'lack of alternative options for the children and an analysis of the evidence that is accepted by the court sufficient to drive it to the conclusion that nothing short of adoption is appropriate for the children'. As Munby LJ stressed,[112] 'the judge must keep at the forefront of his mind the teaching of *Re B*'[113] this being that orders contemplating non-consensual adoption – care orders with a plan for adoption, placement orders and adoption orders – are 'a very extreme thing, a last resort', only to be made where 'nothing else will do', where 'no other course [is] possible in [the child's] interests', they are 'the most extreme option', a 'last resort – when all else fails', to be made 'only in exceptional circumstances and where motivated by *overriding requirements* pertaining to the child's welfare, in short, where nothing else will do'. Over the following few years, this admonition had a chastening effect on childcare adoptions, sharply reducing the number of annual applications submitted, which in turn prompted policy and legislative initiatives aimed at overcoming what had become a judicial line drawn in the sand.

Contested family adoption: the grounds

Under s. 52(1) of the 2002 Act, the same two grounds for dispensing with parental consent apply in the context of a family as in a childcare adoption: either (a) the parent or guardian cannot be found or is incapable of giving consent or (b) that 'the welfare of the child requires the consent to be dispensed with'. Whether contested or not, adoption applications by family members may well be diverted at judicial discretion towards other private family orders – such as special guardianship – unless the applicant/s can show good reason why an adoption order is particularly appropriate.

Human rights considerations

Children's views

The CRC, in its 2016 report, expressed concern that 'many children feel that they are not listened to by their social workers . . . judges, personnel working with children in conflict with the law or other professionals in matters affecting them, including in family proceedings' and recommended that steps be taken to 'ensure that children are not only heard but also listened to and their views given due

110 [2013] EWCA Civ. 813.
111 [2013] EWCA Civ. 1018, para. 20.
112 Ibid, para. 22.
113 *In re B (A Child) (Care Proceedings: Threshold Criteria)* [2013] UKSC 33 [2013] 1 WLR 1911.

weight by all professionals working with children'.[114] Arguably, this could be extended to a requirement that where a child is of an age to make an informed decision, an adoption application should not be granted without the consent of that child unless good reason can be shown.

Unmarried fathers

The decision in *Re L (Adoption: Contacting Natural Father)*[115] that an unmarried mother had the right not to name the father of her child (nor any member of her own family), has constrained the extent to which fathers without parental responsibility or direct care experience, in respect of the child in question, can influence an adoption process. This maternal veto could result in a serious foreclosure of an unmarried father's inherent rights to influence the future upbringing of his child. Moreover, such a step constitutes an abridgement of the adoptee's rights: denying the latter the opportunity to know the identity of the father and have the choice of contacting him; but it also removes any possibility of acquiring information regarding 50 per cent of his or her genetic make-up, including any alert as to possible latent health issues.

Childcare adoptions

Probably most domestic adoptions in this jurisdiction now follow on from dispensing with the need for parental consent on grounds justified by the paramountcy principle. How this principle is applied in circumstances controlled by the local authority during the placement period is critical.

Thresholds for exiting the adoption process

While the above determines whether an adoption order can be made, there still remains the issue of whether, given the particular welfare interests of the child, it should be made. In childcare cases the local authority will have decided in the affirmative during the care planning process, a decision endorsed by the court when it authorised the granting of a placement order, but the grounds for a final determination will still fall to be examined by the court at this stage. As in all adoption applications, at this point the court will consider not just the grounds but also whether, in the circumstances of the particular child, adoption is better than any other form of disposal or none. If it determines in favour of adoption, the court must then consider whether there should be arrangements for any person to have contact with the child and take into account the views of all parties to any such proposed arrangement.[116] Alternatively, and on its own

114 (CRC/C/GBR/CO/5), 2016, paras 30(d) and 31(d).
115 [2007] EWHC 1771 (Fam.).
116 Adoption and Children Act 2002, s. 46(6).

initiative, it may make an order prohibiting post-adoption contact if the circumstances warrant it.[117]

The welfare interests of the child

This principle constitutes the exit threshold from the adoption process. The Children Act 1989, s. 1(3), requires choice of disposal option to be guided by reference to the welfare checklist, as stated above.

Paramountcy

Sectionsl(1) and (2) of the 2002 Act, in compliance with Article 21 of UNCROC, now ensure that the best interests of the child are treated as the paramount consideration by both court and adoption agency. The paramountcy principle governs all decisions, relating to any matter affecting the child's upbringing, whether taken by adoption agency or court at any stage of the adoption process.[118] The principles of no delay[119] and non-intervention[120] are also incorporated. In addition, a welfare checklist is entrenched[121] with some items deliberately calibrated across both the 1989 and the 2002 statutes to ensure consistency of interpretation.[122] In keeping with the childcare checklist, the items listed in the 2002 Act are neither exhaustive nor prioritised and are not necessarily applicable in all cases. The ECtHR endorsed the role of the paramountcy principle in UK adoption law in *YC* v. *United Kingdom*,[123] when it referred to the best interests of the child being paramount, and stated that 'the considerations listed in section 1 of the 2002 Act . . . broadly reflect the various elements inherent in assessing the necessity under Article 8 of a measure placing a child for adoption'.[124]

Consent/views of child and welfare interests

The Adoption and Children Act 2002, while not inconsistent with the requirements of UNCROC, Article 12, does not take any further forward the established legislative position regarding the child's right to be heard on matters affecting him or her in family proceedings. In particular, while it would always be the case that where a child had views in relation to his or her proposed adoption these would be sought and brought before the court by the CAFCASS officer, the child would seldom have the opportunity to express these views either personally and directly

117 Section 51A(6).
118 Section 1(3).
119 Section 1(6).
120 Ibid.
121 Section 1(4).
122 For example, provisions s. 1(3) (a), (d) and (c) of the 1989 Act are replicated in s. 1 (4) (a), (d) and (e) respectively of the 2002 Act.
123 [2012] 55 EHRR 967.
124 Ibid., para. 35.

or through a solicitor. In this jurisdiction, unlike for example Scotland,[125] there is no specific legislative requirement that the child's consent be obtained as well as his or her views.

The blood-link factor

Re G (Children)[126] can be seen as establishing something of a milestone in UK jurisprudence dealing with welfare interests in the context of a parent–child relationship. On the face of it, the case concerned a disputed shared residence order made in favour of two women, whose lesbian partnership had broken down, in relation to two children born by artificial insemination to the one who now had primary care responsibility. However, it in fact led the court into an examination of 'what is a parent?' and 'how much does the blood tie matter?'. Overturning the decisions of the court at first instance and the Court of Appeal, the House of Lords ruled that insufficient weight had been given to the 'important and significant factor'[127] of the biological link between the birth parent and children. In a judgment that claimed to be 'raising no presumption in her favour'[128] the birth mother, argued Baroness Hale, could not be viewed as being on the same footing in relation to the two children as the other 'parent' because she was 'both their biological and their psychological parent . . . in the overall welfare judgment that must count for something in the vast majority of cases'. This important ruling would seem to establish the blood-link as a factor of some legal weight in differentiating between the claims of parents, whether in a same-sex context or otherwise. The decision is open to interpretation as raising the importance attached to the blood-link as a component of a child's welfare interests (integral to developing an authentic identity, with lineage and inheritance connotations, etc.). It also resonates with a more traditional approach that recognizes the inherent stronger legal position of a birth parent (carrying a presumption of care rights and responsibilities) and thereby perhaps devalues the modern emphasis placed on attachment and psychological bonding. Subsequently, however, Lindblom LJ has warned that:[129]

> The repeated reference to a 'right' for a child to be brought up by his or her natural family, or the assumption that there is a presumption to that effect, needs to be firmly and clearly laid to rest. No such 'right' or presumption exists.

Culturally compatible

Contemporary adoption involves older children to a much larger extent than formerly. Many such children will have had time to identify with a particular culture

125 Adoption and Children (Scotland) Act 2007, s. 32.
126 [2006] UKHL 43 [2006] FLR 629.
127 Ibid., para. 44.
128 Ibid.
129 *Re W (A Child)* [2016] EWCA Civ. 793, para. 71; see also *Re H (A Child)* [2015] EWCA Civ. 1284, per McFarlane LJ paras 89–94.

and/or ethnicity and may well have formed relationships with others from that background. Munby LJ, in *Re S; Newcastle City Council* v. *Z*,[130] when faced with the question as to whether a mother was unreasonably withholding her consent to the adoption of her son, on the basis of religious beliefs that were reasonable and genuinely held, concluded that she was as religious belief could not be determinative in that context. Professional practice, in deference to equality principles, has tended to develop a 'culture blind' approach when matching prospective adopter/s and child; an approach now licensed by the Children and Families and Act 2014, s. 3, which removed the previous statutory requirement to give 'due consideration . . . to religious persuasion, racial origin and cultural and linguistic background'.[131] This approach would seem to breach the Article 20(3) UNCROC requirement that 'due regard shall be paid to the desirability of continuity in a child's upbringing and to the child's ethnic, religious, cultural and linguistic background' when placing a child outside their family of origin. An adoption order should respect a child's cultural identity and enable that identity to further develop; the older the child the stronger the presumption that cultural compatibility with adopter/s must be a factor in determining their lifelong welfare.

The orders available

Traditionally, an adoption process concluded simply with the granting or rejection of the order sought; almost always the former, as legal issues were typically resolved before the hearing. This is no longer necessarily the case although most usually the process ends as it has always done.

Additional orders: post-adoption contact

The Adoption and Children Act 2002, s. 46(6), required the court to consider the necessity for post-adoption contact arrangements. This was amended by the Children and Families Act 2014 to permit the making of a contact order at any time, including any time after an adoption order, enabling contact between an adopted child and their parent/s or other members of their birth family. Prior to that amendment, however, in the rare instances where such arrangements were considered to be compliant with the child's welfare, the parties had been encouraged to pursue this informally.[132] That any such arrangement should in future be for the court to make was stressed by the Court of Appeal in *Re P (Placement Orders: Parental Consent)*.[133]

130 [2005] EWHC 1490 (Fam.) [2007] 1 FLR 861. Also, see, *Re T (Minors) (Custody: Religious Upbringing)* (1981) 2 FLR 239, per Scarman LJ, paras 244–5.
131 Adoption and Children Act 2002, s. 1(5).
132 *Re C (A Minor) (Adoption: Access)* [1989] AC 1, HL and *Re R (Adoption: Contact)* [2005] EWCA Civ. 1128.
133 [2008] 2 FLR 625.

Alternative orders

If, during the course of proceedings, the court should consider that grounds of significant harm may exist then, under the 2002 Act, it can as before refer the matter to the local authority. On a subsequent application from the local authority, the court may in turn issue a care order or a supervision order where the significant harm grounds are satisfied and where it considers this to be more appropriate than any other order or no order at all.

Alternative permanency orders are available, reinforced by a directive requiring the court to 'always consider the whole range of powers available to it' under both the Acts of 1989 and 2002.[134] These alternatives include: no order; the special guardianship order,[135] but the court must first consider whether it should couple this order with a contact order;[136] a long-life residence order that will endure in respect of the child concerned until his or her eighteenth birthday;[137] a parental responsibility order in favour of a step-parent applicant;[138] or, finally, a local authority foster parent may apply for any s. 8 order[139] or an extended residence order or a special guardianship order where a child has lived with their foster parents for a minimum period of one year.[140] Of these options, the special guardianship order – as legislatively intended – has proved to be a viable alternative to adoption.[141] The particular merits of this order, relative to adoption, were considered in *Re S (Adoption Order or Special Guardianship Order)*[142] where it was noted that: 'it is a material feature of the special guardianship regime that it is "less intrusive" than adoption . . . it involves a less fundamental interference with existing legal relationships . . . in some cases, the fact that the welfare objective can be achieved with less disruption of existing family relationships can properly be regarded as helping to tip the balance'.[143] Unlike adoption, however, it does not provide a secure lifelong legal relationship between parents and child, nor does it grant inheritance or citizenship rights and there can be no presumption that this order is to be preferred to adoption in cases involving a family placement.

Human rights considerations

Arguably, the courts will need to apply the paramountcy test as determinant of adoption for children in care with caution if they are to avoid ECtHR strictures for

134 Section 1(6).
135 Section 115; amending s. 14 of the 1989 Act.
136 Ibid.
137 Section 114; amending s. 12 of the 1989 Act.
138 Ibid.
139 Section 10 of the 1989 Act as amended by Sched. 3 of the 2002 Act.
140 Section 14A(5) (d) of the 1989 Act as amended by the 2002 Act.
141 In 2014, 3,330 children left care under a special guardianship order compared with 5,050 who were adopted; in 28 local authorities, special guardianship was used more frequently than adoption.
142 [2007] 1 FLR 819.
143 Ibid., para. 49.

employing draconian means of intervention, contrary to Article 8 of the ECHR, compared with the options chosen in similar circumstances by the courts in countries such as France, Norway and Sweden.

Non-consensual adoption: the best option

Munby J made the case for firmly placing the onus on the local authority to prove that adoption and nothing else was in a child's best interests when he remonstrated in *Re L (Care: Assessment: Fair Trial)* that:[144]

> it must never be forgotten that, with the State's abandonment of the right to impose capital sentences, orders of the kind which judges of this Division are typically invited to make in public law proceedings are amongst the most drastic that any judge in any jurisdiction is ever empowered to make. It is a terrible thing to say to a parent – particularly, perhaps to a mother – that he or she is to lose their child forever.

There have been innumerable judicial statements echoing this sentiment, but it was endorsed most emphatically in the case of *Re B-S*[145] and in *Re B*[146] when Baroness Hale pronounced:

> We all agree that an order compulsorily severing the ties between a child and her parents can only be made if 'justified by an overriding requirement pertaining to the child's best interests'. In other words, the test is one of necessity. Nothing else will do.

Again, in *Re V (Children)*, Black LJ stressed the need to justify adoption as opposed to any other disposal option – such as long-term foster care – when he noted that social workers do not always see this as necessary: 'I have searched without success in the papers for any written analysis by local authority witnesses or the guardian of the arguments for and against adoption and long term fostering'.[147] Most recently, in *Re W (A Child)*,[148] Lindblom LJ reprised the 'nothing else will do' benchmark for falling back on adoption as the appropriate default option when other possible arrangements for a child in care are being considered. He offered the view that 'the phrase is meaningless, and potentially dangerous, if it is applied as some freestanding, shortcut test divorced from, or even in place of, an overall evaluation of the child's welfare'.[149] Significantly, however, he added that the phrase 'is no more, nor no less, than a useful distillation of the proportionality and necessity test as embodied in the ECHR'. Essentially, human rights

144 [2002] 2 FLR 730.
145 [2013] EWCA Civ. 1146.
146 [2013] UKSC 33, para. 215.
147 [2013] EWCA Civ. 913, para. 88.
148 [2016] EWCA Civ. 793.
149 Ibid., para. 68.

considerations must apply as a backstop when adoption and other options are being considered for a child in care.

Appropriateness of adoption; alternatives

This jurisdiction makes available a considerable range of public and private family law orders that may be substituted, at judicial discretion, for the adoption order sought by an applicant. However, the most relevant alternative is a special guardianship order, but there is no responsibility placed on local authorities to recruit and train such persons (in a similar manner to foster parents, many of whom could and perhaps should be so trained). In the absence of such a responsibility the availability of this alternative is left to private initiative.

The above mentioned judicial power to make a contact order[150] when granting an adoption application, or at any time thereafter, is unlikely to prevail against the long-standing professional reluctance to make provision for post-adoption contact in the face of adopter resistance. The welfare interests of the child have usually provided the justification for exactly the opposite approach: refusing contact in order to protect developing new attachments and ensure the boundaries and stability of the adopter's family.[151]

The effect of an adoption order

The main consequence of making an adoption order is much as it always has been, even though its more extreme effect may be offset by the issue of a contact order.

Effect on the parties

One immediate effect of an adoption order is the automatic extinguishing of any pre-adoption contact order.[152]

The child

The 2002 Act, s. 67, declares that the adoptee 'is to be treated in law as if born as the child of the adopters or adopter' and as 'the legitimate child of the adopters or adopter'.[153] This phrasing ensures that all the traditional legal attributes of an adoption order are applied, including the nationality, domicile and residence of the adopters and an entitlement to inherit from their estate.[154]

150 The 2014 Act, s. 9, amended the Adoption and Children Act 2002 by inserting ss. 51A and 51B.
151 *Re J (A Child) (Adopted Child: Contact)* [2010] EWCA Civ. 581 and *Re T (A Child) (Adoption: Contact)* [2010] EWCA Civ. 1527.
152 Adoption and Children Act 2002, s. 46(2) (b).
153 See, further, Adoption and Children Act 2002, ss. 66–76, 'Status of Adopted Children'.
154 Ibid., ss. 69–73.

The birth parent/s

The 2002 Act, s. 46, states that the order operates to extinguish 'the parental responsibility which any person other than the adopters or adopter has for the adopted child immediately before the making of the order' and any other order or duty unless specifically exempted.

The adopters

The effect of an adoption order is to vest the adopters with all parental rights, duties and responsibilities in respect of the adopted child. The traditional absolute and exclusive nature of the order may now, however, be compromised by an accompanying order permitting post-adoption contact arrangements while its traditional privacy characteristic may equally be compromised by ongoing public health and social care support services.

Revocation of an adoption order

Only the most exceptional circumstances will justify the legal revocation of an adoption order:[155] a fundamental procedural irregularity will suffice;[156] but injustice will not.[157]

Entitlement to post-adoption support services

The 2002 Act, s. 3(2)(b), introduced a requirement that all local authorities provide support services at any time (i.e. both pre- and post-adoption) and for all parties or others involved in any type of adoption. Such services may be delivered by an adoption agency defined, by s. 8(1) of the 2002 Act, as 'an undertaking, the purpose of which, or one of the purposes of which, is the provision of adoption support services'. Subsequently, the Adoption Support Services Regulations for England (SI 2003) gave adopters, adopted children and birth relatives the right to request an assessment of need regarding contact arrangements and requiring agencies to maintain services to assist such contact arrangements.[158] These provisions have been reinforced by statutory rights to employment leave and payment for parents and adopters, granted under the Children and Families Act 2014.

Services to birth relatives are defined as including assessment, information and advice, support groups, therapy, counselling, intra/inter agency liaison, assistance with indirect contact, casework and advocacy.

155 *Re B (Adoption: Jurisdiction to set aside)* [1995] 2 FLR 1.
156 *Re K (Adoption and Wardship)* [1997] 2 FLR 221.
157 *Webster* v. *Norfolk CC* [2009] EWCA Civ. 59.
158 See also Adoption Support Services Regulations 2005.

Childcare adoptions

In respect of childcare adoptions, the provisions of the 2002 Act are reinforced by the National Standards which apply quite specific requirements in relation to matters such as timescales for service provision, extent of information to be provided, etc.

Human rights considerations

Legal status of adoptee

The modern adoption order maintains the same distinctions traditionally made by the law between an adopted and a 'natural' child and, to that extent, violates the above s. 67 assertion.[159] The fact that UK ICA legislation does not provide automatic British citizenship for children adopted by British citizens in designated countries has attracted criticism.

Extinguishing rights of birth parents

Arguably, the right to religion or belief and the concomitant 'right' of a birth parent to require adopters to respect their wishes regarding the religious upbringing of the adopted child – as upheld in Articles 18 and 29 of UNCROC – are breached by the inadequate protection provided in the 2002 Act. This deficiency is compounded by the above-mentioned removal of the requirement to give consideration to the birth parent/s racial and cultural background.

Information rights: disclosure, tracing and reunification

The 2002 Act introduced some changes to the law governing an area where transparency and access to information have traditionally been deliberately constrained.

Information rights

The 2002 Act, s. 98, gives adopted adults (i.e. over the age of 18) and adult birth relatives ('relative' being defined as 'a grandparent, brother, sister, uncle or aunt, whether of the full blood or half-blood or by marriage') the right to request identifying information relating to an adoptee from a registered adoption agency (either local authority or voluntary) or a registered adoption support agency.

159 Paragraph 30 of Sched. 4 of the Sexual Offences Act 2004, which amends the 2002 Act to continue the legal exception to incest where sexual relations occur between an adopted brother and sister aged 18 or more. Also, s. 74(1) leaves intact the traditional rule relating to consanguinity and prohibited degrees of relationship while entitlement to British citizenship may, in some circumstances, be qualified.

Information disclosure duties

The 2002 Act, s. 98, also gives a registered adoption support agency authority to seek access to the information held by the Registrar General or in the records of a court or adoption agency and gives adult birth relatives a right to request such an agency to discover information and/or make approaches to adopted adults for the purposes of seeking information about them and/or for future contact or reunion.

Maintaining records

Statutory duties require the Registrar General to maintain certain registers and facilitate access to the information therein. Adoption agencies are similarly required to meet certain standards in relation to collating, storing and disclosing information.[160] The 2005 Regulations placed an additional duty on all adoption agencies to keep records on children placed for adoption for at least 100 years and to police access to the information contained therein.

Tracing and reunification

The Adoption Contact Register, established in 1991 and maintained by the Registrar General, first introduced the means whereby the parties to an adoption could make known their wishes for mutual contact. An adopted adult can apply to the appropriate adoption agency for 'protected information' about a person involved in an adoption, such as the adoptee, birth parents or the adoption social worker. The statutory process for tracing and unification directs applicants to registered intermediary service providers which offer counselling programmes as a preliminary to initiating contact arrangements.

Human rights considerations

The opening up of adoption records to provide identifying information to the parties to an adoption has been a very significant concession to human rights considerations.

Veto on information disclosure

The right of an adoptee or birth relative to challenge a decision made by an adoption agency to refuse to disclose information, by applying to an Independent Review Panel, is restricted to adoptions made on or after 30 December 2005. In effect this continues in force the discretionary right of adoption agencies to refuse disclosure of identifying information (usually out of respect for the guarantee of confidentiality given to a relinquishing mother) in relation to by far the majority of adoptions. Moreover, adopted adults can now formally register a qualified or

160 Sections 54, 56–65.

absolute veto with the appropriate adoption agency. The fact that the traditional taboo most strongly associated with adoption is still legally protected and retains the power to impair the fundamental right of an individual to access the information necessary to acquire an authentic identity seems regrettable.

Social media

The fact that the parties to an adoption can use Facebook or other social media outlets to bypass all statutory procedures designed to protect vulnerable individuals, and access identifying information, does present a serious challenge to the right to a private life under Article 8 of the ECHR, but it would seem that little can be done about it.

Conclusion

Adoption legislation came late to this jurisdiction and the volume of orders has faded considerably in recent years, but nonetheless the domestic adoption process has become sophisticated and highly regulated. A particular feature of this process has been the extent to which it has relied upon its own public childcare system rather than on other countries as its primary source for prospective adoptees. Perhaps because adoption in this jurisdiction is much more a matter of public law, necessarily following on from adversarial proceedings with birth parents, it is unsurprising that it has tended to generate many human rights issues. There is a natural linkage between adoption practice and the provisions of the ECHR and UNCROC.

6 The US

Introduction

This, the second of two chapters on common law jurisdictions, unfolds in much the same way as the first. Beginning with a brief background history, it considers some of the early human rights challenges, the shaping of modern principles, policy and practice, explains current adoption types and trends and outlines current adoption law. The chapter then examines each sequential stage of the adoption process, identifying and assessing the relevant human rights concerns. It concludes by reflecting on some of the most characteristic features of the interaction of human rights with adoption law and practice in the US.

Background

Adoption as a formal statutory procedure was introduced in the US by the Massachusetts Adoption of Children's Act 1851[1] which preceded the introduction of similar legislation in England and Wales by 70 years and set out for the first time some of the more basic functions of the law relating to adoption. Although adoption in the US is state business with little scope for federal leadership, nonetheless by 1929 all states had followed the example of Massachusetts and enacted some form of adoption legislation. Some states, like Michigan in 1891, went a step further and introduced laws requiring inquiries to be made as to the suitability of prospective adopters and their home circumstances. Thereafter, adoption became an exclusively judicial process the successful conclusion of which resulted in the issue of an adoption order.

Adoption and human rights: the early challenges

The challenges involved in regulating domestic adoption practice probably first surfaced with the 'orphan train' programme. From 1854 to 1929, a total of perhaps 200,000 homeless or orphaned children were shunted by train from the cities

1 As Anne Estin points out (note to author, 24.09.17) adoption did exist prior to the 1851 Act, although it was much more piecemeal, see, further, at: http://scholarship.law.duke.edu/cgi/viewcontent.cgi?article=1189&context=dlj

to rural sites in the American Midwest where, lined up on train platforms, they would be made available to prospective adopters. This practice eventually led to the introduction of regulatory legislation. Subsequently, issues regarding domestic transracial adoptions arose in the context of a government programme, launched in the late 1950s, to assimilate native Indian children into mainstream Caucasian society. This project, a joint enterprise between the Bureau of Indian Affairs and the Child Welfare League of America, followed on from a failed policy of enforced residential schooling which had involved tens of thousands of children attending some 460 schools across the country. The assimilation programme was equally unsuccessful, it resulted in many forced adoptions, contributed to the degrading of Indian culture, and has corroded relations between Native Americans and the US government ever since.[2]

Shaping modern adoption policy

All law – whether state or federal, statute or administrative – can be and often is tested against the overarching principles of the Constitution. Together with the Bill of Rights, the Constitution (particularly the 13th–15th Amendments) has influenced the development of adoption law as it has all aspects of family law.

A particularly noticeable strand in contemporary adoption policy is the channelling of adoption assistance payments towards parents adopting children from foster care or for families whose adopted children have behavioural, emotional or physical disabilities. Subsidies can cover medical assistance, tutoring, therapy, special equipment and other tools which will enable at-risk children to reach their full potential. The Adoption Tax Credit provides a major financial subsidy for adoption and is available to qualifying adopting families for both domestic and international adoption.

Transracial

While African-American children are currently overrepresented in the care system,[3] there is a scarcity of available African-American foster parents and adopters. White and Hispanic children are underrepresented and black children overrepresented in the adoption process: triggering heated contention with organisations such as the National Association of Black Social Workers vehemently opposing transracial adoptions;[4] and leading to the Multiethnic Placement Act 1994 (see below). Indeed, many black and Hispanic children are often placed for adoption outside

2 Fanshel, D., *Far from the Reservation: The Transracial Adoption of American Indian Children*, New Jersey, Scarecrow Press, 1972.

3 Stehno, S., 'The elusive continuum of child welfare services: implications for minority children and youth', *Child Welfare*, 69 (1990): 551–62; Tatara, T., *Characteristics of Children in Substitute and Adoptive Care: A Statistical Summary of the VCIS National Child-Welfare Database*, Washington, DC, American Public Welfare Association, 1993.

4 *In re Welfare of D. L.*, 486 N.W.2d 375 (Minn. 1992).

the US (several hundred with white adopters in Canada since the 1990s) due to a lack of US adopters available and willing to accept such children.[5] Some researchers have suggested that the reason for this is quite simple: US adopters have a strong preference for non-black children, including Latino children, rather than those of African-American ethnicity.[6]

Principles

Welfare interests of the child

The principle that the welfare interests of the child must be the governing consideration in adoption proceedings has been established since 1856 when the Massachusetts court in *Curtis* v. *Curtis*[7] ruled that 'adoption is not a question of mere property . . . the interests of the minor is the principal thing to be considered'.

Adult adoption

In some states, the adoption process also accommodates the adoption of adults.

Openness[8]

This principle generally refers to the extent to which all parties to an adoption – particularly the child – can access identifying information and details of past and present relationships. It can often extend to include actual contact between adoptive and birth families. It has been estimated that two-thirds (68 per cent) of privately adopted children have post-adoption contact with their birth families as have two-fifths (39 per cent) of those adopted from foster care.[9]

Contemporary adoption trends

As has been recently pointed out 'there is no single source for the total number of children adopted in the United States, and there is currently no straightforward way of determining the total number of adoptions, even when multiple data

5 See, further: Buckwalter-Poza, R., 'America's unseen export: children, most of them black', *Pacific Standard*, 24 June 2014; Payne, E., 'Florida moms, fearing racism, sending babies to Canada for adoption', OttawaCitizen.com, 21 July 2014.
6 See 2010 report compiled by New York University, the London School of Economics and the California Institute of Technology which found that a non-African-American baby is seven times more likely to 'attract the interest and attention of potential adoptive parents than an African-American baby'.
7 71 Mass (5 Gray) 535, 537 (1856).
8 Mullender, A. (ed.), *Open Adoption*, London, BAAF, 1991.
9 Vandivere, S., Malm, K. and Radel, I., 'Adoption USA: a chartbook', based on the 2007 nationwide survey of adoptive parents conducted by the National Survey of Children's Health, US Dept. of Health and Human Services (Office of the Asst. Secretary for Planning and Evaluation), Washington, DC, 2009.

sources are used'.[10] That said, some firm trends are clearly apparent: annual adoptions are steadily decreasing (down 15 per cent from 2001–12);[11] the approximate doubling of children adopted from foster care that followed the introduction of the Adoption and Safe Families Act 1997 has eased somewhat (down 6 per cent from 2008–12);[12] while the sharp decrease in ICAs is being maintained (down 56 per cent from 2001–12).[13] By 2013, the Department of Health & Human Services pictured contemporary adoption as comprising: private domestic adoption (38 per cent), foster care adoption (37 per cent) and intercountry adoption (ICA) (25 per cent); 41 per cent of adoptions being by relatives; 49 per cent of all adoptees were aged 5–12 and 37 per cent were white; while 40 per cent of all adoptions were transracial.[14] Another picture shows that of non-step-parent adoptions, about 59 per cent are from the public childcare system, 26 per cent are from other countries, and 15 per cent are voluntarily relinquished US babies.[15]

The US has a particularly high rate of adoptions relative to live births: approximately 30 per 1,000; which is many times the equivalent rate in England and Wales and all other European countries.[16] For a variety of reasons, the children now becoming available for adoption in the US are more likely to be older and have health or social care issues, have endured failed parental care and have been born within the jurisdiction, than those adopted in the late twentieth century.

Child care adoption

In 2015 the US foster care population reached a high of 427,920: 111,820 of whom were children awaiting adoption; of which 62,378 had had all parental rights terminated in readiness for that possibility.[17] From at least the coming into effect of the 1997 Act, there has been a determined policy to facilitate the adoption of such children, accelerated by the setting up of a federal department designated to deal specifically with planning adoption from care.

Also relevant is the effect of a policy to develop kinship placements as an alternative to foster care; a policy reinforced by the use of guardianship orders. Consequently, the public service tradition of placing children in foster care homes

10 'Trends in US adoptions: 2008–2012', Child Welfare Information Gateway, 2016, at 'Introduction'.
11 Ibid. In 2001, 140,034 children were adopted rising to 146,172 in 2005. By 2008 the number had fallen to 139,647 reaching 119,514 in 2012.
12 Ibid. Public agency adoptions showed an overall increase of 4 per cent between 2001 and 2012 (from 49,945 to 52,042) but this was offset by a decrease of 6 per cent (from 55,264 to 52,042) during the last 4 years of that period.
13 Ibid. Intercountry adoptions reached19,647 in 2001 but fell to 17,456 in 2008 and then to 8,668 in 2012.
14 www.statisticbrain.com/adoption-statistics
15 www.pbs.org/pov/offandrunning/fact-sheet
16 www.un.org/esa/population/publications/adoption2010/child_adoption.pdf
17 AFCARS, report No. 23 (June 2016) at: www.acf.hhs.gov/sites/default/files/cb/afcarsreport23.pdf

declined[18] as kinship placements became steadily more numerous, many of which in time transformed into adoptions. This decline eased through the early part of this decade, with an estimated foster care population of 507,000 in 2004 and 505,000 in 2006,[19] then decreasing quite sharply to 420,000 in 2009 before increasing again in the next decade to reach 427,910 in 2015.[20] In 2015, of the 243,060 exiting foster care: 52,931 (22 per cent) did so through adoption; and 22,303 (9 per cent) did so to live with a guardian.[21]

Foster care

Child care adoption must be seen in the context of a steady annual rise in the number of annual admissions to foster care: of the 2015 total foster care population of 427,920, some 269,000 had been admitted that year; representing a dip in the upward trend of admissions from 293,000 in 2000 to 307,000 in 2010.[22] Despite policy initiatives to drive up adoption and kinship care, the statistics clearly show that most children admitted to the public care system remain in foster care.

Foster parent adoption

Children in the public child welfare system and unable to return to their birth families are, whenever possible: the subject of proceedings brought to permanently extinguish parental rights, and may then be placed for adoption; most often adoption is by the child's foster parents with ongoing State financial support.[23] This practice, whereby State responsibilities for neglected and abused children are in effect privatised and often accompanied by ongoing financial payments, is interesting. In 2015, of the 52,931 (22 per cent) exiting foster care by way of adoption: 26,983 (52 per cent) went to their foster parents; 17,899 (34 per cent) went to relatives including step-parents; but only 7,316 (14 per cent) were third party or 'stranger' adoptions.

Family adoption

As the statistical data clearly demonstrates, by far the largest proportion of all children exiting foster care annually in the US are simply being returned to their

18 General Accounting Office, 1989, as cited by McFadden, E., 'Kinship Care in the United States', in *Adoption & Fostering*, 22(3) (1998): 8.
19 AFCARS, 'Trends in Foster Care and Adoption', 2007.
20 AFCARS, at: www.acf.hhs.gov/sites/default/files/cb/trends_fostercare_adoption 2012.pdf
21 AFCARS, report No. 23.
22 Ibid. The care population, however, decreased annually during the same period from 524,000 in 2,002 to 511,000 in 2005 and to 397,000 in 2012.
23 See the Children's Bureau report (1999) which noted that one-half of all children adopted from foster care were adopted by their foster parents and that 86 per cent of those received adoption subsidies. Note that some states have legislation that expressly prohibits lesbians or gays from adopting children in foster care.

family of origin. This practice is now promoted by public childcare agencies as it provides for minimal disruption to a child's sense of belonging within the family, class, culture and locality of their birth. In 2015, of the 243,060 children who exited the care system, 123,894 (51 per cent) went back to their parents or primary caregiver and 15,621 (6 per cent) went to other relatives.[24]

Step-parent adoptions

Hollinger has noted that 'perhaps half or more of all adoptions are by step-parents; many others are by grandparents or other relatives, who like step-parents, have long been the de facto parents of the children they adopt.'[25] This results in a situation where for the majority of annual adoptions in the US there is judged to be no 'welfare factor', and therefore in most states there is no need for adoption agency involvement, as the child concerned is viewed as having no actual needs which the professional assessment procedure was designed to address. Again, a system which gives a free pass to a placement decision with such long-term welfare implications for a child does raise human rights concerns.

Intercountry adoption

In recent years the US has seen a significant and sustained drop in annual ICAs: down from 22,991 in 2004 to 8,668 in 2012, to 5,648 in 2015.[26]

In 2007 it had been estimated that ICAs totalled some 444,000 (25 per cent of all adopted children) of which 33 per cent were from China.[27] Then, there was every reason to agree with Hollinger that, 'with the implementation of the 1993 Hague Convention on Intercountry Adoption (effective from April 2008), now underway in the United States and in nearly 70 other countries, adoptions of foreign-born children by US citizens may soon exceed 25,000 per year, and the very small number of adoptions of US born children by residents of other countries will rise rapidly'.[28] The fact that the reverse has been the case may be attributed partially to: a scaling back in the flow from such established sources as South Korea and Romania as their domestic adoption and childcare capacity develops; to the US reducing its reliance upon such other sources as Cambodia and Vietnam because of concerns relating to visas and corruption; to the changes in politics and policy of sending nations such as Russia and China; to particular difficulties with prevailing standards in Guatemala resulting in the closure of what has lately been the single most important supply route for US adopters; and to the economic recession which has reduced the pool of those who can now afford the

24 Ibid.
25 Hollinger, J. H., *Adoption Law and Practice*, New York, Matthew Bender/Lexis-Nexis, update 2005, vol. I.
26 www.barkeradoptionfoundation.org/international-adoption-statistics-fiscal-year-2015
27 Vandivere et al., *Children Adopted from Foster Care*, p. 7.
28 Ibid.

considerable expense of ICA.[29] The effect of a reduced flow from particular countries can be seen in the fall from 7,038 to 2,697 adoptions from China during 2004 to 2012, and from 5,862 to 748 from Russia over the same period. The effect of Hague ratification on adoption from non-Convention countries undoubtedly also had an impact. In relation to Guatemala, for example, US adoptions fell from 4,726 in 2007 to 754 in 2009 and to 50 in 2010. By 2013, 52 per cent of the 7,094 intake of children were from non-Convention countries and 3,406 or 48 per cent were from Convention countries – an abrupt contrast to 2005 when 58.2 per cent of the 22,739 were from Hague Convention countries.

This sharp and continuing fall in ICAs masks what Hollinger sees as an interesting trend: the decline is largely limited to young babies. The number of international adoptees aged between 5 to 12 has fallen only slightly since 2004, while the number of children under age 1 fell by 90 per cent. In 2004, children aged 12 months or less accounted for more than 40 per cent of ICAs (now only 10 per cent) while those aged 5 to 12 now constitute 24 per cent (formerly 12 per cent). In 2012, of the 8,668 total adoptions from all countries: just 10 per cent were aged 12 months or less; 58 per cent were aged 1 to 4; and almost one-quarter were aged 5 to 12. It is at least possible that international commercial surrogacy has displaced adoption as the preferred option for those seeking a baby. Bluntly put, where choice rather than altruism is in play, some prospective adopters may simply decide that surrogacy offers better value.

Interestingly, this period is one which has seen the US become a 'sending' country with 26 agencies now accredited by the State Department to process outgoing adoptions. It is estimated that over the past ten years: more than 1,000 US-born children have been adopted in Canada; 300 in the Netherlands; and at least another 100 in the UK.

Adoption related issues in human rights reports

Convention on the Rights of the Child

As the US has still not ratified this Convention it is subject to neither the monitoring procedures nor the requirement for a five yearly report on Convention related standards of practice undertaken by the Committee on the Rights of the Child (CRC). It has also declined to ratify several major human rights treaties.[30] The fact of non-ratification and the consequent absence of such reports in itself gives rise to human rights concerns.

The first universal periodic review (UPR) conducted by the UN in 2010 highlighted concerns regarding the US policy towards immigrant children and noted a

29 The Donaldson Adoption Institute in New York says costs have risen; the cost of an international adoption sometimes exceeds $50,000, at: http://adoptioninstitute.org

30 Including the Convention on the Elimination of All Forms of Discrimination against Women (CEDAW) and the International Convention for the Protection of All Persons from Enforced Disappearance (CAED).

lack of improvement in its second review in 2015. In 2017, Human Rights Watch drew attention to the new policy of separating children from adults when detaining unauthorised immigrants: following deportation of the adults the children can find themselves entering the US public care system; thereafter their future is uncertain.[31]

The current legislative framework

Each state has its own adoption statutes and other related legislative provisions. For the country as a whole it is largely the Adoption and Safe Families Act 1997, in conjunction with the amended Adoption Assistance and Child Welfare Act 1980 and certain other important statutes, which together form a contemporary legislative outline for federally approved adoption practice.[32] This framework is supplemented by the provisions of international Conventions and by the Intercountry Adoption Act 2000.

The legislation: adoption related law; domestic

As Anne Estin points out 'federal law generally comes into play with respect to adoption from foster care, ICA, and in relation to Indian children'.[33] The following are the core pieces of federal legislation (excluding the complex body of child welfare, social security, employee benefits, income tax, jurisdictional, immigration, and citizenship laws, etc. that are also relevant) currently constituting the legal framework for adoption in the US.

Every Child Deserves a Family Act 2013

This legislation provides that any organisation dealing with the foster and adoptive care of children, which receives federal funding, is prohibited from discriminating against prospective adopters in a same-sex relationship or if either identifies as LGBT.

Birthparent Assistance Act 2008

This provides post-placement counselling services for those birthparents who have placed a child for adoption.

31 www.hrw.org/news/2017/03/07/us-plan-tear-more-families-apart

32 Essentially, the following US Constitution and federal statutes are of paramount importance: the Indian Welfare Act (25 USC, Chap 21); the Adoption Assistance and Child Welfare Act 1980 (42 USC, §620); the Child Abuse Prevention and Treatment and Adoption Reform Act (42 USC, Chap 67); and the CRS annotated Constitution. The Code of Federated Regulations (45 CFR, Part 1356) also plays an important role.

33 Note to author (24.09.17); see: www.childwelfare.gov/topics/adoption/laws/laws-federal

Interstate Compact on the Placement of Children (revised 2008)

Developed in 1974, the compact was designed to ensure protection and services to children placed across state lines. It imposes a number of procedural requirements on domestic adoptive placements that involve more than one state.

Children's Health Act 2000

This Act reinforced the Adoption Incentives programme which provides for the payment of incentive funds to eligible states and territories to facilitate the recruitment of adoptive families for children with special needs and increase the number of children adopted from public foster care.

The safe-haven laws

Since 1999 most states have passed 'safe haven' laws in an attempt to prevent unsafe abandonment of babies and neonaticide. These tend to include provisions allowing parent(s), or those designated by the parent(s), to anonymously leave an 'unwanted infant' at a safe-haven centre (hospital emergency room, fire station, police station), no questions are asked, no identification of parent(s) is required and no social or medical history of baby is required. Note that this act – invariably by, or directed by, a birth mother – can constitute a peremptory strike against the human rights of a putative father.

Adoption and Safe Families Act 1997

The principal aim of the 1997 Act is to promote the adoption of children in foster care. It amended but did not repeal the 1980 Act, and introduced two new concepts: the duty of a state to make reasonable efforts at 'permanency planning' once adoption or permanent guardianship becomes the goal; and the concept of 'concurrent planning'.[34] The Act also introduced 'legal guardianship' which provides authority for the transfer of parental rights to a relative enabling them to assume permanent care responsibility for a child failed by parental care.[35] States are eligible to claim financial bonuses from federal funds if they exceed their set quota of annual adoptions.[36] To qualify for federal funds a state scheme must show that 'in determining reasonable efforts . . . to be made with respect to a child, and in making such reasonable efforts, the child's health and safety shall be the

34 42 USC section 675 (E); and see Chapter 2.

35 A 'legal guardianship' order bears a strong resemblance to the English 'special guardianship' order. Both offer a strategic halfway house between long-term foster care and adoption that does not require the extinguishing of birth parents' rights.

36 Federal funds were used as an incentive to encourage states to expedite the adoption of children in the public care system: states would receive $4,000 for every child adopted beyond their best year's total; an extra $4,000 for every child aged 9 and older; $2,000 for every special needs child adopted above the baseline year; and additional federal funds if they exceeded their prior number of completed adoptions.

paramount concern'.[37] This shifted the legal emphasis from family preservation to the priority of child safety. It requires: a clear statement made in court when a care order is issued of the changes to be made by the parents within a 12-month period after which the child will either be returned to parental care or placed for adoption; a permanency hearing to be held 12 months after the issue of a care order; mandatory concurrent planning; and, after a child has been in care for 15 out of 24 months, good reason must be shown as to why a petition to terminate parental rights should not be filed. In effect the 1997 Act imposes a 15-month time limit on the use of financial resources to achieve family reunification after which resource allocation switches to supporting permanency through adoption. This is seen by some as a worrying development:[38]

> This shift of resources into promoting adoption, as opposed to state-managed foster care, as a solution for children in 'dysfunctional' families can be seen as a form of 'privatising' child welfare.

There are also worries that adoption through the foster care system, will be viewed by some as a low cost and 'working-class' alternative to ICA which, at up to $50,000 or more for a child, is an option in practice only open to the more wealthy.

The Adoption Incentives programme began in the fiscal year 1998 as part of the 1997 Act and has since been reauthorised twice: as part of the Adoption Promotion Act of 2003 and as part of the Fostering Connections to Success and Increasing Adoptions Act of 2008. This approach has since been implemented, through replicated state legislation, across the US.[39] The 1997 Act also established the Adoption and Foster Care Analysis and Reporting System (AFCARS), a mandatory data collection system. This provides evidence that the policy drive to use adoption to secure permanency for children unable to return to their birth families is indeed working.

Small Business and Job Protection Act 1996

This legislation prohibits 'a state or other entity that receives federal assistance from denying any person the opportunity to become an adoptive or a foster parent on the basis of the race, color, or national origin of the persons or of the child involved'.

Multiethnic Placement Act 1994

This legislation and its 1996 successor prohibits discriminatory practices by banning the denial or delay of a foster or adoption placement solely on the basis of race,

37 42 USC section 671, section 15.

38 Woodhouse, B., 'The Adoption and Safe Families Act: a major shift in child welfare law and policy', in Bainham, A. (ed.), *The International Survey of Family Law, 2000 Edition*, Family Law, Bristol, 2000, p. 375.

39 US Dept. of Health & Human Services, Children's Bureau, at: www.acf.hhs.gov/programs/cb/focus-areas/adoption

colour or national origin of carer or child. It also compels states to make diligent efforts to recruit and retain foster and adoptive families that reflect the ethnic diversity of 'waiting' children. Two years later it was amended to prohibit any denial or delay in placement on the basis of race, colour or national origin.

Uniform Adoption Act 1994

This formative statute attempts a complete codification of adoption law. It provides, in Article 4, that a custodial parent's unmarried partner, as well as the parent's spouse, may adopt as a second parent, if the custodial parent consents and the court finds the proposed adoption to be in the child's best interests. As Hollinger points out 'the consequence of this kind of adoption is that the custodial parent consents to the adoption, but does not lose, or have to relinquish, his or her parental rights . . . the new adoptive parent becomes a full legal co-parent'.[40] Only a minority of states have adopted the Uniform Adoption Act, in fact perhaps only Vermont.[41]

Adoption Assistance and Child Welfare Act 1980

This, a legislative response to concerns that too many children were being removed from parental care only to disappear into the public care system, established the modern legal framework for childcare. It introduced and positioned within statute law the formative concepts of 'permanency' and 'reasonableness' and provided the basis for a generation of professional intervention focused on rehabilitating children within their families of origin. It authorised the channelling of federal funds to those states that implemented child welfare laws emphasising family preservation and reunification and made 'reasonable efforts' to prevent the removal of children from their families or to reunite them as appropriate. It also funded state initiatives to provide post-adoption support for adopters of hard-to-place children. The human rights dimension to this legislative initiative was reinforced by the decision of the Supreme Court in *Santosky* v. *Kramer*[42] which ruled that states must have 'clear and convincing evidence' that parents would be unable to care for their child before terminating parental rights or such action would be in breach of the 14th Amendment.

This legislation inaugurated an era characterised by public service investment in family reunification but, as Woodhouse pointed out, this was a failing policy:[43]

> An over emphasis on 'reasonable efforts' was preventing children who would never realistically be reunited with their parents from moving on to find safe, permanent families through adoption.

40 Hollinger, *Adoption Law and Practice*.
41 See, further, at: www.uniformlaws.org/Act.aspx?title=Adoption%20Act%20(1994)
42 455 US 755 (1982).
43 Woodhouse, 'Adoption and Safe Families Act', p. 380.

Accordingly, in 1997 Congress passed the Adoption and Safe Families Act in order 'to move abused and neglected kids into adoption or other permanent homes and to do it more quickly and more safely than ever before'.[44]

Indian Child Welfare Act 1978

As was explained in *Adoptive Couple* v. *Baby Girl*,[45] this legislation was designed to stop the practice of unwarranted removal of Indian children from Indian families 'due to the cultural insensitivity and bias of social workers and state courts'. In practice the provisions of the Indian Child Welfare Act often need to be considered in conjunction with those of the Interstate Compact on the Placement of Children.[46]

Other relevant provisions

The Children in Families First Act 2013 was intended to realign structures and reallocate resources in the federal government, and strengthen ICA to the US and around the world. The Fostering Connections to Success and Increasing Adoptions Act 2008, as the title suggests, was intended to increase support for foster parents and improve incentives for adoption. The Adoption Promotion Act 2003 reauthorised the adoption incentive payments programme under part E of title IV of the Social Security Act. The Family and Medical Leave Act 1993 made provision for adoption related tax credits of up to $10,000 per adoption, and subsidies for families who adopt children with 'special needs'.

The legislation: adoption related law; international

On 1 April 2008, the Hague Convention on Protection of Children and Co-operation in Respect of Intercountry Adoption came into effect for all Intercountry Adoptions between the US and other Hague Convention countries.[47] The US has also signed and ratified: the International Convention on the Elimination of all forms of Racial Discrimination; and the Optional Protocol to the Convention on the Rights of the Child on the Sale of Children, Child Prostitution and Child Pornography. It has ratified the Convention on the Civil Aspects of International Child Abduction 1980; signed but not yet ratified the Convention on the Rights of the Child 1989; signed the Convention on the International Recovery of Child Support and Other Forms of Family Maintenance 2007; and is preparing to sign and ratify the Convention on Jurisdiction, Applicable Law, Recognition,

44 Senator Rockefeller of West Virginia, 143 Cong. Rec. 12199.
45 *Adoptive Couple* v. *Baby Girl* 12-399 (2013); 398 SC 625, 731 SE 2d 550 (2012). See 2013 US LEXIS 4916, 2013 WL 3184627.
46 http://law.capital.edu/adoption/#sthash.r0UHEGH0.dpuf
47 Intercountry Adoption Act of 2000, codified at 42 USC sec. 14901 and following sections.

Enforcement and Co-operation in Respect of Parental Responsibility and Measures for the Protection of Children 1996.

Intercountry Adoption Universal Accreditation Act 2012

With effect from 14 July 2014, this domestic statute required adoption service providers working with prospective adoptive parents in non-Convention adoption to comply with the same accreditation requirement and standards that apply in Convention adoption cases. It defined 'adoption services' as including: identifying a child for adoption and arranging an adoption; securing necessary consent to termination of parental rights and to adoption; performing a background study on a child or a home study on a prospective adoptive parent, and reporting on such a study; making determinations of the best interests of a child and the appropriateness of adoptive placement for the child; post-placement monitoring of a case until final adoption; and where made necessary by disruption before final adoption, assuming custody and providing childcare or any other social services pending an alternative placement.

Intercountry Adoption Act 2000

This domestic legislation has provided the legal framework for ICA. It designated the Department of State as the US Central Authority with plenary authority to facilitate and oversee US participation, as both a sending and a receiving country, in inter-Convention country adoptions. It was designed to be consistent with the basic principles and provisions of the Convention and provides that only accredited agencies or approved persons will be allowed to provide adoption services with respect to a Convention adoption in which the US is either a receiving or a sending country. This legislation was closely followed by the Child Citizenship Act 2000 which provided automatic citizenship status for children adopted by Americans.

Hague Convention

The US signed the Convention in 1994, it took effect on 1 April 2008 and since the latter date ICA adoptions are required to be Hague compliant (see Chapter 3).

The legislation: human rights law

The US Constitution is of primary importance. This provides federal recognition of and protection for human rights: the Bill of Rights together with the 13th–15th Amendments, may be considered to provide a body of provisions equivalent to the European Convention on Human Rights. The American Declaration of the Rights of Man, particularly Article 6 concerning the right to a family and to the protection necessary to enjoy that right, and Article 7 which recognises a child's right to protection, is clearly relevant.

International treaties, conventions and protocols, etc.

As a founder member of the United Nations and signatory State to the UDHR, the US, has formally recognised the bearing of international human rights law by: ratifying the International Covenant on Civil and Political Rights (ICCPR); and the International Covenant on Economic, Social and Cultural Rights (ICESCR). Similarly, as founder member of the American Convention on Human Rights, this nation has committed itself, in Articles 17 and 19, to defending the integrity of the family unit and ensuring the protection of children respectively. Other relevant legislation includes the Protocol of San Salvador and the Riyadh Guidelines.

Regulating the adoption process

As there is no national legal framework governing the adoption process, law and regulatory matters continue to be determined separately by each of the 50 states and the District of Columbia, though some umbrella pieces of legislation and judicial decisions bring a degree of commonality to law and practice across all states. Non-consensual placements, however, and Convention adoptions attract standardised regulatory provisions. A distinguishing feature of adoption in the US is that, in keeping with the prevailing 'free-market' ethos, consensual placements are not subject to the type of tight regulatory systems that characterise the way in which other nations, such as the UK, manage the adoption process.

Katz has explained that a twin-track approach, involving either a voluntary relinquishment or an involuntary termination of parental rights, each with its own systems has developed in the US.[48] He defines the first as 'consensual and private, involving non-governmental, non-profit or profit-making agencies or individuals' and the second as 'non-consensual and public, involving state agencies'.

The judiciary

In all states, the adoption process concludes with a judicial hearing. The role of the court, as in the UK, is to ensure that eligibility/suitability criteria are fulfilled by all parties, ascertain or adjudicate on consent requirements, confirm that the proposed arrangements are compatible with the child's welfare and then issue or refuse the order sought.

Government bodies

Adoption agencies

In the US, adoptions are most usually arranged by adoption agencies that are either public child welfare agencies (exempted from accreditation requirements) or

48 Katz, S., 'Dual systems of adoption in the United States', in Katz, S., Eekelaar, J. and Maclean, M. (eds), *Cross-Currents: Family Law and Policy in the United States and England*, Oxford University Press, 2001.

private independent organisations. In either case, such an agency provides the link between children in need of a home and prospective adoptive parents. There are a lot of them: an estimated 1,552, of which 192 focus on ICAs.[49] Following ratification of the Hague Convention, all private adoption agencies involved in ICA have to be state-licensed and also accredited through the US Central Authority.

Adoption agencies assess prospective applicants, arrange suitable placements and process court applications. They accept full legal responsibility for a prospective adoptee when the birth parent/s relinquish their parental rights to the agency. They often provide pre- and post-support services for birth mothers and usually have very long waiting lists. An adoption agency may be liable to adopters for 'wrongful adoption', i.e. a failure to disclose facts about a child's history, including genetic information, that could have had a bearing on their decision to accept a particular placement.[50] An Adoption Committee performs the same functions for an adoption agency in this country as an Adoption Panel does for its UK counterpart, and it usually comprises much the same mix of executive officers, specialist professionals and some independent members. A licensed adoption agency will normally ensure that tasks of confirming the availability of particular children, selecting approved adopters and agreeing matched placements are assigned to such a committee.

All private agencies are required to be licensed and to submit to monitoring, periodic inspection and state regulatory systems. These agencies may be used by public child welfare departments to place children from foster care, and by prospective adopters or birth parent/s wishing to make private adoption arrangements. In the latter case, as an alternative to making a direct placement, a parent may place their child through an agency after having formally relinquished all rights. This is often done on a for-profit basis: 'accredited agencies' must be nonprofit; but 'approved persons' or 'facilitators' – a category that may include large organisations as well as lawyers, social workers and independent consultants – are entitled to operate on a fees-for-service basis. The child may then be advertised for adoption through nationwide media outlets. This commercial component to private placements is a distinctive and long-standing characteristic of the adoption process in the US.

Registration of adoption orders

All states have laws that provide a formal process for the registration of an adoption order by the state Registrar in a Registry of Births. The Registrar is also

49 Quiroz, P. A., *Adoption in a Color-Blind Society*, New York, Rowman & Littlefield, 2007.

50 See, for example, the Ohio case of *Burr* v. *Board of County Commissioners* 491 NE2d 1101 (Ohio 1986) where the tort of 'wrongful adoption' first attracted judicial notice and *Meracle* v. *Children's Service Society* (1986) where an agency was prosecuted for wilful negligence. Also, see Blair, D. M., 'Liability of adoption agencies and attorneys for misconduct in the disclosure of health-related information', in Hollinger, J. H. and Leski, D. W. (eds), *Adoption Law and Practice*, 1998, vol. II, paras 16.01–16.08.

responsible for the issue of a birth certificate naming the adopters as parents of the child, for recording in a separate register the facts relating to the birth parents and for determining rights of access to identifying information.

Human rights considerations

Representation

The arrangements for representing the interests of the parties are much the same as in the UK and the court will have the benefit of the same type of professional reports from the agencies involved.

Due process

The right to due process, both 'procedural' and 'substantive' as enshrined in the 5th and 14th Amendments, requires the legal system its processes and protections to be available to all and that their functions are performed with the utmost propriety. Substantive due process, in this context, has been interpreted to establish a protected interest for parents to raise their children and for those children to be safe. The effect of this due process principle can be seen, for example, in: the requirement that all persons (such as unmarried fathers) are served with notice of proceedings affecting them; that representation be provided to those (such as children) whose interests are being determined; and that full and informed consents (unless statutorily dispensed with) are available.

For-profit adoption agencies

The objectives and methods of such lightly regulated agencies are not always wholly conducive to maximising the welfare interests of children. In particular, concern has been expressed that the regulatory provisions in the Intercountry Adoption Act, s. 203(b)(2), are inadequate to ensure effective policing of 'facilitators' profit-making activities in ICA.[51] On the other hand it has to be said that the existence of so many wholly independent agencies illustrates the existence of a healthy freedom of association environment with opportunities for free speech, advocacy and lobbying which may not be as available in countries where adoption agencies are government or proxy government organisations.

Equality and non-discrimination

Laws relating to equality and non-discrimination have affected adoption in the US as they have in the UK. The resulting difficulties are well illustrated by the travails

51 See, for example, the Donaldson Institute at: www.facebook.com/adoptioninstitute

of the Catholic Charities adoption agencies. State administrators had required Catholic Charities, because it accepted public funds, to provide adoption and foster care services to same-sex couples in the same manner that they serviced different-sex couples. Rather than comply, Catholic Charities closed most of its Illinois affiliates forcing the state to transfer more than 1,000 children from the charity's custody to secular agencies. The consequent disruption to the care arrangements for so many children, including the probability of losing the opportunity for adoption, clearly impacted upon their human rights.

Moreover, racial inequity if not outright discrimination has also been a constraint in determining which children enter the adoption process. While African-American children are overrepresented in the care system,[52] there is a scarcity of available African-American foster parents and adopter preference overall is for white children. Consequently, there is a stronger probability that black children will be denied access to adoption. Indeed, Hollinger estimates that as many as 500 infants, most of whom are black, leave the US through outgoing adoption every year.[53]

Legal orphans

Court removal of parental rights, a necessary precondition for admission to the adoption process, has not necessarily led to that outcome for those concerned. Many children now remain in the public care system as 'legal orphans' with no ties to any family. This is clearly a serious human rights issue. In the period 2000–5, for example, while the number of children whose parental rights had been terminated ranged from 73,000 to 65,000, those adopted annually remained relatively constant in the low 50,000s.

Thresholds for entering the adoption process: eligibility, suitability and placement

The adoption process in the US is a curious mix of public and private interests with the law extending considerably more latitude to the latter than is the case in the UK.

Role of adoption agency

The lack of a central regulating agency allows for some variation across the states in how the domestic adoption process is defined. In all states there is little

52 Stehno, 'Elusive continuum of child welfare services'; Tatara, *Characteristics of Children in Substitute and Adoptive Care.*

53 Buckwalter-Poza, R., 'America's unseen export: children, most of them black', *Pacific Standard*, 24 June 2014, at: www.psmag.com/navigation/politics-and-law/outgoing-adoption-americas-unseen-export-children-black-84084; see also Selman, P., 'The rise and fall of intercountry adoption in the 21st century: global trends from 2001 to 2010', in Gibbons, J. and Rotabi, K. (eds), *Intercountry Adoption: Policies, Practices, and Outcomes*, Farnham, Ashgate, 2012.

professional involvement in step-parent adoptions and no statutory support services available for such adopters nor for those who acquire children through intercountry processes.

Pre-placement counselling

While post-adoption counselling is now a mandatory requirement across all states, the public and private adoption agencies in most if not all states are also required under the Birthparent Assistance Act 2008 to provide pre-placement counselling services for those birth parents who have placed a child for adoption regarding their legal rights and the options available. Counselling must also be offered to prospective adopters.

Eligibility and suitability of the parties

A registered adoption agency has the responsibility of ensuring that all parties entering the adoption process satisfy the statutory eligibility and suitability criteria, subject to the less stringent approach required in respect of kinship adoptions.

The child

The availability of a child for adoption is determined by either the existence of parental consent, or the absence of any need for it (i.e. being orphaned or abandoned) or the presence of grounds for dispensing with it (i.e. judicial removal of parental rights) as set out in the Adoption and Safe Families Act 1997. An interesting feature of the process in the US is that all states, with the exception of New Jersey, permit adult adoption – most without any caveats, save for the consent of all parties.

The birth parent/s

Where the parents of the child to be adopted are or have been married to each other, then the consent of both is required, or grounds for dispensing with this must be available. In relation to ICA, evidence is required that the birth parent/s are dead or have abandoned the child (including abandoned to institutional care) or – since mid 2008 – otherwise fit within the ambit of the Immigration and Naturalization Act.

The consent of an unmarried mother, or grounds for dispensing with it, must always be available. Most states have laws stipulating a minimum time period following birth of a child before the mother can give a valid consent to adoption; but in some it is valid within hours of birth. Until the early 1970s, the unmarried father of a child relinquished by the mother had no legal standing in adoption proceedings; his consent was not required and he was not even entitled to formal legal notice of such proceedings. This situation was altered by the case of *Stanley*

v. *Illinois*[54] in which the Supreme Court in a footnote to its judgment added that such a father should be given the opportunity to be heard in adoption proceedings. Subsequently, in *Lehr* v. *Robertson*,[55] the Supreme Court held that a putative biological father who had never established an actual relationship with his child did not have a constitutional right to notice of his child's adoption by the man who had married the child's mother. Currently, in about 30 states there are now birth father registers which allow a man who is the father of a baby, or thinks he might be, to record his interest in the child. Once registered, such a father must be notified where feasible that adoption proceedings in respect of his child have been, or will shortly be, commenced. Most states, in compliance with developing international law, now also require that the consent of an involved father be obtained or that grounds for dispensing with it be shown.[56] However, the courts have ruled that a father would need to appropriately evidence any such 'involvement'.[57]

The birth parent/s and rehabilitation

As has often been judicially emphasised, the right of a parent to maintain a relationship with his or her child is among the interests included in the constellation of liberties protected through the 14th Amendment.[58] Therefore, before authorising a non-consensual adoption placement the court first has to be convinced that sufficient evidence exists to overcome the legal presumption that a birth parent is entitled to the custody of their child.[59] Except in cases of extreme abuse or neglect, such evidence will be best adduced by reports to the court detailing the outcome of unsuccessful rehabilitation programmes. The capacity – and willingness – to provide such discretionary but resource intensive programmes varies from state to state.

The adopters

In the US, as in the UK and as emphasised in a number of ECtHR rulings, there is no legal right to adopt.[60] Again, as in the UK, adopters must satisfy conditions

54 405 US 645 (1972) at fn 9 where in reference to 'custody or adoption proceedings' it is stated that: 'Extending opportunity for hearing to unwed fathers who desire and claim competence to care for their children creates no constitutional or procedural obstacle to foreclosing those unwed fathers who are not so inclined' (p. 657). For further Supreme Court rulings positively affecting the *locus standi* of unmarried fathers, see *Quilloin* v. *Walcott*, 434 US 246 (1978), *Caban* v. *Mohammed*, 441 US 380 (1979) and *Lehr* v. *Robertson*, 43 US 248 (1983).

55 463 US 248 (1983).

56 *Caban* v. *Mohammed* 441 US 380 (1979).

57 *Adoptive Couple* v. *Baby Girl* 12-399 (2013); 398 SC 625, 731 SE 2d 550 (2012).

58 *Troxel* v. *Granville* (99–138) 530 US 57 (2000) 137 Wash. 2d 1, 969 P.2d, affirmed.

59 The parental right to custody has been deemed a fundamental right by the US Supreme Court (*Santosky* v. *Kramer* 455 US 745 (1982)).

60 *Lindley for Lindley* v. *Sullivan*, 889 F.2d 124 (7th Cir. 1989).

relating to age, domicile/habitual residence, improper payments and duration of placement – though these have always been most stringent in relation to third party prospective adopters but more flexible and readily satisfied by kinship adopters. Adoption agencies are not required to assess step-parent applicants, although their eligibility and suitability remain to be judicially assessed (usually based upon a home study report, background checks and the mandatory consent of the child's noncustodial parent), a minimum period of care is not normally required. Since April 2008, ICA adoptions have been governed by Hague Convention requirements and the criteria applied to assess adopters are therefore the same as in other signatory States (see Chapter 3). Issues such as the upper age limit of adopters, willingness to accommodate contact arrangements and the availability of state financial support have generated much the same the same level of controversy as in the UK. Transracial adoption has been and continues to be a particularly sensitive matter for policy and practice.

While neither the Uniform Adoption Act nor state legislation modelled upon it place any restrictions on adoption by unmarried applicants, there is still some ambivalence regarding unmarried couples as adoption applicants, and an outright ban in some 12 states including Louisiana. The protracted legal proceedings of *Adar* v. *Smith*[61] illustrate the difficulties (see below).

LGBT adopters

Where gay marriage has not been permitted in law, the constraints on adoption by unmarried couples have usually been sufficient to also rule out gay couples. Since the leading Hawaiian case of *Baehr* v. *Lewin*,[62] however, the judiciary in most states where the issue has arisen have accepted that adoption by same-sex couples can be compatible with the welfare interests of the children concerned. As the law has changed to make gay marriage lawful in most states, some have also introduced legislation to specifically prohibit discrimination on the basis of sexual orientation in assessing the suitability of prospective adoptive parents.[63] In addition, some states disqualify those suffering from physical or mental disabilities or impose 'reputability requirements' which exclude individuals with a history of criminal convictions or employment instability.

Placement with consent

Placement choice, as exercised by the birth parent, often takes the form of a relinquishing birth mother choosing from agency profiles of prospective adopters registered with an adoption agency; and it may extend to face-to-face meetings. A

61 *Adar v. Smith*, 622 F.3d 426 (5th Cir. 2010). The appeals rested on a claim that the Full Faith and Credit Clause and Equal Protection Clause of the US Constitution binds states to respect and uphold the judgments issued by courts in other states.

62 852 P 2d 44 Haw (1993); though this was not a 'same-sex' case.

63 For example, New York: see, 18 NYCRR §421.16[h][2].

singular feature of the adoption process in the US is that in the majority of private placements, the suitability of adopters is decided by the birth mother. While this is most obviously the case in step-parent adoptions it is also, in effect, the reality in agency adoptions when prospective adopters are encouraged to prepare a videotape – in which they relate their qualities – for distribution to birth mothers. The latter's choice may well be influenced by financial considerations as brokered by the agency.

In a private adoption context, placement decisions with third parties are mostly made by adoption agencies at their discretion following formal parental relinquishment of the child to the agency: most states continue to permit private adoption placements; only four restrict placement to agencies in non-relative adoptions. Prospective adopters may, however, make a direct personal approach to a birth mother or to do so through the mediation of a third party or perhaps by placing an advertisement in local, national or international journals or on the internet. Many but not all states also permit independent persons, such as lawyers, to make placement arrangements.

Placement by the birth parent/s

In the US, the right of a birth mother to place her child for adoption with whomsoever she chooses, or to authorise another person to do so on her behalf, has been embodied in the laws of all but four states which restrict the right to placement with a relative.[64] Indeed, as Hollinger has noted: all but a handful of states permit direct non-agency placements, and most domestic adoptions of infants are the result of voluntary direct placements.

Placement without consent

In a public childcare context, the placement is made by the relevant government agency following judicial termination of parental rights. Courts have often referred to the presumption (albeit a rebuttable one) that the 'natural bonds of affection lead parents to act in the best interests of their children'.[65] Grounds for the termination of parental rights, in circumstances of parental neglect or abuse as set out in the Adoption and Safe Families Act 1997, are provided by the child welfare laws of all states and if satisfied will enable the child to be placed by the relevant public service agency with selected prospective adopters, and in due course allow the latter to commence adoption proceedings.

Welfare interests

As Justice Stevens has pointed out, 'the constitutional protection against arbitrary State interference with parental rights should not be extended to prevent the states

64 Colorado, Connecticut, Delaware and Massachusetts.

65 See, for example, *Parham* v. *J. R.*, 442 US 584, 602 (1979); *Casey*, 505 US, at 895; and *Santosky* v. *Kramer*, 759.

from protecting children against the arbitrary exercise of parental authority that is not in fact motivated by an interest in the welfare of the child'.[66] However, any such 'arbitrary exercise of parental authority' or presumably neglect must be such as to result in termination of parental rights before welfare interests can permit an adoption placement.

Placement supervision

The Interstate Compact for the Placement of Children, endorsed by all states, provides procedures to safeguard children in pre-adoption placements.

Human rights considerations

The US adoption process provides much more scope than its UK counterpart for decision-making that serves private and commercial interests. This important difference arguably leaves the process more vulnerable to abuse.

Parental right to place

The fact that in many states birth parents are free to place their child for adoption purposes with whomsoever they like, and most domestic placements of infants are made on that basis, allows this crucial decision to bypass all professional scrutiny. As an alternative to making a direct placement, such a parent may place their child through an agency after having formally relinquished all rights, or they might be approached directly by prospective adopters before having done so. The child may be advertised for adoption through nationwide social media outlets. Often a profit motive is involved. Because such practices may imperil the welfare interests of the child concerned, leaving him or her vulnerable and exposed to potential abuse, they are prohibited by Article 29 of the Hague Convention and have long been prohibited in the UK; their continuation in the US therefore gives rise to human rights concerns.

Gay adopters

Although same-sex marriage was legalised countrywide by the ruling in *Obergefell* v. *Hodges*,[67] adoption by same-sex couples continued to be banned in many states: several such as Florida, had legislation expressly prohibiting lesbians or gays from adopting children in foster care;[68] not until 2016 was the prohibition on adoption by same-sex couples repealed in Mississippi and not until 2017 was the law changed to allow same-sex couples in Arkansas to be named as such on a child's birth certificate.[69] These rulings by the USSC have finally ended the legal inconsistency

66 *Santosky v. Kramer*, per Stevens J.
67 576 US _ (2015).
68 *Lofton* v. *Sec'y Dept Children & Family Services* 358 F.3d 804 (11th Cir. 2004).
69 *Pavan* v. *Smith* 582 US _ (2017).

across the US regarding the eligibility of same-sex and LGBT persons to adopt. In so doing the federal court would seem to have resolved the human rights implications of the decision in *Adar* v. *Smith*[70] which concerned a gay couple who adopted their Louisiana-born son in 2006 in New York where a judge issued an adoption decree. They had then sought an amended birth certificate for their child (declaring both adopters to be the child's parents) in Louisiana but were advised by the state registrar that this was not possible because Adar and Smith were not married, and Louisiana does not recognise adoption by unmarried parents. Ultimately, the USSC refused to interfere with that decision. It was then estimated that over 90,000 adopted children could potentially be affected if other states followed Louisiana's position, because, according to 2009 data from the US Census Bureau: an estimated 47,000 unmarried, different-sex couples currently were raising over 64,000 adopted children in the US; additionally, an estimated 20,000 same-sex couples were raising nearly 30,000 adopted children. In this context, the USSC ruling in *V. L.* v. *E. L.*[71] is an important milestone. This case concerned two women, partners for 16 years, who had three children (one aged 13, and twins aged 11) conceived by IVF and then adopted by both in Georgia before the family moved to Alabama. Following their separation, the biological mother denied her former partner access to the children and the Alabama courts at first instance issued a decree of shared custody. This was overturned by the Alabama Supreme Court which declined to recognise the adoption order on the grounds that the Georgia court had been wrong to vest parental rights in a lesbian couple, and the matter duly came before the USSC. Upholding the validity of the initial adoption order, the USSC warned that 'a State may not disregard the judgment of a sister State because it disagrees with the reasoning underlying the judgment or deems it to be wrong on the merits'.

Faith-based adoption placements

The Freedom to Serve Children Act, introduced in the Texas legislature in 2017,[72] is perhaps an indicator of a new front opening up in this country's endemic culture wars which will see religion used to push back the LGBT norms now legally established, if not yet wholly accepted, across the US. This legislation proposes to give children's service providers, including adoption agencies, the right to decline services to individuals based on 'the provider's sincerely held religious beliefs'. The ACLU has protested that this initiative 'would allow child welfare service providers that contract with the state to use taxpayer money to discriminate against LGBT individuals and families in foster care, adoption and other services'.[73]

70 *Adar* v. *Smith*, 622 F.3d 426 (5th Cir. 2010). The appeals rested on a claim that the Full Faith and Credit Clause and Equal Protection Clause of the US Constitution binds states to respect and uphold the judgments issued by courts in other states.
71 577 US _2016.
72 HB 3859.
73 www.aclutx.org/en/press-releases/avalanche-proposed-religious-refusal-bills-would-allow-use-religion-justify

This development needs to be viewed against a backdrop which has seen adoption championed by religious organisations as a means of ensuring the salvation of the souls of children. An evangelical adoption culture has been cultivated by those of fundamentalist Christian beliefs, with thousands of Christians attending annual adoption conferences and with denominations like the Southern Baptist Convention actively encouraging their members to adopt.[74] Arguably, when religion becomes the driving force – for or against adoption – then the welfare interests of children and their human rights are at risk.

Constraints on ICA

While human rights concerns in this context rightly focus on the potential for trafficking and the profit-driven motivation of commercial agencies, other aspects of ICA practice also give rise to similar concerns. Arguably, for example, the recent and continuing sharp decline in ICA is attributable in part to tighter regulatory practices which may breach a child's fundamental right to freedom of movement. For many child subjects of ICA processes, the US ratification of Hague in 2008 had the immediate negative effect of stalling those processes and leaving them and their prospective adopters in limbo – often for years. In Guatemala, for example, some 4,000 US adoptions (some at an advanced stage) came to an abrupt halt when the standards of practice governing the legal availability of children were judged to be non-Hague compliant.[75] Similar issues arose in the aftermath of the Haiti disaster. Not dissimilar consequences flow from the sudden imposition of political constraints as occurred when Russia terminated ICA in 2014 and China prohibited gay adopters (and others) from accessing its ICA programme.

Also of concern is that when private agencies assess, match and place a child, their responsibilities and legal authority end with the adoption order. The self-reporting obligation that rests on adopters to update the agency for six months post-adoption is voluntary, without any statutory means of enforcement, and has led to the deaths or 'rehoming' of many adoptees.[76]

74 See, for example, the Christian Alliance for Orphans which, as stated on its website, 'unites more than 140 respected Christian organizations and a national network of churches. Working together, our joint initiatives *inspire* and *equip* Christians to reflect God's heart in caring for orphans in adoption', at: www.christianalliancefororphans.org; see also Joyce, K., 'The evangelical orphan boom', *New York Times*, 21 September 2013; Joyce, K., *The Child Catchers: Rescue, Trafficking, and the New Gospel of Adoption*, New York, Public Affairs, 2013.

75 'Stalled adoption program in Guatemala leaves families in limbo', *New York Times*, 8 December 2012.

76 See, for example, Washington's Department of Social and Health Services (Office of the Children's Ombudsman), *Severe Abuse of Adopted Children* (September 2012), at: www.dshs.wa.gov/pdf/ca/SevereAbuseofAdoptedChildrenReport2012.pdf

Transracial

It has been estimated that four in ten of all US adoptions are transracial. This generates controversy as to whether they violate an adoptee's right to develop an authentic culturally affirmed identity. It is a practice that has been and continues to be a difficult human rights issue.[77]

The hearing and the grounds

A judicial hearing, held in camera and subject to the usual reporting restrictions, but managed in a more relaxed manner than other court proceedings, provides the context for determining all adoption applications across the US. In compliance with the due process principle, all persons (such as unmarried fathers) are served with notice of proceedings affecting them, representation is provided to those (such as children) whose interests are being determined and full and informed consents (unless statutorily dispensed with) must be available.[78]

Where consent is available

As has been noted: 'a court cannot approve an adoption without proof that a child's birth parents have executed voluntary and informed consents, or, alternatively, that their parental rights were terminated because of their failures to perform parental duties . . . without a voluntary relinquishment or forfeiture of parental rights, the state has no license to remove children from their parents in order to seek a "better" placement'.[79] An informed consent – in writing and either witnessed and notarised or executed before a judge or other designated official – from both birth parents is a standard requirement in all states. Where the consent of all parties is available in a kinship application the court is unlikely to pursue any further enquiries.

Consent of unmarried father

Only the consent of an unmarried father with established paternity rights is necessary. As previously mentioned, most states have a putative father registry in which an unmarried birth father may record his paternity and contact details in a prescribed manner and within a designated time period. This officially recorded data provides the basis for serving notice on an unmarried father of the fact that an

77 See, for example, the Evan B. Donaldson Adoption Institute report, *Finding Families for African-American Children: The Role of Race and Law in Adoption from Foster Care*, May 2008, which depicts transracial adoption as inappropriate for many African-American and other minority children in foster care.

78 See, further, Child Welfare Information Gateway, *Consent to Adoption*, Washington, DC: US Department of Health and Human Services, Children's Bureau, 2013.

79 Donaldson Adoption Institute, *Finding Families.*

adoption application has been lodged, and an opportunity for him to register his consent or refusal of consent to the making of an adoption order, in respect of his child.

Consent of a minor

The informed consent of an older child is a precondition for their adoption in virtually all states. The age limit varies from state to state but in most it is set at age 14 and in some it is required from 10 years old. Many states make provision for a child's consent to be dispensed with.

Where consent is not available

On the application coming before the court it will rule on whether or not it can dispense with the necessity for parental consent and will accede if satisfied that: good reason exists for so doing such as abandonment, failure to support the child, mental incompetence, or a finding of parental unfitness due to child abuse or neglect; and this is compatible with the welfare interests of the child. In contested private adoptions, the rights of the parties under the Constitution will play a significant role in what will be more adversarial proceedings than is normally the case in other modern western nations and where the outcome is more likely to be an order other than adoption; guardianship being a probable option.

Child care adoption: the grounds

The Constitution, as interpreted by the USSC, requires a state to show compelling reason for infringing rights of family privacy and for overriding parental autonomy as these fundamental liberties are protected by the 14th Amendment and its guarantee of due process.[80] The court will require evidence that the grounds of child abuse or neglect, as set out within parameters established by the Adoption and Safe Families Act 1997, can be satisfied.

Contested family adoption: the grounds

In the context of private adoptions, where an application by a parent or relative is contested by a birth parent who withholds consent, the court must proceed to a full hearing, receiving evidence from the parties and perhaps from expert witnesses, making findings of fact, ruling on the respective rights of the parties and ultimately making a determination on the merits of the case and in accordance with the welfare principle.

80 *Meyer* v. *Nebraska* 262 US 390 (1923), *Stanley* v. *Illinois* 405 US 645 (1972) and *Wisconsin* v. *Yoder* 406 US 205 (1972).

Human rights considerations

Independent assessment of welfare interests

The type of court that provides a venue for adoption hearings varies somewhat across the states with few being held in family courts. Consequently, the courts tend to be largely reliant upon the reports filed by adoption agency staff for assessments on the parties involved. There is no equivalent to the UK model of court officials (now CAFCASS, formerly a *guardian ad litem*) designated and trained to undertake impartial assessments – particularly in relation to the factors constituting the welfare of a child – solely on behalf of the court.

Unmarried fathers

The fact that the onus rests on such a father to declare his interest is arguably contrary to the welfare interests of the adoptee and jeopardises the latter's human rights. He may choose not to do so. The adoptee, the court and all professionals involved are then left reliant upon the mother to disclose the father's identity. Should she choose not to do so then the adoptee and adopters will be deprived of important genetic data relating to the father, which may have implications for the adoptee's health, and social background information the lack of which may well impair his or her ability to develop an authentic identity.

Thresholds for exiting the adoption process

The established priority given to 'permanency planning' in law and practice, together with the policy of regarding long-term foster care as undesirable and the absence of a range of alternative orders, have elevated adoption to become the judicial disposal option of choice where family reunification is impractical.

The welfare interests of the child

In all states, the court, in response to proceedings commenced by prospective adopters, will determine whether or not an adoption order should be made. This decision rests on the principle, well established in the US and defined by a list of considerations specified with slight variation in the relevant legislation of each state, that the adoption order must accord with the welfare interests of the child.[81] In ascertaining whether the proposed adoption is in keeping with such welfare interests, the court will have the benefit of assessment reports from professional social workers responsible for monitoring the placement.

81 *Curtis* v. *Curtis* 71 Mass (5 Gray) 535, 537 (1856); cited by Katz, 'Dual Systems of Adoption in the United States', p. 283.

Paramountcy

While the welfare interests of the child are of critical importance in determining an adoption application, it cannot be said that this factor is given a paramount weighting in law. Essentially, the paramountcy principle would be incompatible with the constitutional rights of birth parents, as established by the USSC in *Santosky* v. *Kramer*.[82] This presumption of a right to custody can only be vitiated by voluntary relinquishment or by 'clear and convincing' evidence that birth parents are unfit to care for their child.

Consent/views of child and welfare interests

Where the child is of an age to give an opinion, then, in many states, the court will consult with him or her as to their perception of what would be in their best interests and in some this is a statutory requirement. Whether or not articulated in statute law, the right of a 'mature minor' to assert their views, identify matters constituting their welfare interests and often to determine their future care arrangements is well established in the courts of the US.

Culturally compatible

In the multicultural melting pot that constitutes contemporary society in the US, the issue of cultural compatibility as a necessary component of welfare interests in the determination of an adoption application still has the capacity to be contentious. While it is statutorily barred from impeding transracial adoptions, and rarely arises in the context of ICA, it is very much a live issue in relation to the proportion of Afro-American children in foster care who are adopted by Caucasians. It is also one which arises in relation to children with Native American ancestry. The Indian Child Welfare Act 1978 requires that a court considering a fostering or adoption application in respect of such a child must give first priority to placement with a relative, then another member of their tribe and then with another Indian family. Only when those options have been exhausted can consideration be given to third party unrelated non-Indian adopters. Although the ruling in *Adoptive Couple* v. *Baby Girl*[83] narrowed the constraints imposed by this cultural imperative it remains a potent caveat to welfare interests where children with even a tenuous genetic connection to an Indian ancestry are involved.[84]

The orders available

In the US, as in other western common law jurisdictions, the granting of an absolute and permanent adoption order, with attendant if qualified rights of access to information and to possible ongoing support, is the most usual outcome of an

82 455 US 745 (1982).
83 398 SC 625, 731 SE 2d 550.
84 *Carter, et al.* v. *Washburn, et al.* No. 15-CV-1259, US Dist. Ct. for the Dist. of Arizona. See, further, at: www.bu.edu/bulawreview/files/2013/11/EDITORS-FOREWORD1.pdf

adoption process. The adoption order will be for 'full adoption' which conforms to the traditional common law model and once granted, the adopters receive an official decree and a birth certificate with the adopters' name listed as the parent.

Additional orders: post-adoption contact

Where all parties agree, including the child concerned (if aged 12 years or more), then an adoption order can be made subject to a contact condition. The question of whether or not there will be post-adoption contact between an adoptee and members of his or her family of origin is one usually resolved informally: state laws do not prohibit post-adoption contact; adopters may make their own decisions; and the birth parent/s may well have agreed such arrangements at time of relinquishment. In the latter instance, where a written contractual agreement has been drawn up between the parties, stating the type and frequency of the contact or communication, this can be legally enforced in 22 states under statute law.

Alternative orders

In this jurisdiction, unlike others such as the UK, the alternatives to an adoption order are limited. In order of preference, the judicial options to secure permanency are either safe reunion with parent/s or family of origin, adoption or permanent legal guardianship. The latter is recommended in circumstances where reunification with parent/s or family of origin is not possible and adoption is inappropriate. Intended for use by those relatives who may not wish to see a complete severance of ties between child and family, it is seen as particularly appropriate in relation to older children. The order does not terminate parental rights but instead transfers custodial rights to a named guardian leaving intact other legal rights such as those relating to inheritance. Permanent legal guardianship is the next preferred option to adoption and is intended for use by relatives of the child. Long-term foster care is the least preferred option.

Human rights considerations

Non-consensual adoption; the best option

For children whose parents have been judicially stripped of all parental rights there has for some years been an established policy of pursuing adoption rather than foster care. As in the UK, however, in practice it is mainly foster parents who end up adopting the children they have been caring for: a trend that some regard as indicating that government is privatising its *parens patriae* responsibilities;[85] by providing incentives that include ongoing professional support and financial

85 A doctrine whereby the inherent power and authority of the monarch and subsequently the State is used to protect persons who are legally unable to act on their own behalf.

assistance. Arguably, consigning a large proportion of the childcare population, freed up from the parental rights of those who have abused or neglected them, to the limbo of 'legal orphans' is a high price to pay for securing the adoption of a minority.

Appropriateness of adoption; alternatives

The introduction of permanent legal guardianship orders should have broken the above either/or options and allowed or required foster parents to secure their care arrangements without necessarily altering the status of a child who may well be old enough to have retained a degree of attachment to members of their birth family.

Accommodating kafala

All developed western countries are struggling with the need to accommodate Islamic law and practices within their established legal systems. As the leading common law nations receive increasing numbers of migrants from devastated Islamic countries so also is the pressure increasing to bridge religious and cultural differences. The difference between *kafala* and adoption is one important aspect of such differences which has yet to be resolved and the failure to do so may well leave the human rights of many Muslim children unprotected.[86]

ICA and political intervention

More so than other countries, the adoption process in the US would seem prone to obstruction by external political intervention with consequences for the human rights of prospective adoptees. This was the case in 2013 when the ICA adoption process in respect of 27 Russian children scheduled to be placed with their US adopters was halted by the Russian government. The resulting court proceedings found that the human rights of the children to family life under Article 8 of the ECHR had been violated.[87]

The effect of an adoption order

An adoption order has the legal effects traditionally associated with it for all parties involved but with some distinguishing characteristics.

Effect on the parties

The child

On the granting of a domestic adoption order, the child concerned ceases to have any legal ties to their birth parents, assumes the name, residence and citizenship of

86 See, further, Global Muslim Women's Shura Council, *Adoption and the Care of Orphan Children: Islam and the Best Interests of the Child*, 2011, at: www.wisemuslimwomen.org/wp-content/uploads/2017/10/WISE-UP-Adoption.pdf

87 *A. H. and Others* v. *Russia* (Nos 6033/13 and 22 other applications), 2016.

the adopters and will have the same legal rights as a birth child including those of inheritance; although in a number of states, statute law still allows adopted children to inherit from their birth parents. Unlike other common law jurisdictions, however, the adoptee may be an adult. Under the Child Citizenship Act 2000, which became effective on 27 February 2001, ICA adoptees automatically become US citizens when at least one parent is a US citizen, the child is under 18 years of age, has been the subject of a full and final adoption and has been admitted to the US as an immigrant.

The birth parent/s

In this as in other common law jurisdictions, the making of an adoption order terminates all parental rights and responsibilities of birth parents.[88] In some but not all states, birth parents may retain a right to continued anonymity.

The adopters

An adoption order permanently and exclusively vests all parental rights and responsibilities in respect of the child concerned in the adopters.

Revocation of an adoption order

In all states, the general rule is that an appeal cannot lie against the granting of an adoption order and it cannot be revoked at the behest of any of the parties concerned. It remains indissoluble other than on the usual grounds of illegality, mistake, etc.

Entitlement to post-adoption support services

Ongoing post-adoption support services have been available since the introduction of the 1997 Act and almost all childcare adoptions receive financial subsidies. ICA and private domestic adoptions are now also more likely to receive support services on request: such as social work guidance, group training for parents and mentoring for children. Hollinger[89] has drawn attention to the 'considerable controversy among policymakers as to whether children adopted from other countries who have special needs because of illness, mental or physical disabilities, or "attachment disorders"[90] should be able to qualify for the kinds of public or other financial assistance programs for which US-born adoptees are eligible'.[91]

88 See, for example, *Suster* v. *Arkansas Dep't of Human Services*, 314 Ark. 92, 858 SW 2d 122 (1993).

89 *Adoption Law and Practice*, LexisNexis, 2010 (as updated), ch. 11.

90 Ibid., citing Tepper, T. S., *Parents Network for the Post-Institutionalized Child*, www.hagueregs.org/History%20Stuff/April2Meeting.htm

91 *Adoption Law and Practice*, citing: www.childwelfare.gov/adoption/postadoption; International Adoptions-Financial Resources, at www.pueblo.gsa.gov/cic_text/children/adoption/interb.html

Human rights considerations

Rehoming

'Rehomed' adopted children are those who are voluntarily transferred by their adopters to new families through a basic 'power of attorney' document – a notarised statement declaring the child to be in the care of another adult. It would seem to be a practice confined to the US and, by some estimates, may involve as many as one in four ICA adoptions.[92] The new guardians are able to enrol a rehomed child in school, claim a tax deduction and draw government benefits. Following a Reuters investigation into this practice[93] the US Government Office of Accountability (GOA) released a report[94] and some states – Wisconsin, Ohio, Colorado and Florida have since introduced legislation aimed at protecting children from rehoming. Needless to say, this practice which bypasses the adoption process and all relevant professional screening is little more than a form of 'trafficking' and as such seriously violates an adoptee's human rights and may well breach those of the birth parents.

Information rights: disclosure, tracing and reunification

This has for many years been an area of heated controversy and currently there is no consistency in state responsibilities for ensuring provision of post-adoption information disclosure and tracing/reunification services.

Information rights

Most states traditionally sealed their adoption records in a practice that has been criticised as 'a relic of the culture of shame that stigmatised infertility, out-of-wedlock birth and adoption'[95] now all allow the release of such information on the basis of mutual consent: about a dozen will release the original birth certificate when the child concerned is 18 or 21; and about half of all states have intermediary 'search and consent' procedures.[96] The Uniform Adoption Act 1994 allows access to identifying information upon mutual consent, in cases of medical need, and requires non-identifying information to be released upon simple demand by adoptive parents or adult adoptees. For contemporary adoptions, access to identifying information is not an issue as all parties are identified.[97]

92 https://adoptionland.org/rehoming-international-adoption
93 'The child exchange: inside America's underground market for adopted children', Reuters, 9 September 2013, at: www.reuters.com/investigates/adoption/#article/part1
94 'Child welfare: steps have been taken to address unregulated custody transfers of adopted children', GAO-15-733, 16 September 2015, at: www.gao.gov/products/GAO-15-733
95 Bastard Nation: The Adoptee Rights Organisation, 'A history of sealed records in the US', Basic *Bastard*, 2003, at: www.bastards.org
96 www.childwelfare.gov/pubPDFs/infoaccessap.pdf#page=4&view=Access
97 The author acknowledges the advice of Joan Hollinger on these matters.

Information disclosure duties

Currently, the move is towards greater transparency. In most cases the judiciary have ruled that an adoptee is entitled to access at least the name of his or her birth parents and may access related court records and documents with a court order on showing good cause (i.e. in New York, California, Michigan, Washington, Wyoming and New Jersey).[98] In states which maintain adoption registries (e.g. Pennsylvania, Colorado, Florida and Rhode Island) adopted children may access the medical records of their birth parents.

Maintaining records

State laws govern the type of information required or permitted to be collected, by adoption agencies on adopted persons and their birth families. This information generally relates to medical and genetic history, family and social background, and mental health history. For the adopted child or youth, it may also include placement history and any history of abuse or neglect. It clearly differentiates between 'identifying' and 'non-identifying' information. The law specifies those variously permitted to access such information (usually with particular regard for accessing birth certificates), details the terms and processes for doing so, and states the minimum period for which adoption agency records must be archived. Most states now maintain registers in which the adopted adult and the birth parent/s can register their mutual permission for the registrar to disclose identifying information.

Tracing and reunification

Independent agencies, providing services for all parties to an adoption – on a continuum from counselling, through information gathering and tracing to possible reunification – are now well established in the US with many operating on an interstate and for-profit basis. The fact, however, that the law governing access to birth records is shrouded in controversy and varies from state to state results in an uneven patchwork of such services.

Human rights considerations

Accessing identifying information

This issue is clearly one of conflicting human rights: that of birth parents to privacy (and to have pledges of confidentiality given on relinquishment to be honoured); and that of adoptees to have access to the personal information necessary to develop an authentic identity. Disclosure vetoes, by which an adoptee may access their original birth certificate only if their birth parent does not object, continue to

98 See, for example, *In re J.N.H.*, 2009 Colo. App. LEXIS 569 (Colo. Ct. App. 16/04/09).

constrain adoptees in some states. There is also widespread provision for contact vetoes and other intermediary systems. The strong resistance to open access from organisations representing the interests of birth parents is to some extent a distinguishing feature of modern adoption practice in the US.[99]

Conclusion

Adoption in the US very much reflects the values of its social context. Although this statutory process has been in existence for nearly twice as long as in the UK, it is far from being a standardised State-regulated public service. The process is universally judicial in nature, the procedural checks and balances are much the same, but the adoption laws differ considerably across the various states and at federal level there is still a resistance to ratifying some important international treaties and conventions which could facilitate more uniformity of practice and greater human rights protection.

Arguably, the distinctive and representative characteristics of the adoption process in the US are those that also leave it vulnerable to human rights abuses. Perhaps most obviously these would include the private placement rights of parents, the role of commercial adoption agencies, State financial incentives for foster parent adoption, rehoming, the vetoes on identifying information and the long-established recourse to non-Hague compliant countries for ICA purposes. The recent rash of conservative Bills, designed to push back on LGBT issues, introduced in the Texas legislature is also concerning. It may, perhaps, indicate a growing tension between religious beliefs and human rights which could spread more widely as a factor influencing adoption law and practice.

99 Nations currently facilitating access to records include the UK, Sweden, the Netherlands, Germany, South Korea, Mexico, Argentina and Venezuela.

Part III

Contemporary law, policy and practice in a civil law context

7 France

Introduction

This chapter is primarily concerned to identify and examine those distinctive features of this archetypal civil law jurisdiction that distinguish the legal aspects of the adoption process from its common law counterpart and to identify any related human rights implications. Beginning with an overview of adoption principles and policy, with particular attention being given to the distinction between simple and plenary adoption and the role of the maternal right to anonymity, the chapter then considers contemporary trends in the different types of adoption. It outlines the relevant legislative and regulatory frameworks as a prelude to assessing the interaction between human rights and adoption law at each stage of the adoption process. The chapter concludes with a summary of the main areas of concern.

Background

The social construct of 'family' as defined in French law is quite singular.[1] For legal purposes the rules and proceedings governing family matters are to be found in the Civil Code, as amended, but the Code itself is a product of the Napoleonic era and is conceptually rooted in the revolutionary ideology that gripped France at the turn of the eighteenth century. Consequently, the concept of 'filiation' came to be central to the meaning attached to 'family': matters of individual and cultural identity, the role of the family unit in society and the acquisition of status-based relationships, are more socially ascribed than acquired by birth.[2] This continues to be of key significance in family law and the development of adoption law[3] and practice in France has to be viewed in the overall context of 'filiation'.

1 Fuchs, R. G., *Contested Paternity: Constructing Families in Modern France*, Baltimore, MD, Johns Hopkins University Press, 2008.

2 Fulchiron, H., 'Egalité, vérité, stabilité: the new French filiation law after the Ordonnance of 4th July 2005', *International Survey of Family Law*, Bristol, Jordan, 2006, pp. 203–16.

3 Ancel, M., *L'Adoption dans les legislations modernes*, Paris, Sirey, 1958 pointed out that between 1804 and 1939 a provision in the Civil Code provided that adoption did not remove a person from his family of origin; the function of adoption was to add to the adopted person's rights, not take away (paras 62–3).

Adoption and human rights: the early challenges

A key characteristic of the French adoption process, distinguishing it from that of many other countries, particularly the common law nations, is the distinction made between plenary and simple adoption. Other prominent characteristics include the right of a relinquishing mother to anonymity,[4] the heavy reliance upon intercountry adoption (ICA) and the not unrelated resistance to childcare adoption.[5]

Shaping modern adoption policy

The traditional characteristics continue to play a prominent role in shaping contemporary adoption law and policy in France.

Of major importance is the distinction between full adoption, or *adoption plénière*, and simple adoption. The first, available since 1939, corresponds to the common law form by wholly terminating the legal relationship between birth parent and child and replacing it with the rights and status of the adopting family. Simple adoption, on the other hand, does not sever the relationship between birth parent and child, it creates a new legal relationship to exist alongside the original one. In 2012 there were: 3,287 plenary adoption orders; 6,661 simple adoption orders (not all concerning persons under the age of 18);[6] and 1,569 ICA of which 83 per cent were plenary.

Another distinctly French characteristic is the right of a mother, under Article 341 of France's Civil Code, to give birth anonymously. This was formerly known as '*accouchement sous X*' (because the birth mother was recorded on the birth certificate as 'X' and the child was referred to as '*né sous X*') but records now refer simply to an 'anonymous delivery' and to the mother as 'X'.[7] The right to anonymity, added to the Civil Code in 1993, has existed in one form or another since 1793 when, under the National Convention of the French Revolution, secret pregnancies and births were protected by law.[8] It is the absence of recognition by the mother of the child (or denial of filiation) to whom she had given birth anonymously, that removes the necessity to obtain her consent for the child to be taken into State care.[9] Currently, improvements in the social conditions for

4 As also in Luxembourg, Italy and the Czech Republic.
5 See, further, Mignot, J.-F., 'Full adoption in England and Wales and France: a comparative history of law and practice (1926–2015)', *Adoption and Fostering*, London, Sage, 2017, pp. 142–58.
6 But see Belmokhtar, Z., 'L'adoption simple et plénière en 2007: des projets différents', *Infostat Justice*, 106 (2009): 1–6 where it is estimated that some 10,000 simple adoptions occur annually of which perhaps 85 per cent concern adults.
7 Article 341 of the Civil Code, introduced in 1993, precludes a child born to X from establishing any legal tie to the mother, even if her identity should be discovered. The law has been relaxed somewhat by Statute n° 2009-61 of 16 January 2009. See also Art. 325 of the Civil Code.
8 Statute of 27 June 1904 and Décret-Loi of 2 September 1941. See also Donovan, K., 'Real mothers for abandoned children', *Law & Society Review* (2002): 1.
9 Article L. 224-4, point (1), of the Social Action and Families Code.

unmarried mothers, together with the introduction of the Act of 3 December 2001 which eliminated the discrimination in inheritance rights that traditionally disadvantaged children 'born out of wedlock',[10] has resulted in far fewer babies '*né sous X*' becoming wards of state as a first step to adoption.[11] Probably no more than 1,000 babies a year are currently voluntarily relinquished by their parents, taken into care and adopted.[12]

The other two necessarily closely related characteristics of modern adoption law and policy in France are the reluctance to resort to adoption for children in the public care system, for reasons to do with filiation (the rights of known parents prevail), and the established practice of looking overseas for potential adoptees (see below).

Principles

The welfare interests of the child

The best interests of the child (*intérêt supérieur de l'enfant*), are held to be the guiding principle in all proceedings affecting that child. However, when the ECtHR ruled in *Odièvre* v. *France*,[13] that denying children given up at birth the right to discover their biological parents' identity did not violate the human rights of their children, it thereby diluted the relative weighting given to the welfare interests of the child. Subsequently, the Committee on the Rights of the Child (CRC) urged France to incorporate the concept of the child as a subject of rights in all policies, programmes and projects.[14]

Adult adoption

The Civil Code introduced the adoption of adults which has ever since been restricted to the simple form and used primarily to secure rights of inheritance.

Permanence through foster care

As has been noted 'France . . . regards successful integration into a foster family as a satisfactory form of permanence'.[15] Such an arrangement, which protects the

10 Note that the marital status of parents no longer determines the legal status of their children: whether married or not their child will have exactly the same legal status (Ordonnance n° 2005-759 of 4 July 2005, as since ratified by the Statute n° 2009-61 of 16 January 2009).

11 For an outline of the law and procedure governing an '*accouchement sous X*', see *Kearns* v. *France* [2008] 2 FCR 19.

12 Initial report to CRC, 1993, as cited by Selwyn, J. and Sturgess, W., *International Overview of Adoption: Policy and Practice*, University of Bristol, 2000, p. 37.

13 *Odièvre* v. *France* [2003] 1 FCR 621.

14 CRC, *Concluding Observations of the Committee on the Rights of the Child*, France, UN Doc. (CRC/C/15/Add.240) (2004), para. 5.

15 Selwyn and Sturgess, *International Overview of Adoption*, p. 37.

filiation between child and known birth parent/s, illustrates the importance of this principle for all French family law, including adoption.

Openness

As illustrated by the legacy of '*accouchement sous X*' there is little in the way of a culture of 'openness' in the French adoption process. Moreover, as the challenge to the '*né sous X*' right to anonymity was unsuccessful in *Odièvre* v. *France*[16] it remains the case that technically such children cannot be viewed as unduly discriminated against.

Contemporary adoption trends

Adoption in France has been in decline for some years: the total number of legally adoptable children ('wards of the state') fell from 100,000 in 1950 to 46,000 in 1970, 5,000 in 1990 and fewer than 2,500 in 2016.[17] Partly this has been due to very few children entering the process from a childcare context (although a few are adopted this is almost invariably by their foster parents, with only a handful becoming otherwise available to domestic adopters). It is also a consequence of the dwindling availability of '*né sous X*' children and wards of the state. In the main, however, the cause lies in the drying up of external sources of supply.[18] As the queues of prospective adopters lengthen, the sources of potential adoptees are rapidly disappearing.

Transracial

France's colonial past ensured that it would have an early introduction to transracial adoption. Children from Vietnam, Mali, Burkina Faso, Haiti and other countries to which France had strong ties have for many decades found their way into the French adoption process and given it a strong transracial dimension.

Childcare adoption

Responsibility for childcare and protection rests with the local Child Welfare authority, or Aide Sociale à l'Enfance (ASE). In recent years this government agency has seen an increase in the number of court orders relating to child protection issues but a decrease in adoptions. In order to cope with the greater numbers in the public childcare system it has invested in more small residential

16 *Odièvre* v. *France*.

17 Verdier, P., *L'enfant en miettes*, Toulouse, Edouard Privat, 1986 and Observatoire National de L'Enfance en Danger, *La situation des pupilles de l'État:* Observatoire National de L'Enfance en Danger, *La situation des pupilles de l'État, synthèse de l'enquête au 31 décembre 2015.*

18 Halifax, J., 'Why are there so many international adoptions in France?', at: www.uea.ac.uk/swp/icar2/pdf's/Halifax99.pdf

units and has increased its diversity of services and programmes with trained professionals and multidisciplinary teams offering support to foster carers.

In 2010 the French childcare population was 273,000 or some 1.9 per cent of all children, a dramatic increase in the 20-year period since 1990 when the figures were 112,800 and 0.8 per cent respectively and high compared to other western European countries.[19] In practice, only a fraction of the total childcare population ever becomes available for adoption: in 2012 some 731 were adopted from the public childcare system[20] compared with 3,450 in England;[21] most are much more likely to spend their childhood in long-term foster care or in an institution.

'Wards of the state' (pupille de l'État)[22]

This collective term is used in respect of those children who: are otherwise without legal status, because of a lack of filiation, being *né sous X*, or have been abandoned;[23] are orphans without family guardianship; or have been removed by court order from their parents who have been stripped of parental rights. The State, as carer of last resort, assumes total parental rights and duties in respect of all such children. In two-thirds of cases, the local Child Welfare Service assumes care responsibility for the child, following rejection by – or death of – their birth parents. Falling from 24,000 in 1977 to 7,600 in 1987, the number of wards of the state had stabilised at approximately 3,300 in 1997 but had declined further to 2,347 by 31 December 2010.

Although it's a legal requirement that a ward of the state must be promptly placed for adoption, this is not always achieved.[24] By the end of 2003, out of 2,882 such wards (average age 2 years and 10 months), only 1,009 had been placed for adoption and by 2010 this was true for about one-third, a proportion that had been stable for several years.[25]

19 Compared with: the Netherlands, 0.24 per cent; Austria, 0.5 per cent; Portugal, 0.6 per cent; and Luxembourg, 0.7 per cent.

20 Observatoire National de l'Enfance en Danger, 2007–13.

21 Department for Education, 2013.

22 Not to be confused with *pupilles de la nation* who are the children of a parent killed or severely wounded while defending the nation and who are not taken into care, but remain at home, usually with their mothers. See, further, Mergnac, M.-O., *Orphelins et Pupilles de la Nation*, Guides de généalogie, 2016.

23 An 'abandoned child', under Article 350 of the French Civil Code, is one who has been in the care of a private person, or an institution or the child welfare service for a full year during which the parents have shown no interest in him or her. At the end of that period the court may issue a declaration of abandonment, unless the parents are in 'great distress', and vest full parental rights in the carers.

24 Article L 225-1 of the Code de l'action sociale et des familles.

25 ONED reports show that 757 children were adopted in 2010 as opposed to 714 in 2009. These children were very young (77 per cent less than 1 year old) and were adopted through para. 1 of article L.224-4 of the CASF (73 per cent) and by a *département*-registered family (84 per cent).

Foster care

There is a strong traditional preference for relying on long-term foster care as a more appropriate option than adoption for furthering the welfare interests of a child in care. In special circumstances, a non-parent (e.g. a foster parent, grand-parent or other relative) can apply to the *juge des tutelles* (guardianship court) for a *tutelle* order (guardianship).

Foster parent adoption

Wards of the state 'fostered with a view to adoption' are children fostered with a family approved for adoption or for whom the foster family has submitted an adoption application. They must share the home of their future adoptive parents for at least six months before the plenary adoption decision.[26]

That the adoption of children from the public care system is not a general policy objective is reflected in the fact that in 2011 of the 273,000 children in care only 2,350 were adopted. A clear distinction is drawn between filiation (biological or adoptive relationships) and child protection: the latter is focused on disposal options that aim to support families in need; by means of education, control and assistance measures, that enable parents to retain and protect their children.

Family adoption

The use of adoption by a parent or relative of a child in order to legally consolidate a reformed family unit, is well established in France. Article 345–1 of the Civil Code provides for the plenary adoption of a child by the spouse of the child's parent while Article 360 provides for the simple adoption of a child by the parent's spouse. Leaving aside step-parent adoptions, most adoptions by relatives are simple rather than plenary in nature.[27]

Step-parent adoptions

A large proportion of annual adoptions have been by step-parents; and these have largely been simple adoptions undertaken for inheritance reasons.[28] The applicant step-parent must be married to the birth parent of the child to be adopted.[29] Same sex step-adoptions, where one person for example adopts the child of their divorced lesbian partner, have been possible since the decision in *E. B.* v. *France*[30] (see below). The Loi Famille 2014 introduced provisions giving step-parents

26 Article 345 of the French Civil Code.
27 Robcis, C., *The Law of Kinship: Anthropology, Psychoanalysis and the Family in France*, Cornell University Press, 2013.
28 Mignot, J.-F., 'Simple adoption in France: revival of an old institution (1804–2007)', *Revue française de sociologie English edition*, 56(3): 525–60.
29 Art. 343 of Civil Code. The law is to be amended.
30 Application No. 43546/02, 25.01.08.

recognition as persons entitled to hold a level of parental rights and intended to obviate the need for adoption. So, a child's parents could sign a *mandat d'éducation* giving a step-parent the right to undertake 'daily tasks' in respect of the child.

ICA

The worldwide contraction in ICA has also affected France and, in common with other countries, the range of children now being adopted by this means is changing to accommodate a higher proportion of children who are older and/or have health or social care needs.

For some years France has had a high ICA dependency, being second only to the US in the number of foreign children adopted: mostly coming from countries that had not ratified the Hague Convention; in 2003, 90 per cent of all adoptions were intercountry, falling to 72 per cent in 2008.[31] At the turn of the century the high numbers of annual ICAs, averaging 3,200–4,000 during the period 1998–2010, were largely drawn from Vietnam[32] and Haiti. In 2006, for example, France concluded an accord with Cambodia, where standards of practice are particularly susceptible to abuse, a matter which has long been of concern to the CRC[33] and continues to be so. Moreover, a high percentage of ICAs are not made through accredited bodies but through individual channels, which accounts for the sustained level of annual adoptions and for the low age range of children being adopted. By 2011, however, total ICAs had fallen to 1,995 and continued to fall annually thereafter: falling, in fact, by 67 per cent between 2004 and 2013; though still constituting the highest proportion of annual adoptions. In 2015 there were only 815 adoptions of children born abroad. In its 2015 report, INED (French National Institute of Demographic Research) concluded that 'the decline in adoptions is not without consequence in a country such as France: we can anticipate an increase in requests for medically assisted reproduction and gestational surrogacy'.[34]

Adoption related issues in human rights reports

The UN CRC, in its 2015 report, noted the existence of 'information indicating that 80 per cent of children are placed into care by the child welfare services on account of their parents being poor' and 'recommended that France: avoid the placement of children in alternative care as a result of low parental income'.[35] It

31 www.europarl.europa.eu/RegData/etudes/BRIE/2016/583860/EPRS_BRI(2016)583860_EN.pdf
32 In 1998, a total of 1,343 children were adopted from Vietnam, falling to 469 in 2010 (source: Selman, *Adoption Advocate* No. 44: Global Trends in Intercountry Adoption: 2001–10).
33 CRC, *Concluding Observations*, para. 33.
34 Mignot, J.-F., 'Why is intercountry adoption declining worldwide?', *Population and Societies*, 519 (2015): 1–4.
35 UN Human Rights Council, *Compilation: [Universal Periodic Review]* A/HRC/WG.6/15/FRA/2, para. 37.

also requested information as to 'what measures have been taken to ensure the right of all children to be properly informed, to express their views and to have them taken into account in decisions regarding their placement into out-of-home care'.[36] Furthermore, the Committee of Experts raised issues concerning the adoption of children from countries not parties to the Hague Convention on the Protection of Children and Cooperation in Respect of Intercountry Adoption. This is a long-standing issue of concern which continues in seriousness if not in scale as the number of children involved shrinks.

Human Rights Watch has criticised the French authorities for their policy towards unaccompanied migrant children noting that 'some are unable to access services or receive protection as guaranteed by the law'. In 2014 it reported that France was detaining up to 500 unaccompanied children each year in transit zones at the borders, where they were being denied the protection and due process rights afforded other unaccompanied children on French territory.[37] Presumably, the legal security and protection that access to the adoption process would offer is among the services denied.[38]

The current legislative framework

The legislation: adoption related law; domestic

The present adoption system, first introduced in the 1804 Civil Code has since been subject to periodic reviews and updating. Currently the statutes (66–500 of 11 July 1966, as amended) and Part VIII of the Civil Code ('Of Adoption') constitute the primary legal framework for adoption in France. In particular: Articles 343 to 359 deal with plenary adoption, Article 345–1 provides for the plenary adoption of a child by the spouse of the child's parent; while Articles 360 to 370–2 deal with simple adoption, Article 360 provides for the simple adoption of a child by the parent's spouse.

Statute n° 2007-308 of 5 March 2007

This statute, amending Article 388-1 of the Civil Code, provides that 'the discerning child has the right to express his/her view in any judicial proceeding that concerns him/her (e.g. in an adoption process). The hearing of the child (always in private) cannot be refused by a judge where this hearing is at the child's request.' As Francoz-Terminal comments, this was 'a reform that greatly strengthened the right of a child to be heard and to express his/her views before a judge'.[39]

36 CRC, 71st session, CRC/C/FRA/Q/5, *List of Issues in Relation to The Fifth Periodic Report of France* (23 July 2015), para. 10.
37 www.hrw.org/news/2015/01/20/france-migrants-asylum-seekers-abused-and-destitute
38 www.hrw.org/news/2017/06/29/submission-universal-periodic-review-france
39 Note to author (20.12.2013).

Statute n° 2005-744 of 4 July 2005

This statute introduced some technical reforms. It aimed to improve the adoption process by harmonising the approval process across the country (the administrative procedure, at the end of which the candidate is 'assented' to adopt, managed by local authorities – the Conseils généraux). The reform also aimed to improve the support to adopters, especially those engaged in ICA, and created the Agence Française de l'adoption[40] to assist such adopters. It strengthens the assistance and support given to adopters, once children have been entrusted to their care, by introducing mandatory post-adoption service provision to be delivered either by the adoption service of the local authority or by the Agence Française de l'adoption.[41]

Statute n° 2002-304 of 4 March 2002

This statute introduced provisions concerning parental authority.

Statute n° 2002-93 of 22 February 2002

This statute granted former adoptees and wards of the state the right to access their records. It also created a new commission, the Conseil national pour l'accès aux origines personnelles (CNAOP), to mediate between the interests of adopters, adoptees and birth parents.

Statute n° 2001-1135 of 3 December 2001

This law abolished any distinction in adoption procedure based on the type of filiation: whenever filiation has been established, father and mother must consent to the adoption. The rights of all children, legitimate, natural or adopted, have since been identical in respect of: the rights of the surviving spouse and of children born out of wedlock; all discrimination against children born out of wedlock was abolished in respect of inheritance.

Statute n° 2004-111 of 6 February 2001

This statute introduced provisions relating to ICA.

Statute n° 98-771 of 1 September 1998

This statute establishes the arrangements for appraising applications for authorisation to adopt a child in State care (Articles 1, 4 and 5).

40 www.agence-adoption.fr/home

41 An alternative view of the impact of this law has been expressed by Terre des Hommes which asserts that: 'since the passing of a law on 4 July 2005, the involvement of the French Central Authority in "strictly private" adoptions with non-contracting states has noticeably diminished. The situation is therefore highly alarming' (Lammerant, I. and Hofsetter, M. (eds), *Adoption: At What Cost?*, Lausanne, Terre des Hommes, 2007, p. 12).

Statute n° 96-604 of 5 July 1996

This statute (the MATTEI Act) makes adoption easier by relaxing certain restrictions and simplifying administrative procedures, for example by reducing the time limit for withdrawing consent from three to two months.

Statute n° 93-22 of 8 January 1993

This statute removed obstacles, in existence since the Napoleonic Code, to bring proceedings alleging paternity in respect of a child 'born out of wedlock' but left a plaintiff with a heavy burden of proof. It also states that an application for disclosure of details identifying the natural mother is inadmissible if confidentiality was agreed at birth.

Statute n° 66-500 of 11 July 1966

This statute introduced the two legal forms of adoption that now exist in France: plenary adoption which severs the links between the child and its birth family and creates a new set of parental relationships; and ordinary (or 'simple') adoption which institutes a second set of relationships with the adopting parent/s without severing the links with the family of origin. Whereas previously *legitimation adoptive* was restricted to two non-separated spouses, *adoption plénière* was now available to an unmarried person. Moreover, consensual adoption for both 'legitimate' and 'illegitimate' children was introduced for circumstances where both mother and father have given their consent. The presence of 'legitimate' children in the prospective adopter/s family was no longer a bar to adoption.

Other relevant provisions

The Loi Famille 2014 gives recognition to the role of step-parents for the first time and makes provision for that role to be vested with a degree of parental responsibility.

The legislation: adoption related law; international

France is a signatory of all major international treaties, conventions, protocols, etc. including: the UN Convention on the Rights of the Child and its three Optional Protocols; and The Hague Convention on Protection of Children and Cooperation in Respect of Intercountry Adoption 1993.[42] It has signed but not ratified the European Convention on the Adoption of Children which came into force on 24 April 1968 (see Chapter 3).

42 Signed on 5 April 1995 and ratified on 30 June 1998.

The legislation: human rights law

France, of course, has the distinction of being the nation that established the founding proclamation of human rights – the Declaration of the Rights of Man and of the Citizen in 1789 – which subsequently inspired not dissimilar documents in many countries. Currently, the cornerstone of its domestic human rights provisions is the Preamble to the Constitution of the French Fifth Republic. This is supplemented by the provisions of many major international human rights conventions, etc. including the Universal Declaration of Human Rights (UDHR) and the Charter of Human Rights of the European Union (see Chapter 3).

Regulating the adoption process

The adoption process in France, being essentially consensual in nature and catering for both simple and plenary adoption orders, in domestic and intercountry proceedings, is subject to a lighter regulatory regime than is applied in most modern common law countries. The process requires two successive steps: an administrative procedure, which leads to the grant of an assent (*agrément*), and then a judicial procedure leading to the adoption order. The Head of the District Council (President du Conseil General du département), an elected local authority, together with his internal agents, in particular the Childhood Welfare Service (ASE – Aide Sociale à l'Enfance) and the Assent Commission (Commission d'agrément) are the lead government regulators of the administrative stage of the process. Also, as noted in the 2015 CRC report, France has expanded the mandate and the means of the Office of the Ombudsmen so that it can address children's issues.[43] The French National Consultative Commission on Human Rights may also be relevant.

The judiciary

Adoption in France, although including a significant administrative component, is essentially a judicial process. It falls ultimately to the District Court (Tribunal de Grande Instance) to either grant or refuse the adoption order sought, and this is also the body responsible for overseeing all international adoptions.[44] The Cour de Cassation, France's highest court, is the final court of appeal for difficult points of law.

Government bodies

The Child Welfare Service plays a pivotal role in the French adoption process. The 'assent' of that agency has been compulsory for adopting a ward of the state since the statute of 6 June 1984, and for adopting a foreign child since that of 5 July

43 CRC considered report of France (14 January 2016), at: www.ohchr.org/EN/NewsEvents/Pages/DisplayNews.aspx?NewsID=16950&LangID=E

44 Statute n° 2009-526 of 12 May 2009.

1996 (Article 11.-I). This 'assent' process has since been harmonised throughout the country by Statute n° 2005-744 of 4 July 2005 and ancillary statutory instruments.[45] Assent or refusal to assent must be communicated within nine months after the initial request from the applicant.[46] Once granted, the assent remains valid for five years, but adopters must confirm their application each year to the adoption service of the Child Welfare Service (ASE).[47]

The National Council for Access to Personal Origins (CNAOP) was established in 2002 by a statute that also granted former adoptees and wards of the state the right to access their records and discover the names of their parents, relatives and their medical conditions.[48] The role of the agency is to mediate between the interests of adults who wish to know their origins, those of pregnant women wishing to maintain their anonymity, and those of children who have the need to access the information necessary to form an authentic sense of personal and cultural identity.

The Mission de l'Adoption Internationale, located within the French Ministry of Foreign Affairs, was established in order to coordinate the process of international adoption. It acts as a central authority for Hague purposes and is responsible for authorising and supervising ICA agencies.

Adoption agencies

Government policy in respect of adoption is the joint responsibility of the Foreign Affairs Department and the Family Department (attached to the Department of Health and Social Care) with the Conseil interministériel pour l'adoption holding responsibility for coordinating the roles of government bodies. The relevant government bodies are the Conseil supérieur de l'adoption, the Agence Française de l'adoption (created by the Act 2005-744 of 4 July 2005) local authorities (Conseil généraux) and the authorised adoption agencies. Adoption must be undertaken through an accredited and registered body. Most usually this means the Aide sociale service – in relation to a ward of the state or a foreign child – which being a public body does not charge fees. There are private agencies like Famille adoptive française or Les Nids de Paris which operate largely but not exclusively on an intercountry basis and are entitled to charge for expenses. Other foreign adoption agencies, such as those based in the US, may offer services to French citizens but do so on a strictly commercial basis.

Registration of adoption orders

For an adoption order to be recognised and for the adopted child to acquire French nationality an application must be filed with a Tribunal de Grande Instance de France.

45 Decree n° 2006-981 of 1 August 2006 and n° 2006-1272 of 17 October 2006. The legal provisions have been integrated to art. R225-1 to R225-11 of the Social Welfare and Family Code.

46 See art. L225-2 of the Social Welfare and Family Code.

47 Ibid., art. R225-7.

48 Loi n° 2002-93 du 22 janvier 2002 relative à l'accès aux origines des personnes adoptées et pupilles de l'État.

Human rights considerations

Regulating ICA

There are grounds for concern regarding the number of private commercial agencies involved in ICA activity. Terre des Hommes has asserted that there seems to be an official acceptance of private adoptions and a lack of effective regulatory control.[49] It points out that there is no legal requirement that French prospective adopters pursue their application through an accredited body, they may instead do so privately and most choose that option: Terre des Hommes estimate that in France 'private adoptions constitute two-thirds of intercountry adoptions'.[50] Agence Française de l'adoption (created by the Act 2005-744 of 4 July 2005) as lead government body in relation to ICA would seem to be functioning more as a facilitator for private adoptions, than as an impartial regulator, in countries that are non-Hague compliant. However, as Jean-François Mignot points out, the situation has changed over the past decade as by 2015 'only' 25 per cent of ICAs to France were realised privately.[51] Nonetheless, this would seem to suggest that the standards intended to be applied by Hague are being subverted.

Thresholds for entering the adoption process: eligibility, suitability and placement

Role of adoption agency

Normally, the parent/s relinquish their child to an approved adoption agency which will then take full responsibility for placement selection.

Pre-placement counselling

There is no explicit statutory obligation resting on any specific agency to provide a pre-placement counselling service to the birth parent/s but as a matter of good practice, in relation to domestic proceedings for plenary adoptions, this would be undertaken by the Child Welfare Service.

Eligibility and suitability of the parties

The child

Children eligible for adoption are those who are either: wards of the state, with administrative consent of the appropriate authorities; the subject of a judicial declaration of abandonment; or whose birth parents have given their consent. In the case of an *adoption plénière* the child must also in principle: be under 15 years

49 Lammerant and Hofsetter, *Adoption*, pp. 12–13.
50 Ibid., p. 26.
51 Note to author (19.10.17).

of age (up to 20 years in certain cases); and have lived for at least six months in the adopter's home.

The birth parent/s

The French adoption process continues to permit the birth parent/s to relinquish their child anonymously, i.e. without any accompanying information.[52] However, in January 2002 this right was modified by the introduction of a law allowing mothers who have a baby in secret to place their name in a sealed envelope thus leaving open the possibility to decide later in life if they wish to know their mother's identity (and thus possibly to contact or meet her).

The birth parent/s and rehabilitation

Before a ruling is made, under Article L224-4 of Social Welfare and Family Code, that a child may be placed for adoption – the parent/s having been stripped of all parental responsibility following their conviction (for criminal abuse, neglect or failure to protect) – rehabilitation to care in the family of origin must be attempted. An agreed plan or *projet pour l'enfant* will be drawn up between authorities and the parent/s allowing for all options to be explored and tested. This may take the form of a *placement a domicile* (permitted under the policy of *service d'adaptation progressive en milieu naturel*) where essentially a child is returned home as part of an intensive professional investment designed to improve parenting skills, or a supervised parent and child residential placement, an *accueil sequentiel*, which allows for a time-share arrangement between family home and a specialised training unit. The adoption of a child in circumstances of failed parental care is viewed very much as a last resort because of the resulting filiation implications.

The adopters

Article 343 of the Civil Code states that:

> Adoption may be applied for by a married couple who have not been judicially separated and have been married for more than two years or are both over twenty-eight years of age.

There is no upper age limit nor is there a required maximum age difference between adopter and adoptee. Third party adopters must be not less than 15 years older than the child whom they propose to adopt.[53] There are no requirements regarding race or religion. The suitability of the prospective adopters is assessed by the Child Welfare Service in accordance with the usual criteria relating to

52 *Odièvre* v. *France*.
53 Articles 344 of the French Civil Code.

psychological, financial, social, educational and family situation.[54] A married person may apply alone. If not judicially separated, however, then his or her spouse's consent is required unless incapable of expressing their intentions.[55] An unmarried couple cannot make a joint application;[56] only one of the partners can be the child's adoptive parent. Where the applicant is a single person, he or she must be over 28 (though in practice getting approval from the Child Welfare Service can be difficult).[57]

Where both spouses are applying to adopt the child of one of them, then: there is no age limit nor any requirements regarding duration of marriage;[58] there must be an age difference of ten years between adopter/s and the child concerned[59] other than in exceptional circumstances;[60] In step-adoptions, a plenary adoption is permitted only if the child has a legally established filiation exclusively with the applicant spouse;[61] if the parent other than the spouse has been completely deprived of parental authority; or if the parent other than the spouse is dead and has left no first degree relatives, or if these have obviously lost interest in the child.[62]

LGBT adopters

Statute n° 2013-404 of 17 May 2013 legalised same-sex marriage and provided parity of legal status with heterosexual marriage.[63] Consequently gay couples now have the right to adopt a child and either spouse can adopt the child (either biological or adoptive) of his/her spouse. Moreover, as stated by the Cour de Cassation, France's top civil court,[64] French law allows 'by adoption, the establishment of a family link between a child and two people of the same sex, without any restriction relative to the mode of conception of the child'. However, the wording of this ruling simplifies the difficulties that have arisen for many French gay couples who, over the past ten years or so, have been caught in a grey area where the laws of adoption and surrogacy intersect. The main problem being that as surrogacy is illegal in France, such couples have entered into surrogacy arrangements overseas and then sought to adopt the child in France with

54 See new art. R225-3 of the Social Welfare and Family Code as amended by the Decree n° 2006-981 of 1 August 2006.
55 Articles 343 and 343-1 of the French Civil Code.
56 Ibid., Article 346.
57 Ibid., Articles 343-1, 343-2 and 343.
58 Ibid., Article 343-2.
59 Ibid., Article 344.
60 Ibid., Article 344.
61 Ibid., Article 435-1 bis of the Civil code as amended by the Statute n° 2012-404 of 17 May 2013 added a new category, viz.: where the child has been adopted as a single person exclusively by the said spouse.
62 Ibid., Article 345-1.
63 Following the ruling of the ECtHR in *E. B.* v. *France*, Application No. 43546/02, 22 January 2008.
64 Ruling (23 September 2014).

consequent problems arising in relation to the eligibility of the non-biological parent applicant and as regards the citizenship of the child.

Placement with consent

Except in the case of a family adoption, prospective adopters must have consent from the Department of Social Welfare for Children (ASE), under the authority of the President of the General Council of their administrative department. Once such consent has been obtained, they must file an application to adopt the child (whether full or simple) at the regional court of the place in which they live. The decision is recorded in the civil status register in the child's place of birth and is mentioned in the family record book (*livret de famille*). A birth parent's consent may be in respect of a child of any age: it can be revoked within two months, or up to one year if both have parental responsibility; at the end of the revocation period the child is declared a ward of the state and is thereafter adoptable.

Placement by the birth parent/s

In compliance with Article 29 of Hague, French adoption law prohibits a birth parent from making, or arranging for others to make, an adoption placement of their child with a person chosen by the parent.

Placement without consent

A child is defined as 'abandoned' if the whereabouts of the birth parents is unknown and they have had no contact with their child for a full year. A court order then strips the parents of all rights and an adoption placement can then be made without any need for parental consent. Consent to adoption is never required from a woman who has given birth anonymously under the '*accouchement sous X*' process as legally she's no longer recognised as the mother. In such circumstances the consent to place for adoption is given by the appropriate State authority. Such a placement, by virtue of the provisions of Article 352 of the Civil Code, constitutes a bar not only to the return of the child to the mother but also to any declaration of filiation or recognition.

Welfare interests

Of all the possible categories of children who may be eligible for adoption it is really only those who fall within the ambit of Article L224-4 of the Social Welfare and Family Code for whom their welfare is a positive influence at the placement stage. Only for that very small minority, who have been abandoned or so abused by their parents that the latter have been judicially stripped of their right to custody, can it be said that a breach of the welfare threshold is the trigger for their entering the adoption process. For all others, welfare is a default factor or one that comes into play later.

Placement supervision

The child is usually placed with his or her prospective third party adopter/s two months after consent has been given on a trial basis – the *placement en vue d'adoption*. If, after the expiry of that period, consent has not been withdrawn, the placement then becomes one for adoption[65] which precludes any restitution of the child to their family of origin.[66] Where the intending adopter/s are related to the child and the latter is at least 2 years of age, then application to the court usually follows directly after acquiring parental consent (i.e. without an intervening supervised placement).[67]

The placement is monitored by the Child Welfare Service from the child's arrival until the adoption application is determined. The 2005 statute strengthened the requirement to safeguard the welfare of the child and assess the progress of the placement: there is now a mandatory post-placement assessment and support process to be undertaken by either ASE or by the French Adoption Agency (Agence française de l'adoption);[68] the prospective adopters are required to lodge an application within 6 months of the child being placed.

Human rights considerations

Welfare interests at time of placement

The fact that the welfare interests of the child are not professionally assessed by the ASE prior to a family placement is a weakness. The implication that the welfare of such a child requires less attention from the State than one placed by an adoption agency may amount to a form of discriminatory treatment.

Surrogate LGBT parents and legal status of the parties

French law regards surrogacy agreements as null and void,[69] although a series of rulings by the Cour de Cassation[70] has gradually ironed out specific legal inequities relating to LGBT couples returning to France with children conceived through overseas surrogate arrangements and seeking to use adoption as a means of establishing a legal framework for their new families. However, French law continues to permit a distinction to be made between the status of biological and non-biological surrogate parents. This was apparent in a 2017 ruling by the Cour de Cassation which refused a request that French authorities automatically

65 Article 348-3 of French Civil Code.
66 Ibid., Article 352.
67 Ibid., Article 347.
68 Statute n° 2005-744 of 4 July 2005.
69 Articles 16–7 of the French Civil Code.
70 Civ. 1st, 17 December 2007, n° 07-20.468; Civ. 1st, 6 April 2011, n° 09-17.130, n° 10-19.053, n° 09-66.486 and confirmed afterwards (Civ. 1st, 13 September 2013, n° 12-18.315 and n° 12-30.138; Civ. 1st, 19 March 2014, n° 13-50.005).

recognise the two parents listed on the foreign birth certificate but permitted the father's partner to apply to adopt the child; probably meaning simple adoption. While this allows children born to surrogate mothers to establish filiation with both commissioning parents, it legally differentiates between the parents which may compromise the child's right, under Article 8 of the ECHR, to family life.

An unmarried cohabiting prospective adopter

Given the fact that a large proportion of French families are non-marital, the prohibition on joint adoption applications from a cohabiting couple would seem discriminatory. As the law restricts the right to adopt to only one of the partners it raises questions regarding the parental rights and responsibilities of the other. Arguably, the net result is that an adopted child in that situation is disadvantaged relative to a child of married parents, which again raises issues of discrimination.

Child's right to a family

A considerable proportion of children admitted to the public care system will spend their childhood in a residential unit, due to a lack of foster parents and a policy of not prioritising adoption from care. This itself is clearly a concern but is made more so by the fact that France is also one of the few European countries with a high proportion of children aged less than 4 in its childcare population.[71] The correlation between a high incidence of young children in residential care and a high level of recourse to ICA may indicate an unaddressed policy issue in respect of the needs of the former group for permanent family-based care. Contrary to Article 8 of the ECHR, very many young abused or neglected children are being denied an opportunity to form the secure and durable emotional attachments that life in a permanent family home would offer.

Non-adoptable Muslim children

The fact that the Civil Code prevents a child from entering the adoption process if adoption is prohibited by law of his or her country of origin, must adversely affect the very many orphans and unaccompanied children who arrived in France from such predominantly Islamic countries as Libya, Syria and Iraq during the 2015–17 migrant crisis.

The hearing and the grounds

The hearing is held in the local district court. If the request is for plenary adoption, the court can examine the request only after a six-month placement period.[72]

71 Chou, S. and Browne, K., 'The relationship between institutional care and the international adoption of children in Europe', *Adoption & Fostering*, 32(1) (2008): 40–8, 45–6.

72 Articles 348-3 of the French Civil Code.

Where consent is available

The majority of adoption applications are third party – relating to ICAs, '*né sous X*' and wards of the state – and are almost invariably consensual. Whether married or not, both birth parents share parental responsibilities and both must give their consent to adoption. Where one is dead, unable to give consent or has lost parental rights, the consent of the other is sufficient. Where both have died without leaving any instructions, or both have lost parental rights, then consent is given by the family council (*conseil de famille*) after consultation with the person with actual care responsibility for the child. Birth parents may retract consent within two months.[73]

Consent of unmarried father

Where the identity and whereabouts of the unmarried father are known, his consent is required unless grounds exist for it to be dispensed with. However, this is only the case where filiation is established: the consent of a putative father, without any legal link to the child in question, is neither required nor sought.

Consent of a minor

For both simple and plenary adoption the personal consent of the child concerned is also required if he or she is aged 13 years or older;[74] validity is not conditional upon the child having sufficient understanding.[75] Retraction of consent is not permitted.

Where consent is not available

Where a child is a ward of the state or is otherwise in the public care system and the parents have not consented then this is provided by the family council responsible for the child. No consent is needed for the adoption of children whom the courts declare to have been abandoned.[76]

Childcare adoption: the grounds

The court may grant an adoption order if it determines that consent has been unjustifiably, or abusively, refused by one or both of the birth parents, or if they are disinterested in the child or if they are at risk of endangering the child's health or morality.[77]

73 Ibid. See, also, *Kearns* v. *France*.
74 Article 348-3 of the French Civil Code as amended by Statute n° 2010-1609 of 22 December 2010.
75 Ibid., Articles 345 and 360.
76 Ibid., Article 350.
77 Ibid., Article 348-6.

Contested family adoption: the grounds

Again, if the court determines that consent has been unjustifiably, or abusively, refused by a birth parent, or that a parent is disinterested in the child or is at risk of endangering the child's health or morality then this would provide sufficient grounds for granting an adoption order.[78]

Human rights considerations

Paternal rights and a child 'né sous X'

Clearly, a maternal decision to veto disclosure of any information regarding the child she decides to relinquish for adoption, wholly extinguishes all possibility of the father exercising his rights in respect of that child. In particular, it nullifies any right he may have to give or withhold his consent to the adoption. This gender-specific discretionary power is discriminatory and seriously compromises the paternal right to family life. Jean-François Mignot adds the following important comment:[79]

> As far as I know this is a matter of fact, not of law. A birth-giving woman has no legal right to prevent the father from taking care of their child; she may have the material possibility, but not the right. So, if the father knows where she gave birth and he can find his child quickly, he can definitely establish a filiation link with it and raise it as its own child, even without the mother.

The fact remains, however, that the frequently exercised maternal veto does foreclose the rights of others.

Minor's retraction of consent

As the consent of a minor, aged 13 or more, is treated equally in law as that of other parties to an adoption it would seem at least incongruous and possibly discriminatory to deny the minor a correspondingly equal right to retract that consent.

Thresholds for exiting the adoption process

In France there is no right to adopt or to be adopted, nor any general right to start a family.[80] This gives rise to a cautious judicial approach towards adoption.

78 Ibid., Article 348-6.
79 Note to author (19.10.17).
80 See Beignier, B., 'Freedom to conceive a child', *Dr. fam.* 3 (2004): 4, for an argument that procreation is not merely a right but a freedom.

The welfare interests of the child

An adoption order will only be granted if the District Court finds that 'the conditions offered at the family, educational and psychological levels correspond to the needs and best interests of the child'.[81] In *Harroudj* v. *France*[82] it was unable to make such a finding. This case concerned the refusal of permission for a French national to adopt an Algerian baby girl already in her care under *kafala* (see Chapter 1). The court held that there had been no violation of Article 8 of the Convention. It found that a fair balance had been struck between the public interest and that of the applicant, the authorities having sought, with due regard for cultural pluralism, to encourage the integration of *kafala* children without immediately severing the ties with the laws of their country of origin. It would seem that the ruling was essentially to the effect that a legal equivalence existed between *kafala* and simple adoption which did not leave the Islamic child deprived of any rights. That being the case, *kafala* had a sufficient degree of recognition in French law to make a transition to full adoption unnecessary.

Surrogacy, often followed by adoption, also gives rise to difficulties. *Mennesson and Others* v. *France* and *Labassee* v. *France*,[83] for example, concerned the refusal to grant legal recognition in France to parent–child relationships that had been legally established in the US between children born as a result of surrogacy. In both cases the ECtHR held that while there had been no violation of Article 8 in respect of the applicants there had been such a violation concerning the children's right to respect for their private life. The court observed that the French authorities, despite being aware that the children had been identified in the US as the children of Mr and Mrs Mennesson and Mr and Mrs Labassee, had nevertheless denied them that status under French law. It considered that this contradiction undermined the children's identity within French society. It further noted that the case law completely precluded the establishment of a legal relationship between children born as a result of lawful surrogacy treatment abroad and their biological father which overstepped the wide margin of appreciation left to States regarding decisions relating to surrogacy.

Paramountcy

There is no suggestion in the Civil Code or related statutes that the welfare interests of the child concerned are to be accorded a paramount legal weighting in adoption proceedings.

81 Article R225-4 of the Social Welfare and Family Code.
82 Application No. 43631/09, 2012.
83 Application Nos 65192/11 and 65941/11, 2014; see also *Foulon and Bouvet* v. *France*, Application Nos 9063/14 and 10410/14, 2016; *Laborie* v. *France*, Application No. 44024/13, 2017.

Consent/views of child and welfare interests

Article 388-1 of the Civil Code states that where a child requests to be heard then this request must be granted.[84] As mentioned earlier, in both forms of adoption the consent of the child is required if he or she is aged 13 years or older.[85]

Culturally compatible

The fact that most adoptions in France have been intercountry suggests that cultural compatibility has not been a prominent consideration.

The orders available

The outcome of an adoption application will most usually take the form of a granting or refusal of an adoption order. An appeal may be lodged within 15 days by the applicant, the Procureur de la République, or by any third party who was notified of the decision.

Plenary adoption order

A full or plenary adoption order is most usual. It may be granted to a birth parent following the death of their unmarried partner, who was the other birth parent of the child concerned, but only if the deceased leaves no first-degree relatives (e.g. grandparents) or if these have clearly taken no interest in the child.[86]

Simple adoption order

Where the subject is the birth child of a spouse then the other spouse, as applicant, is only eligible for a simple adoption order during the lifetime of their spouse.

Additional orders: post-adoption contact

There is no suite of additional or alternative orders available to the court. Should post-adoption contact be indicated, then this would suggest that simple adoption would be appropriate.

Alternative orders

In response to an application for a plenary adoption, the court is entitled to make an order for simple adoption. In special circumstances, a carer (e.g. a foster parent,

84 The author gratefully acknowledges the advice of Laurence Francoz-Terminal on this matter.
85 Article 348-3 of the French Civil Code as amended by Statute n° 2010-1609 of 22 December 2010.
86 Article 345-1 of the French Civil Code.

grandparent or other relative) can apply to the *juge des tutelles* (guardianship court) for a *tutelle* order (guardianship).

Human rights considerations

Non-recognition of foreign orders

The case law illustrates that by refusing to recognise the legal status granted by foreign courts, to the parties involved in surrogacy arrangements, the French courts are violating the human rights of the children concerned.

Kafala *may be discriminatory in a Civil Code context*

It would seem right that access to plenary and simple forms of adoption should be available to any French citizen able to satisfy the necessary eligibility and suitability criteria. *Kafala* as a forced default option would seem discriminatory and therefore non-compliant with Article 2 of UNCROC.

The effect of an adoption order

The effects of an adoption order are as stated in Articles 370 to 375 of the French Civil Code and depend entirely on whether it is simple or plenary.

Effect on the parties

The child

Plenary adoption confers on the child a filiation with their adopters that substitutes for their original filiation. The adopted child assumes the same relationship as a child born to the adopter/s. Any legal bond with the original family is extinguished. The adopted child automatically assumes the surname and nationality of the adopter/s. The child loses all inheritance rights in respect of their birth parents and instead acquires the same such rights in respect of their adopters as a marital child.

In simple adoption, the adopted child becomes a member of their new family but retains most legal ties to their family of origin: he or she keeps their original family name and some other legal bonds; does not automatically acquire the adopters nationality; and is legally prohibited from marrying any ascendants or relatives of the adopters.[87] Also, the adoptee retains their inheritance rights in relation to their family of origin; the simple adoptee (and their children and step-children) can inherit from both families; but the adoptee cannot inherit from the parents of the adoptive parents.[88] While the adoption gives rise to a maintenance obligation (*obligation alimentaire*) between the adoptee and adoptive parent, it

87 Ibid., Article 366.
88 Ibid., Article 368.

does not completely extinguish that which lies between the adoptee and their birth parents. If the adoptee dies and leaves successors, rights of inheritance are determined by common law. If not, the inheritance is divided, half going to the birth family and half to the adoptive family.

The birth parent/s

The effect of a plenary adoption order is that birth parents lose all parental rights in respect of their child and are freed from all duties. All such rights and duties are transferred to the adopter/s. A simple adoption order does not irrevocably extinguish all legal ties. For example, birth parents remain bound by their duty to maintain the adoptee (the *obligation alimentaire*) but in practice this can only be activated if the adoptee first establishes that he or she could not obtain such maintenance from their adoptive parents

The adopters

In simple adoption, the adopters are vested with parental rights and responsibilities including a maintenance obligation (*obligation alimentaire*) in respect of the adoptee.

When the child is adopted, by the cohabitee or registered partner of the birth parent, who has custody, then the latter loses parental authority over the child, which results in the present judicial approach of refusing to order a simple adoption in relation to the child of unmarried birth parents.[89]

Revocation of an adoption order

Under French law a full or plenary adoption is irrevocable.[90] A simple adoption order can be revoked, but only in exceptional circumstances and only after a full judicial hearing. It may also be transformed into a plenary adoption.[91] French law has no particular procedure for the annulment of an adoption, although the decision may be set aside, for example because of a formal defect.

Entitlement to post-adoption support services

Statute n° 2005-744 of 4 July 2005 introduced a duty to provide post-adoption support services to assist adopters. The responsibility for service provision rests with either the adoption service of the local authority or the Agence française de

89 Cour de Cassation 20 February 2007 n° 06-15.647 and n° 04-15.676. The two cases concerned same-sex couples, but sexual orientation was irrelevant. Adoption was considered as contradicting the best interest of the child since it would thereby deprive the birth mother of parental responsibility for her children (author acknowledges with thanks the advice of Laurence Francoz-Terminal on this matter).

90 Article 359 of the French Civil Code.

91 Ibid., Article 345.

l'adoption. Legal responsibility rests on each *département* to make available post-adoption support services for all parties of both domestic and ICAs. Organisations such as CLSC Plateau Mont Royal offer various post-adoption services, free of charge, in the form of group sessions and individual counselling. Adoption Counselling and Advisory Services (COCAs) are available to provide post-adoption support.

Human rights considerations

Simple adoption and welfare interests

For a child, simple adoption offers little security and imposes such constraints on their long-term welfare interests (in terms of legal status, filiation, inheritance rights, citizenship entitlement, etc.) that arguably it is not conducive to protecting their human rights.

Information rights: disclosure, tracing and reunification

Rights of access to information are dependent upon the type of adoption order granted.

Information rights

In a full or 'plenary' adoption, the provisions governing access to public records give adopted and adopting persons access to official documents (full copies of birth certificates) that state the fact of adoption but not the identity of birth parents as the original birth certificate will have been annulled. In its place there will be a copy of the adoption order giving identification details relating only to the adopter/s. In simple adoption, the child concerned and other parties to the adoption have rights of access to relevant official documents (e.g. full copies of birth certificates) on which the identity of the birth parent/s may be recorded, as the original birth certificate will not have been annulled. However, the limited factual information recorded on an adoptee's original birth certificate, the process for gaining access to it and the extent of information required to be kept on agency files, combine to make it difficult for an adoptee or birth parent to obtain a full factual picture of the adoption to which they were parties.[92] The ECtHR has found this lack of openness to be justifiable. In *Odièvre* v. *France*[93] an adopted person had sought the release of information identifying her birth mother. As the latter had expressly reserved her right to confidentiality, the Parisian Child Welfare Authorities refused her request. The ECtHR held that the decision was not in breach of either Articles 8 or 14 on the grounds that France had a pressing reason to respect the privacy of

92 Dekeuwer-Defossez, F., 'Adoption and secrecy of origins (in French law)', at: http://ciec1.org/Etudes/ColloqueCIEC/CIEColloqueDefossezAngl.pdf

93 Application No. 42326/98 [2003] ECHR 86.

the mother, namely that mothers might abandon or abort their children if confidentiality on adoption could not be guaranteed. Nonetheless, in 2009, the CRC 'reiterated its previous recommendation that France take all appropriate measures to fully enforce the child's right to know his or her biological parents and siblings, as enshrined in Article 7 of the Convention'.[94]

Information disclosure duties

The general rule is that an adopted child has access to all the documents in his or her administrative file, upon request if the child is of age, otherwise via his or her legal representative. However, in practice the exercise of this right is subject to a parental right to veto disclosure of identifying information.

Maintaining records

There are no adoption registers as such in France. The registrars' office (*bureau de l'état civil*) in the local town hall, which maintains registers of birth, marriage and deaths (*naissances, mariages, décès*), will include a record of adoptions registered with it. These records will typically provide the place, date and time of registration; the date and place of birth; the child's surname and forenames, the parents' names (with mother's maiden name), and the names, ages, and professions of two witnesses. A duplicate of these records is held in the Archives Départementales which provides a centralised nationwide system of record-keeping for all citizens.

Tracing and reunification

Legislation passed in 2002 put in place a national government body with the power to determine requests from adopted children and their birth parents for identifying information and to assist those seeking to trace birth relatives. This legislation, may well provide the means for an applicant to contact his or her birth mother. Consequently, the practical value and relevance of the *Odièvre* judgment is now questionable. The absence of any unconditional right of access to identifying information regarding family of origin, has so far obviated the need for contact registers, etc.

Human rights considerations

Access to personal information: 'né sous X'

Until the 1960s, an estimated 2,000 babies a year were '*né sous X*', or born to mothers who had exercised their right to anonymity and left no trace of parental

94 UN CRC, Concluding Remarks of its fifty-first session (2009), at: http://reliefweb.int/report/mauritania/committee-rights-child-concludes-fifty-first-session

identity on their children's birth certificates or on any other official records.[95] Although the numbers have since decreased appreciably. This has resulted in a situation where tens of thousands of people, mainly adoptees, have been left searching for origins information that has been officially edited out by the State. The legal guarantee of maternal anonymity with the inevitable accompanying identity issues for the children concerned has been a matter of concern to the CRC.[96] For the ECtHR to rule that denying children given up at birth the right to discover their biological parents' identity does not violate the European Convention is troubling.[97] Access to the sole means for acquiring the private life, personal and cultural identity protected under Article 8 of the ECHR seems essential and the ECtHR decision anomalous.

Access to personal information: general

Leaving aside the particular difficulties relating to '*né sous X*' adoptees, the general official approach to making information available to those who have been parties to an adoption is such as to bring into question whether appropriate standards are in place to ensure that Article 8 rights can be given full effect. There does not seem to be a national system for coordinating adoption-specific information which could link the full range of adoption agencies, courts and registrars, provide clear pathways for the different parties, with inbuilt counselling opportunities, and allow for sequential stages of tracing and contact if such should be mutually agreed.

Conclusion

France belongs to the civil law tradition. Adoption, here, reflects the principles that currently hold the balance in French family law, particularly around the central concept of filiation, and is set within the distinctively egalitarian culture of this nation as shaped by more than two centuries of adherence to the Declaration of the Rights of Man and of the Citizen.

The consensually based and judicial nature of the French adoption process has some characteristics that distinguish it from that of other jurisdictions – but also bring it into conflict with human rights. Most obviously, the concept of anonymous births, known as '*accouchement sous X*', though once a feature of adoption law in the UK is now relatively rare: this maternal veto on disclosure of the information necessary for her adopted child to be alerted to potential genetically based health

95 The exercise by any woman of this right, which is enshrined in Article 326 of the Civil Code and which the legislature has to date shown no intention of reconsidering, is governed by the provisions of Article L. 222-6 of the Social Action and Families Code, as amended by the Act of 22 January 2002.

96 UN CRC, Concluding Remarks of its fifty-first session. CRC reiterated its previous recommendation that France take all appropriate measures to fully enforce the child's right to know his or her biological parents and siblings, as enshrined in Article 7 of the Convention.

97 *Odièvre* v. *France*.

risks and to build an authentic sense of identity is clearly in breach of basic human rights. Also of interest is the distinction made in French adoption law between plenary and simple adoptions: a two-tiered system which allows for a meaningful differentiation of legal status to match distinctions of filiation; but one which arguably – if unintentionally – discriminates against those, such as Muslim migrant children, who cannot fit within the filiation rules.[98] The fact that the consent of a child older than 13 is a prerequisite for his or her adoption is also atypical as is the lack of any upper age limit on prospective adopters: the former being wholly ECHR compliant but the latter somewhat questionable in terms of a child's welfare interests. In the context of an unusually high rate of child abuse, a high level of children in public care and the highest total of young children under 3 in institutional care in the EU, the low rate of adoption from the public childcare system is very evident as is the corollary that such children are being deprived of their Article 8 right to family life. This has to be contrasted with the fact that French prospective adopters have an established dependency on overseas sources for children and, increasingly, on surrogate mothers who can be paid to produce them; this emphasises the growing commercial dimension to adoption practice in France.

98 However, as Jean-François Mignot argues: while many Muslim children are inadvertently the victims of the fact that French adoption law respects Muslim-countries' legal frameworks, which prohibit adoption; many other Muslim children, from the few Muslim countries which acknowledge adoption (Tunisia, Turkey, Indonesia), do not suffer from any disadvantage in France. In short, the fault does not lie with French law as it does not directly discriminate against Muslim children: it simply never takes religion into account (note to author, 18.10.17).

8 Germany

Introduction

This chapter begins by examining the background social factors that have shaped the modern German adoption process. It identifies and assesses recent trends in the flow of adoption orders and the more characteristic principles that have come to shape current adoption practice. It then details the legislative framework for adoption, on both a domestic and intercountry basis, giving consideration to the policies that inform statute law. It outlines the German adoption process, explains the role of its regulatory bodies and adoption agencies, and tracks the path taken by the parties through the sequence of stages that end with the making of an adoption order. At each stage it identifies and discusses what appear to be the main human rights issues. The chapter then considers the availability of post-adoption support services, information disclosure rights and arrangements for tracing and reunification. It concludes by reflecting on the more distinctive hallmarks of contemporary adoption law and practice in Germany and their implications for human rights.

Background

Adoption in Germany has taken some time to overcome the distortions in its social role resulting from the impact of two world wars and the racially driven ideology of the Third Reich; a historical background well documented and analysed by many academics.[1]

Adoption and human rights: the early challenges

Shaping modern adoption policy

It is a fundamental principle of German family law that recognition will only be given to the legal status of parenthood if this established by ancestry or by adoption.

1 For a brief historical overview, see, for example, Bosch, *Entwicklungen und Probleme des Adoptionsrechts in der Bundesrepublik Deutschland, Zeitschrift fur das gesamte Familienerecht*, 1984.

Principles

The welfare interests of the child

The basic principle that adoption should serve the best interests of the child is stated in the Civil Code.[2] However, the Committee on the Rights of the Child (CRC) noted with concern that this principle had not been fully incorporated into federal legislation and the prioritization of the child's best interests was not yet integrated into all areas of the legislative, executive and judicial branches of government.[3]

Adult adoption

The adoption of adults is not uncommon in Germany, but this would be restricted to specific circumstances and to adoption in its simple form.[4]

Openness

The traditional approach of secrecy and anonymity for all parties is provided by the Civil Code: no information regarding the identity of the adoptee, the fact of their being subject to an adoption process or of an eventual adoption order may be disclosed; any breach may result in judicial penalties.[5] Indeed, barring certain exceptional circumstances, enquiries from official or private sources to a family seeking confirmation that a child has been adopted are explicitly prohibited and it has been established that it is permissible for the parties concerned to deny the fact of adoption.[6]

However, in practice open adoption is often accommodated, subject to the consent of all parties: allowing for arrangements to be made to facilitate some level of contact between the biological parent and the child throughout the latter's life. Moreover, adoption agencies encourage adopters to advise adoptees from an early age about the fact of their adoption.[7]

Contemporary adoption trends

Germany ranks quite low in the international league table of adoptions; there are relatively few adoptions in relation to the size of its population. The annual statistics show a steady decrease in annual adoption orders: from 8,687 in 1993, to

2 Civil Code (Bürgerliches Gesetzbuch), s. 1741, para. 1.
3 UN CRC, *Concluding Observations on the Combined Third and Fourth Periodic Reports of Germany*, 25 February 2014, CRC/C/DEU/CO/3–4, at para. 26, at: www.refworld.org/docid/52f8a2074.html [accessed 19 August 2017].
4 Civil Code, s. 1772.
5 Ibid., s. 1758.
6 *Munchener Kommentar zum Burgerlichen Gesetzburch, Band 8, Familienrecht* II, §1758, No. 6.
7 Recommendations, No. 5.2.

5,909 in 2001, 4,060 in 2011 and down to 3,812 in 2015. They also reveal a heavy weighting favouring domestic over intercountry adoption (ICA), though the latter have abruptly shrunk: in 2000, of the total of 6,373 adoptions, 5,495 were domestic; in 2003, the figures were 5,336 and 4,584; and by 2015 they were 4,013 and 3,812. However, if adoptions by step-parents and relatives were deducted, the annual rate of traditional third party adoptions by 'strangers' of children born within the jurisdiction would be seen to be in steep decline. The domestic adoption of children in Germany is one of the three highest in Europe (accompanied by the UK and Poland)[8] but adoption by non-relatives continues to fall: peaking at 7,669 in 1978, falling to 4,008 in 1986, to 1,448 in 2013 and reaching 1,362 in 2015.[9]

Transracial

As a consequence of Germany's relatively low and falling annual rate of ICA, its experience of transracial adoption is also correspondingly lower than that of other developed nations. In this context, it is relevant to note that German ICA – against the trend in other western nations – does not seem to include any adoptions from China.

Childcare adoption

As adoption is essentially a consensual process, there are very few adoptions of children from the care system although Jugendamt, the Youth Office, is required to consider whether adoption is legally possible for every such child.[10] According to the German Association for Child Protection in 2010, the number of children entering the public care system increased by 81 per cent in the previous four years[11] but in that year only 250 left it by way of non-consensual adoption. The children found by the court to have been failed by parental care are placed in foster homes, with other relatives, or in residential care. The proportion of the childcare population consigned to residential care has always been relatively high; contrary to the principle declared in the Preamble to the Convention on the Rights of the Child that children should grow up in a family environment. In 2005, for example, there were some 61,806 children in residential homes and 81,310 in 2015; considerably more than in foster care.[12] As has been pointed out 'the development of international child rights norms and standards shows that the

8 www.europarl.europa.eu/RegData/etudes/BRIE/2016/583860/EPRS_BRI(2016)583860_EN.pdf

9 www.destatis.de/EN/FactsFigures/SocietyState/SocialStatistics/SocialBenefits/PublicChildrenYouthWelfare/Adoptions.html.

10 Social Code VIII, s. 36, para. 1.

11 www.dw.de/new-child-protection-law-aims-to-strengthen-families-rather-than-divide-them/a-6329547

12 'Foster care research in Germany: a critical review', at: www.thefreelibrary.com/Foster+care+research+in+Germany%3a+a+critical+review.-a0202649731

placement in institutions should only be used as a measure of last resort, when it is absolutely necessary and when it is in the best interests of the child'.[13] In 2015 of the 77,600 children in the public care system very few exited by the adoption route.[14]

Unlike other countries such as the UK and the US the increase in the care population does not seem to trigger policy debates in Germany leading to law reforms that might enable the adoption option to be available to a greater proportion of that population.[15]

Foster care

At any given time, there are approximately 50,000 children in full-time foster care (0.3 per cent of the under 18 population) and that has been the case for some years: in 2005 there were 50,364 children and young people in family foster care; and in 2015 there were 71,501.[16] The preferred foster care placement is with a relative. Of the total foster care population in 2005, approximately 60 per cent of the children were in kinship placements.[17] The CRC expressed concern about 'the increasing number of children deprived of their family environment and taken into public care'.[18] It has been pointed out that 'for the past 20 years controversy has continued as to whether foster families should see themselves as replacing the child's birth family or complementing it – an argument that has polarised almost all the service agencies'.[19]

Foster parent adoption

There do not seem to be any official statistics relating to adoption by foster parents.

Family adoption

Adoptions by a parent, step-parent or close relative constitute the majority of all adoptions in Germany. In 1999, there were a total of 6,399 adoptions of which

13 Report of the Special Rapporteur on the sale of children, child prostitution and child pornography (27 February–24 March 2017), para. 17, at: https://documents-dds-ny.un.org/doc/UNDOC/GEN/G16/440/24/PDF/G1644024.pdf?OpenElement
14 www.destatis.de/EN/FactsFigures/SocietyState/SocialStatistics/SocialBenefits/PublicChildrenYouthWelfare/Tables/EducationalAssistenceN.html
15 However, see Botthof, A., 'Die Annahme als Kind als Alternative zur Dauerfplege', *FamRZ* (*Zeitschrift für das gesamte Familienrecht*) 2016, pp. 768–73; see also at: www.dji.de/ueber-uns/projekte/projekte/expertise-und-forschungszentrum-adoption-efza.html
16 See n. 14.
17 Walter and Blandow, 2004, at: www.dji.de/fileadmin/user_upload/pkh/blandow_verwandtenpflege.pdf
18 UN CRC, *Concluding Observations*, para. 46.
19 Wolf, K., 'Foster care research in Germany', *Adoption & Fostering*, 32(2) (2008): 19–30, 20, citing Gehres, W. and Hildenbrand, B., *Offentliche Sozialisation: Aufwachsen in Pflegeverhaltnissen*, Wiesbaden. VS Verlag fur Sozialwissenschaften, 2008.

4,406 involved children located in their family of origin when adopted. In 2003, the corresponding figures were 5,336 and 3,594 respectively. The statistics for 2013 reveal that 3,793 children were adopted: 2,232 (59 per cent) by step-parents and 113 (3 per cent) by relatives.[20]

Step-parent adoptions

Presently, adoption is the only way for a step-parent to gain full parental responsibility for a stepchild. Step-parent adoptions are available to heterosexual spouses, since 2005 to registered partners[21] and now to homosexual spouses. Since 1991 more than a half of all adoption orders have been made in favour of a spouse of the biological parent. In 2009, for example, of the almost 4,000 adoption orders made, about half were in favour of step-parents, and by 2013 the proportion had risen to almost 60 per cent. As the law in Germany vests total custody in the mother of a child born to an unmarried couple then,[22] in the event of her marriage to someone other than the child's father, this simplifies a subsequent step-parent adoption application as consent from the child's father is not required.

ICA

Contemporary practice, has seen a considerable drop in annual ICAs. In 2004, for example, there were a total of 475 such adoptions: 163 from Hague-compliant countries; and 312 from non-Hague (of which almost half were from Russia).[23] Terre des Hommes estimates that between 2000 and 2005 there was a decrease in annual ICAs from 878 to 547[24] and by 2015 they had fallen to 201.

Adoption-related issues in human rights reports

In its 2014 report, the CRC repeated earlier concerns regarding the lack of a national comprehensive and integrated data collection system on all children and urged that this be established together with indicators on children's rights which could be used to analyse and assess progress in the realisation of those rights.[25] It also strongly urged 'the State party to take all the measures necessary to end the practice of anonymous abandonment of children and to strengthen and promote

20 www.destatis.de/EN/PressServices/Press/pr/2014/08/PE14_275_225.html
21 Civil Code, s. 1741(2); and Lebenspartnerschaftgesetz [Registered Partnership Act], s. 9(7).
22 But see *Zaunegger* v. *Germany* (Application No. 22028/04), IHRL 3698 (ECHR 2009).
23 Annual Adoption Statistics for Receiving States: Germany, 2005, at: www.hcch.net/upload/adostats_de.pdf
24 Lammerant, I. and Hofsetter, M. (eds), *Adoption: At What Cost?*, Lausanne, Terre des Hommes, 2007, p. 23.
25 UN CRC, *Concluding Observations*, op cit.

alternatives as soon as possible'.[26] The report drew attention to a problem that was already apparent but would become much worse in the following years – the welfare of child migrants – many unaccompanied by adults. It warned that the principle of the welfare interests of children 'is frequently disregarded in cases concerning children from educationally and socioeconomically disadvantaged families, including refugee and asylum-seeking children'.[27]

The current legislative framework

Adoption was initially legalised by incorporating provisions into the Civil Code on 18 August 1896 which took effect on 1 January 1900. There was a major reform of the law relating to children in 1998. However, the law concerning the guardianship of minors has yet to be revised. The Procedure in Family Matters Act 2009 (FamFG) had the effect of transferring adoption proceedings to the jurisdiction of a new and enlarged Family Court.

The legislation: adoption-related law; domestic

The Adoption Placement Act 1976, as amended in 1993, together with the Law Concerning Adoption Procedures and their Implementation (both of which took effect from 1 January 1977), have long constituted the main legal framework for adoption in Germany. A lengthy period of family law reform concluded in February 1998 with a legislative package that included four statutes: the Guardianship Act; the Parentage Law Reform Act; the Equal Status in Inheritance Act and the Child Maintenance Act. Of these the first is most relevant for present purposes. Other legislation with a bearing on adoption has since followed.

Civil Code (Burgerliches Gesetzbuch)

This provides the basic, overarching, federal civil law framework, within which family law provisions address childcare and adoption. Provisions relating to childcare are to be found in ss. 1630–98b and address such matters as: the parental duties of care and protection; the remit of the Guardianship court and the suspension or removal of parental rights; and the appointment and duties of a guardian or curator. Provisions relating to the adoption of minors are to be found in ss. 1741–66 and deal with issues such as: consent; eligibility to adopt; the effect of an adoption order; and the cancellation of an adoption. The adoption of adults is addressed more briefly in ss. 1767–72.

Social Code

The Child and Youth Services Act (Kinder und Jugendhilfegesetz) is incorporated into the 8th Book of the Social Code. Sections 33–43 govern the service provision

26 Ibid., para. 31.
27 UN CRC, *Concluding Observations*, para. 26.

duties of the regional Child and Youth Services Department, together with their local offices, to support vulnerable families, protect children and provide care arrangements for those children who cannot remain in their family home. Section 51 specifically addresses the duty to provide counselling, guidance and support to birth parents and to children engaged in adoption proceedings.

Procedure in Family Matters Act 2009

This legislation replaces the Non-Contentious Proceedings Act 1898 (as amended in 1992) which dealt with the jurisdiction of the guardianship courts in adoption proceedings and provided for the recognition of foreign adoptions. It updates and consolidates family law proceedings previously to be found in the 1989 Act and in several other statutes. Among the changes introduced, this Act provides for a new and enlarged Family Court to have jurisdiction for adoption matters.[28]

Parentage Law Reform Act 1997

One consequence of this statute, which came into effect on 1 July 1998, was to give adopted children the same legal status as birth children in relation to their respective parents. Primarily, however, the Act strengthened the legal position of the father of a non-marital child by requiring the consent of both birth parents for the child to be relinquished for adoption.[29]

Guardianship Act 1997

As Frank has explained, this statute, which came into effect on 1 July 1998, 'sets out the extent of the parents' right to custody of an illegitimate child'.[30] As he points out, the new law was highly controversial because of 'the danger that the mother could conceivably choose not to reveal the identity of the father'.[31] This would effectively allow her to prevent the father from seeking any rights in relation to their child and give her exclusive discretion to relinquish the child for adoption.

Adoption Placement Act 1976

This legislation, as amended in 1993, addresses all aspects of arrangements to be made in relation to child adoption. It states the legal requirements relating to matters such as: adoption placements; the functions of adoption agencies, their accreditation and the role of professional staff; prohibitions regarding advertising and solicitation; adoption support services; and notification duties.

28 Procedure in Family Matters Act 2009, s. 1, 111 No. 4, 186ff.
29 Parentage Law Reform Act 1997, s. 1747 1.
30 Frank., R., 'Germany: parentage law reformed', in Bainham, A. (ed.), *The International Survey of Family Law*, The Hague, Martinus Nijhoff, 1997, pp. 167–82, p. 167.
31 Ibid., p. 168.

Adoption Act 1976

Modern German adoption law began with this legislation. It changed the adoption of minors from being a private contract matter to one requiring a court order.

Other relevant provisions

From 1 May 2014, the law has permitted women to give birth with complete anonymity.

The legislation: adoption-related law; international

Germany has ratified: the International Covenant on Civil and Political Rights; the Convention on the Rights of the Child; the European Convention on Human Rights; the European Convention on the Adoption of Children in 1980; and the Hague Convention. UN declarations and resolutions – including the Universal Declaration on Human Rights (UDHR) – are assumed to be binding. It has implemented the Hague Convention by way of the Adoption Placement Act and two separate statutes: the Adoption Convention Implementation Act which concerns ICA placements and cooperation between national Central Authorities; and the Effects of Foreign Adoption Act which regulates the recognition of foreign adoption orders.[32]

The legislation: human rights law

The German Constitution (Grundgesetz), which guarantees all rights proclaimed in the UDHR, provides the main source of domestic human rights law.

Regulating the adoption process

The German adoption process is judicial in nature, with registered adoption agencies playing a key role, and requiring a court order on successful completion.[33]

The judiciary

The Family Court (Familiengericht) determines all adoption applications in accordance with ss. 1741–72 of the German Civil Code (Burgerliches Gesetzbuch) and the Procedure in Family Matters Act (Familienverfahrensgesetz).[34]

32 As Andreas Bottoff points out, the following should also be included *Europäisches Übereinkommen über die Adoption von Kindern (revidiert) vom* 27 November 2008 (BGBl. 2015 II S. 2, 3). Note to author (16.10.17).

33 Civil Code, s. 1752.

34 The enlarged Family Court assumed jurisdiction for adoption applications in 2009. Author acknowledges with thanks the advice of Nina Dethloff on this matter (note to author, 9.10.2014).

Appeals lie to the superior district court (Oberlandesgericht). As regards ICA, if either the prospective adopter/s or the child is resident in Germany,[35] then the Family Court has jurisdiction to hear the application with the local office of the Child and Youth Social Services Department acting as the adoption agency if no accredited body is involved.[36]

Government bodies

The Federal Prosecutor General acts as the designated national Central Authority (Bundeszentralstelle fur Auslandadoption) for the purposes of Hague while each of the 16 German states have established their own Central Authority to process ICAs.[37] The relevant files, prepared by a public or private agency, will be processed through the Federal Central Authority – but only if so requested by the applicants – otherwise, the applicants can bypass Central authority oversight.

The regional Child and Youth Social Services Departments, together with their local offices, were established by the Child and Youth Social Services Act. They bear responsibility for providing childcare services and for ensuring the provision of adoption services which are coordinated by the Central Adoption Section of that Department and delivered through the registered adoption agencies. In the latter context, they are responsible for matters such as: the registration and supervision of voluntary adoption agencies; conducting annual reviews of children under 14 years of age in the care system who may be eligible for adoption; arranging staff training; and maintaining regional lists of hard to place children to facilitate the identification of possible matching placements. The regional youth offices act as Central Authorities for the purposes of the Hague Convention.

Adoption agencies

There are a mix of such agencies: some are public sector bodies, either the regional Child and Youth Social Services Departments or the local offices of those departments; and some are independent agencies; those engaged in ICA are designated 'accredited bodies' and regulated accordingly. The role and functions of adoption agencies (*Adoptionsvermittlungsstellen*) are as defined by the Adoption Placement Act which require all agencies to be registered, and to be subject to government supervision. A range of independent non-profit adoption agencies operate in Germany, as permitted and regulated by the Adoption Placement Act.[38] These are usually affiliated to churches or child welfare organisations and operate with professionally trained social work staff.[39] Some 12 independent agencies (*Annerkannte Auslandsvermittlungsstellen*) are accredited bodies authorised by special licence, issued

35 Procedure in Family Matters Act, s. 187.
36 Social Code, VIII, para. 1, s. 50.
37 Adoption Placement Act, s. 2(1) and (2).
38 Ibid., s. 2(2).
39 Ibid., s. 3(2).

under s. 4(1) of the Adoption Placement Act, to make ICA placements. Agency duties include: the provision of counselling – as well as medical, psychological, psychiatric and legal expertise – as necessary to support the local authorities.

Since ratification of Hague, as Terre des Hommes point out, 'the placement of children is usually carried out by specialists, thus improving its quality' and it also noted 'a decrease in child trafficking in the area of adoption, as well as in the number of private adoptions'.[40]

Registration of adoption orders

Instead of a central registration system for recording births, marriages and deaths each state has established its own separate system of civil registration. Adoptions are included in the records of births, marriages and death maintained by the civil registration office (*Standesamt*) in the local towns. Whether the order granted was in respect of a domestic or ICA, the adopted child's details must be recorded by the Registrar for the district in which the adopters reside.[41] If the child was born outside Germany, then the adopters may apply for a new birth registration which will be kept in the Registrar's office in Berlin.[42]

In relation to the 'simple' adoption of an adult, as this does not confer citizenship status, the Registrar will not record the adoption in the birth register. An appeal against a decision of the Registrar lies to the lower district court.[43]

Human rights considerations

Regulating adoption placements

Given that the actual placing of a child is the most critical part of the adoption process, it is worrying that both domestic and ICA placements would seem vulnerable to abuse. The former is so because it is not illegal for a recipient prospective adopter to accept a child on that basis. In the latter case a considerable proportion of ICA placements are acknowledged[44] to bypass the regulatory process. Arguably, such practices amount (or may amount) to 'trafficking' which is illegal and violates Art 35 of UNCROC.

Long-term residential care

Unusually in Europe, a high proportion of children entering the German public childcare system are channelled into long-term residential care – rather than

40 Lammerant and Hofsetter, *Adoption*, p. 23.
41 Personenstandsgesetz, s. 15, para. 1, No. 3 (many sections of the Personenstandgesetz are out of date).
42 Ibid., s. 41, para. 2.
43 Ibid., s. 45.
44 Botthof, *Perspektiven der Minderjährigenadoption*, pp. 166ff.

foster care – which may well constitute a breach of their basic human right to a family life.

Baby refuge

While not unusual, the provision of designated safe refuges where mothers can relinquish their babies, safely and anonymously, is still practised in Germany and has been condemned as violating the human right of the children to an identity. In its 2014 report the CRC 'strongly urges the State party to take all the measures necessary to end the practice of anonymous abandonment of children and to strengthen and promote alternatives as soon as possible'.[45] It also urged the State party to increase its efforts to study and address the root causes of the abandonment of infants. The response should include the provision of family planning and reproductive health services, adequate counselling and social support in cases of unplanned pregnancy, the prevention of high-risk pregnancies, and support for families in need.

Thresholds for entering the adoption process: eligibility, suitability and placement

Access to the German adoption process is subject to scrutiny by the professional staff of registered adoption agencies, applying the usual eligibility and suitability criteria, and to judicial oversight.

Role of adoption agency

In Germany, the gateway to the adoption process is manned by both public (*Adoptionsvermittlungsstelle des örtlichen Jugendamtes*) and private adoption agencies (*Adoptionsvermittlungsstelle in freier Trägerschaft*). Both sets of service providers bear responsibility for assessing the eligibility and suitability of prospective adopters and then submitting their findings to the court[46] in a home study report, in accordance with matters specified in the Recommendations.[47]

Pre-placement counselling

The Child and Youth Social Services Department has a legal duty to offer pre-placement counselling to the birth parents and advise them of the alternative options available. Any wishes the parents may have regarding the placement of their child must be noted, taken into account and given effect, in so far as they are judged to be compatible with the welfare interests of the child. Once legal proceedings are underway, relinquishing parents should be further counselled on the

45 UN CRC, *Concluding Observations*, para. 31.
46 Adoption Placement Act, s. 7.
47 Recommendations, No. 3.3.

course of adoption proceedings and given advice as to the consequences of an adoption order.[48] Where proceedings are initiated to dispense with the need for parental consent, then the local office must advise the parents accordingly. Counselling is not required in circumstances where the child has been living with the prospective adopters for a protracted period or where this might endanger the child's physical or mental health.

Eligibility and suitability of the parties

The child

The adoption of minors is regulated by ss. 1741–66 of the Civil Code and adults by s. 1767 but is only possible if morally justified (*sittlich gerechtfertigt*). There is no upper age limit for adult adoption but for a child that limit is their eighteenth birthday. In the case of an adult adoption, where the adoptee is a married person, the consent of their spouse is necessary.[49] The law requires a full report on all matters relevant to the welfare interests of the particular child, including a profile of their family of origin, to be submitted to the court.[50] If a child already has adherence to a particular religion,[51] this has to be respected by an adoption agency and choice of placement should ensure religious compatibility. Most adoptees are related to their adopters.

The birth parent/s

The court will require a full report on the birth parents and their family background: this will need to address the reasons and circumstances of their voluntary relinquishment of the child; or, alternatively, a full explanation of the reasons for their refusal to consent to the proposed adoption. The report must include details of any counselling offered or provided to the birth parents.

Where the unmarried mother has sole custody then her consent to the adoption of her child can be determinative. The father's consent need not be sought if this would lead to the denial of an adoption order and have a consequent disproportionate effect on the welfare of that child.[52] German law on parental responsibility was reformed in 2013 to ensure that fathers who are not married to the mother of their child can gain joint custody even against the mother's wishes, provided that

48 Social Code, VIII, s. 51.
49 Civil Code, s. 1767(2).
50 Recommendations concerning adoption procedures, etc. 1994 (the Recommendations), No. 32.
51 Federal Law on the Religious Education of Children (15 July 1921; 12 September 1990).
52 Civil Code, s. 1748(4). Although, as Andreas Botthof points out 'The effect of this section is very limited due to case law, i.e. BVerfG, 04.2006 – *1B* v. *R 286*' (note to author, 16.10.17).

this is not inconsistent with the child's best interests, and will then be in a position to refuse consent to an adoption placement.[53]

The birth parent/s and rehabilitation

The Child and Youth Social Services Departments have a duty to make appropriate efforts to reunify a family, within a reasonable time following the admission of a child into the care system,[54] while birth parents of a child in foster care have the right to request reunification services at any time.[55] Critically, birth parents enjoy a presumptive right to maintain contact with their child in foster care, unless a family court rules that contact endangers the welfare of that child.[56] In that context, it is significant that the ECtHR has in two cases concerning contact of fathers with their children found German law to be unsatisfactory and to violate the rights of fathers.[57]

However, as Wolf points out, 'in Germany there is substantial criticism of the practice of reuniting children with birth families'. He asserts that 'efforts to support the birth family are sparse . . . it is usually only after several years living in foster care that the issue of return to the birth family is raised . . . much more rarely than in the UK, birth families are reunited'.[58] In fact it has been estimated that out of all those in full-time foster care, reunification will be possible for only one-quarter[59] which, in the virtual absence of non-consensual adoption, leaves by far the majority to remain in the care system until they age out.[60]

The adopters

The minimum age limit for eligibility is now 25, though to be aged 20 is permissible in exceptional circumstances.[61] A married couple must apply jointly[62] (except where one spouse is legally incompetent or under age).[63] Unmarried, single people, as well as one member of an unmarried heterosexual couple, can adopt and either parent is an eligible adoption applicant in respect of their non-marital child. The Recommendations emphasise the need for a thorough assessment of an

53 Katrin Lack, *Ein Jahr Gesetz zur Reform der elterlichen Sorge nicht miteinander verheirateter Eltern*, [2014] FamRZ 1337.
54 Social Code VIII, s. 37.
55 Civil Code, s. 1632.
56 Ibid., s. 1666.
57 *Sahin* v. *Germany*, Application No. 30943/96 and *Sommerfeld* v. *Germany*, Application No. 31871/96; judgments 11 October 2001.
58 Wolf, K., 'Promoting the positive development of foster children: establishing research in Germany', *Adoption & Fostering*, 36(1) (2012): 40–51, 49.
59 Erzberger, C., *Strukturen der Vollzeitpflege in Niedersachsen*, Bremen, GISS, 2003.
60 www.dji.de/fileadmin/user_upload/pkh/DJI_Handbuch_Pflegekinderhilfe.pdf
61 Civil Code, s. 1743.
62 Ibid., s. 1741(2)(2).
63 Ibid., s. 1741(2)(4).

adopting step-parent's motives, family dynamics, the welfare interests of the child and the sustainability of the new family unit.[64]

Intercountry adopters must fully comply with the normal assessment procedures and a failure to do so when adopting a child overseas will violate German public policy.[65] Where the applicants and child are habitually resident in Hague signatory States then the assessment of adopters and related proceedings are as set out in the Convention (see Chapter 3).[66]

LGBT adopters

Gay adoption has in theory been possible since 2005,[67] but not until a ruling of the Federal Constitutional Court in 2013 did it become possible for one member of a civil partnership to adopt their partner's stepchild or adopted child.[68] The decision was in response to a challenge from a woman who was denied permission to adopt a Bulgarian girl whom her partner had adopted. The court found that the German constitutional provision that 'marriage and the family shall enjoy the special protection of the State', could be used to justify ruling out same-sex partners adopting the other partner's adopted child. As Kirchhof J then explained 'in marriage as in a civil partnership, adoption provides the child in the same way with legal security and material advantages in terms of care, support and inheritance law'. This sentiment was given legislative effect in June 2017 when Germany legalised gay marriage and since then LGBT adopters have had the same adoption rights as heterosexual couples.

Placement with consent

Authority to make adoption placements is as stated in the Adoption Placement Act. This requires consensual placements to be made by professionals and in practice they are made by local registered adoption agencies which may be independent bodies, the regional Child and Youth Social Services Departments or the local offices of those departments.[69] Each may have responsibility for domestic adoptions and also for arranging intercountry placements[70] acting in accordance with powers delegated by the state Central Authority.

Where all parties favour an open adoption, then the adoption agency may facilitate a placement direct from hospital within eight weeks of the baby's birth,

64 Recommendations, No. 3.43.

65 *AG Hamm*, 3 February 2006 – XVI 41/05; see also Botthof, *Perspektiven der Minderjährigenadoption*, pp. 142–56.

66 Convention on Protection of Children and Co-operation in Respect of Intercountry Adoption, Article 2.

67 Registered Partnership Act 2001, s. 9(7)(1), as amended.

68 German Constitutional Court, judgment of 19 February 2013, 1 *B* v. *R* 3247/09.

69 Social Code s. 2(1).

70 Ibid., s. 2a(4).

even though the birth parents are unable to give a valid consent until the child is at least 8 weeks old.[71]

Placement by the birth parent/s

Birth parent placements are prohibited in German law but there is good reason to suspect that some do occur and there is no specific law prohibiting prospective adopters from accepting a child.

Placement without consent

If a court has terminated the birth parent/s custody rights,[72] then the placement is made in accordance with that authority. If a birth parent has not formally consented to adoption, he or she must at least have agreed to the placement with the prospective adopters.[73]

Welfare interests

The welfare needs of a child do not constitute criteria for admission to the German adoption process. The threshold merely requires that adoption should serve the best interests of the child. This is generally interpreted as predicting that the child's circumstances will improve and that this will be evident in the child's psychosocial development.

Placement supervision

A probationary adoption placement (*Adoptivpflegschaft*) is generally a prerequisite for an adoption application,[74] whether the proceedings are domestic or intercountry in nature. It is treated by the professionals concerned not as 'probation' but as a therapeutic settling in period.[75] During this time, parental rights are suspended, and all related matters are treated as *sub judice*.[76] The local office of the Child and Youth Social Services Department assumes guardianship responsibilities. There are no prescribed time limits. At the conclusion of this period, the supervising agency must provide an evaluative report to the guardianship court detailing emerging family dynamics. Should the placement break down, the court must be notified, and it then determines the least harmful alternative care arrangement for the child. One option may be that the birth parents resume care responsibility.[77]

71 Civil Code, s. 1747, para. 3.
72 Ibid., s. 1666.
73 Subject to exceptions in the Civil Code, ss. 1747(4) and 1748.
74 Ibid., s. 1744.
75 Recommendations, No. 4.4.
76 Civil Code, s. 1748.
77 Code of Procedure in Non-Contentious Matters, section 49, para. 1, No. 1 m.

Human rights considerations

Step-parent and relative applicants

In Germany by far the majority of all children entering the adoption process are known to, if not related to, their adopters and are remaining within their home and framework of relationships. The customary queries regarding the tendency of this use of adoption to distort family relationships therefore applies with greater force than usual. The risk of an adoptee not having an opportunity to develop a fully informed individual identity is similarly accentuated.

Children in residential care

Unlike other European countries, an unusually high proportion of children entering the German public care system are denied the human right of family life – by way of adoption or foster care – as they are consigned to residential care.

Child migrants

In 2015 alone, the child protection services in Germany took custody of over 42,300 unaccompanied refugee children.[78] How many such children ultimately enter the adoption process is unknown, but the scale of this problem is such as to swamp domestic service provision and must place at risk the human rights of those involved.

Welfare interests of ICA children

As Terre des Hommes report:[79]

> adoptive parents resident in Germany manage in practice to bring adopted children into the country without any recourse to private or public bodies. The German authorities recognize that they have few means to control such adoptions which are considered as private, and which frequently later receive legal recognition.

This causes the editors of the report to conclude that, as regards ICA, a 'discordant reality' prevails in Germany because alongside the accredited bodies, other bodies also openly engage in ICA; and some adopters bypass them all. The circumstances of many ICA children thus evade the regulatory and professional processes designed to protect their human rights and provide for 'due process'.

78 Federal Statistics Office of Germany.
79 Lammerant and Hofsetter, *Adoption*, p. 28.

Unmarried fathers

German law affords little protection for the human rights of unmarried fathers. This is particularly evident in the maternal right to claim anonymity which deprives the father of any notice of an intention to place his child for adoption.

The hearing and the grounds

All adoptions are heard by the Family Court (Familiengericht), in private, following submission of an application,[80] and are determined by it. Proceedings are as outlined in the Procedure in Family Matters Act. The court is required to protect the anonymity of the applicant adopters,[81] investigate and examine all relevant facts *ex officio*,[82] and it must hear submissions from the adoption agency[83] and the child.[84] The agency involved is required to submit a report that includes an assessment as to whether child and adopters are appropriately matched.[85] The court will hear submissions from the local Child and Youth Social Services office and from the Child and Youth Social Services Department in ICAs.

Where consent is available

The birth parent/s consent is necessary: the mother's must be given a minimum of eight weeks after the child's birth;[86] an unmarried father's is valid even if given before the birth; it lapses if an adoption order is not issued within three years.[87] Neither birth parent is entitled to withdraw their consent.[88]

Consent of unmarried father

Since 1998, the *locus standi* of unmarried fathers, in relation to children for whose adoption the mother had given consent, has been the same as that of married fathers. Paternity may be established merely by the father's acknowledgement of such.[89] Once paternity has been ascertained, the local office of the Child and Youth Social Services Department must counsel him regarding his rights.[90] The ECtHR ruled in *Zaunegger* v. *Germany*[91] that the legal right of an unmarried

80 Civil Code, s. 1752(1).
81 Ibid., s. 1758.
82 Procedure in Family Matters Act, s. 26.
83 Ibid., s. 189.
84 Ibid., s. 192.
85 Ibid., s. 189.
86 Civil Code, s. 1747(2) 1.
87 Ibid., s. 1750(4) 2.
88 Ibid., s. 1750(2) 2.
89 Ibid., s. 1592(2). Note, also, the introduction of the Paternity Contestation Law Amendment Act (13 March 2008).
90 Ibid., s. 1600 and s. 1747 (2); see also Child and Youth Services Act, s. 51(3).
91 (Application No. 22028/04), IHRL 3698 (ECHR 2009).

mother to refuse the father the possibility of his obtaining, with her, joint custody of their child was discriminatory, in relation to their equal right to private and family life, and constituted a breach of Article 14 of the ECHR when taken together with Article 8. Where a birth father has applied for custody, an adoption order cannot be made until after the court has ruled on his application.[92]

Consent of a minor

The consent of the child is a prerequisite for his or her adoption:[93] but a child is not actually entitled to give an autonomous consent, it must be accompanied by that of their guardian;[94] if the child is less than 14 years of age or legally incompetent, then it is the consent of their guardian that must be given;[95] a child aged 14 or older may withdraw their consent at any time prior to the making of an adoption order – with or without the permission of their guardian.[96]

Where consent is not available

Where a birth parent is dead, incapacitated by mental illness, or their whereabouts are unknown, then the court may dispense with the need for their consent.[97] Also, the welfare principle enables consent to be dispensed with in circumstances where a failure to do so would constitute a grave disadvantage for the child,[98] where the parents are permanently incapacitated, or where not to place the child with the adopters would gravely impair his or her development. Again, where the birth parents are indifferent towards the welfare of their child, but not culpable of abuse or neglect, then the need for their consent may be dispensed with three months after they have received counselling as to their rights.[99] However, it would seem that these provisions are seldom used.[100]

Childcare adoption: the grounds

The court may dispense with the need for consent where the birth parent/s custody rights have been terminated following convictions for child abuse or neglect, abandonment or failure to provide financial support for more than one year.[101]

92 Civil Code, s. 1747(3) Nr 3.
93 Ibid., s. 1746(1) 1.
94 Ibid., s. 1746(1) 3.
95 Ibid., s. 1746(1) 2.
96 Ibid., s. 1746(2).
97 Ibid., s. 1747(4).
98 Ibid., s. 1748(1) 1.
99 Ibid., s. 1748(2) 1 and the Code of Social Law (Sozialgesetzbuch), Vol. VIII, s. 51(1).
100 Botthof, *Perspektiven der Minderjährigenadoption*, pp. 81–2.
101 Civil Code, s. 1748(1) 1 and 2.

Contested family adoption: the grounds

As noted above, the court may dispense with the need for the consent of a non-consenting birth parent in circumstances where their refusal constitutes a grave disadvantage for the child.

Human rights considerations

Consent of an unmarried father

An unmarried father has no *locus standi* in adoption proceedings[102] – unless he first claims paternity – even if he is cohabiting with the child's mother. Only when he has formally acknowledged paternity – whether before or after the child's birth[103] – will he then be entitled to give or withhold his consent. Much the same legal difficulties apply in the context of surrogacy arrangements: German law will recognise the birth father (and mother) as the legal parent/s; the commissioning prospective parent will be denied *locus standi.* Arguably, this is more than merely disadvantageous to the adult parties involved, it nullifies the opportunity for the child to enjoy their rights under Article 8 of the ECHR to family life as he or she will be left with a birth parent or parents who never had any intention of parenting and may well resent having to undertake unwanted care responsibilities.

Consent of child

The fact that a child aged 14 or more, the subject of adoption proceedings, is entitled to give consent but only if this is endorsed by that of their guardian seems anomalous, may well be discriminatory and could constitute a denial of their individuality.

Thresholds for exiting the adoption process

The lack of a range of alternatives, coupled with an inability to attach conditions, means that the court's ambit of discretion is restricted to either making or refusing an adoption order.

The welfare interests of the child

The Civil Code, s. 1741, declares that:

> A child may be adopted if such adoption will serve the welfare of the child and if it is to be expected that a parent–child relationship will develop between the adopter and the child.

102 Civil Code, s. 1747(1).
103 Ibid., s. 1594.

An adoption carried out without taking the interests of the child into account violates German public policy and cannot be recognised[104] but a foreign adoption can be, even if legally flawed, as long as it serves the interests of the child and is consistent with the essential principles of German law (s. 109 FamFG).[105] This was reaffirmed in the 2014 ruling by the Federal Supreme Court which held that the Californian registration of a gay couple, as the legal parents of a surrogate child, should be recognised in German law; in part because one of the parents was genetically related to the child.[106] The court took the view that any consideration of whether a foreign court decision is contrary to German public policy (*ordre public*) must take into account the child's right to respect for his or her private and family life under Article 8 of the ECHR, citing the ECtHR decisions in *Mennesson* and *Labassee*.[107]

Paramountcy

No inference can be drawn from the above s. 1741 that the welfare interests of a child (*Kindeswohl*) is to be treated as of paramount significance: there is no suggestion that the welfare test should be applied to assess the child's best interests on a lifelong basis; the requirement is no more than to ensure that adoption and welfare are compatible. However, the provisions in s. 1748 of the Civil Code do lend added weight and extend the reach of the principle relative to the innate rights of birth parents.

Consent/views of child and welfare interests

Participation in court proceedings may be provided by the appointment of a *Verfahrensbeistand* (guardian *ad litem*) if this is necessary in order to preserve the interests of the child, for example where the decision may include the separation of a child from his/her family.[108] This may be the case in a step-parent adoption where the court considers that the application gives rise to a conflict of interests that may jeopardise the child's welfare and it may then appoint independent representation for the child.[109] The judge must hear a child in person if the 'inclinations, ties or wishes of the child are important for the decision'. Therefore, in German adoption proceedings, unlike the position in almost all other countries, the court is required to hear directly from the child their views as to the proposed adoption.[110] While no age limit is specified, any child aged 14 or older must always be heard personally.[111]

104 *KG Berlin*, 4 April 2006-1 W 369/05.
105 *AG Hamm*, 17 April 2006 – XVI 44/05.
106 Federal Supreme Court judgment of 10 December 2014, XII ZB 463/13.
107 *Mennesson and Others* v. *France and Labassee* v. *France*, Application Nos 65192/11 and 65941/11, 2014.
108 Procedure in Family Matters Act, s. 158.
109 Civil Code, s. 1796.
110 Procedure in Family Matters Act, s. 192.
111 Ibid., s. 159; subject to some exceptions listed in this provision

Culturally compatible

Birth parents have the right to stipulate the preferred religious upbringing of their child and the Guidelines require that the child's religion be taken into account. In effect, a guarantee must be given that the child will be free to practise his or her religion.[112] This is a significant concession to the human right to hold a cultural identity and one not always given recognition in the adoption law of other countries.

The orders available

Under German law, an adoption application can only be granted or rejected. There is no provision for interim orders nor for any form of conditional adoption order. Where an order has been made by a foreign authority in the course of an ICA it must then be approved in a German court if it is to be legally recognised in this jurisdiction.[113] Acquiring a German adoption order removes all uncertainty as to legal status and confirms entitlement to residence permit, filiation, citizenship and access to social benefits.

Plenary adoption order

This is now the only form of adoption order issued by the German courts.

Simple adoption order

This adoption order was effectively ended by the 1977 law reform except in respect of the adoption of adults which will still almost always takes a 'simple' rather than the 'full' form.

Additional orders: post-adoption contact

There is no tradition of post-adoption contact arrangements between birth family members and an adoptee, instead the law has tended to assume that any such arrangements should not be encouraged. The issue arose in *I. S.* v. *Germany*[114] where the applicant complained of not being able to have regular contact with, and receive information about, her biological children who had been adopted by another couple. She submitted that the German courts' decisions on contact and information with regard to her children had breached her human rights. She alleged that she had been promised contact with and information about the

112 Guidelines, No. 3.316.

113 Procedure in Family Matters Act, ss. 108 and 109 and *Adoptionswirkungsgesetz*, s. 5(4). Note that in *LG Dresden, 26 January 2006-2 T 1208/04*, the court ruled that the relevant point in time for assessing whether the recognition of the foreign adoption violates German public policy is when deciding about the recognition.

114 Application No. 31021/08 (2014).

children, which had not been respected. The ECtHR held that there had been no violation of Article 8. It found that, by consenting to the adoption, the applicant had knowingly given up all rights as regards her biological children. The arrangements concerning information about them had in particular been based on a mere declaration of intent by the adoptive parents. It found that the German courts' decision, to favour the children's interest in developing in their adoptive family without disruption over the mother's right to respect for her private life, had therefore been proportionate.

While the law continues not to make any facilitative provisions for contact, in practice it is now not unusual for the parties to make informal arrangements for post-adoption contact, if only by means of an annual exchange of letters and photographs.

Alternative orders

Guardianship and custody orders provide alternatives to adoption for some in certain circumstances. There are no legal orders, let alone a continuum of private family orders, designed specifically to offer optional frameworks for undertaking varying quotients of parental responsibilities.

Human rights considerations

Welfare interests as a determining factor for an adoption order

The Convention on the Rights of the Child and other international instruments stress that this factor should be of central importance in decisions regarding a child's upbringing. The Civil Code, s. 1741, fails to give effect to that requirement, indeed there could hardly be a more perfunctory reference to it, which is symptomatic of a more general failing German adoption law, policy and practice in relation to adoption and perhaps to children more generally.

Lack of alternatives to adoption

The absence of alternative private family law orders, other than guardianship, removes the possibility of a more flexible judicial response to an adoption application which could authorise ongoing contact with birth family members.[115]

The effect of an adoption order

The order granted has the traditional permanent and exclusive effects: essentially legally terminating the relationship between child and birth parents and transforming the relationship between adopter and child to that of parent and child.[116]

115 Botthof, *Perspektiven der Minderjährigenadoption*.
116 Civil Code, s. 1754.

Effect on the parties

The child

Only a full order can be issued in respect of a child adopted by a third party and its effect is to end the adoptee's legal relationship with his or her birth parents and substitute an equivalent relationship with their adopters whose surname they will assume thereafter.[117] The usual accompanying legal indicators of such a change of status also apply: an entitlement to maintenance from adopters; full inheritance rights; and, as the adoptee and adopters are held to come within the prohibited degrees of consanguinity, they are prohibited from marrying each other.[118] As German citizenship is based primarily on the principle of *jus sanguinis*, a child adopted by a German citizen becomes a German national automatically if aged less than 18 on the date the application for adoption was made.[119] Children born on or after 1 January 2000 to non-German parents acquire German citizenship at birth if at least one parent has a permanent residence permit and has been residing in Germany for at least eight years.

The birth parent/s

On the granting of a full adoption order, all legal ties between the adoptee and their family of origin are terminated[120] (except in cases of kinship adoption).[121]

The adopters

The effect of an adoption order is to fully vest in the adopters all parental responsibilities that were previously held by the birth parents.[122] Thereafter the legal relationship between adopters and child is as if the child had been born to them and of their marriage.

Revocation of an adoption order

A German adoption order is theoretically permanent and irrevocable. However, if it was legally flawed from the outset, then it may be repealed.[123]

117 Ibid., s. 1757.
118 Note, however, that s. 1766 of the Civil Code expressly addresses the legal consequences for the adopter and adoptee in the event of their marrying each other: the adoption status (rather than marital status) is then cancelled.
119 German Nationality and Citizenship Act 1913, as amended in 1993, s. 3, No. 3 and s. 6.
120 Civil Code, s. 1755.
121 Ibid., s. 1756.
122 Ibid., s. 1751(1).
123 Ibid., s. 1759.

Entitlement to post-adoption support services

There is official recognition that the adopters and child will require ongoing support,[124] which may take the form of financial aid, and their entitlement to access the full range of normal family and community public services must be explained and facilitated.[125] Adoption agencies and the local offices of the Child and Youth Departments are required to provide ongoing counselling and support services to all parties following an adoption on request.[126] In particular, assistance should be made available to the adopters and adoptee.[127]

Human rights considerations

Lack of the flexibility needed to protect contemporary welfare interests

Given that simple adoption has no application to children, the fact that only the most traditional form of that order – full, exclusive, unqualified and permanent – is available, may impose constraints on the human rights of an adoptee. The rigid effects of such an order offer few opportunities to accommodate the fluid realities of modern family life which often feature serial parenting arrangements and households of tenuously related children. This is particularly likely to be the case with older children, or those with siblings, where established relationships need to be retained if rights under Article 8 of the ECHR are to be adequately protected.

Information rights: disclosure, tracing and reunification

The German Constitution is guarded on the subject of information rights. It asserts that individuals have a fundamental right to develop their own personality, but it also warns that this is conditional upon no infringement of either the rights of others or of public morals.[128]

Information rights

The law continues to reinforce the traditional interpretation of adoption as a 'closed' and private matter and in particular provides secrecy for the adopters and adoptee. Access to information regarding the identity of the adopters and adoptee, or even to establish the fact of an adoption, is legally protected: no information may be released without the consent of the adopters and adoptee.[129]

124 Recommendations, No. 4.4.
125 Social Code, VIII, ss. 27–41.
126 Adoption Placement Act 1976, s. 9.
127 Social Code, ss. 27–41, and the Recommendations, No. 4.4.
128 Federal Constitution, Basic Law, Article 2.
129 Civil Code, s. 1758.

Information disclosure duties

The German Federal Constitutional Court has upheld the constitutional right of every person to know his or her biological origins;[130] but for an adoptee this right is subject to their adopter's discretion as to how and when it should be exercised. In practice, an adoptee aged 16 or older may access the public register, which records the facts relating to his or her origins,[131] and may also access their adoption file.[132] However, this must be interpreted in the light of the frank acknowledgement of the Federal Supreme Court that according to German law, the right to know one's ancestry is not guaranteed by the German local register of births, marriages and deaths.[133]

Maintaining records

The Personal Status Law (*Personenstandsgesetz*) requires the name and identifying data of an adopted child to be registered under the family name of the adopters.[134] An adoptee's birth certificate will simply name the adopters as the birth parents with no indication that the child has been adopted.[135] The original birth certificate is kept on file by the Registrar and is not publicly accessible. The adoptee is entitled to copies of his or her birth certificate on application to the Registrar.

Tracing and reunification

The parties to an adoption do not share an equality of rights to subsequently access information: agency disclosure of information relating to an adoptee sought by birth family members is wholly dependent upon the consent of adopters and adoptee. Those wishing to access official adoption data sources are likely to find that adoption case material is archived among court files rather than in an adoption agency. Facilitating adopted persons engaged in a search for information relevant to establishing their identity is acknowledged to be a public service duty and related counselling services are available. In the event of the necessary consents being given, then the relevant adoption agency is obliged to mediate between the parties and assist in an exchange of information if satisfied that there are valid reasons for so doing.

Human rights considerations

Maternal veto on information disclosure

The maternal right to relinquish her child anonymously – leaving no information whatsoever – with a State guarantee that her anonymity will be thereafter

130 Decision of the German Constitutional Court, BVerfGE 79, 256; FamRZ 1989, 255.
131 *Personenstandsgesetz*, s. 61(2) 1.
132 Adoption Placement Act, s. 9b(2).
133 Federal Supreme Court judgment of 10 December 2014, XII ZB 463/13.
134 *Personenstandsgesetz*, s. 15, para. 1, Nos 3, 4.
135 Ibid., s. 63.

protected, imposes a serious constraint upon the human rights of the child to access the information necessary to develop his or her individual identity. This right has greatly concerned the CRC which has strongly urged that 'the State party should keep a confidential record of the parents, to which the child could have access at a later stage'.[136] The right to anonymity is compounded by the requirement that in any event an adoptee's access to identifying information is subject to the informed agreement of both birth parents and adopters.

Conclusion

Adoption in Germany is very much a part of private family law: used essentially to redraw legal boundaries for reforming family units; accommodating both child and adult adoptees; available in full and simple forms (limited as regards the latter); and continuing to be subject to very traditional characteristics, particularly the maternal right to anonymity. While the dramatic rise in the number of children now being consigned to the public childcare system has not challenged the consensual nature of Germany's adoption process it is exacerbating the constraints on the human rights of the children involved. There would appear to be a reluctance to re-examine policies that for some decades have resulted in a current population of some 70,000 children who are left to age-out in State care: instead of adoption, some 80 per cent are offered only the protective umbrella of guardianship; and an unusually high proportion are left in long-term residential care. Such policies inevitably have the effect of depriving very many children of their right to family life – whether through rehabilitation with their birth family or by way of a fresh start with adopters.

136 UN CRC, *Concluding Observations*.

Part IV

Contemporary law, policy and practice in an Asian context

9 Japan

Introduction

Adoption is very popular in Japan: the current rate of some 80,000 a year places Japan among the world leaders in this particular form of family building.[1] However, it bears very little resemblance to adoption as it is known elsewhere: children are rarely adopted. Japanese adoption would seem to be focused in the main not on creating a new family unit but on salvaging an old one. Its characteristics are so singular as to constitute a re-definition of adoption.

This chapter begins by exploring the origins of adoption law in Japan: it briefly considers its social role; provides an overview of the law relating to adoption and human rights; and outlines current adoption legislation together with the related regulatory framework. It examines the statistical data on trends in the contemporary use of adoption: noting characteristic aspects; it gives particular attention to the distinction between 'ordinary' and 'special' forms of adoption. The chapter then identifies the main points of intersection between human rights and adoption law at each of the sequential stages in the adoption process and considers their significance.

Background

Japanese adoption has always been mainly about succession and for some time this has meant adopting adults. 'Death without an heir', as Hozumi once observed 'was considered to be the greatest filial impiety'.[2] In circumstances where there was a failure of male issue, it was the duty of the family 'head' to acquire a son by adoption: preference being given to a male from within the extended family or clan to preserve lineage; which could even be achieved posthumously by provision in a deceased's last will and testament.[3] The social significance of adoption is very important in Japan. In 1912, some 14 years after enactment of the Civil Code, it

1 Buchanan, K., 'Many adoptions in Japan are not about raising children', Library of Congress (5 April 2017), at: https://blogs.loc.gov/law/2017/04/many-adoptions-in-japan-are-not-about-raising-children

2 Hozumi Nobushige, *The New Japanese Civil Code*, 1912, p. 56.

3 Civil Code, Article 848.

was noted to be the 'corner-stone of family law'.[4] Like marriage, it continues to be viewed as a means of conferring status: on adopters as much as on the adopted, in fact 'in all times past it has been held to be almost as important a factor as marriage itself in the making of families'.[5] As Morris observed, when considering the social role of adoption in the late nineteenth century, 'certainly its most important function in Japan, is in the case where it is employed as a means for transferring the headship or *katoku*, and the property of a house'. The placement of a son in a combined marriage and adoption arrangement with a family with a daughter but no male heir, was a not uncommon practice; the adoptee/son-in-law being known as a *muko yoshi* (adopted husband).[6] The marriage had to occur first. Girls were also adopted (known as *yojo*), sometimes to provide care for the elderly but for many other reasons as well. A married couple could be adopted into an unrelated family.

For the Japanese adoption process, the adoption of children has always been of marginal significance. Private adoptions, arranged directly between birth parent/s and adopters, first began to become subject to State control in 1875 when the Meiji government introduced compulsory family registration which included a requirement that adoptions be registered. In 1896 the Japanese government established the Civil Code, which was modelled closely on European law as derived from Roman precedents but not to the exclusion of traditional law and custom. As Morris at the time remarked: 'while their Civil Code contains many Articles on the subject of adoption which are taken almost word for word from certain European Codes, and have an undoubted ancestry in the *Corpus Juris Civilis*, there is also a great quantity of material relating to customs indigenous to Japan.'[7]

Adoption and human rights: the early challenges

The contemporary adoption process only began to evolve in the years following the end of the Second World War. In response to an urgent need to provide for the many war orphans and refugees, within the framework of the revised Civil Code then imposed upon the defeated nation, the State and other parties began to develop their present roles. This was given some urgency by the reported cases of 'baby farming' and led eventually to the setting up of the first adoption agencies which commenced their mediatory function, later attracting State subsidies, of arranging the placement of children with suitable prospective adopters. In 1948 Ms Miki Sawada established a home to care for the children of mixed race abandoned by their mothers and arranged for their adoption, often in the US. The first formal adoption agency commenced in 1961, *Katei Yogo Sokushin Kyokai* (society for promoting childcare at home) in Osaka and Kobe but not until 1988 was the 'western' adoption process statutorily introduced.[8]

4 Hozumi, *New Japanese Civil Code.*
5 Morris, R., 'Adoption in Japan', *Yale Law Journal*, 4 (1894): 145.
6 Civil Code, Ch. 4 and 5, Act No. 9 of 1900, Art. 788, para. 2.
7 Morris, 'Adoption in Japan', 143.
8 The author acknowledges the advice of Satoshi Minamikata on these matters (note to author, 18.10.17).

Shaping modern adoption policy

There has been little evidence of anything resembling a coherent strategy or programme for adoption and related services. Adults and children may be adopted. There are no prescriptive provisions requiring greater weight to be given to the welfare interests of an abused/neglected child than to the parental right to withhold consent to the adoption of that child. Birth parents wishing to relinquish their children for adoption may choose from a number of different routes. Adoption agencies are free to develop their own individual approaches to prospective adopters. The interface between childcare law and adoption law remains in practice almost impermeable. Few children with 'special needs' are admitted to the adoption process. For adopters the prospect of adopting an unrelated child remained tarnished by the traditional taboo of *doko no uma no hone ka wakaranai* (you don't know from which horse the bone comes), reflecting the importance placed upon bloodlines and lineage.

The introduction of the revised Child Welfare Act in April 2017 promises to mark a significant change in the development of Japanese policy towards children in care, in particular as regards the use of adoption and foster care as opposed to the history of reliance upon institutionalisation. This legislation follows on from the 2015 government commitment to increase the use of foster parents from the current level of 15 per cent up to 30+ per cent, as well as reducing the number of institutions down to two-thirds by 2029.

Transracial

Given the importance attached to 'family' – to bloodlines, lineage and ancestors, etc. – it is unsurprising that transracial adoption, being the most overt and socially conspicuous breach of traditional family boundaries, is regarded with considerable caution in Japan.

Principles

Despite its singular characteristics, many of the principles prominent in the adoption law of other developed nations clearly also govern adoption practice in Japan and others tend to be quietly accommodated.

Adult adoption

This use of adoption is not only permitted, it is and has long been the main purpose of the Japanese adoption process. Bryant identifies its three primary uses as the adoption of sons-in-law, adoption of extramarital lovers[9] and adoption to reduce income tax (recent legislation has made this less of an incentive).

9 The adoption process has long served as a means whereby a married person may legally adopt his or her lover – with or without the consent of their spouse. See, further, Bryant, T. L., 'Sons and lovers: adoption in Japan', *American Journal of Comparative*

Adoptions to secure heirs have steadily escalated from 73 per cent of all Japanese adoptions in the mid-twentieth century to over 98 per cent of all adoptions in 2004; the vast majority of the adoptees are childless adult males. Of the 78,910 adoptions in Japan in 2016 only 744 were children adopted through the courts: which is consistent with the data recorded by Bryant more than 20 years earlier.

Satoshi Minamikata points out that adult adoption is open to abuse and that there have been a number of cases in recent years where the adopted adult has used his acquired status to defraud adopter/s of their property.[10]

'Ordinary' and 'special' adoptions

These conform to the 'simple' and 'full' typology typical of France and other civil code jurisdictions.

'Ordinary' adoption, based on a simple agreement between the parties, is used in respect of adults and minors. In respect of adult adoptees, it does not require judicial endorsement. It creates a legal parental relationship between the adopters and the adoptee, whether adult or child, but not wholly to the exclusion of legal links between the latter and his or her birth parent/s. If the child to be adopted is a minor, then leave from the Family Court is required, though not if the minor is a lineal descendant of the adopter/s, or a child of the adopter's spouse.

'Special' adoption, introduced in 1988 and intended to be the modern equivalent of other western models, is a formal statutory process in which the legal rights of the parties involved are recognised and given some protection. It tends to be regarded as the default option reserved for complex situations. In addition, consent of the child's parents is required except where this is unobtainable or where the child has suffered abuse, serious neglect or been abandoned by the parent/s. It is only permitted in relation to children aged 6 years or less, requires a probationary placement period of at least six months and the Family Court must then determine whether or not the proposed adoption is compatible with the child's welfare interests.

The welfare interests of the child

The Japanese adoption process has little trace of the altruism generally associated with the process in other countries. Instead it has largely evolved to reflect the purposes and needs of adult adopters and is designed more to achieve the latter's benefit than the welfare of an adoptee. The 'welfare' of a male child, for example, may have little to do with his need for nurture and attachment but be interpreted as

Law, 38 (1990): 299–336. The fact that same-sex marriages are not legally permitted makes this use of adoption an expedient means of securing inheritance rights.

10 The author acknowledges advice from Satoshi Minamikata on this matter (note to author, 18.10.17).

consonant with prospective socio-economic benefits, indicating that his welfare would be best furthered through adoption by those in need of an heir to perpetuate their family, family name or business. Moreover, the lack of weight given to this principle within the Code is such that it can fail to protect a child from discrimination.[11]

Family-based care

Article 3.2 of the revised Child Welfare Act, introduced in April 2017, establishes family-based care as the new governing principle to determine the placement of children entering the Japanese childcare system. In future preference will be given to placing such children in a family setting, such as adoption and foster care, while institutionalisation will be restricted to those cases where family-based care is 'not appropriate'.

Openness

The introduction of principles of 'openness' to adoption practice has proved problematic; there is much in the traditional ethos of Japanese social relations that is inimical to transparency and insistence on such an approach may prove counter-productive in an adoption context. As Hayes and Habu explain:[12]

> The open philosophy is somewhat at odds with the traditional Japanese cultural emphasis on reserve, social duty and the masking of individual feelings. There are also potential conflicts of interest between an agency and parents; if an adoption agency is too forthcoming about the backgrounds of the children in its care, then this may make their placement more difficult. This means that a policy of openness is not necessarily an advantage in helping as many needy children as possible.

11 CRC, *Concluding Observations of the Committee on the Rights of the Child: Japan*, UN Doc. CRC/C/15/Add.90 (1998) which states that: 'The Committee is concerned that legislation does not protect children from discrimination on all grounds defined by the Convention, especially in relation to birth, language and disability. The Committee is particularly concerned about legal provisions explicitly permitting discrimination, such as Article 900 (4) of the Civil Code which prescribes that the right to inheritance of a child born out of wedlock shall be half that of a child born within a marriage, and about mention of birth out of wedlock in official documents. It is also concerned at the provision of the Civil Code stipulating a different minimum age of marriage for girls (16 years) from that of boys (18 years)' (para. 14). These same matters were the subject of concern for the Committee in its reports of 2004 (paras 22 and 23) and 2010 (paras 31, 33, 37 and 38). However, as Satoshi Minamikata points out 'Article 900 was revised and no discrimination now exists between legitimate and illegitimate children after the Supreme Court decision in 2013 (4 September 2013 Minshu 67–6-1320)'. Note to author, 18.10.17.

12 Hayes, P., and Habu, T., *Adoption in Japan: Comparing Policies for Children in Need*, New York, Routledge, 2006, p. 45.

Contemporary adoption trends

Adoption in Japan developed from and remains embedded in the overriding principle that the integrity of family boundaries should be preserved and bloodlines protected. This influence may account for the long-established use of adoption within the extended family as a means of strengthening bloodlines and kinship bonds. It also explains the relatively low numbers of children adopted from either the care system or from overseas.

Child care adoption

Cases of child neglect and abuse in Japan are governed by the Welfare of Children Act, s. 28. Children enter the care system either on a consensual basis because parents cannot cope and voluntarily relinquish them, or on a coercive basis following a family court order obtained on grounds of parental neglect or abuse.

Few children in the care population are adopted. The main reason for this is 'the long-standing predisposition of Japan's child guidance centres – which determine the placement of children needing such care – towards institutionalizing children rather than placing them in adoption or foster care'.[13] There is no financial support, let alone incentive, for foster parents to transform their status to adopters. Moreover, parents retain inherent rights including the right to withhold consent to adoption, so very few children subsequently transfer to the adoption process. This is not due to an absence of legal provisions permitting such a transfer: both the Welfare of Children Act and the Civil Code enable a family court to dispense with the need for parental consent in respect of the proposed adoption of a child that has suffered abuse at the hands of that parent. However, it would seem that there is some resistance to making the children concerned available for adoption.[14]

This is borne out by statistics from the Ministry of Health, Welfare and Labour which reveal that although in 2011 there were 303 adoptions from the childcare system, almost 90 per cent remained unadopted.[15] This was a matter of concern to the Committee on the Rights of the Child (CRC) which has noted 'the lack of a policy on alternative, family-based care for children without parental care, the increase in the number of children taken into care away from their families, the inadequate standards of many institutions, in spite of efforts to provide small-group and family-type care, and the reportedly widespread abuse of children in alternative care facilities'.[16] Following the introduction of the Child Welfare

13 Ministry of Health, Welfare and Labor, 'Reference material: current state of alternative care', March 2014 (as cited in Human Rights Watch, 'Without Dreams' report, p. 4).

14 For example, according to the judicial statistics for 2012, the outcome of 184 applications to the Family Court for the forfeiting and suspending of parental rights and duties was: 32 granted; 17 rejected; and 129 withdrawn by the parties (child's relatives, authority and other interested persons).

15 Ibid., p. 2.

16 CRC, Fifty-fourth session (CRC/C/JPN/CO/3), 25 May–11 June 2010, para. 52.

(Amendment) Act in April 2017, it is expected that the policy of preferencing institutional care over foster care will be reversed.

Foster care

Japan has a far lower incidence of children in State care than many other countries but unlike those other countries it has designated institutional care rather than foster care as the primary form of provision for such children. In 2010/11, 12 per cent of Japanese children in care were placed with foster parents compared with 93 per cent in Australia, 77 per cent in the US and 71 per cent in the UK.[17] In 2016 there were 9,949 registered foster parents caring for 4,731 children. As mentioned, the revised Child Welfare Act is intended to radically change the Japanese approach to foster care.

Foster parent adoption

Some foster parents are specifically approved as potential adopters and children are placed with them in the expectation that they may eventually be adopted. Approximately 17 per cent of all foster parents have this dual status. In March 2009, the government issued a 'Notice on Adoption Administration' which directed Child Guidance Centres (CGCs) to give a higher priority to making such placements and by 2016, 222 children were so placed.

Family adoption

A small but not insignificant number of children are placed with members of their extended family who have been approved as foster parents for that purpose. In 2016, 702 children were in such kinship placements. Most 'ordinary' adoptions occur in relation to children and adults who are related to their adopters. This may help explain the consequent failure to develop adoption as an option for children in public care.

Step-parent adoptions

The majority of domestic adoptions of children are step-adoptions. Step-parent adoption in Japan is not without its issues. The fact that there is no obligation to engage with the non-custodial parent is particularly problematic: not only is there no consent requirement but there is no necessity to notify either before or after the adoption.

ICA

As a 'receiving' nation, Japanese courts currently process some 300–500 intercountry adoptions (ICAs) annually (a figure which excludes those children

17 www.hrw.org/news/2016/05/27/revised-child-welfare-act-principle-family-based-care-now-guaranteed-law

whose adoptions are finalized before entering the jurisdiction).[18] It is very noticeable that only a small proportion of such adoptions are 'special' (i.e. conforming to the usual ICA model where a 'full' adoption order is granted to third party adopters).[19] Currently, Japan has neither ratified nor signed the Hague Convention, while its role in ICA is further complicated by restrictive immigration laws.

Adoption related issues in human rights reports

Institutionalisation and the right to family life

In 2010, the CRC stated that it was 'concerned at the number of institutionalized children and the insufficient structure established to provide alternatives to a family environment for children in need of special support, care and protection'.[20] This was also of concern to Human Rights Watch, in its 2014 report *Without Dreams: Children in Alternative Care in Japan*,[21] which criticized over-institutionalization and called for fundamental reform. It pointed out that: the vast majority of children in the public care system (over 85 per cent) are placed in government-run institutions, which in 2013 housed just under 34,000 children; the rest are with foster parents or are placed in smaller 'family homes', where five to six foster children are cared for in one family; a relatively tiny number, 303 in 2011, are eventually formally adopted. This continued heavy reliance upon institutionalised care clearly violates the right to family life in Article 20.3 of the Convention on the Rights of the Child.

ICA

The CRC has declared its concern 'at the lack of necessary safeguards to ensure the best interests of the child in cases of intercountry adoption'[22] and 'recommends that the State party take the necessary steps to ensure that the rights of the child are fully protected in cases of ICAs and to consider ratifying the Hague Convention of 1993 on Protection of Children and Cooperation in Respect of Intercountry Adoption'.[23]

Failure to implement recommendations

International bodies have repeatedly made the same recommendations for improving human rights in Japan and have noted a consistent failure in

18 Hayes and Habu, *Adoption in Japan*, p. 82.
19 Judicial Statistics 2012 record: adoption orders, 326; and special adoption orders, 29.
20 CRC, Fifty-fourth session (CRC/C/JPN/CO/3), para. 18.
21 www.hrw.org/report/2014/05/01/without-dreams/children-alternative-care-japan
22 CRC, Fifty-fourth session (CRC/C/JPN/CO/3), para. 17.
23 Ibid., para. 38.

government implementation; a fact formally recorded by the Chairman of the Human Rights Committee (HRC) during the Committee's 2014 review.[24]

The current legislative framework

The law governing adoption was initially stated in the family and succession part of the Civil Code in 1898, but completely revised in 1947, Parts 4 and Part 5 of which now govern family matters. The revised provisions required all adoptions by non-relatives of children under the age of 20 years to be approved by the Family Court in accordance with the welfare principle. Where the child was less than 15 years of age the consent of birth parent/s or legal representative was necessary.[25] The Civil Code defined two types of adoption in Japan: *futsu yoshi*, or 'ordinary' adoption and *tokubetsu yoshi*, or 'special' adoption.

The legislation: adoption related law; domestic

Child Welfare (Amendment) Act 2016

Hailed as a great opportunity for a fundamental improvement of Japan's alternative care system, this legislation embeds a new principle of 'entitlement to family life' which should transform the childcare system and facilitate an increased flow of children from it into the adoption process.

*Family Affairs Proceedings Act 2011 (*Kaji Jiken Tetsuzuki Ho*)*

This replaced the Domestic Proceedings Act 1947 (*Kaji Shimpan Ho*) and now provides the procedural framework that governs the jurisdiction of the Family Court on many family matters, including adoption. Like its predecessor, it provides for Family Court authorisation of adoption agreements in respect of minors (under 15 years of age) and for that court's determination of 'special' adoptions. Otherwise, there is no body of adoption specific legislation, associated procedures and case law precedents to guide an understanding either of current Japanese adoption law or of its historical development.

Child Abuse Prevention Act 2000

This Act, as amended in 2004 and 2007, sets out the responsibilities of the government departments and the prefectures in respect of preventing child abuse and neglect.

24 HRC considered the report of Japan (6th periodic report pursuant to ICCPR requirements), 16 July 2014, at: www.ohchr.org/EN/NewsEvents/Pages/DisplayNews.aspx?NewsID=14878

25 Civil Code, Articles 797 and 798.

Adoption Act 1988

Although often referred to as the Adoption Act 1988, in fact the provisions constitute Articles 817-2 and 817-11 of the Civil Code. It introduced 'special' adoption to make Japanese adoptions more compatible with international norms and to give more protection to adopted children under 6 years of age. A 'special' adoption severs the child's ties, rights and privileges with regard to the birth parent/s and any prior adoptive parent/s. The child must be under the age of 6 at the time the adoption petition is filed or under the age of 8 and have been in the continuous care and custody of the prospective adoptive parents since before their sixth birthday. All persons with legal custody of the child, including the birth and adoptive parents, must consent to the adoption. It also strengthened the legal position of adoptive parents. However, as most annual adoptions continue to be of the traditional 'ordinary' form, which does not require a complete severance of all such legal links, the Japanese adoption process as a whole is more compromised than its common law counterpart.

Child Welfare Law 1947

State control of care provision for orphans and abandoned children was initiated by this legislation while all those in institutions automatically became subject to its provisions. Where a child was voluntarily placed in a CGC or children's home by the parent/s who thereafter ceased contact with their child, then the parent/s were designated as 'missing'. The first step being for the child to be brought to the attention of the CGC which then sought authority under Articles 27–28 from the local Family Court to remove him or her to either: a childcare home (institution); or foster care (foster parents registered to local authority); or for adoption (usually spending some time in the childcare home or foster home). This legislation provided the legal framework for establishing a national foster care system with paid foster parents and for the current network of child guidance centres. It also prohibited adoption agencies from profit-making.

Other relevant provisions

The sheer lack of legislation relating to children is a characteristic of Japanese law.

The legislation: adoption related law; international

Japan is not a signatory to the Hague Convention 1993 on the Protection of Children and Cooperation in Respect of Intercountry Adoption, but it ratified the Convention on the Rights of the Child in April 1994, submitted its initial report for this convention in May 1996 and its last in May 2010. Japan signed and ratified the International Covenant on Civil and Political Rights (ICCPR) in 1979. However, Japan has yet to make the adjustments necessary to ensure Convention compliance in respect of some of its laws relating to children (as noted above).

The Diet ratified the 1980 Hague Convention on the Civil Aspects of International Child Abduction in June 2013.

The legislation: human rights law

The Constitution of Japan is the main domestic source of the country's human rights law which is influenced by the Universal Declaration of Human Rights (UDHR) to which Japan acceded in 1956. The Human Rights Bureau under the Ministry of Justice, the Human Rights Volunteers and the Human Rights Conciliator System are also relevant. Work is ongoing in relation to the Human Rights Protection Bill and the establishment of a National Human Rights Commission. In its 2014 report, the HRC noted the absence of an independent national human rights institution.[26]

Regulating the adoption process

In this jurisdiction, it is perhaps a misnomer to refer to 'the adoption process' when in practice neither the subjects, the official bodies, the role of professionals nor the outcomes are standardised components; and there is a conspicuous lack of data regarding annual adoptions. The gradual legislative creation of such a process involving the State, adoption agencies and professional staff did not displace but simply added to traditional informal practices. In reality, the contemporary domestic adoption process consists of two parallel routes: one which includes a number of different types of agencies (government, independent and hybrid) operating alongside private initiatives, to bring a very small number of proceedings concerning children before the Family Court, and which may conclude with either a 'special' adoption or an alternative judicial determination; and the other, consisting of tens of thousands of applications relating to adult adoptees, which may elude adoption agency involvement, and require only that the parties submit an adoption notice to the family registration office.

The ICA process is also far from straightforward. As Japan is not a signatory to Hague it does not have a central authority. ICAs are facilitated by private adoption agencies which, since the introduction of the Adoption Agency (Regulation) Act 2016, are now required to be registered.

The judiciary

The adoption process in Japan is mainly administrative rather than judicial in nature. The Family Court is the sole determining body with authority to adjudicate on 'special' adoption applications, but these constitute a small minority of annual adoptions, and it must approve 'ordinary' adoptions where the child is not a lineal descendant of the prospective adopters. When a lineal descendant is

26 HRC considered the report of Japan.

adopted, even if the adoptee is a minor, a court decision is not needed for the adoption. This includes children adopted by stepparents and grandparents.[27]

Government bodies

The CGC network (broadly equivalent to UK local authority social services departments) of 206 centres are crucially placed in relation to the 'special' adoption process. They arrange placements and home study reports and issue the all-important certificate identifying the child placed as a 'child who requires protection' which will be required by the Family Court in respect of all 'special' adoptions. However, the following comments of Ayako Harada must be borne in mind:[28]

> Generally speaking, Child Guidance Centres do not attempt to find an adoptive family for children in social care, even when family reunification is deemed impossible. Neither the Child Welfare Act nor the Child Abuse Prevention Act requires Child Guidance Centres to initiate adoption services for the child who cannot be reunited with his or her parents. It seems that Child Guidance Centres provide adoption services only when the parents express a wish to place their child for adoption.

This resonates with a point made by Hayes that 'the low numbers of children in adoption and foster care is related to a strong reliance on private institutions where there is considerable autonomy over childcare decisions, and where there is a financial incentive to retain children in institutional care.'[29]

Adoption agencies

A distinctive feature of the Japanese adoption process is the nature and role of adoption agencies: there are no government adoption agencies nor have there been any 'accredited bodies': all Japanese adoption agencies are private; but since the introduction of the Adoption Agency (Regulation) Act 2016 all are now required to be approved and supervised by the relevant government body.

Private arrangements, whether involving agencies or other third parties, are facilitated by the fact that in Japan, unlike other modern developed nations, there is no central regulating agency authorised to coordinate the roles and responsibilities of all parties, professionals and other agencies that comprise the adoption process. Adoption agencies may evade registration by restricting their activities to

27 Moriguchi, C., 'Child adoption in Japan, 1948–2008: a comparative historical analysis', *Economic Review*, 61(4) (2010): 344

28 Harada, A., 'The Japanese child protection system: developments in the laws and the issues left unsolved', in Atkin, B. (ed.), *The International Survey of Family Law, 2010 Edition*, Bristol, Jordan, 2010, p. 231.

29 Hayes, P., 'Intercountry adoption: a comparative analysis of its effect on domestic adoption rates', Full Research Report, ESRC End of Award Report, RES-000-22-1840. Swindon: ESRC, 2009, p. 5.

placements ostensibly for reasons other than adoption but which over time are converted to become adoption placements. The practice of using 'contracts' with unmarried mothers, to secure the relinquishment of their baby or perhaps unborn child, is strongly associated with unregistered adoption agencies. Until 2016, the role played by unregistered agencies had been a source of concern, particularly as regards those engaged in placing Japanese children for adoption in other countries.[30] The ISSJ, which facilitates domestic adoptions and specialises in ICA, is a private agency but one registered and supported by the Ministry of Health.

Registration of adoption orders

The City Office cannot legally register the adoption decree until the Family Court has heard and determined the application, has waited two weeks to see if the decision is challenged, and has then given its approval to the adoption. In cases where the 'ordinary' adoption involves a minor who is a descendant of one of the adoptive parents, the City Office may register a regular adoption without any necessity for prior approval by the Family Court.

Human rights considerations

Lack of a coherent system

The general lack of a coherent professional regulatory framework with clear provision for 'due process' has attracted repeated criticism from the CRC.[31] This includes legislative weaknesses – such as the fact that Japan is still not a signatory to Hague and the absence of any statutory recognition given to the welfare interests of a child as a governing principle – which jeopardise human rights.

Inadequate control of ICAs

Most such adoptions are privately organised, bypass regulatory processes, and result in only a small proportion of 'special' adoptions; consequently, far fewer Japanese ICA adoptees will enjoy the human rights protections guaranteed to their counterparts in other western countries.

Adoption agencies

The introduction of the 2016 legislation to regulate the activities of private adoption agencies is improving matters but the fact that these agencies are wholly private, with no government control over service costs, leaves the human rights of

30 Cited by Hayes and Habu, *Adoption in Japan*, p. 10.

31 Concluding Observations of the Committee on the Rights of the Child, Japan, UN Doc., CRC/C/15/Add.231 (2004): 'The Committee is concerned that there is limited monitoring or control of domestic and intercountry adoptions, and that there is very limited data available on domestic and intercountry adoptions' (para. 39). See also the 2010 report (para. 14).

all parties vulnerable to abuse. In the past, as the ISSJ has pointed out, some agencies 'charge as much as $60,000'[32] and it has alleged that 'it seems like some private agencies are "selling" new born babies for very high prices'.[33]

The significance of independent lobbying groups

Arguably, without groups like Human Rights Watch helping to raise awareness about the damage to the welfare of children caused by institutionalisation, it is unlikely that the Japanese government and the public more generally would have considered it necessary to push for the changes now embodied in the revised Child Welfare Act. This illustrates the importance of the fundamental human rights to freedom of association and expression.

Thresholds for entering the adoption process: eligibility, suitability and placement

The criteria for entering the adoption process in Japan are complicated. This is to be expected in a jurisdiction where: the purpose of adoption is most often for reasons other than to secure the welfare of a child; the law recognizes two different types of adoption; provision is made for the adoption of both adults and children; and where parents are permitted considerable discretion to make private adoption arrangements.

Role of adoption agency

Pre-placement counselling

There has never been any requirement that Japanese adoption agencies provide pre-placement counselling for those birth parent/s who may be considering voluntarily relinquishing their child for adoption, though many do. For example, locating the birth parent/s, providing pre-placement counselling and ensuring that adoption is the only option for them, is standard practice for the ISSJ.[34] The 2016 Act has now introduced a counselling requirement.[35]

Eligibility and suitability of the parties

The child

A child eligible for 'special' adoption is a 'child who requires protection'. This is further defined under the Civil Code,[36] but in general the child concerned is most

32 HCCH, 'Country profile for intercountry adoption: Japan', the Permanent Bureau, 2013, para. 9.c.
33 Ibid., para. 11.b.
34 HCCH, 'Country profile for intercountry adoption', para. 2.1.C.
35 Author acknowledges advice from Satoshi Minamikata on this matter (note to author, 18.10.17).
36 Civil Code, Article 817, 7.

often either: a non-marital child; an abandoned infant; a child whose parent(s) has/have died or disappeared; a child whose parents are incapable of providing support; or an abused child. The CGC is the only body authorised to confirm the status of such a child and will do so by issuing a declaration to that effect where the child is in the public childcare system, following recourse to the Family Court, but not where he or she is the subject of a private placement. In this context, a Supreme Court ruling should be noted establishing the principle that discrimination against the legal interests of a child born out of wedlock is unconstitutional.[37]

The Civil Code requires a child adoptee to be less than 6 years of age at the time an application is made for his or her 'special' adoption. An exception is allowed for a child up to the age of 8 who has been in the continuous care and custody of the prospective adoptive parents since before the child's sixth birthday.[38] Where the procedure is for an 'ordinary' adoption then the child concerned must be less than 20 years of age, if less than 15, then the consent of a legal representative (usually a parent with full parental rights) is required.[39] The parties must obtain the prior approval of the Family Court.

Most usually, adults are adopted to provide descendants for a childless family or for business purposes. In such circumstances the traditional requirement for 'ordinary' adoptions that the adopters be older than the adoptee, but that the age difference need only be one day,[40] continues to apply.

The birth parent/s

By far the majority of child adoptions result from the consensual relinquishment of babies by young and unmarried mothers shortly after birth. The proportion of children born outside marriage is very low and the social pressure for their consensual adoption is high.

Traditionally, an 'ordinary' adoption took the form of a placement within the extended family, an arrangement made with the approval of the male head of the family, for reasons associated with perpetuating the bloodline in matters of lineage, inheritance, business or simply as a means of keeping alive the family name. However, this is no longer necessary under the current Civil Code and the legal concept of 'the head of the family' does not exist. Adoption of an adult takes the form of a contract to that effect between two adult parties.

The birth parent/s and rehabilitation

Where their child has been admitted to the anonymous care of an institution, and thereafter available for visits, there is little incentive for parents to engage in a

37 Supreme Court (4 June 2008) in 2002 Hanrei Jiho; 1267 Hanrei Taimuzu 92; though this was not an adoption case.
38 Civil Code, Article 817, 5.
39 Ibid., Article 797.
40 Ibid., Articles 792 and 793.

rehabilitation programme. This is reinforced by the institutional financial incentive to retain childcare responsibility. A combination that severely compromises the right of such a child to family life.

The adopters

In 'special' adoptions the Civil Code requires that adopters: be a married couple; both of whom must jointly adopt unless one is a birth parent and the other a step-parent;[41] one must be aged 25 years or more and the other be at least 20 years old;[42] and they must have provided direct care for the adoptee for at least six months immediately prior to making their application to adopt.[43] In 'ordinary' adoptions, the status requirements are more relaxed:[44] adopters are usually married but may, occasionally, be a single applicant; if a relation (e.g. grandparent or step-parent), then recourse to the courts is unnecessary. In neither is there a requirement for a minimum age difference between adopter and adoptee. Japanese adoption law makes no provision for suitability criteria: the statutory emphasis given in common law nations to matters of health and income, etc. are not addressed. The Family Court, however, will require information regarding health, finances and other relevant matters such as living conditions. However, the CGC, through which all 'special' adoptions are arranged, does undertake an approval assessment of prospective adopters, which deals specifically with these matters, the suitability of the home and the 'matching' of child and adopters. In the case of foreign applicants pursuing an ICA of a Japanese child, the matching is finalised by the adoption agency which negotiates directly with the foreign agency representing the adopters.

A single person of either gender is viewed by adoption agencies such as the ISSJ as an acceptable, but not ideal, applicant for a special adoption and he or she must first obtain the consent of the Family Court to proceed which is not always granted. If a family court should approve the adoption of a minor by a cohabiting couple, only one party will be the adopting parent, the other is regarded as a partner of the adopting parent.[45] While there is no specific legal obstacle to prevent cohabiting couples from adopting, in practice whether or not the applicants are of the same gender, the ISSJ does not accept unmarried couples and a family court rarely makes such orders.

LGBT adopters

As of 2017, there is still no national law governing such marriages or addressing LGBT issues in general. Same-sex couples are currently not viewed as suitable

41 Ibid., Article 817, 3.
42 Ibid., Article 817, 4
43 Ibid., Article 817, 5.
44 Ibid., Article 795.
45 Ibid.

applicants for 'special' adoptions: for example, they are not accepted by the ISSJ for either domestic or ICAs. The 'ordinary' adoption of one person by another is an established means of formalising a same-sex relationship and continues to be so in the absence of same-sex marriage.

Placement with consent

As in most other developed nations, orders in favour of step-parents now constitute the highest proportion of annual family adoptions. However, voluntary relinquishment by the birth parent/s has been and remains the normal circumstance catered for by Japanese child adoption law.

Where the child is placed with a family member, with the consent of all concerned, then an 'ordinary' adoption is effected without any need to involve the Family Court. Where the placement is with a married couple unrelated to the child, then, even though the consent of all parties is available, recourse to the Family Court is necessary to ensure the complete and irrevocable vesting of parental rights and duties in the adopters. In the case of an 'ordinary' adoption, the placement may involve a consensually relinquished baby and be made informally in the traditional manner, either directly by the birth parent/s or by an authorised relative. Alternatively, the placement may be made by an intermediary such as a doctor, lawyer, nurse, etc., or an independent private adoption agency, acting on behalf of the birth parent/s. In circumstances where the arrangement to place a child is made by a CGC it is subject to statutory provisions and in practice cannot commence until the prospective adopters are first registered as foster carers. In some but not all cases, where the arrangement is made by a private agency, the same procedure may be followed. The parent/s can exercise considerable influence over placement selection.

In 'special' adoptions there are two alternative processes. First, the placement may be made by the CGC. Following an initial introductory meeting of child and prospective adopters (registered as foster parents) arranged by the CGC, and successful completion of a one–three-month period of mutual familiarisation, the CGC makes a positive decision regarding the feasibility of adoption. An application is lodged with the Family Court and a full six-month probation period ensues after which, following a positive investigative report from a family court officer, the court then makes an adoption order. The placement is accompanied by financial support in accordance with national payment rates for foster carers. Second, it may be made by a private agency. Following an initial agency interview of the prospective adopters, the agency investigates and confirms that the requirements for special adoption are satisfied and the child is placed with the applicants. An application is then made to the Family Court, a six-month probation period ensues after which, following a positive investigative report from a Family Court officer, the court then makes an adoption order.

Placement by the birth parent/s

Direct placement of a child by the birth parent/s or by an intermediary acting on behalf of the birth parent/s, with relatives or non-relatives, for adoption purposes, has long been and continues to be a characteristic of the adoption process in Japan. It is legally permitted even in relation to 'special' adoptions.

Placement without consent

Where the birth parent has abandoned the child, custody is then vested in the Director of the local CGC who can consent to a placement with registered foster carers 'with a view to adoption' pending the decision of Family Court proceedings.

Welfare interests

In practice, while neither the CGC nor the Family Court will countenance an adoption that is clearly incompatible with welfare, the principle has at best a marginal relevance to the adoption process (see below). Adult adoptions proceed on a private contractual basis in which 'welfare', as normally understood, is not a factor.

Placement supervision

In 'special' adoptions, during the six-month trial period from placement to application, the guardianship rights of a child voluntarily relinquished remain with the birth parent/s. A social worker from the placing agency (usually a CGC social worker) will visit and at the end of that period and, in the absence of any contra-indications, will advise the couple to make application to the Family Court and submit a report to the court regarding the quality of family relationships and recommend accordingly.[46]

Human rights considerations

Definitions of 'child' and 'adoption'

While 'special' adoption clearly conforms to the western definition of 'adoption', and therefore offers a corresponding degree of security and permanency, not every child entering the Japanese adoption process will qualify for it. For example, usually a child aged 6 years or more will be ineligible for a 'special' adoption. Such an arbitrary criterion of entitlement to family life is innately discriminatory (though, as Satoshi Minamikata comments, this may only be so from the perspective of western society).[47]

Financial barriers barring children in care from the adoption process

Most children in the public care system in Japan are accommodated in private children's homes, though usually under strict control and supervision by the

46 Civil Code, Article 817, 8.
47 Note to author (27.10.17).

government.[48] Arguably, the system thus contains a built-in disincentive for proactively managing the transfer of abused and neglected children into the adoption process. Much the same financial disincentive governs foster care: foster parents wishing to transform their relationship with a child to one of adoption will incur a financial loss. It may be that a new independent professional assessment service needs to be provided to filter out those children whose needs would be more appropriately met in an adoption context. This should be governed by a legal presumption that a child's human right to permanent family life must prevail, unless there is hard evidence to the contrary.

Unadoptable children in the care system

It is no coincidence that mixed race children are overrepresented in the care system but underrepresented in the adoption process. The CRC has expressed its concern that discrimination persists against children belonging to ethnic minorities, children of non-Japanese nationality, children of migrant workers, refugee children and children with disabilities.[49]

Birth parent preference for institutional care

The birth parent veto on foster care or adoption because of 'loss of face', together with the ongoing discretionary opportunity to retain relationship with a child in an institution, is an obstruction to planning a better future for their children. Arguably this constitutes a flaw in the State's duty of care to children who have become 'wards of the state'.

Maternal consent

The practice developed by some agencies, requiring a mother to sign a 'contract' agreeing to an adoption placement, within 36–72 hours of the birth of the child (often in circumstances where agency payment of costs for the hospital accommodation of mother and child are at least implicitly conditional upon contract completion), may be legally valid but elsewhere it would generally be construed as improperly induced.[50]

Direct adoption placements by the birth parent/s

The right of the birth parent/s to directly place their child with whomsoever they choose, for adoption purposes, is clearly open to abuse and jeopardises the human rights of the children concerned.

48 Social Welfare Act, Articles 2 and 7.
49 CRC, Fifty-fourth session (CRC/C/JPN/CO/3), para. 33.
50 Hayes and Habu, *Adoption in Japan*, pp. 56–68.

Direct adoption placements by third parties

Placements may be made by an intermediary such as a doctor, lawyer or nurse. Again, this bypasses professional assessment as to whether the placement satisfies the best interests of the child test.

Non-assessment of family and step-adoptions

The fact that the adoption of a child, who is a lineal descendant of either the adoptive parent or the adoptive parent's spouse, may take place without judicial oversight or authorisation from the Family Court has been denounced by the CRC as a failure to protect the human rights of such children.[51]

Non-consent in step-adoptions

Step-adoptions may proceed without notification to, nor the necessity for the consent of, the other non-involved birth parent, which pre-empts any possibility of the latter exercising their human rights.

Ineligibility of gay adopters

The fact that gay couples are not acceptable as prospective 'special' adopters would appear to be discriminatory.

Baby hatches

As the stigma attached to being an unmarried mother retains its traditional potency, a 'baby hatch' or *konotori no yurikago* is available in Kumamoto where parents can safely and anonymously leave infants for whom they are unable to continue providing care. In 2016, it was revealed that 13 babies were placed in the Kumamoto baby hatch of which one was non-Japanese. This practice is condemned by the CRC as foreclosing the fundamental human right of a child to access in the future the information necessary to develop an authentic identity.

Adult adoption for tax purposes

That by far the majority of adoptions are of adults, and are motivated by tax or inheritance benefits[52] or other rewards for the adopters, may not present any human rights issues but is so anomalous and incongruous as to question whether

51 CRC, Fifty-fourth session (CRC/C/JPN/CO/3), para. 55.

52 Heisei 28 (ju) 1255, SCrt. (31 January 2017). See also Sayuri Umeda, 'Japan: adoption of grandchild in order to save on inheritance tax can be valid', *Global Legal Monitor* (23 February 2017) at: www.loc.gov/law/foreign-news/article/japan-adoption-of-grandchild-in-order-to-save-on-inheritance-tax-can-be-valid/?loclr=bloglaw

the Japanese adoption process as presently constituted can be properly compared with others.

The hearing and the grounds

All applications for 'special' adoptions must be made to the local Family Court and most 'ordinary' adoptions must be approved there. In the latter case, if the child concerned is a not a lineal descendant of the adoptive parents, the Family Court must adjudicate the adoption but if he or she is a descendant of one of the adoptive parents – as where a child is adopted by a grandparents or spouse of a parent – then the City Office may register a regular adoption without prior Family Court approval.[53] Adult adoptions do not come before a court.

Where consent is available

Consent for the adoption of a child must be available from either a sole surviving parent, a legal guardian, both parents (if both parents are living and remain married), by the birth mother (in the case of a non-marital child), or from the governor of the institution vested with parental rights and duties in respect of the child in the absence of both parents and any guardian.[54] According to the Family Affairs Proceedings Act 2011, s. 164(3), the court must hear the intention/wish of the birth parent(s) in the case of 'special' adoption. This requirement is important in circumstances where the parents of the child to be adopted are not married, either because they never were, or because of divorce. Section 797(2) stipulates, 'where a person to be adopted is cared for by one of his/her parents and that parent does not have parental authority in relation to the person but cares for the person in accordance with s. 766, a legal representative shall obtain the consent of that parent before giving the consent referred to in the preceding paragraph'.

Where an unmarried mother is 20 years of age or older then custody of her child is held to be vested exclusively in her (*shinkensha*) and her consent must be obtained unless the necessity for it can be judicially dispensed with.

Consent of unmarried father

The consent of an unmarried father must be obtained only if he has been vested with parental rights and duties by a court; which happens only after he acknowledges paternity of a child or a family court makes a determination of paternity. The Civil Code provides: a father shall only exercise parental authority with regard to a child of his, to whom he is affiliated, if both parents agree that he shall have

53 Civil Code, Article 798.

54 In the case of an adult adoption, one spouse can apply without the consent of the other, but, in that event, the adoption binds only the adopter and adoptee to the exclusion of the non-consenting spouse.

parental authority (s. 819(4)); and when the parents do not, or cannot, make the agreements referred to in paragraph (1), paragraph (3), and the preceding paragraph, the Family Court may, on the application of the father or the mother, make a ruling in lieu of agreement (s. 819(5)). In no other circumstances is the consent of an unmarried father required.[55]

Consent of a minor

Where the child to be adopted is 15 years of age or older, then his or her consent must also be sought. Where the relinquishing mother is under 20 years of age she is in law a minor and therefore the consent required is that of her parent or guardian.[56]

Where consent is not available

The Civil Code provides that where the director of the local CGC has given consent to a placement with registered foster carers 'with a view to adoption' then the Family Court judge will determine whether the need for parental consent can and should be dispensed with. Where the parent is 'missing' then, typically, if after three years there has been no contact the court is usually prepared to dispense with the need for consent.

Child care adoption: the grounds

The Civil Code provides that the need for parental consent may be judicially dispensed with in circumstances where the birth parent is 'unable to declare [his or her] intention or where there is cruel treatment, malicious desertion by the father and mother, or any other cause seriously harmful to the benefits of a person to be adopted'.[57]

Contested family adoption: the grounds

Contested family applications are a rarity in Japan.

Human rights considerations

Lack of judicial scrutiny

Figures show that 98% of adoptions in Japan do not come before a court; including the adoption of many children by step-parents or other relatives. This in itself

55 The author acknowledges advice from Satoshi Minamikata on this matter.

56 Civil Code, Article 833. This applies to an unmarried minor mother but not to a married mother (a minor is regarded as an adult if she is married; Civil Code Article 753).

57 Ibid., Article 817, 5, 6. The ground is 'unable to declare [his or her] intention' (Fukushima Family Court determination 14 September 1992 Katei Saiban Geppo 45–10–71).

affords the human rights of the parties concerned less protection than they would receive in other countries.

Consent of an unmarried father

As an unmarried mother, aged 20 or more, is held to be exclusively vested with all parental authority in respect of her child, she determines whether or not an uninvolved father is notified of adoption proceedings. Again, this pre-empts the opportunity for a concerned but uninformed father to claim any rights he may have under Article 8 of the ECHR.

Thresholds for exiting the adoption process

The legislative intent behind the introduction of the 'special' adoption procedure was to provide a formal, professionally managed adoption process, equivalent to that of other modern developed nations, which would become the accepted route to adoption for most if not all future adoptions. This has not happened. The 'special' route, while important for many of Japan's vulnerable children and offering a secure legal basis for their future welfare, has not displaced 'ordinary' adoption which continues to be the preferred route for most applicants.

The welfare interests of the child

It is now a legal requirement that the welfare interests of the child be promoted by their proposed adoption.[58] However, in practice the welfare principle does not constitute a uniformly applicable threshold for exiting that process. As mentioned above, 'welfare' may be legitimately interpreted as material advantage; an interpretation more likely to be made in 'ordinary' adoptions, most obviously where the subject is an adult. Moreover, 'ordinary' adoptions do not usually come before the court, so the welfare test is not necessarily applied; this is particularly the case where the adopters are related to the child.

The limitations of the welfare principle as a threshold for successfully exiting this process are very evident in relation to the 'special' adoption of a child in the public care system. Despite provision in the Civil Code for the judiciary to dispense with the need for parental consent in such cases, there is little evidence of a willingness to do so. In the words of Hayes and Habu 'this has meant that unless the parents co-operate, the function of "special" adoption as a way of protecting children from abuse within the family has remained latent'.[59]

Paramountcy

There is no sense in which welfare interests are given the paramount weighting required by Article 21 of the Convention on the Rights of the Child. The

58 Ministry of Foreign Affairs 2001: 113, 143.
59 Hayes and Habu, *Adoption in Japan*, p. 5.

requirement that an applicant's success in the Japanese adoption process depends on the proposed adoption being compatible with the subject's welfare interests falls well short of according governing authority to the principle.

Consent/views of child and welfare interests

Not only is there no requirement that the court hear and take account of the child's views but in most cases it may proceed without his or her consent. The consent of a child, under the age of 15, is not required but a legal representative is appointed to protect their interests and the Family Court may hear opinions of the minor at its discretion. If the child is 15 years of age or older, then their consent is required.[60]

Culturally compatible

Culturally more homogeneous than most western nations, Japan uses its adoption process largely as a means of safeguarding the integrity and continuity of family life, guided by an awareness of bloodlines, which of necessity ensures a high degree of cultural compatibility.

The orders available

There is more variance in the outcome of adoption applications in Japan than in most other modern developed nations. For example, in 2012, the Judicial Statistics reveal that: there were 1,075 applications for 'ordinary' adoption of minors, of which 1,092 were determined, 744 granted, 39 dismissed and 297 withdrawn; while of the 660 'special' adoption applications, 585 were determined, 495 granted, 18 dismissed and 70 withdrawn.[61]

A successful application to the Family Court for an 'ordinary' adoption results in the issue of a certificate allowing 'Permission to adopt' (*yoshi to suru koto o kyoka-suru*). A similar outcome in respect of a 'special' adoption application concludes with the Family Court issuing a final adoption decree (*tokubetsu yoshito-suru*).

Additional orders: post-adoption contact

In practice 'special' adoption is judicially viewed as incompatible with post-adoption contact arrangements. Where it is envisaged that ongoing contact with members of the birth family would be in the welfare interests of the child then the Family Court is likely to consider that an 'ordinary' adoption would be more appropriate.

60 Civil Code, Article 797; see also Family Affairs Proceedings Act, Article 161(1).
61 Judicial Statistics 2016, chart 3. The author is indebted to Satoshi Minamikata for this information.

Alternative orders

In Japan there is no equivalent to the range of public and private orders that can be found in other jurisdictions and which provide opportunities for the judiciary to reject adoption in favour of a more appropriate alternative for furthering the welfare interests of a particular child. The Family Court may reject an application for a 'special' adoption. In that event, a child will be returned to their birth parent/s, or foster parent/s, or to an institution depending on the circumstances, unless an application is lodged for an 'ordinary' adoption. Alternatively, the CGC may decide to simply continue the foster care status and responsibilities of the applicants in respect of the child. Public guardianship may be available under the Civil Code, Articles 834 and 838.

Human rights considerations

'Ordinary' adoption and the welfare of a child

That some children can be assured of the higher degree of protection that their welfare interests receive under a 'special' adoption while others must settle for the lesser protection afforded by an 'ordinary' adoption may constitute discriminatory treatment.

Consent/views of the child

The CRC has recommended that 'the State party strengthen measures to promote the rights of the child to express his/her views fully in all matters affecting him/her in all contexts, including . . . in courts and administrative bodies and also in policy-making processes'.[62]

The effect of an adoption order

The effect is dependent upon whether the adoptee has been the subject of an 'ordinary' or a 'special' adoption process and in the former case whether that subject was an adult or child. In either case, finalising an adoption triggers the rules of consanguinity to proscribe sexual relations between the adoptee and the adopters or other family members within the prohibited degrees of relationship.[63]

Effect on the parties

The child

As in a common law context, the primary legal effect of a 'special' adoption on the child concerned is to 'legitimate' him or her and thereby place that child in the

62 CRC, Fifty-fourth session (CRC/C/JPN/CO/3), para. 44.

63 Note, however, that s. 734 (1) of the Civil Code permits marriage between an adoptee and adoptive sibling.

same legal relationship with their adopters as if born to them and of their marriage. An 'ordinary' adoption also has the effect of conferring the status of 'legitimacy' on the child but the latter is not wholly legally severed from his or her birth family and may, for example, retain rights of inheritance in relation to that family as well as an obligation to support his/her birth family members.[64]

Where the adoptee is an adult then again the primary effect is to place him or her, and invariably the adult is a male, in the same legal relationship with their adopters as if born to them and of their marriage.

The birth parent/s

An 'ordinary' adoption relieves the birth parent/s of their rights and duties in respect of custody and guardianship. It does not wholly and permanently sever the legal links between a child and his or her birth parent/s and such links may be maintained, for example, through the child's inheritance rights. The consequences of a 'special' adoption for the birth parent/s, however, are very similar to those in common law nations: all legal incidences of parental responsibility, including any affected by court orders relating to the child in question, are permanently and irrevocably extinguished.

The adopters

In an 'ordinary' adoption, the legal rights vesting in the adopters are essentially those of custody and guardianship including the responsibility of administering the assets/property of a child adoptee. It does not vest parental responsibilities permanently and absolutely in the adoptive parents. The adoption of an adult for succession and tax avoidance purposes has been a very common practice with complex implications for adopters and birth family members, though now slightly curtailed by legislation.[65]

Revocation of an adoption order

Whether or not an adoption order can be revoked depends on the circumstances and on whether it was an 'ordinary' or a 'special' adoption. An ordinary adoption can be readily dissolved with the mutual consent of the parties. A 'special' adoption conforms closely to the common law model and dissolution is very rare, but when it occurs then the child is returned to his/her birth parents.[66]

Entitlement to post-adoption support services

The financial support provided by the State to adopters offers an inducement for the latter to choose the statutory 'special' adoption process rather than the

64 Civil Code, Article 877.

65 Succession Tax Act article 15(3); see also Bryant, 'Sons and lovers', 321–5.

66 Civil Code, Article 817, 10. In 2016 there was one application and one withdrawal (judicial statistics 2016, chart 3).

traditional 'ordinary' route which does not attract any entitlement to financial support.[67]

Human rights considerations

Distortion of legal function

For most parties to most Japanese adoptions the intended effect of the order is to place adopters and adoptees in a position to claim a fiscal or other similar benefit: it's essentially a 'paper exercise'. For a small minority the intended effect is to safeguard the welfare of a child. That the same adoption order – whether 'ordinary' or 'special' – should satisfy both sets of needs may have no human rights implications but it does give rise to a concern that this adoption process is being largely misused; at least from a western perception.

A non-custodial parent

There is no requirement to notify a non-custodial birth parent that their child has been adopted which would seem to constitute an abridgement of their human rights.

Information rights: disclosure, tracing and reunification

There is no counterpart to the voluntary and statutory services available in the developed western nations, particularly the US and the UK, which facilitate arrangements for contact, tracing and reunification between adoptee and members of their family of birth. On the other hand, the official registry where family records are kept is open for inspection to those who can show good reason for accessing the information. So, for any adult parties to an adoption, acquiring the information necessary to establish contact between them is not very difficult.

Information rights

While an adult adoptee, the subject of a 'special' adoption, has a legal right to access identifying information held in official records, no other party has a corresponding right. Otherwise, the principle is that any person with legitimate reason is entitled to access the *koseki* system.

Information disclosure duties

Generally, the adoptive parents take the evidence of court approval and register the facts relating to the adoption at the City or Ward Office, though in relation to 'special' adoptions this is not strictly necessary as the order terminates all

67 Human Rights Watch, 'Without Dreams', p. 75.

inheritance rights the adoptee had in respect of their family of origin. In those 'ordinary' adoptions which are not brought before the court, the parties simply bring the facts and related documentation to the City or ward Office for registration in the *koseki* which is an official government file held by the City Office or Ward Office that provides a consolidated record of the legal status of each and every citizen including dates of birth, marriage, death and other milestones.[68] An entry in the *koseki* serves as proof of a valid adoption. In a 'special' adoption, the *koseki* will show the names of the adoptive parents, as though they were the birth parents, if the child was under the age of 6 years when adopted;[69] should the child be older when adopted then the *koseki* will show the names of the birth parents. In the case of an 'ordinary' adoption, both the birth and adoptive parents' names are shown.

Maintaining records

All birth and adoption records are held and maintained by the City or Ward office including the *koseki*. The ISSJ has declared that it permanently maintains all files relating to an adoption.[70] In the case of an ordinary adoption (whether of minor or adult), the difficulty of tracing through the *koseki* files may be avoided by referring instead to the Resident Registration System which enables a birth parent to track down the new address of their child and identify the adopters, should they wish to do so.

Tracing and reunification

There is no Japanese counterpart to the statutory services and processes in common law jurisdictions that carefully differentiate and regulate the rights of parties to an adoption in circumstances where one or more wish to locate and make direct contact with others. However, the ISSJ 'assists adoptees if they want to be reunited with birth family. We provide counselling to both sides and make sure that ISSJ intervene at their meeting.'[71]

Human rights considerations

Lack of tracing services

It is possible that in Japan there is not the same need for such services as in other developed nations. It may well be that there are deeply rooted cultural

68 Matsushima, Y., 'Japan: what has made family law reform go astray?', *The International Survey of Family Law*, The Hague, Martinus Nijhoff, 1999, pp. 193–206.
69 Civil Code, Article 817, 2.
70 HCCH, 'Country profile for intercountry adoption', p. 11.
71 Ministry of Health, Welfare and Labour, 'Reference Material: Current State of Alternative Care', March 2014 (as cited in Human Rights Watch, 'Without Dreams' report, p. 12).

disincentives for services that probe the ancestry of those known to belong by birth to different and therefore suspect bloodlines. While access to the information necessary for an adoptee to develop a sense of identity is a human right, and one not facilitated by State services, it is perhaps a right without a corresponding need for many of the parties to the Japanese adoption process.

Conclusion

In Japan the concept of adoption or *yoshi* has a much wider meaning than in modern western nations: it has never been particularly concerned with either providing children for infertile couples nor with finding homes for children in need; its purpose has always very largely been to candidly benefit adopters rather than children; indeed, very few children are adopted. The Japanese adoption process is so different from the others presently being considered as to make a comparative analysis quite challenging.

10 China

Introduction

Beginning with a brief history of the social role of adoption in China, this chapter provides profile data on trends in the contemporary use of adoption, noting jurisdiction-specific characteristics: the fact that this has long been a primary 'sending' nation for intercountry adoption (ICA) purposes; the effect of the one-child policy; the nature and consequences of a poor regulatory regime; and the currently rapid growth in domestic adoptions. It considers the relevance of certain key adoption principles, before outlining the current adoption law and human rights legal framework together with a description of the remit and effect of related regulatory bodies. As with the preceding chapters, it then goes on to identify and discuss the interaction between human rights and adoption law at each stage of the adoption process.

Background

Adoption and human rights: the early challenges

Perhaps the most prominent cultural component, and one with particular implications for adoption in this country, is the traditional preference given to males.[1] Not only has it always fallen to the males to continue the family name, and all that this had come to represent in the community, but they also had the exclusive responsibility of performing ancestor worship duties.[2] There was an expectation that boys would grow up to fulfil the traditional duties of their gender: ensure the continuation of the family lineage and assume responsibility for the care of elderly parents. For a family without boys, daughter-in-law adoption had provided one way of increasing the chances of securing a male heir, but that possibility was ended with the introduction of the Marriage Law 1950 which included provisions for its prohibition.

1 Wolf, A. and Huang, C., *Marriage and Adoption in China: 1845–1945*, Stanford University Press, 1980; Wang, F. and Lee, J., 'Adoption among the Qing nobility and its implications for Chinese demographic behaviour', *History of the Family*, 3(4) (1998): 411–27.

2 Menski, W., *Comparative Law in a Global Context: The Legal Systems of Asia and Africa*, Cambridge, University Press, 2000.

Shaping modern adoption policy

The 'one child' policy,[3] introduced in 1979, instituted a set of regulations that limited the number of children per family, in an attempt to reduce poverty and hunger in what was then the world's most populous nation. Unsurprising it quickly led to a surplus of girls. As Greenhalgh and Li noted in 1995, in the province of Shaanxi consistently more girls than boys were given away for adoption or abandoned in response to policy dictates.[4] This abandonment of many disabled or female babies overwhelmed the nation's orphanages and generated a black market in which children – particularly male babies and toddlers – were treated as commodities, to be bought or stolen and sold on by unscrupulous traffickers,[5] despite such practices being specifically prohibited.[6] It is against such a policy background that the government enactment of the Adoption Law in April 1992, and its amendment in 1998, must be viewed.

The Adoption Law was initially restrictive. Adopters had to be childless, over the age of 35 and meet residency requirements if they were eligible to adopt any of the many thousands of abandoned children in China's overcrowded orphanages. It was relaxed somewhat in 1998 when the upper age limit was reduced to 30 and the childless restriction was removed in order to encourage domestic adoption of orphaned, abandoned or disabled children. Zhong, in 2002, stated that the official goal was to place eight children domestically for every ICA.[7] Since then, steps have been taken to progress this strategy. The Ministry of Civil Affairs declared in its 2003 report that 'adoption is now seen as the best option for children'[8] and in the 2005 report to the UN Committee on the Rights of the Child (CRC) it was stated that 'China's policy with regard to adoption issues can be expressed as, 'Domestic adoptions first, intercountry adoptions as appropriate'.[9]

As the one-child policy was relaxed, but rates of abortion and infertility continued to reduce the children available, so domestic adoption increased. Over

3 White, T., *China's Longest Campaign: Birth Planning in the People's Republic, 1949–2005*, Ithaca, NY, Cornell University Press, 2006; Scharping, T., *Birth Control in China, 1949–2000: Population Policy and Demographic Development*, New York, RoutledgeCurzon, 2003; David, D., '"Never mind if it's a girl, you can have another try": the modification of the one-child family policy and its implications for gender relations in rural areas', in Delmen, Ostergaard and Christiansen (eds), *Remaking Peasant China: Problems of Rural Development and Institutions at the Start of the 1990s*, Denmark, Aarhus University Press, 1990, pp. 81–91.

4 Greenhalgh, S. and Li, J., 'Engendering reproductive policy and practice in peasant China: for a feminist demography of reproduction', *Signs*, 20(3) (1995: 601–41.

5 Some level of insight into the world of trafficking in China may be found in Garrow, J., *The Pink Pagoda*, WND Books, 2012; but see, further, at: http://research-china.blogspot.co.uk/2012/03/review-of-jim-garrows-pink-pagoda.html

6 Adoption Law, Article 31.

7 Zhong, J., 'China domestic adoption', at: www.chinesechildren.org/Newsletter%5CWindow%20to%20China/WTC_03_2002.pdf

8 Ministry of Civil Affairs, *People's Republic of China, China Country Report*, 2003, p. 52.

9 UN CRC, *Second Periodic Report of States Parties Due in 1997, China*, 15 July 2005 (CRC/C/83/Add.9), para. 162, at: www.refworld.org/docid/43f305580.html [accessed 30 August 2017]

time, a distinct policy emphasis emerged which focused on progressing China's Waiting Child programme – being primarily concerned with finding homes for children with special needs. In 2011 quite stringent additional restrictions were imposed upon intercountry adopters which greatly increased the waiting time for a child, resulting in a sudden and radical reduction in the number of children adopted along that route.

Transracial

The overwhelming majority of Chinese, at 91.59 per cent, are of Han ethnicity. China, therefore, has had little opportunity to practise domestic transracial adoption. Indeed, there is little evidence of transracial adoption in the domestic adoption process. However, China in fact has a very strong association with transracial adoption: for many decades ICA by Caucasians in the US and Europe consisted very largely of Chinese and Korean children who have undoubtedly made the largest contribution to total international transracial adoptions.

Principles

The welfare interests of the child

The 2005 report to the CRC submitted that 'there is no law, from basic laws such as the General Principles of Civil Law and the Criminal Code, to specific statutes such as the Marriage Act, the Education Act and the Inheritance Act, that does not reflect the "greater rights and interests of the child"'.[10] However, references to the interests of the child in both the Law for the Protection of Minors and the Adoption Law are at best cursory and this continued to be of concern to the CRC in its 2013 report when it stated that 'the best interests of the child is not always fully reflected and incorporated in key child-related acts and policies' and recommended that 'the right of the child to have his or her best interests taken as a primary consideration and their right to be heard are fully taken into account in all decisions regarding custody, residence, contact or other issues which have an important impact on the life and development of the child'.[11] There is no suggestion that such interests attract a priority weighting or that any advocacy or assertion of such rights would warrant specialist legal representation. As China has ratified the International Convention on the Rights of the Child it must be assumed that this country considers itself bound by the Convention but there is little evidence that China's domestic laws have been adjusted to fully embody

10 Ibid., para. 33.

11 UN CRC, *Concluding observations on the combined third and fourth periodic reports of China (including Hong Kong and Macau Special Administrative Regions)*, adopted by the Committee at its sixty-fourth session (16 September–4 October 2013), 4 October 2013 (CRC/C/CHN/CO/3-4), paras 30 and 54, at: www.refworld.org/docid/5263de9d4.html [accessed 9 September 2017]

Convention principles and less that their implementation gives full effect to Convention rights.

Openness

There is no culture of 'openness' in Chinese adoption law and practice. In fact, the Adoption Law, Article 22, specifically provides for the opposite (see below). It may also be the case that, for foreign adopters, part of the attraction of adopting from China lies in the fact that their adopted child will not have any ties with their family of origin: as only 'orphans' or 'abandoned' children are available for ICA, this precludes ongoing contact arrangements of any form.

Contemporary adoption trends

There has been a noticeable decrease in the children available: on a domestic basis, this is due in part to increased prosperity which has resulted both in fewer children being abandoned, the continued relaxation of the 'one-child policy' and an increase in the number of families choosing to have more than two or more children and pay the related fine; on an intercountry basis, there are simply fewer children available for foreign adopters. Although this country is invariably associated with ICA, unsurprisingly given the sheer volume of children involved and the duration of its record as a sending country, a sense of perspective is needed: domestic adoptions have always outnumbered those flowing along the intercountry route. Johnson reports that for the 1990s 'the number of domestic adoptions from orphanages certainly exceeded the number of international adoptions at the beginning of the decade'.[12] In 2001, as the UN reported, while China had 8,644 ICAs, these constituted only 19 per cent of total adoptions for that year.[13] By 2014 there were only 2,774 ICAs but domestic adoptions had increased considerably.

Childcare adoption

The Law for the Protection of Minors, Article 8, requires parents to 'fulfill their responsibility of guardianship and their obligations according to law to bring up minors' and specifically directs that they 'shall not maltreat or forsake the minors', while Article 52 warns that criminal proceedings will be initiated against 'whoever maltreats a minor family member in a vicious manner', but there is no authority permitting implementation of preventative child protection measures. Although Article 12 provides for the removal of parental rights in circumstances of child abuse and neglect, and Article 4(3) of the Adoption Law provides authority for

12 Johnson, K., 'Politics of international and domestic adoption in China', *Law & Society Review*, 36(2) (2002): 387.

13 UN Dept. of Economic and Social Affairs, 'Child adoption: trends and policies', 2009, p. 214.

the adoption of children under the age of 14 where 'parents are unable to rear them due to unusual difficulties', these provisions are very rarely used. Article 8, however, frees up orphans, abandoned infants or children under the care of social welfare institutes – whose own parents cannot be ascertained and found – for possible adoption. It would seem that while parental absence is viewed as an acceptable basis for adoption, parental failure is not.

Frost makes the point that 'child abuse and neglect not only is not the emphasis in the current Chinese adoption system, but is also not the main reason for building a legal adoption relationship'.[14] Instead, as the 2003 report goes on to explain, the care strategy is focused on orphaned or abandoned children for whom the service provision is as follows:[15]

> in general, a placement for the child is first sought in the community, with the orphaned child's extended family, following traditional patterns of care. Where such community care is not possible, children are placed in social welfare institutions, from which adoption or fostering opportunities can be assessed. In locations where local conditions mean that social welfare institutions do not exist, dispersed foster care is found for this group of children.

It needs to be said, however, that the term 'orphan' is suspect: mostly, the children in orphanages or otherwise in the care of social welfare institutes have a live parent or parents but have been abandoned by them: for reasons of poverty; because their parents have left them and moved to cities in search of employment; or because of a disabling condition, other health issues, or because they are not of the desired gender.

Orphanages are where children available for domestic and ICA are accommodated. There are now over 1,000 orphanages in China containing children who, because they are orphans or have been abandoned, cannot be reunited with their birth family. While the China Center of Adoption Affairs (CCAA) permits and regulates the small minority of orphanages designated as suitable for ICA, there are hundreds, perhaps thousands, of orphanages that are not so officially designated but quite probably have informal arrangements with those that are.

Foster care

China is in the process of changing from its traditional reliance upon institutional care to developing an emphasis on foster care.[16] In 2000 the Ministry of Civil Affairs made a policy commitment to promote foster care in response to the problem of increasing numbers of orphaned and abandoned children as the most

14 Frost, N., *Child Welfare: Child Placement and Children Away from Home*, New York, Taylor & Francis, 2005, p. 122.

15 Ministry of Civil Affairs, *People's Republic of* China, p. 52.

16 See, for example, Beckett, C. and Thoburn, J., 'Family placements from a Chinese institution', *Adoption & Fostering*, 26(3) (2002): 19–27.

appropriate means of facilitating their reintegration into family life. It is the view of the Ministry that 'this policy is one of the most important approaches to the "socialisation of social welfare", that is the development of civil society and community approaches in welfare provision'.[17]

Foster parent adoption

For many years it has been standard practice for social welfare institutes to place some children in foster care under the direct supervision of institute staff. In certain circumstances where the foster parents meet the eligibility criteria, then, with the permission of the institute, they may later adopt that orphaned or abandoned foster child. Article 26 of the Marriage Act declares that:

> The State shall protect lawful adoption. The relevant provisions of this Act governing the relationship between parents and children shall apply to the rights and duties in the relationship between foster-parents and foster-children. The rights and duties in the relationship between a foster-child and his natural parents shall terminate with the establishment of his adoption.

Family adoption

A strong family ethos, traditionally an important characteristic of Chinese culture, continues to be respected and reinforced by the childcare authorities. Where members of the birth family are dead or cannot be located then an abandoned child will often be fostered, without remuneration, with other relatives who seldom consider adoption. Adoption by relatives (*qinqi*) retains its attraction as a means of strengthening bloodlines, vesting legal status and responsibility in step-parents and assisting family members compromised by the one-child policy. It must also be borne in mind that an unknown number of informal adoptions and illegal adoptions occur, particularly in rural areas of China, in accordance with traditional customs, which avoid registration.[18]

As domestic adoption gathers momentum in China, a singular characteristic is the preference given by adopters to the adoption of a child to whom they are related, however distantly (*goo Guoji*, or 'agnatic adoption').[19] The adoption of a relative raises no issues in terms of family bloodlines and indeed their strengthening may often be a motivating factor for kinship adoption.[20] The cultural significance of kinship adoptions would seem to be recognized by Article 7 of the Adoption

17 Ministry of Civil Affairs, *People's Republic of* China, p. 54.

18 Zhang, W., 'Child adoption in contemporary rural China', *Journal of Family Issues*, 27 (3) (2006): 301–40.

19 Author acknowledges advice from Weiguo Zhang on this matter (note to author, 3.11.2014).

20 Cohen, M. L., *Kinship, Contract, Community, and State: Anthropological Perspectives on China*, Stanford University Press, 2005.

Law, as revised in 1998, which facilitates the 'adoption of a child of a collateral relative by blood of the same generation and up to the third degree of kinship'.

Step-parent adoptions

Adoption by a stepfather or stepmother is specifically facilitated in China under Article 14 of the Adoption Law. It is free from most constraints governing the eligibility of adopters.

ICA

ICAs from China began in 1992 and grew very rapidly. As Johnson has noted:[21]

> Since 1994 China has been among the top three 'sending countries' and from 2000 to 2010 it has been the world's number one source of intercountry adoptees in all but one year. In 2005, the peak year of ICA from China and near peak for all ICA, China contributed 14,000 of the 44,000 children adopted internationally, and 8,000 of the roughly 22,700 ICAs to the USA.

However, since 2005, when China signed the Hague Convention, the annual number of ICAs has fallen dramatically. The process has now become time-consuming, arduous and expensive with a six-year waiting list. It has also become very largely a process for channelling older or special needs children towards overseas care. Indeed, whereas in 2005, 9 per cent of children adopted from China were defined as having special needs, by 2009 the number had jumped to 49 per cent, according to the CCAA. New rules, introduced by the CCAA, which took effect on 1 May 2007 and were further refined in 2017, have restricted the eligibility of adopters and increased the bureaucracy of the process.

Adoption related issues in human rights reports

The UN Committee on Economic, Social and Cultural Rights (CESCR) in its 2014 report[22] addressed some issues of varying relevance for adoption. It noted, for example, that China does not have a comprehensive anti-discrimination law that protects all marginalised and disadvantaged individuals and groups,[23] that gender inequality persists[24] and urged that coercive measures, such as forced

21 Johnson, K., 'Challenging the discourse of intercountry adoption: perspectives from rural China', in Gibbons, J. J. and Rotabi, K. S. (eds), *Intercountry Adoption: Policies, Practices and Outcomes*, Ashgate, Surrey, 2012.
22 *Concluding observations on the second periodic report of China, including Hong Kong, China, and Macao, China*, 13 June 2014, E/C.12/CHN/CO/2, at: www.refworld.org/docid/53c77e524.html [accessed 30 August 2017]
23 Ibid., para. 14.
24 Ibid., para. 16.

abortions and forced sterilisation,[25] be prohibited. While welcoming the decision to revise the 'one-child policy' by allowing couples to have a second child when one of the parents is an only child, it recommended that 'the State party take all necessary measures, including the revision of its family planning policies, to ensure that everyone can freely and responsibly decide on the number and spacing of their children'.[26] The CRC, in its 2013 report, expressed more pointedly its dissatisfaction with the current management of the adoption process and called upon the authorities to 'urgently review the current mechanisms and procedures for domestic and intercountry adoption'.[27]

The current legislative framework

The legislation: adoption related law; domestic

Adoption law in China began comparatively recently with the Adoption Law of the People's Republic of China, which took effect on 10 November 1992,[28] was subsequently amended on 1 April 1999,[29] and has governed all adoptions in China ever since. This formative legislation was augmented, on 10 November 1993, by the Implementation Measures on the Adoption of Children by Foreigners. As noted by the CRC, there are also a great many national laws relating to children including: the Law for the Protection of Minors; the Law on the Prevention of Juvenile Delinquency; Provisions for the Management of Social Welfare Institutes; and Provisions for the Further Development of Welfare for Orphans.[30]

Other relevant provisions

The Criminal Code (as amended in 1997), Article 240, defines the offences associated with trafficking children.

The legislation: adoption related law; international

For present purposes it should be noted that China signed the Convention on Protection of Children and Cooperation in Respect of Intercountry Adoption and

25 Ibid., para. 26.
26 Ibid., para. 25.
27 CRC, sixty-fourth session (16 September–4 October 2013), 4 October 2013, para. 56(a).
28 Adopted at the 23rd Meeting of the Standing Committee of the Seventh National People's Congress on 29 December 1991, promulgated by Order No. 54 of the President of the People's Republic of China on 29 December 1991, effective 1 April 1992.
29 Adopted at the 23rd Meeting of the Standing Committee of the Seventh National People's Congress on 29 December 1991, and amended in accordance with the 'Decision on Revising the Adoption Law of the People's Republic of China' at the Fifth Session of the Standing Committee of the Ninth National People's Congress on 4 November 1998, effective 1 April 1998.
30 UN CRC, *Second Periodic Report of States Parties Due in 1997*, para. 6.

has ratified: the UN Convention on the Rights of the Child in 1992; the International Covenant on Economic, Social and Cultural Rights, the International Covenant on Civil and Political Rights and the Optional Protocol to the Convention on the Rights of the Child on the Sale of Children, Child Prostitution and Child Pornography in 2002; and the Hague Convention on Protection of Children and Co-operation in respect of Intercountry Adoptions in 2005. It began implementation of the latter on 1 January 2006.

The legislation: human rights law

The Constitution of the People's Republic of China affirms the equal status before the law of all citizens and provides legal protection for the rights of children. The General Principles of Civil Law, the Rights and Interests of Women Act, the Protection of Minors Act, the Marriage Act and other statutes also stipulate the rights that children should enjoy.

As noted by the UN CESCR in its 2014 report, China has established 25 new government institutions with similar functions to those of a national human rights institution and committed to a National Human Rights Action Plan (2012–15). Nevertheless, the Committee recommended that China 'establish an independent national human rights institution with a broad mandate to promote and protect human rights, including economic, social and cultural rights, in line with the Paris Principles, and provide it with adequate financial and human resources'.[31]

Regulating the adoption process

The CCAA is the government body with responsibility for regulating the adoption process. The Adoption Law provides the authority and identifies the subject matter for CCAA regulation.

The judiciary

The adoption process is exclusively administrative rather than judicial in character. Essentially, this is because there are no determinative legal issues, as all available children are held to be either orphans or abandoned and therefore, by definition, there is no need to seek parental consents: all legal rights in respect of such children are viewed as vested in the State; and, as a matter of government policy, adoption is the predetermined option judged to be most compatible with their welfare. The decision to approve or reject an adoption application is made by the CCAA.

It was the view of the UN CESCR in its 2014 report that there were deficiencies in the judicial grasp of human rights and it therefore urged that all necessary legislative and administrative measures be taken to guarantee the full

31 CESCR, *China*, 13 June 2014, para. 8, at: www.refworld.org/docid/53c77e524.htm l [accessed 30 August 2017]

independence and impartiality of the judiciary and that systematic human rights training be provided.[32]

Government bodies

The CCAA is the regulatory body for all domestic adoptions and ICAs. As the Central Authority responsible for all ICAs, it processes all such applications which must be submitted through a registered adoption agency. It is also responsible for the welfare of children in social welfare institutes (or orphanages) that are available both for domestic adoption and for ICA.

These institutes are complex facilities providing care for a range of children and adults with social and healthcare needs. Established by government or by local collectives, they include orphanages which provide care and guardianship and arrange appropriate education for orphans and abandoned children throughout their childhood. They also provide specialist health and care services for children with more profound physical and intellectual disabilities. As mentioned, some of the children are placed in the homes of local families under the supervision of institute staff, others are adopted by domestic or intercountry adopters. The Adoption Law, Article 5(2), expressly permits the Institutes to place children for adoption.

Adoption agencies

The CCAA maintains a register of adoption agencies and will only accept adoption applications that are channelled through those agencies. While there are no registered domestic Chinese agencies that operate on a for-profit basis, some international agencies based in the US or Europe and engaged in arranging adoptions from China, do so.

Registration of adoption orders

The *hukou* system, or family register, is probably the nearest equivalent to the register of births, marriages, deaths, etc. maintained under the oversight of a Registrar in common law countries. It provides a record of household registration as required by law which usually includes the births, deaths, marriages, divorces, and moves, of all family members and registers any formally completed adoption. The system does not register the very many de facto or customary adoptions which may total two or three times the number registered.

Human rights considerations

Article 3 of the Adoption Law stipulates that 'adoption shall not contravene laws and regulations on family planning'. This clause makes obvious the legislative (and

32 Ibid., para. 10.

political) intent that the government's family planning programme is to provide the governing policy framework for adoption in China.

Due process

The lack of a judicial process rests on the premise that as the prospective adoptees are all orphans or abandoned children there are no consent issues requiring adjudication. This premise is questionable – particularly given the 2015 ECPAT report estimating that nearly 70 million children have been left behind in rural villages as their parents migrate to the cities to seek employment[33] – in many cases, the children have parents who could be located. Arguably, the absence of an inquisitorial legal capacity can leave the Chinese adoption process open to challenge on the grounds of not always being in a position to: guarantee the rights of the children involved under Article 6 of the Convention on the Rights of the Child when determining an application; nor to be certain that orphanages when admitting children to that process are acting in a manner wholly compliant with the requirements of Article 21.

Incoherent child protection and adoption processes

The Law for the Protection of Minors, Article 4(3), fails to provide any link between the provisions of Article 12 (under which all parental rights may be stripped from those found guilty of abuse or neglect of their children) and provisions of the Adoption Act (under which children are defined as eligible for adoption). This legal lacuna operates to deny the possibility of a route whereby any such children could enter the adoption process (or, indeed, the childcare system) and as such violates the right of a child, under Article 20 of UNCROC, to a family environment.

Thresholds for entering the adoption process: eligibility, suitability and placement

Role of adoption agency

In domestic adoption, the placement is made by the local orphanage for a one-month probationary period. Under Article 12 'if the parents of a minor are both persons without full civil capacity, the guardian(s) of the minor may not place out him (her) for adoption, except when the parents may do serious harm to the minor'. The child protection caveat clearly licenses the appropriate State authority to act unilaterally in placing a child at risk of abuse or neglect for adoption.

The placement process for an ICA must take place in China but the monitoring of that placement takes place in the adopters' country after adoption. The CCAA

33 www.ecpat.org/wp-content/uploads/2016/10/3.-SECTT-CHINA.pdf

requires adoption agency reports from the 'receiving' country to confirm that the child and the placement are developing satisfactorily.

Pre-placement counselling

There is no formal requirement in Chinese law that any of the parties to an adoption should receive pre-placement counselling. That does not necessarily mean that counselling will not be offered: it will certainly form part of the application process in ICA; and most probably will occur, to some degree, in relation to third party domestic adoption.

Eligibility and suitability of the parties

The child

The Adoption Law, Article 4, states that a child may be eligible for adoption if under the age of 14, and is either: an orphan; an abandoned infant or child whose parents cannot be ascertained or found; or a child whose parents are unable to rear them due to unusual difficulties. Article 8 adds that 'orphans, disabled children or abandoned infants and children, who are raised in the social welfare institutes, and whose biological parents cannot be ascertained or found, may be adopted irrespective of the restrictions that the adopter shall be childless and adopt one child only'. Article 25 of the Marriage Act declares that 'children born out of wedlock shall enjoy the same rights as children born in wedlock'.

The birth parent/s

The Adoption Law, Article 10, states that: 'where the parents intend to place out their child for adoption, they must act in concert. If one parent cannot be ascertained or found, the other parent may place out the child for adoption alone.' This right to place may be mediated by orphanage directors or others.

The birth parent/s and rehabilitation

In the 2005 report to the UN CRC it was stated that:[34]

> The ultimate objective of children's welfare institutions is to help children return to their family and society. To this end, civil administration bureaux are to enhance their promotion of adoption, foster-care and semi-fostering by families, and to introduce family-style care in children's welfare institutions to the extent possible.

34 UN CRC, *Second Periodic Report of States Parties Due in 1997, China*, para. 165.

There is no indication that in fact such institutions have the responsibility, resources or skilled staff to undertake the 'failed parenting' work necessary for the safe rehabilitation of a child to their family of origin. They will, however, make every attempt to place the child and care responsibility within the broader kinship network.

The adopters

The Adoption Law, Article 6, states that the prospective adopters must be: childless; capable of rearing and educating the adoptee; have no illness which is deemed medically as inappropriate for the adopter to adopt children; and must have reached the age of 30. Articles 8 and 9 add, respectively, that: the adopter may adopt one child only, male or female; and where a male person without spouse adopts a female child, the age difference between the adopter and adoptee shall be no less than 40 years. Article 10 imposes the condition that 'where a person with spouse adopts a child, the husband and wife must adopt the child in concert'. Some of the criteria – such as the age requirement – are the same for both domestic and intercountry adopters, but most differentiate between the two and apply more stringently in respect of the latter. There is no residency requirement.

Article 7 of the Adoption Law states that 'the adoption of a child belonging to a collateral relative by blood of the same generation and up to the third degree of kinship' is to be free of the restrictions in Articles 4, 5 and 9 as well as the restriction to a minor under the age of 14. Further, as regards adoption by a Chinese citizen resident overseas, the same Article declares that 'in adopting a child belonging to a collateral relative by blood of the same generation and up to the third degree of kinship, may even be not subject to the adopter childless status'. Again, the kinship preference is evident also in Article 18 which declares that 'where a spouse places out a minor child for adoption after the death of the other spouse, the parents of the deceased shall have the priority in rearing the child'. In addition to the above general eligibility/suitability requirements of prospective adopters, Article 21 of the Adoption Law outlines the stages to be followed by intercountry adopters which, since implementation of Hague in 2006, now complies with the related procedure (see Chapter 3). This has been supplemented by the more specific and restrictive CCAA eligibility criteria for intercountry adopters issued in 2007 and 2011 which are as follows –

> Couples must be heterosexual and married: for a first marriage, the couple must be married over 2 years; if either spouse has 1–2 divorces, the current marriage needs to be a minimum of 5 years; where one or both spouses have 3 or more divorces they are ineligible. The married couple must be aged 30 to 50 years old: 30 to 40 for a child 6 to 18 months old; 40 to 45 for a child 12 to 36 months old; 45 to 50 for a child of 36 months; or 30 to 55 years of age

31 CESCR, *China*, 13 June 2014, para. 8, at: www.refworld.org/docid/53c77e524.htm l [accessed 30 August 2017]

> if applying for a special needs child. Both parents must have received education at or above high school or vocational skill training. The following prohibitive criteria now apply: diagnosed with major depression or any other severe mental health concerns; current diagnosis of depression or anxiety or currently on medication for depression or anxiety (must be treatment and medication free for over 2 years, no history of alcoholism within the last 10 years); history of cancer; blindness or deafness; any infectious disease or disease which requires long-term treatment and which affects life expectancy (malignant tumors, epilepsy. lupus, nephrosis, etc); BMI of 40 or more; and any major surgery or transplant within the last 10 years, or use a wheelchair or mobility aid or have missing limbs. The applicants must show a positive net worth (assets vs. liabilities) of at least $80,000.00 with an income earning of over $10,000 per person in the household, including the adopted child. Adoptive parents must demonstrate an annual minimum combined income of $30,000. Families are not eligible to adopt if any of the following apply: current warrants or currently on probation; history of drug use or charges; any arrest for a violent crime (e.g. assault); history of domestic violence, sex abuse, abandonment or abuse of children, even if not arrested or incriminated; any felonies. There may be some flexibility where the parent has less than three criminal records of slight severity with no serious outcomes with ten years passed or less than 5 traffic law violations with no severe outcomes.
>
> The CCAA limits the number of children in the household to a maximum of five. The following couples may adopt: couples with less than 5 children under 18 years old living in the household; couples with adult children (not living in the home); couples with more than 4 children in the family, but not all living at home. If there are more than 4 children living in the household, the applicants are restricted to special needs children. An applicant who has recently given birth must wait until the child is 12 months old. Applicants with religious beliefs that prohibit any kind of medical treatment, including blood transfusions, for the child, will not be eligible to adopt.[35]

Since 15 March 2011, the CCAA has permitted applications from single females, provided they are applying for a special needs child and can fulfil certain restrictive criteria. Further amendments to adopter eligibility criteria were added in 2017. In all cases, the mandatory home study must be performed by a licensed social worker employed by an adoption agency registered with the CCAA.

LGBT adopters

Adoption by gay couples is prohibited. Rules introduced in 2006 required adopters to be a heterosexual couple married for at least two years. In 2012, for the avoidance of all doubt, the CCAA prohibited single adopters; a stricture that may be relaxed in relation to prospective adopters of special needs children. The

35 http://cccwa.mca.gov.cn/article/PoliciesRegulations

prohibition was specifically targeted at eliminating applications from single women in same-sex relationships who had accounted for up to one-third of ICAs to the US in the late 1990s.[36]

Placement with consent

The Adoption Law of the People's Republic of China, Article 5, declares that the following citizens or institutions are entitled to place a child for adoption: the guardians of an orphan; social welfare institutions; and parents unable to rear their children due to unusual difficulties.

Placement by the birth parent/s

Birth parent placements are specifically permitted, under Article 5 of the Adoption Law, in circumstances where 'parents are unable to rear their children due to unusual difficulties': it is unclear how this provision is interpreted and exercised; it may be that it is confined to placements with first party or other relatives.

Welfare interests

Government policy decrees that adoption is the best option for meeting the welfare interests of abandoned or orphaned children.

Placement supervision

Domestic adoption procedures allow for a one-month probationary period. As the placement is made by the orphanage director in the exercise of his or her guardianship authority, it is probable that the director will undertake such visits as are necessary to ensure the care and safety of the child. In ICAs, the regulatory process focusses on post- rather than pre-adoption placement supervision to ensure that the matching and subsequent family assimilation of the child are satisfactory. The requirements of the Guarantee of Adopted Children's Rights and Interests by Intensive Protection Measures, introduced in April 2011, imposed new duties upon the CCAA including requirements that it intensify its post-placement work: the time for submitting post-placement reports is extended; the content of the reports must address specified areas of concern; and the frequency of reporting is increased.

Human rights considerations

Birth parent placements

While permitted by the Adoption Law, such a placement clearly breaches a child's human rights and is contrary to the Hague Convention, Article 29, which

36 Ibid., at p. 59.

prohibits direct contact between birth parents (or a child's guardian) and prospective adopters before professional assessments are concluded to verify the status of the child as legally adoptable and the prospective adopters as eligible and suitable.

The 'one child' policy

This policy clearly breaches the human rights of parents.[37] Also, however, when combined with the preference for male children, it has placed the human rights of female children at risk as gender discrimination leads to girls being disproportionately represented in orphanages and in ICA.

Adoption as a forced option due to lack of State family support services

The CRC has expressed its concern about the widespread abandonment of children in mainland China, particularly children with disabilities and girls, and has urged 'the State party to take all necessary effective family-support measures to avoid the separation of children from their family environment by . . . providing appropriate assistance and support services to parents and legal guardians'.[38]

Trafficking

For some years there has been a suspicion that many children enter the Chinese adoption process illegally. As noted by the CRC 'thousands of children are estimated to be abducted, trafficked and sold every year, including for illegal adoption purposes'. It urged that 'China investigate all cases of abductions and unlawful adoptions of children, including from hospitals and "orphanages"'.[39]

Eligibility restrictions on adopters

Many of the restrictions on adopter eligibility introduced in recent years – such as those on same-sex couples, on single persons, on gay couples, or on those with a record of minor offences or of depression, etc. – would not be constraints on applicants in their country of origin because of a lack of any evidence that they have a bearing on child welfare. Some would constitute discrimination.

The hearing and the grounds

The legal adoption process in China is not adjudicative and does not require a formal 'hearing' as such. The resulting lack of any associated caselaw is a feature of the adoption process in this country.

37 The detrimental effects of this policy are far reaching. As Margaret Ryznar points out 'asylum claims based on the 1-child policy have been rejected by courts in the US' (note to author, 11.10.17)
38 CRC, sixty-fourth session, para. 51.
39 Ibid., paras 55 and 56(c).

Where consent is available

Chinese adoption is unequivocally consensual. As stated in Article 11 of the Adoption Law, 'adoption of a child and the placing out of the child for the adoption shall both take place on a voluntary basis'. In practice, all parental rights and responsibilities in respect of an abandoned child are legally vested in the State (the social welfare institute or orphanage), which greatly simplifies the process of obtaining the necessary consents.

Step-adoptions in particular are treated favourably. Under Article 14, 'a step-father or step-mother may, with the consent of the parents of the step-son or step-daughter, adopt the step-son or step-daughter', and that such an adoption may be free from the restrictions specified in Articles 4, 5 and 6 of the Adoption Law, as well as from the restrictions that the adoptee must be under the age of 14 and the adopter may adopt one child only.

Consent of unmarried father

The Adoption Law, Article 10, requires birth parents to 'act in concert' when placing a child for adoption but states that if one parent 'cannot be ascertained or found, the other parent may place out the child for adoption alone'. In practice, while the consent of an involved father will be required most usually an adoption proceeds on the basis that he is not known.

Consent of a minor

The Adoption Law, Article 11, states that 'where the adoption involves a minor aged 10 or more, the consent of the adoptee shall be obtained'.

Where consent is not available

In almost all third party adoptions, whether domestic or intercountry, parental consent is unavailable and that of the orphanage director acting under the authority of his/her guardianship powers will be routinely substituted. Interestingly, as Article 12 of the Adoption Law makes clear, a parental lack of decision-making capacity – for mental health or other reasons – does not of itself justify dispensing with the need for that consent.

Childcare adoption: the grounds

In circumstances where parents have 'unusual difficulties'[40] or may cause serious harm to their child,[41] this will provide grounds for adoption.

40 Adoption Law, Article 5.
41 Ibid., Article 12.

Human rights considerations

Rights of the birth parent/s

It is a singular characteristic of the adoption process in China that for third party adoptions, whether domestic or intercountry, the birth parents have no role to play: as only children without parents are eligible for adoption by a non-relative, the birth parents are defined out of the process.

Childcare adoptions

While there is provision in Chinese law for parental consent for adoption to be dispensed with in circumstances where 'children whose parents are unable to rear them due to unusual difficulties' the fact that this is very rarely if ever availed of may constitute a failure by the State to provide appropriately, as required under Article 20 of UNCROC, for children deprived of their family environment.

Step-parent adoptions

These have long been treated with caution within western adoption processes. The fact that they are regarded so favourably in China, avoiding the scrutiny necessary to ensure that they are compatible with a child's welfare interests, may jeopardise the human rights of some children.

Thresholds for exiting the adoption process

Successful completion of an adoption process would seem to be entirely dependent upon applicant capacity to satisfy eligibility requirements. Once the matching stage is completed only applicant withdrawal can prevent an adoption.

The welfare interests of the child

The Adoption Law, Article 2, states that:

> Adoption shall be in the interest of the upbringing and growth of adopted minors and in the protection of the legitimate rights of the adoptee and the adopter, in conformity with the principle of equality and voluntariness, and not in contravention of social morality.

Further, the Ministry of Civil Affairs declares that 'in both domestic and international adoption, the principle of "best interests of the child" is applied'. However, in practice it would seem to attract no more than a cursory acknowledgement that an adoption should be welfare compatible. In domestic adoptions, while the welfare interests of the child constitute a formal criterion for adoption, there is no legal guidance as to how this is to be interpreted. In ICAs, evidence is required to confirm that the welfare interests of the child are being met – but such evidence is sought after the adoption has been finalised.

Paramountcy

There is no evidence to suggest that the welfare principle is of paramount importance at the point when the adoption application is determined. The absence of provisions for non-consensual adoption in circumstances of parental abuse itself indicates the low importance given to this factor relative to parental rights.

Consent/views of child and welfare interests

The Adoption Act, Article 11 (in keeping with Articles 12 of the General Principles of Civil Law and 21 of the Marriage Act), stipulates the right of children to express their personal views, in so far as their own interests are concerned, and that the consent of a child aged 10 or more is a prerequisite for his or her adoption. However, there would appear to be an absence of any legal mechanism for providing advocacy on behalf of the child concerned at the determination of an adoption application.

Culturally compatible

The history of ICA illustrates how little influence this factor has had upon the outcome of the adoption process; although there have been recent initiatives to provide post-adoption support services for those of the Chinese adoptee diaspora who wish to reaffirm cultural affinities.

The orders available

Such is the extent of preliminary screening that most usually the outcome of an adoption process is the granting of the application, though in the case of ICAs the process may take an inordinate length of time.

Additional orders: post-adoption contact

The above-mentioned Article 15 gives permission for voluntary post-adoption conditions to accompany an adoption order. It states that 'should the parties involved in the adoptive relationship wish to conclude an adoption agreement, a written agreement on adoption shall be concluded'. However, aside from family/kinship adoptions, post-adoption contact between an adopted child and members of their birth family is not an option as orphanage adoptees are defined as not having parents or family.

Alternative orders

The Adoption Law, Article 17, provides an alternative to adoption for applicants who are relatives or friends of the family. It states that 'orphans or children whose parents are unable to rear them may be supported by relatives or friends of their parents' and that 'the adoptive relationship shall not apply to the relationship between the supporter and the supported'. Otherwise, the continued guardianship provided by the orphanage or an associated foster care arrangement are in practice the only alternatives available.

Human rights considerations

Giving effect to the welfare principle

There is no counterpart to the independent professional input in western nations, designed to present an impartial and thorough analysis of what exactly constitutes the welfare interests of a child in accordance with a checklist of factors. Moreover, the many constraints on intercountry adopters successfully completing the adoption process have little direct relevance to the welfare interests of the children concerned. The failure to give adequate recognition and weighting to the welfare principle at that crucial juncture would seem to be non-compliant with Article 12 of UNCROC.

The effect of an adoption order

The Adoption Law, Article 15, declares that 'the adoptive relationship comes into force on the date of its registration' while Article 23 states its legal effect corresponds to its counterpart in the common law countries.

Effect on the parties

The child

The Adoption Law, Article 23, states the main legal effect of an adoption order to be that: 'the rights and duties in the relationship between an adopted child and his or her parents and other close relatives shall terminate with the establishment of the adoptive relationship'. Article 24 adds that 'an adopted child may adopt his or her adoptive father's or adoptive mother's surname, and may also retain his or her original surname, if so agreed through consultation between the parents concerned.

The birth parent/s

The Adoption Law, Article 22, declares that:

> The rights and duties in the relationship between an adopted child and his or her parents and other close relatives shall terminate with the establishment of the adoptive relationship.

Article 19 adds that 'the parents of a child adopted by others may not bear any more child in violation of the regulations on family planning on the ground of having placed out their child for adoption'.

The adopters

The Adoption Law, Article 23 proclaims that an adoption order will have the traditional common law effect of transferring all parental rights and duties to the adopters.

Revocation of an adoption order

An adoption order in China is not irrevocable, it may be dissolved by mutual consent of the parties. While Article 26 declares that 'no adopter may terminate the adoptive relationship before the adoptee comes of age', it then adds 'except when the adopter and the person having placed out the child for the adoption agree to terminate such relationship'. Further, in such circumstances, 'if the adopted child involved reaches the age of 10 or more, his or her consent shall be obtained'. Articles 26 and 27, respectively, provide that an adoption may also be terminated on grounds of fault or of a breakdown in relationships. Article 29 adds that should dissolution occur then the legal relationships between the parties shall revert to their pre-adoption status.

Entitlement to post-adoption support services

All receiving nations have their own network of post-adoption support agencies and groups, some government sponsored, others voluntary, that provide services specific to the needs of intercountry adopters and their children from China – but here is no Chinese equivalent service provision in respect of domestic adoption. In a reversal of the usual State support provision of western countries, China places an onus on intercountry adopters to submit evidence that they are managing satisfactorily, that the welfare of the child is being progressed and that his or her Chinese cultural identity is being nurtured.

Human rights considerations

Prohibition on birth parents having more children

The punitive Article 19 addendum, warning that birth parents must never bear any more children, would seem to violate their basic human rights.

Dissolution of an adoption order

The singular characteristic of Chinese domestic adoption – that it may be dissolved by mutual consent of the parties – undermines the 'unique selling point' of an adoption order. The legal guarantee of permanence is in practice reduced to the discretionary intent of the parties which may result in a decision, or threat of a decision, that would breach the human right of an adoptee to family life.

Lack of State support services

Not only does the State not provide post-adoption support, it imposes a considerable financial levy in respect of all third party adoptions whether domestic or intercountry. Given that Chinese policy now has an emphasis on placing special needs children for adoption – by both the domestic and intercountry routes – then, if domestic adopters are to be encouraged, as Zhong urged 12 years ago, 'the government should also provide medical assistance, financial help, tax benefits and incentives to families who wish to adopt handicapped children'.[42] Its failure to do so risks violating the State obligation, under Article 20 of UNCRO, to support children deprived of care in their family of origin.

ICA and cultural identity

The scale and duration of Chinese involvement in ICA raises questions about State regard for the cultural identity of the many tens of thousands of Chinese children it has entrusted to the care of Caucasians. Arguably, even though there are now some outreach programmes in place to support those children who may wish to establish links with their country of birth, the overall effect of State policy may be in breach of its obligation to assist the preservation of adoptees' ethnic, religious, cultural and linguistic affiliation as required by Article 20 of UNCROC.

Information rights: disclosure, tracing and reunification

China would appear to have no equivalent to the information disclosure procedures and associated tracing and reunification services that are now part of the post-adoption landscape in most developed nations. As a large proportion of all adoptions, domestic and intercountry, are in respect of orphaned or abandoned children for whom no family history is available, the lack of such procedures and services is perhaps unsurprising.

Information rights

The Adoption Law, Article 22, states that 'when the adopter and the person placing out the child for adoption wish to make a secret of the adoption, others shall respect their wish and shall not make a disclosure thereof'. This specifically confers rights of privacy and anonymity upon birth parents and adopters: an adoptee's post-adoption access to information is at the discretion of those parties.

42 Zhong, 'China domestic adoption'.

Information disclosure duties

The fact that a large proportion of adoptees are classified as 'abandoned' or orphans dictates future disclosure options. For domestic adopters, whose motivation is usually to fill the gap caused by infertility issues, the associated cultural and social stigma may help explain why they do not necessarily need disclosure procedures. For adoptees, the cultural expectation of lineage loyalty may well dissuade them from making enquiries that might yield information that could be compromising both for them and members of the wider family.

The social status that accompanies *hokou* registration has important implications for adoption. It provides the basis for public service entitlements, but only families and children registered as living in an area can access the government services for that locality. An exception is provided for children without any known family for whom guardianship responsibility has been assumed by a social welfare institute.

Maintaining records

The Adoption Law, Article 15, requires every adoption to be registered at the provincial Civil Affairs Bureau, and adds that 'in cases of adoption of abandoned infants or children whose natural parents cannot be traced, the civil administration shall announce the adoption publicly before effecting the registration'. Article 16 directs that 'the Public Security organ shall register the adoptee in the household registry in accordance with the relevant national regulations'. Apart from this requirement to register an adoption at the Civil Affairs Bureau and to make the necessary adjustments to the relevant *hokou* registration documents, there does not appear to be any form of adoption register or registration process.

Tracing and re-unification

There is no Chinese equivalent to the domestic tracing and reunification services that have become so prevalent in western nations. However, in the context of ICA the CCAA and relevant orphanages very willingly offer adoptees and adopters ongoing contact arrangements with pre-adoption carers. Moreover, both in China and in receiving countries, there are networks that offer support services specifically for those engaged in Chinese adoptions.

Human rights considerations

Veto on disclosure of identifying information

The above-mentioned Article 22 discretionary right of birth parents and adopters to keep the fact of adoption a secret can, if exercised, constitute a denial of the basic human right of an adoptee, under Articles 7 and 8 of UNCROC, to access the information necessary for an authentic personal identity.

Hokou *registration*

The *hukou* registration system results in poverty-stricken or migrant parents abandoning children (particularly those who are disabled and in need of expensive services) to the care of institutes as a means of ensuring their access to services such as healthcare and education. It also leads to many de facto adoptees being passed off as birth children by their adopters in order to acquire *hukou* registration. The CRC, in its 2013 report, recommended that the *hokou* registration system be abandoned 'in order to ensure birth registration for all children, especially for children of migrant workers'.[43]

Negation of birth parents' identity

In third party adoptions, whether domestic or international, the birth parents have been virtually edited out of the process by the State at a very preliminary stage. There is, therefore, limited information about them and few opportunities for their post-adoption involvement. Arguably, the Chinese adoption process has an in-built systems failure in that it is not constructed to provide verifiable data in respect of the identity and whereabouts of birth parents nor in respect of the status of its 'orphaned' and 'abandoned' children. Arguably, the system fails to provide adequately for the recognition and protection of birth parents rights, with knock-on negative effects for the identity rights of adoptees.

Conclusion

Human rights has most relevance to the Chinese adoption process as regards: the focus on and definition of 'orphaned' and 'abandoned' children; the lack of a domestic cohort of legal and social work practitioners trained to independently assess and represent the welfare interests of children; and the absence of any role for the judiciary. Perhaps the most pressing human rights concern lies in the evidence of a continuing criminal trade in abducting, trafficking and selling babies and young children for the purpose of illegal adoption.

43 CRC, sixty-fourth session, paras 39(b) and 48.

Part V

Contrasting tensions and implications

11 Adoption and human rights

National tensions and international standards

Introduction

This chapter considers whether there are any themes emerging from the intersection of adoption law and human rights as noted in the preceding six jurisdiction-specific chapters. It begins with an overview of the varying extent to which those jurisdictions comply with the international framework of relevant human rights treaties, conventions, protocols, etc. in so far as they relate to adoption law. This is paired with a similar overview of relevant aspects of the corresponding regulatory frameworks and their respective alignment with international human rights standards. The main body of the chapter then summarises and compares jurisdictional performance in relation to key human rights indicators at each stage of the adoption process from entry, through determination of an application, to exit and post-adoption information rights. This is followed with an assessment as to whether the noted jurisdictional differences conform to any pattern. The chapter concludes by reflecting on the significance of the findings including a brief review of the extent to which they may be explained by intrinsic differences between common and civil laws.

National compliance with international human rights

The existence of a growing body of international instruments designed to structure a network of principles and standards that should govern national law and practice in relation to adoption – and many other matters – has not resulted in uniform compliance. This is partially due to differences in cultural context. The fact that not all relevant countries subscribe to the same instruments, that many Hague signatory States often maintain bilateral agreements with non-Hague-compliant countries and the lack of any enforcement mechanisms, undoubtedly make a significant contribution. It is also partially due to a failure to ratify, and to the number of derogations from key provisions. However, another factor is that some signatory States simply fail to abide by the terms of the instruments.

International treaties, conventions, protocols, etc.

The main components of the international human rights framework as it relates in general terms to children are the Universal Declaration of Human Rights 1948

(UDHR), the European Convention for the Protection of Human Rights and Fundamental Freedoms 1950 (ECHR) and the United Nations Convention on the Rights of the Child 1989 (UNCROC). Of specific importance for adoption is The Hague Convention on Protection of Children and Co-operation in Respect of Intercountry Adoption 1993, the United Nations Declaration on Social and Legal Principles relating to the Protection and Welfare of Children with Special Reference to Foster Placement and Adoption Nationally and Internationally 1986, and the European Convention on the Adoption of Children 2008, which together provide the framework for regulating intercountry adoption.

National compliance

Of the six jurisdictions studied, France and China are not signatory States to the UDHR while England, France and Germany are among the 47 that subscribe to the ECHR. The US is the only one of the six not included among the almost 200 nations that to date have become parties to UNCROC. All six have signed and ratified the Hague Convention and, although few signed the United Nations Declaration on Social and Legal Principles relating to the Protection and Welfare of Children with Special Reference to Foster Placement and Adoption Nationally and Internationally 1986, this provided a starting point for consideration of further international initiatives to regulate ICA such as the European Convention on the Adoption of Children 2008 to which European Council members such as France, Germany and England are parties.

Governing principles

The principles now found in national adoption law have largely been drawn from those established by the above international framework of adoption related conventions, protocols, etc. As mentioned, this does not necessarily mean that national practice conforms accordingly; in particular, principles relating to improper costs, respect for cultural background and trafficking are regularly abused.

Full adoption

The traditional adoption order with its typical legal characteristics – absolute, permanent and exclusive – is available in all the jurisdictions studied. The extent to which these characteristics have been modified in recent years is an important area of jurisdictional difference.

The welfare interests of the child

In accordance with Article 3 of UNCROC, the national law in all jurisdictions studied have entrenched this principle to govern the adoption process and outcome. In practice, the existence or otherwise of statutory guidelines to aid interpretation and application of the principle is crucial, this can vary considerably.

The paramountcy principle

The weighting given to the welfare interests of the child by the paramountcy principle, as required by Article 21of UNCROC and reinforced by Hague, has become a general benchmark for the law relating to decisions affecting the upbringing of children. However, the extension of its functional role to passporting children from the public care system into the adoption process, thereby downgrading other options such as long-term foster care, is one that has proven to be jurisdictionally divisive.

Openness

Adoption practice reflects social, political, economic and moral changes and the move towards openness in adoption is in keeping with general trends in society.[1] The Hague statement of principle, as reinforced in UNCROC, that children requiring adoptive placements are entitled to know and have access to information about their family background and cultural heritage and maintain or develop cultural identity, has done much to prompt this development in contemporary adoption practice. However, it is far from being accepted in all jurisdictions and in some it generates heated controversy.

Regulating the adoption process

Ensuring that the functions of a process are appropriate, that when operational it meets standards of transparency, efficiency and propriety and that there is accountability for outcomes, are among the key tests applied by all regulatory bodies. In relation to national adoption processes the regulatory emphasis will naturally vary in accordance with cultural context and result in complexities which make a comparative analysis of national experiences problematic. However, even after taking into account differences in cultural context, regulating an adoption process still requires each national regulatory body to satisfy the same international matrix of human rights. In practice this also varies considerably.

The judiciary

In all jurisdictions presently being considered, the necessity for proper processes to access justice and for an adoption process to be subject to an independent and impartial tribunal established by law, are requirements underpinned by Article 10 of the UDHR. This is supported by Article 6 of the ECHR which governs the European signatory States, while Article 21 of UNCROC – which is binding on all those jurisdictions except the US – requires adoption to be authorised only by competent authorities.

1 Grotevant, H. and McRoy, R., *Openness in Adoption*, London, Sage, 1998, p. 196.

There can be no greater safeguard for the human rights of all parties to an adoption than if that process concludes in court where an independent judiciary can scrutinise the roles of the various bodies involved, adjudicate on issues affecting the parties and determine all applications in accordance with the welfare interests of the child. While this is the norm in England, the US, Germany and France, in both Japan and China the process is managed and determined by administrative bodies; exclusively so in the latter case. Administrative rather than judicial oversight leaves the adoption process prone to political influence and without either the independence or the span of authority to rigorously examine the background circumstances of an adoption application. It also means that the workings of the adoption process are more 'closed': legal issues are not placed in the public domain: instead of published judgments and established case precedents, internal practice guidance tends to be issued to the agencies and professionals concerned.

Due process

Articles 6 and 8 of the ECHR, together with Article 10 of the UDHR, require the adoption process in signatory nations – such as England, Germany and France – to adhere to due process, as does section one of the 14th Amendment to the US Constitution. This explicit legal safeguard is absent in Japan and China.

Arguably, in England the discretionary ambit of decision-making available to local authorities can permit an undermining of due process as may also be the case with some private adoption agencies in relation to ICA in France, Germany and the US.

Representation for a child

Enforcement of human rights requires the interests of the parties affected to be represented in any forum established for determining related issues. Article 8 of the 1986 Declaration provides that such representation should be made available to children in the adoption process and this is probably also an implied requirement in the above Article 6 of the ECHR.

Unless proceedings are contested, legal representation is not normally provided specifically for the child subject of an adoption process in any of the jurisdictions studied. Given that adoption has become much more complex than formerly – involving older children, many with health or social care needs, some with siblings, who often bring with them cultural, racial or religious complications – there is a strong argument that such representation should now be provided in all adoptions if this aspect of the process is to be human rights compliant.

Government bodies

Where government policy and funding promote the non-consensual adoption of children in the public care system – as in England and the US – this places bodies such as local authorities on the interface between the human rights of children and their parents. When this occurs in a legal context governed by the paramountcy principle, and where an ever-increasing number of approved adopters queue for the opportunity to adopt, the human rights of birth parents are exposed to a heightened level of risk.

Adoption agencies

The 'trafficking' of children for adoption purposes is prohibited by the Optional Protocol on the Sale of Children, Child Prostitution, and Child Pornography 2000 (Sex Trafficking Protocol) 2000, by Hague and by Article 35 of UNCROC. Adoption agencies offer a legally sanctioned gateway into the adoption process and one legislatively intended to filter out such practices.

The pivotal position of such agencies means that the responsibility of policing the human rights interface between all parties falls largely to them, at least initially. Laws requiring the registration and regulating of all adoption agencies are therefore clearly vital. This would seem to be most satisfactorily addressed in England. In the US, the licensing of such agencies accommodates those operating on a commercial basis which, particularly in relation to ICA, can lead to aggressive competition in a shrinking market and to sourcing prospective adoptees in non-Hague-compliant countries, with a consequent danger of human rights violations. In Japan, where adoption agencies have been mostly neither registered nor regulated, the scope for such violation is considerable. In China, there is evidence to suggest that a lack of regulatory control has resulted in serious human rights violations in the provinces involving orphanages accepting abducted children for adoption purposes and levying fees for arranging placements.

Because of their key role, adoption agencies are also the primary archivists of information relating to the parties of each adoption. Effective regulatory control of adoption agency data collection is essential if adoptees are to later access the information needed to form an authentic identity.

Registration of adoptions

The right of every child to an identity, and to have it entered in public records, is established by Article 8 of the Declaration on Social and Legal Principles relating to the Protection and Welfare of Children, with special reference to Foster Placement and Adoption Nationally and Internationally 1986, as affirmed by Article 7 of UNCROC and endorsed by Hague.

One means of giving effect to this right is through a system which records information relating to the fact of every adoption, identifies the parties involved and thereby contributes to a national database that profiles the legal status of all citizens. Such adoption registers are well established, either on a national or regional basis, in all countries presently studied – with some caveats in relation to those in Japan and China. In the latter country, because the *hukou* system fails to provide a satisfactory and complete record of all adoptions, it also risks breaching the human right of an adoptee to access the information necessary to acquire an identity.

Entry to the adoption process

Although generally associated with children – and for the purpose of securing their absolute, exclusive and lifelong welfare interests with adoptive parents – in fact the adoption process also permits entry to adults, for reasons that may have little if anything to do with their welfare, may be deliberately inclusive of relationships with the birth family and need not be maintained on a lifetime basis. For the purposes of comparing like with like, however, the following account of jurisdictional differences at each stage of the adoption process largely proceeds on the assumption that the subject is a child.

Entry thresholds

State intervention in family affairs for child protection purposes, that may lead to ushering a child into the adoption process, will only be human rights compliant if such intervention first demonstrates that every reasonable effort has been made to retain the child in parental care.

Right to care in family of origin

Article 8 of the ECHR declares a right to respect for private and family life, Article 9 of UNCROC requires the State to ensure that a child shall not be separated from his or her parents against their will while Article 18 requires the State to render appropriate assistance to parents and legal guardians to facilitate the upbringing and development of their children.

Where there is no prospect of family care – as when a child has been voluntarily relinquished or orphaned – then such State intervention is uncontroversial. Queries may, however, be raised in relation to the definition of 'orphan' and as regards the evidence available to substantiate that status: which is a particular problem in ICAs from China. Again, where the State is responding to a reconfigured family care arrangement – as in step or kinship adoptions – then, generally, there is similarly little scope for dispute. Childcare adoptions, on the other hand, trigger heated controversy.

The absence of powers permitting State intervention for the specific purpose of facilitating non-consensual entry to the adoption process is a feature of the child protection/adoption law interface in the vast majority of developed nations – but not in England, the US and nor, to a lesser extent, in Germany. Whereas in France, Scandinavia and other European countries this has resulted in adoption being dependent upon domestic birth parent consent or on ICA, and explains its rapid decline, in the three countries mentioned the rate of decline in annual domestic adoptions is slower. However, if national recourse to non-consensual adoption is to be human rights compliant the State must first address the onus placed upon it by international human rights provisions to invest in appropriate family support services. A precondition for valid State sponsored childcare adoption is that it first satisfies a family rehabilitation threshold. The CRC has drawn attention to the fact that the onus rests more heavily on the State when, as in England, parental coping capacity can be undermined by poverty.

Intercountry routes into the adoption process

As stated in Article 17 of the 1986 Declaration, restated in the preamble and in Article 4(b) of Hague, and reiterated in Article 21 of UNCROC, a child born outside the jurisdiction may enter the adoption process of that jurisdiction only in circumstances where other care alternatives – such as an adoption or foster care placement – are not available in his or her country of origin. The priority given to retaining a child in need of alternative care within their country is reinforced by Article 24 of the Declaration and Article 20 of UNCROC, particularly 20.3, which stress the importance of cultural roots and continuity of environment to forming a child's identity.

In all countries studied, however, there exist means whereby agencies and individuals can bypass Convention requirements – sometimes by way of national bilateral agreements with non-Hague-compliant countries. As formerly high volume sending countries, including Korea, Philippines and China now restrict their contribution to the ICA flow and others such as Russia, Ethiopia and Ukraine remain outside the Convention, so agencies are competing to locate and develop new sources for potential adoptees. This results in many children entering the adoption process by routes that are not subject to Convention safeguards, which is perhaps most likely to be the case in Germany and in the US, with a consequent greater likelihood of human rights violations affecting the children involved.

Role of adoption agencies

The fundamental right to freedom of association, as guaranteed in Article 20(1) of the UDHR, is subject to legitimate regulatory constraint. This also impacts upon adoption agencies.

The role of such agencies – as prescribed in Articles 10, 11 and 12 of Hague – is crucial to any adoption process and they perform essentially the same functions in all jurisdictions. This includes responsibility for ensuring that: adoption applicants satisfy eligibility and suitability criteria; the requisite consents are available; an appropriate placement is made and supervised; and that assessment reports are provided for the court. Profiteering, in particular, is prohibited by Articles 11 and 32 of Hague, by the above-mentioned Protocol 2000, and by Article 21 of UNCROC. Whereas national adoption law governing this role is generally Hague compliant, it may be at times inadequate to curb an agency siphoning off profits. It is questionable, for example, whether the costs levied by some adoption agencies in Japan, the US and by the CCAA in China are in that respect wholly Hague compliant.

Moreover, adoption agencies seldom have any role to play in step-parent adoptions which may leave the children concerned relatively unprotected in comparison with other adoptees and raises questions as to whether this is compatible with the prohibition on discriminatory practice as stated in Article 2 of UNCROC.

Pre-placement counselling

The informed consent of birth parents has traditionally marked the starting point for an adoption process. This is recognised by Article 21 of UNCROC which, among other matters, requires the provision of such counselling as may be necessary before parental consent for adoption is obtained.

In England, as in the US and Germany, there is an explicit statutory obligation resting on adoption agencies to provide a pre-placement counselling service for this purpose. The absence of any equivalent duty on adoption agencies in France, Japan and China arguably constitutes a failure to ensure adequate protection for the crucial human right to provide an informed consent on matters of such importance.

Eligibility and suitability of the parties

The criteria for determining rights of access to the adoption process are not dissimilar in the jurisdictions presently being considered, at least as regards the parties to a full adoption. There are, however, some issues that cause difficulty.

Status of 'child'

Although the process is normally associated with the adoption of children, usually young children, in some jurisdictions – such as Germany, exceptionally in France and in some states of the US – the adoptees can be adults and in Japan these constitute by far the majority of all annual adoptions. Given the overall preponderance of step and kinship adoptions, and bearing in mind the ICA contraction, it is probable that in general contemporary adoption is now motivated less by altruism and more by family repair considerations; overall, most adoptees are related to their adopters.

As regards third party adoptions, the professional filtering processes established by the provisions of Hague and UNCROC, as given effect through national legislation, are usually sufficient to ensure that children are legally free from ties to birth parents before entering a 'full' adoption process. Where problems arise, it is often due either to an absence of evidence to substantiate the status of 'orphan' or to deliberate criminal activity by 'traffickers'. Both sets of problems have been prevalent in Chinese domestic and international adoptions. In France, arguably, the same problem persists in relation to the interpretation of children legally defined as 'abandoned' and therefore available for adoption.

Issues also arise in relation to the placement of Muslim children. While such children can be, and often are, placed in *kafala* care arrangements this affords them less protection than would a statutory adoption order. The religious constraints – and the legal gap between national and Islamic law – preventing the adoption of Islamic children in need of a home, may well discriminate against the latter's Article 8 rights to family life when compared with the statutory protection available to their non-Islamic counterparts.

Unmarried father/maternal veto

The right of an unmarried father to contest the proposed adoption of his child has only been established relatively recently in the jurisdictions studied and is dependent upon him first acquiring official recognition, usually either through being granted parental rights or at least by registration of paternity. In practice, where the father is uninvolved or is not aware of the birth then, unless the birth mother chooses to divulge his name and contact details when relinquishing the child for adoption, which she may decline to do, he will not be in a position to register his interest. In all jurisdictions studied the exercise of a maternal veto on information disclosure – particularly in France – is legally sanctioned and often exercised, which results in the child's human rights under Article 7 of UNCROC being compromised. The use of 'baby hatches' to facilitate the anonymous surrender of babies – although potentially lifesaving – leads to the same human rights deficit.

Same-sex applicants

While there is no human right to adopt, same sex couples should be as entitled as anyone else to apply to become prospective adopters and denying them such an opportunity, for that reason, would be discriminatory, in violation of Article 8 of the ECHR and may potentially breach Article 3 of UNCROC. The Chinese prohibition on such adopters presents the most overt challenge to these provisions as is the similar ban in Japan in relation to 'special' adoptions. It is possible that the cautious approach in some states of the US could also have the same effect.

Placement

The placement decision is critical to the success of an adoption process. The lesson firmly established by *Children Who Wait*[2] is that any delay accompanying this decision may be so emotionally damaging for the children concerned as to threaten the likelihood of that success.

Alternatives to an adoption placement

Articles 3 and 4 of the 1986 Declaration, reinforced by other Convention principles, state that in the event of a failure of parental care and kinship care being unavailable, then care by 'another substitute – foster or adoptive – family or, if necessary, by an appropriate institution should be considered'.

2 Rowe, J. and Lambert, L., *Children Who Wait*, London, ABAA, 1973.

Clearly, any such third party adoption placement can only be the preferred choice when others options are available but have been discounted on the basis of the welfare interests of the child concerned. Where, as in Japan – and also, until comparatively recently, in China and to a lesser extent in Germany – the State gives precedence to institutional care, this effectively precludes domestic adoption placements. Similarly, where, as in France and perhaps Germany, the State prioritises foster care then adoption placements are also less likely. If an alternative care arrangement requires a legal framework less extreme than an adoption order, then the State must make available a range of private and public orders so as to avoid that order becoming the default option. The guardianship orders, accompanied by financial assistance, available in England and the US, offer a feasible alternative to adoption.

Government funding arrangements: whether benefiting non-coping birth parents or adoption agencies; and whether channelled through adoption allowances, foster parent salaries or residential care funding; can considerably influence decision-making in regard to placement options. A policy of financially incentivising adopters to provide a post-family breakdown service, rather than financing preventative family support public services or private family parental responsibility orders, could leave a State open to the challenge that it has chosen to avoid its human rights obligations under Articles 16 and 25(2) of the UDHR, Article 8 of the ECHR and Articles 9 and 18 of UNCROC.

Adoption placement by birth parents

Article 29 of Hague, in deference to the welfare principle, specifically prohibits direct adoption placements by birth parents.

While adoption law in England, France and Germany (although here a child may be lawfully received for that purpose) has long endorsed the prohibition on permitting a birth parent to place, or direct others to place, their child with prospective adopters chosen by them, this is not the case in Japan, China nor in almost all states of the US. Recognition of the human right of a child to have their welfare interests treated as a matter of paramount importance in such a context is not given statutory effect in those jurisdictions. Such derogation from an internationally established principle constitutes a violation of human rights under Article 29 and also increases the risk that it may lead to a violation of Articles 3 and 21 of UNCROC.

Adoption placement and cultural matching

Article 20(3) of UNCROC, as mentioned above, requires that 'due regard shall be paid to the desirability of continuity in a child's upbringing and to the child's ethnic, religious, cultural and linguistic background' when placing a child outside their family of origin.

This principle has proven controversial. In England, the former statutory requirement to consider religious, racial, cultural and linguistic factors when making an adoption placement was deleted by the Children and Families Act 2014 and this could, arguably, license an infringement of the above human right of a child. While in the US and Japan, the overrepresentation of black and mixed-race children available, but not placed, for adoption may indicate that the adoption process is operating in a discriminatory fashion in violation of Article 2 of UNCROC.

A more incidental aspect of this issue, perhaps, concerns the right of the birth parent/s to stipulate that a placement should be with prospective adopters who share their religious affiliation. In some jurisdictions such a stated preference is statutorily required to be respected by an adoption agency which should ensure that choice of placement provides for religious compatibility.

Determining an adoption application

Ensuring that eligibility and suitability criteria are satisfied in respect of all parties, confirming that all necessary consents have been given or can be dispensed with and ascertaining that, if granted, an adoption would be in keeping with the welfare interests of the subject, while giving consideration to any possible post-adoption arrangements, are always the key matters to be addressed at this stage.

Consensual

The fundamental right of a parent to relinquish their child is specifically recognised in Article 4(b) of Hague and in UNCROC. Accordingly, all jurisdictions require such a decision to be evidenced by a formal and informed consent, or the necessity for it to be dispensed with, as a precondition for an adoption. The necessity for parental consent is obviated for children found to be 'orphans' or 'abandoned' or where their parent/s lack the capacity to give a valid consent.

Maternal consent

The European Convention on the Adoption of Children 1967, Article 52, para. 3, states that any consent given by a mother to the adoption of her child is invalid if given within six weeks of that child's birth; she can, however, give a valid consent to placement within that period.

While the spreading practice of providing 'baby hatches' clearly circumvents the Article 52 provision so, arguably, does that of permitting agency placements direct from hospital, as happens not infrequently in England and probably elsewhere. In some states of the US, a mother can give a valid consent to the adoption of her child within hours of its birth which again violates this principle.

Consent of unmarried father

The 2008 Convention on the Adoption of Children requires 'that the father's consent be obtained in all cases, even when the child is born out of wedlock'.

In England, the consent of such a father is not a strict requirement, though he should be served with notice of intended adoption proceedings, and he will not be in a position to give or withhold consent unless he first acquires legal recognition as a 'parent'. Moreover, a mother may legitimately refuse to either disclose to the father the fact of his paternity or to others the identifying information necessary for him to be contacted and advised of her decision to relinquish their child for adoption. Should he be so advised then in some jurisdictions – e.g. Japan – his consent is not required unless and until he acquires parental rights.

Consent of a minor

The 2008 Convention on the Adoption of Children is unequivocal in requiring that 'the child's consent be obtained if the child has sufficient understanding to give it'. This is reinforced by Articles 13 and 14 of UNCROC which emphasise a child's right to self-determination including the right to make informed decisions.

This is not a statutory requirement in English adoption law but, even if restricted to teenage children, it is in France and Germany (where it requires adult endorsement), in Japan for those aged 15 or older, in China where the lower age limit is set at 10 years and in most if not all states of the US. Clearly the absence of a requirement that the adoption of a child with a discerning capacity must be conditional upon their consent, could result in the child being excluded from decision-making that is crucially important for their future, which would breach his or her human rights.

Non-consensual

Singularly in China, it is reported that the designation of 'orphan' or 'abandoned' has been somewhat routinely applied to many children admitted to the ICA programme, even though it was probable that some had a live parent with a discoverable identity. Consent of the relevant orphanage director may be substituted for that of a parent. In all other countries studied the absence or withholding of parental consent is a matter that must be addressed in adoption proceedings but one that causes most controversy in the context of children in the public care system.

Childcare adoption: grounds for dispensing with parental consent

International human rights instruments, such as Articles 3 and 13 of the 1986 Declaration, recognise that in general where care in the family of origin is not possible then adoption may be necessary. Some, such as Articles 9 and 20.3 of UNCROC together with the 2009 UN Guidelines, go further and acknowledge that a failure of parental care may require removal of a child and his or her possible adoption. All, however, avoid defining the circumstances in which parental fault would constitute such a failure of care in the family of origin as to justify non-consensual adoption. Article 8 of the ECHR, in particular, while making such an acknowledgement, endeavours to balance in principle the supportive and coercive roles of the State in family affairs.

The hearing in respect of a child admitted to the adoption process from the public childcare system will require evidence that statutory grounds for dispensing with parental consent can be satisfied. Broadly, where such grounds exist they are formulated around circumstances of parental inadequacy, neglect or culpability; the latter taking the form of instances of child abuse. The fact that such grounds exist and can be satisfied does not, of course, mean that this will necessarily be sufficient to justify adoption in a particular case.

In England, the synchronising of grounds for dispensing with consent with those of admission to the care system, around the central principle of paramountcy, means that at this stage the ambit of judicial discretion is effectively limited to confirming that the evidence justifying public rather than family care subsists. In the absence of new evidence showing that the significant harm threshold is no longer relevant and a return to parental care is now feasible, a finding that the child is available for adoption will be readily made leaving only the issue as to whether the order should be granted. Similarly, in the US, to a lesser extent in Germany but rarely in Japan, a parental conviction on the grounds of child abuse or neglect will result in the removal of all parental rights leaving the court at the adoption hearing in a position to make an adoption order. In France, as in China, only if the hearing is able to confirm that a child has in effect been 'abandoned' by their parents will adoption be possible.

Family/kinship adoption

First party applications, where one applicant is genetically related to the subject, have always and in all jurisdictions been treated with less rigour than those by third parties at the time of hearing: there is an assumption that an adoption which keeps a child within familiar boundaries – of relationships, culture, family identity and often of location – will be in keeping with their welfare interests. Recognition for the right of a family to protection from State intervention when making such arrangements is not explicitly addressed in international law but can probably be found within the broad parameters of Article 8 of the ECHR.

Although traditionally rarely contested, the likelihood of such applications being disputed is increasing, particularly in the context of step-parent adoptions. Generally, in all jurisdictions and in the absence of fault, where an applicant can offer a degree of continuity in home and family relationships they are most likely to succeed unless an alternative order is available and determined to be more appropriate.

Exiting the adoption process

The outcome of an adoption process is usually assumed to be, and traditionally has been, the grant or refusal of an adoption order. As family law in general becomes more flexible so also is the approach to adoption. While the welfare interests of the subject are crucial, an interesting indicator of jurisdictional flexibility is the existence or otherwise of a range of alternative disposal options. The availability of alternatives is as important a consideration at the conclusion of the adoption process as it is at the placement stage.

Welfare interests

While the law in all jurisdictions provides that an adoption order can be made – on a consensual and even, with some variation, on a non-consensual basis – it treats the issue of whether it should be made quite separately with significant jurisdictional differences. There is little indication from national legislation or case law of the need to broadly interpret and apply this concept so that it: focuses not just on a snapshot of circumstances prevailing at the time of hearing but is also projected to consider likely future scenarios on a lifetime basis; takes into account the fact that the younger the child the greater the probability that their welfare is bound up with an attachment to their primary carer; takes also into account that the older the child the stronger the likelihood that a break with their relationships to grandparents and other members of the extended family, to friends, home, school and physical surroundings, etc. will impact negatively on their welfare; and that concern for a child's welfare must also consider and weigh up the effect of the proposed adoption upon the welfare of any other sibling.

At this secondary stage, the role played by the 'welfare interests' of the subject, is critical.

The paramountcy principle

The principle that adoption should be in the interests of the child was established in international law by the 1967 European Convention, Article 8, para. 1. The elevation of this principle to a 'primary consideration' in decisions relating to children was achieved by UNCROC, Article 3, and its further elevation to one of paramount importance in the adoption process was due to Article 21 as reinforced by Hague.

An inherent difficulty with the paramountcy principle is that the overriding weighting thereby given to the welfare interests of a child necessarily reduces the relative importance, and protection available to, all other relevant human rights. While it directly impacts upon the human rights of birth parents, it must also dilute the related processes and proceedings, divert professional aims and objectives and ultimately constrain an objective weighing of all options at an adoption hearing. It tends to separate out the interests of a child and in so doing it undermines the significance of bonds of attachment between that child and his or her direct primary care giver – most usually the mother, or both birth parents, or grandparents, or some significant other such as foster parents – bonds which are integral to the child's welfare and if broken can only damage it, at least in the short term. The principle may indeed be correct but managing its application so as to safeguard the human rights of all concerned, especially those of the child which may be inextricably bound up with those of their carer, becomes most challenging at the hearing.

In England, application of the paramountcy principle has come close to negating the adjudicative function: government policy has been strongly advocating adoption as the preferred exit strategy for children in care; administrative decision-making on welfare grounds by social workers and others, seemingly raised a presumption that their pre-adoption placement arrangements were necessarily in keeping with the principle; by the time the matter came to court the presumption, entrenched by facts on the ground, had become difficult to judicially displace. In the US, the human rights guarantee provided by the 14th Amendment has ensured a more rigorous approach that delineates, and differentiates between, the rights of the parties rather than one that defaults to the paramountcy principle. Nor does this principle play any part in the domestic adoption legislation of France, Germany, Japan or China.

Alternative orders

Statements of principle in UNCROC and Hague, emphasising that adoption is a service for children rather than for an adult seeking to acquire a child, recognise that the adoption option is justified only if it fits the needs of the child concerned. This presupposes that options other than adoption are legislatively available: an outcome that balances the human rights of the parties concerned is only possible if there are alternatives which allow for choice on a 'best fit' basis. However, while the existence of statutory alternatives can offer the possibility that an outcome of the adoption process may be an order other than the one applied for, the probability of that occurring depends greatly on a willingness to accept that any such alternative might be more appropriate.

Private family law orders

Article 3 of the 1986 Declaration, as mentioned above, clearly states that where care cannot be provided for a child within their family of origin then consideration should be given to the following alternative care frameworks in descending order of priority: 'care by relatives of the child's parents, by another substitute foster or adoptive – family or, if necessary, by an appropriate institution'; in no sense therefore is adoption viewed as the only or the primary option. This cautionary approach to alternative care is evident also in UNCROC, Article 20.3, which adds that 'when considering solutions, due regard shall be paid to the desirability of continuity in a child's upbringing'.

In England, legislative intent has for some time been to provide alternatives to adoption for those wishing to legally reconfigure family boundaries following family breakdown and divorce. A range of orders, some of which can be used in a complementary package are available, of which special guardianship has most recently been launched and has become widely used. In the US, France and Germany, but not in Japan nor China, a guardianship order is also an alternative, though virtually the only alternative, to adoption in such circumstances.

Public law orders

The above cautionary approach towards adoption, as advocated in the 1986 Declaration, etc., applies also to non-consensual proceedings: the fact that care cannot be provided for children within their families of origin, due to parental fault or default, should not mean that adoption is the best or only option to secure the future welfare of every child so affected. In a public law context, as in private, an absence of available alternatives may force reliance upon adoption, the draconian effects of which increase the probability of human rights violations particularly as regards the birth parents.

The outcome of the adoption process in England may be any one or more of the private family law orders, or no order or possibly a continuation of the care order which would allow the child to be retained in a long-term foster care placement. However, as in private family law, the absolute security of adoption has come to be regarded as the gold standard and all other orders and arrangements, such as foster care, tend to be viewed as second best alternatives. This is also true of policy in the US where the alternatives are fewer and the preference for adoption is stronger. In France and Japan, the court has the option of issuing a 'simple' adoption instead of the requested 'plenary' order where a less exclusive and enduring care arrangement would seem sufficient. In Germany and China, the choice is to either grant or refuse the adoption order and, in the latter case, to continue the guardianship arrangement allowing the child to remain in the care of foster parents or in an institution.

Post-adoption contact orders

The 'openness', represented by Article 7 of UNCROC and in the 2008 European Convention requirement that 'a better balance be struck between adopted children's right to know their identity and the right of the biological parents to remain anonymous', is facilitated by the capacity to authorise post-adoption contact arrangements at the time of hearing. Any such arrangement was until recently widely regarded as threatening the integrity of the adoption relationship and, if desired, was not an issue for the hearing but a private matter for the parties to address later. However, as older children and those with complex health or social needs enter the adoption process, providing for a continuation of established relationships has become recognised as a necessary component of their welfare interests.

For some time, it has not been unusual for the English judiciary to grant an adoption accompanied by a contact order authorising contact arrangements between an adoptee and the birth parent/s and/or with other members of their family of origin. This is also the practice in the US but in many states the arrangements take the form of a private, though enforceable, contract between the parties. Legislative provision for such arrangements do not exist in France, Germany and Japan and are impractical in China where most adoptees come from orphanages, which must relatively inhibit the opportunities in those jurisdictions for meeting the 'openness' requirements as stipulated in the above Conventions.

An adoption order and its effects

An adoption process most usually concludes with the issue of an order providing for the permanent and exclusive transfer of all rights and responsibilities in respect of a child to the adopter/s. However, it can also allow for the possibility of relationships and responsibilities to be openly shared between adopters and members of the family of origin and permit the adoption bond to be legally severed at the discretion of those involved.

Effect on the parties

The legal effects are wholly dependent upon whether the status of the order is one for full or simple adoption and to an extent the risk of a human rights violation varies accordingly.

The adoptee

There is no right to be adopted. Rather, as explained in the UN Guidelines for the Alternative Care of Children 2009, para. 12, the purpose of adoption is to provide a stable and permanent home for a child in need of alternative care which will meet their basic need for safe and continuous attachments to their care givers.

While it is clear that in all jurisdictions studied the 'full' or 'ordinary' order issued in respect of child adoptees at the conclusion of the adoption process is legislatively intended to have that effect, it is equally apparent that such exclusiveness is not the intention in *kafala*, nor in the lesser form of 'simple' adoption that may be result from that process in France and Japan. However, while the legal characteristics of the former type have retained their traditional effect – placing the child in much the same position in relation to the adopters as if he or she had been their birth child – this has been moderated by the availability of contact and information rights. For a child the subject of a 'simple' adoption the legal ties to their adopters are not so absolute and exclusive as links with their birth parents, embodying reciprocal rights and responsibilities, are maintained. Although Article 27 of Hague permits the conversion of 'simple' to 'full' adoption this is wholly discretionary and dependent upon the consents of all parties which, for religious/cultural reasons, may be withheld.

Arguably, the 'simple' form of adoption, like *kafala*, is an inadequate and inappropriate means of securing the boundaries of a child's human right to the permanency of family life under Article 8 of the ECHR. Indeed, it is possible that if the opportunities for securing family life for a child are restricted to such forms of adoption this could be construed as violating the prohibition on discriminatory treatment under Articles 14 of the ECHR and 2 of UNCROC.

The adoption of adults is generally restricted to the 'simple' order, except in Japan, and is available in France, Germany, Japan and some states in the US. In Japan, where 98 per cent of all annual adoptions are of adult males aged 20–30, this form of adoption is utilised so as to place the adult in the same legal relationship to the adopters as if born to them, for purposes of inheritance and tax benefits. This singular, culturally defined use of adoption in Japan would seem to have no relationship with or implications for human rights: other than, perhaps, to raise a question as to its appropriateness, this interpretation would seem at variance with international Convention definitions; also, the resulting distorting effect on the status of family members, relative to each other, may impinge upon their human rights.

The birth parent/s

The 'full' or 'ordinary' order issued in all jurisdictions studied has the intended legislative effect of stripping the birth parents of all legal rights and duties in respect of their adopted child; however, the traditional absolute nature of the order may now be ameliorated by contact orders and information rights. Where the adoption takes the 'simple' form then, whether the adoptee is an adult or a child, the birth parents retain sufficient legal links and relationship ties to maintain their innate role as parents. In France, Germany and some states in the US – but not in England, Japan nor, for other reasons, in China – the right of birth parents to anonymity severely compromises the human rights of adoptees under Article 7 of UNCROC to access information regarding their identity; the same infringement results from birth parent use of 'baby hatches'.

The adopters

While the basic human right, under Article 12 of the ECHR, to marry and have a family does not include a right to adopt, the State is obliged under Article 27 of UNCROC to 'recognise the right of every child to a standard of living adequate for that child's physical, mental, spiritual, moral and social development', a right which the Convention acknowledges may be given effect through adoption. Once the adoption has been granted, the adopters assume full parental responsibility for the welfare of the adoptee as though he or she was born to them and of their marriage. This will be the case in all jurisdictions studied when the 'full' form of adoption is utilised. In France, Germany and Japan a 'simple' adoption will result in reduced responsibilities for ancillary matters such as inheritance, shared family name, involvement with birth family members, etc. Moreover, in Japan the adopters of an adult adoptee, for tax and/or succession purposes, will become responsible for specific contractual obligations relating to the latter's future fiscal and inheritance prospects.

Revocation of adoption

Immutability has long been one traditional effect of an adoption order, but this is not necessarily the case in all jurisdictions.

'Full' adoption

This form of adoption, available in all jurisdictions studied, offers certainty to the parties but primarily it satisfies the right of an adoptee to the security of permanent family life as provided for under Article 8 of the ECHR. The fact that it is virtually irrevocable, except in China, guarantees that the right will continue to be respected by all parties.

'Simple' adoption

Together with *kafala*, this form of adoption may be terminated: in Japan, at the discretion of the parties; but in France and Germany (where it's restricted to adults) this requires special reasons and judicial sanction. The insecurity accompanying the possibility of revocation would seem to breach Article 8 rights and be non-compliant with Article 3 of UNCROC.

Entitlement to post-adoption support services

Article 9(c) of Hague requires the provision of post-adoption services.

In England the local authorities and adoption agencies are statutorily obliged to provide a full range of such services for all involved in any type of adoption and, as in the US, these are most likely to accompany childcare adoptions. Similar service provision obligations rest on government and voluntary bodies in France, Germany and Japan, although in the latter case the duty is confined to the parties of a 'full' adoption, while in China there is no equivalent domestic requirement to provide such services.

Post-adoption information rights

A right of access to information regarding the identity of the parties to an adoption, and the circumstances surrounding it, marks the official end of the adoption process; tracing and contact services are best regarded as ancillary and these are generally left to the discretion of voluntary or commercial bodies and are frequently the subject of social media searches. Traditionally, a right of access to identifying information has been controversial because of the opportunity it offers to discover facts which one or more parties may have gone to some lengths to conceal and as to which they could well have received firm guarantees of permanent secrecy. In a modern human rights context, however, while it must be recognised that adoption substitutes a new identity for the one a child was born with, when an adult that adoptee needs to reconcile both if he or she is to be psychologically in a position to move on and develop their own authentic persona.

Information rights

Article 7 of UNCROC, supported by a statement of principle in Hague, clearly establishes the right of an adoptee to access the information necessary to form an independent and authentic identity.

While practice in England would seem wholly compliant with this human right, the situation is different in many states of the US where, although federal law allows access to identifying information on contemporary adoptions with the mutual consent of the parties, files on past adoptions can remain legally sealed in deference to the recorded wishes of birth parents. In Germany access is wholly dependent upon the consent of both birth parents and adopters, while in France it is unconditional in relation to 'simple' adoptions but is otherwise severely restricted and made more so by a traditional respect for the maternal veto. In Japan, only adoptees aged 28 or more have rights of access to identifying information; which would seem to compromise the human rights of younger adult adoptees. In China statutory law expressly protects the anonymity of birth parents and adopters, which results in an adoptee's post-adoption access to information being wholly at the discretion of those parties. Clearly, Convention declarations of the human right of an adoptee to identifying information are widely ignored.

Information disclosure duties

Information disclosure depends in the first instance on the courts, the relevant government bodies and on adoption agencies having properly archived that information and then on the terms on which they are obliged to provide access to it.

Maintaining records

Adoption agencies have always been the main custodians of adoption information. While statute law now requires the retention and conditional disclosure of identifying data this does not necessarily apply to information recorded many decades ago and given under conditions of guaranteed confidentiality. Many such agencies have since ceased to exist, or have destroyed their records or consider that they are still bound by confidentiality agreements. In all jurisdictions studied the human right of adoptees to access identifying information is frequently compromised by adoption agency inability or unwillingness to provide it.

Registration systems

Government systems for recording the fact and details of adoption orders are not always efficient; perhaps particularly as regards the registration of 'simple' adoptions.

In England the centralised offices of the Registrar General are well practised in collating and retrieving such data, which is also the case with state based systems in the US, and both maintain contact registers. In France and Germany, the records maintained by Registrars are not adoption specific but with guided searching will disclose basic adoption details. In Japan and China the registration systems of *koseki* and *hokou*, respectively, would seem to be flawed as regards the accurate collating of relevant adoption data. Essentially, the capacity to realise the human right to access identifying information varies considerably in accordance not only with prevailing law but also with the relative efficiency of national information retrieval systems.

Pattern of jurisdictional differences: legal tradition, adoption and human rights

The six chosen jurisdictions, representing a mix of different legal traditions, provide an opportunity to conclude the study by considering whether the differentiating jurisdictional characteristics conform to a discernible pattern and, if so, to reflect on the extent to which this may be attributable to differences in legal tradition.

Common law, civil law and Asian hybrid

While England and the US clearly belong to the common law tradition and France and Germany to civil law, the legal tradition of Japan and China would seem to be built mostly on civil law but with additional Asian strands. All have become variously and voluntarily subject to a supranational layer of treaties, conventions, protocols, etc.

Common law and civil law

Any temptation to delve into the large body of academic work relating to the differences between these legal traditions can be safely avoided as, for present purposes, it is sufficient to restrict the inquiry to a focus on the more obvious aspects of each tradition that seem likely to help explain the above jurisdictional differences in the intersection of human rights and adoption law.

The French Civil Code and the German *Bürgerliches Gesetzbuch* are classic models of the civil code. From the earliest stage of the code's development, under Justinian's *Corpus Juris Civilis*, adoption was recognised, legally defined and treated, as an expedient social construct.[3] As noted earlier (see Chapter 1), the flexible nature of the civil code allowed the legal definition of adoption to be such that it could be used to fill in the gaps in the law relating to the family. Constructed essentially around an evolving core of statutes, as the civil code built up an ancillary classification system of rules and processes, so it permitted a loose arrangement of different situations in which adoption could be used. For civil law countries, acceding to an additional supranational layer of human rights entailed incorporating it alongside the established codified legislation and working through any conflicts as they arose. In the absence of conflicts coming before the court, the existing statute law remained in place.

The law relating to adoption evolved somewhat differently in the common law jurisdictions than in those of the civil law. Paradoxically, in England and the US, it was not until its incorporation into statute that adoption law acquired its fixed and distinctive common law characteristics. The late Victorian social context in which it was launched ensured that the legal definition of adoption, reflecting status concerns, was quite rigid: the circumstances for its use and its legal attributes – absolute, permanent and exclusive – were established from the outset. The common law being constructed around judicial principles laid down in case law, with statute law narrowly construed to fit with case precedents, the courts maintained their definition of adoption and the restricted circumstances for its use until statute law directed otherwise. Arguably, being principle based, human rights were more readily taken into account by the common law judiciary and integrated into their decision-making.

Asian hybrid

The legal systems of both Japan and China draw heavily from the civil code tradition; the latter with a considerable leavening of socialism. The social context within which adoption law and human rights operate is culturally more enclosed and different from that of the other four jurisdictions. Contemporary jurisdictional differences are very apparent in the legal definition and social role of adoption in Japan and in the extent to which these are subject to centralist control in China where human rights are viewed more as secondary to national laws rather than as a supranational source of authority.

Pattern of jurisdictional differences and legal tradition

The catalogue of indices of jurisdictional difference is lengthy. It includes: the role of private adoption agencies; a birth parent's right to place; LGBT adopters; the right of a child to consent; State financial support to adopters; the maternal veto, etc. However, in so far as there is any discernible pattern, this might be centred around substantive matters such as the definition of 'adoption', the relationship between adoption and the public childcare system, the use of ICA, the outcome of the adoption process and post-adoption information rights.

Definition of 'adoption'

A fundamental jurisdictional difference, from which others flow, is that adoption can be defined as 'full' or 'simple' reflecting, respectively, its common law or civil law origins. A further definitional distinction is that the latter can accommodate adult adoptees. While this would seem to be largely confined to civil law, it's not exclusive to that legal tradition as is apparent from its availability in some states of the US.

The centrality of the child to the common law model of adoption probably owes something to late Victorian concerns about legal and social status. This may explain why that model retained its abiding legal characteristics – absolute, permanent and exclusive – and why principles such as 'the welfare interests of the child' and 'paramountcy' came to be of crucial importance. In contrast, the looser boundaries and focus of the civil law model has required it to accommodate a balance of principles and permit greater flexibility in their application.

Adoption and the public childcare system

Only the common law jurisdictions have a firm policy commitment, evident in national law and practice, of expediting the transfer of children in care to the adoption process – grounded on a policy of mainstreaming adoption as the preferred childcare disposal option – but this would not seem attributable to anything inherent in the common law tradition. Instead, arguably, there is a cultural predisposition in those jurisdictions towards moving children from an expensive public care system, proven to negatively impact a child's long-term life chances across a range of indicators, to private alternative family care which is demonstrably better for the children concerned. Policy in the civil law jurisdictions shows a stronger emphasis, if not in preventative service provision, then in the rehabilitation of children to parental care or to care by others within the extended family of origin, or to foster care arrangements that maintain family links and hold open the possibility of eventual return. This policy may owe something to an innate respect for family or 'filiation' in the civil code which is most strongly apparent in France, but is also evident in Japan and to an extent in China.

Use of ICA

The modern use of adoption has relied heavily on ICA; for some countries such as France, it now virtually defines the national experience of adoption. Among the common law jurisdictions studied, however, there is no consistency in the use of ICA: while the US is the world leader as a receiving nation and in recent years has developed a slight profile as a sending nation, England's record is exactly the opposite. This is also apparent in the civil law jurisdictions: France, unlike Germany, has heavily relied upon ICA for many years. China, in sharp contrast, as a sending nation was for many years the world leader, while Japan has never had much more than a marginal role as such but has a modest profile as a receiving nation though, curiously, most often the adoptee children are the subject of simple rather than full adoptions. In both the policy emphasis has been on providing care for children in orphanages rather than in foster care or by way of adoption.

Again, jurisdictional differences would seem more attributable to cultural context than to legal tradition. As the tightening framework of Hague induces a broader compliance so the ICA flow is slowing to a trickle and being displaced by commercial surrogacy with consequences for the adoption process which are not dependent upon legal tradition.

Adoption process outcomes

While the outcome of the adoption process in the common law nations is invariably a full adoption order, and almost always in respect of a child, neither are necessarily the primary outcome characteristics in the civil law jurisdictions. In the former, the traditional characteristics of absoluteness and exclusiveness have become qualified by the 'openness' principle which now frequently permits an adoption to be compromised by a contact order and, more often than not, facilitates some level of ongoing relationship between all three parties. In the latter, while the 'simple' form of adoption always required such 'openness', the 'full' form does not. Moreover, as the common law adoption process becomes increasingly a childcare exit route, so too does the acceptance that adoption need be neither exclusive nor permanent: the rate of childcare adoption breakdown is growing steadily higher in England as in the US; with many adoptees eventually returning to their families of origin. So, to that extent there is a degree of convergence in the adoption process outcomes of both legal traditions.

The corresponding outcomes in China and Japan bear little resemblance to that of their western counterparts. The Chinese process is predicated on the absence of birth family relationships, so openness in adoption is really a ***non sequitur***. In Japan, by far the majority of adoptees are adults for whom the process ends in an 'ordinary' adoption with complete openness, but for the small minority of 'special' adoptions of children less than 6 years of age the process is unlikely to involve ongoing relationships between adoptee and their family of origin.

Post-adoption information rights

Principles of transparency and accountability now impact upon the adoption process as on others. The common law jurisdictions remain variously constrained by the historical assurances of permanent confidentiality, given mainly to birth parents and also to many adopters, but generally such assurances can no longer bind the parties in contemporary adoptions. Both the US and England now legislate for the disclosure of identifying information although at the same time both also permit practices that privilege maternal rights regarding anonymity and disclosure of paternal identity. The civil law jurisdictions adhere more strongly to traditional secrecy rights: in France the right of a birth mother to claim anonymity is resolutely maintained; in Germany the law makes provision for the confidentiality of adoptees and adopters to be protected.

The singularity of the adoption process in an Asian cultural context is also apparent in the approach to post-adoption information rights. In China, the pre-adoption status of a child as 'orphan' or 'abandoned' precludes the possibility of post-adoption information sharing between the parties. In Japan, the fact that almost all are adults when adopted dispenses with any possibility of secrecy and anonymity; the few child adoptees can readily access identifying information later in adulthood. For all, regardless of principles of transparency and accountability, the prevalence and penetration of social media has virtually extinguished privacy rights.

Conclusion

Some jurisdictional characteristics of the adoption process would seem to correspond to a distinction between the common law and civil law: in particular the status of adoptee, the 'simple' and 'full' forms of adoption and the importance attached to retaining family links. Others are clearly more cultural: such as the significance of adult male adoptees, commercial adoption agencies, designating children as 'abandoned' and the practice of 'rehoming'. Still others are perhaps arbitrary: including the need for the consent of a child adoptee, the birth parent's right to make an adoption placement, the maternal right to anonymity, her right not to disclose paternal identity and the use of 'baby hatches'. In short, there is no firm pattern which would allow jurisdictional differences to be confidently credited to genesis in a particular legal tradition.

The significance of this is simply that there cannot be a systemic human rights approach to jurisdictional variation in adoption law: auditing the common law and civil law adoption processes against the same fixed schedule of human rights; with non-compliance attributed solely to a characteristic feature of a legal tradition. Anyway, it is apparent that the legal traditions are losing some of their distinctiveness under the homogenising pressure of multi-jurisdiction litigation and international conventions, etc. The cultural context of adoption law and practice will itself ensure that human rights compliance is assessed more in accordance with principles such as 'proportionality' than with legal tradition.

Conclusion

Adoption, in law as in life, has always been part of 'the family', a unit customarily viewed as indispensable to society. Article 16(3) of the Universal Declaration of Human Rights (UDHR) proclaims the family to be 'the natural and fundamental group unit of society and is entitled to protection by society and the State' while the preamble to the UN Convention on the Rights of the Child (UNCROC) declares the family as 'the fundamental group of society and the natural environment for the growth and well-being of all its members and particularly children, should be afforded the necessary protection and assistance so that it can fully assume its responsibilities within the community'. In the developed nations of the twenty-first century, however, such pronouncements can no longer be assured of tacit endorsement.[1]

These sentiments are a legacy from a time when the law was concerned to recognise and protect the status of the marital family unit – and rights of property, inheritance, family name etc – as the necessary foundation for citizenship and a civil society. A time when its integrity was protected from being undermined by 'illegitimacy', illicit sexual relationships, cohabitation, and by ease of access to divorce, etc. Family law was then a coherent body of rights and duties deemed to be vested in members of the marital family, which grounded associated status designations (child of the family, husband and wife, etc.). Private family law and the statutory processes for conferring or extinguishing status were limited in number, clearly defined, absolute and permanent in their effects and rigorously policed by the courts. Public family law was non-interventionist and largely directed towards policing parental behaviour that threatened or did not conform to the norms represented by the marital family. Adoption functioned as one of a set of discrete legal proceedings (including guardianship and wardship) for securing a child's future. It offered an expedient means for 'legitimising' the child of an unmarried mother and transferring care responsibility to a respectable marital family unit.

1 As, seemingly, acknowledged by the UN in its 2016 report 'Family policies and the 2030 Sustainable Development Agenda', at: www.lifesitenews.com/news/un-report-there-is-no-definition-of-the-family

Since the closing decades of the twentieth century the context of family, family law and society that has always shaped adoption has undergone profound change in all the developed nations. Adoption has had to change accordingly. The challenge now is whether the adoption process, as it has been known to different legal traditions, can survive.

Society, family and the law

Residual traces of the Victorian patriarchal model family, resting on monogamous marital union for life and providing the foundations for the entire body of family law, have given way to the fluidity and flexibility of modern globalised western society. Consequent developments on both the private and public fronts of family law have directly impacted upon the number of children in need of care away from their family of origin.

A modern family law context for adoption

The cornerstones that supported family law for many generations have crumbled. On both the private and public fronts there has been a retreat from the traditional presumption that the legal integrity of the family unit should be upheld and from a concern that the associated status designations should be protected.

Parenting

Being a parent is now largely a matter of private individual choice;[2] mostly to be made by women. Serial parenting arrangements, together with the medical developments which allow adults to choose or reject the option of parenthood, have undone the central significance that the nuclear marital family unit once had within the body of family law while equality and non-discrimination legislation has done much to redress the status imbalance between family members. This has led to a decisive switch in legal focus: from the family unit, whether marital or non-marital, to the child. As the structures for 'society' and 'family' have become less certain so the law has fallen back to defend the lowest and most vulnerable common denominator.

Parental responsibility

The displacement of parental rights by the principle of parental responsibility has marked a shift in emphasis in family law from structure to content, from status to duty. Parents are legally empowered to reconfigure their adult-to-adult relationships but have the duty to do so in ways that enable them to continue being responsible for their children; and to bear responsibility for such others as may share the family home. The new priority given to protecting the welfare interests of children has led to a hardening of the onus resting on those in such a position

2 Though not in China, where it remains a matter subject to public policy directives.

to provide that protection. Certain concepts such as 'fault' have lost their traditional currency; spouses and parents will now in law be as free to break as to make family commitments, but they will be held accountable for the consequences whether intended or not. Other concepts such as 'unreasonableness' now pervade family law as indicators of failure to uphold the responsibilities of spouse or parent and justifying removal of their rights as such.

The child: welfare and rights

In all modern western jurisdictions, whatever parenting decisions are taken and however families are to be constituted or reconstituted, the law will now regard the welfare interests of the child as of paramount importance in all decisions affecting his or her upbringing. From a position where such interests were required to be taken into account, in a restricted number of proceedings and in relation to specified matters, it has now acquired a paramount weighting which is gradually permeating all family law in most jurisdictions.

The step from protecting the welfare interests of a child to advancing their rights has been one of the most important developments in recent family law. It has been made in order to equip children to take their place on an equal basis in an adversarial court system where the numbers of adult litigants, the costs and the shortage of court time has in the recent past caused their interests to be treated in a cursory, subservient and paternalistic fashion. Nonetheless, the balance to be struck between a child's welfare interests and their rights is a contentious issue in many jurisdictions.

Family breakdown

Marriage no longer means what it once did for family and society.[3] The marriage rate has been in decline for some decades and the institution itself has shed the characteristics – heterosexual, monogamous and for life – that defined it for centuries. Whether marital or not, the family is experiencing soaring rates of breakdown[4] and it is this phenomenon that generates the main flow of children into the adoption process in contemporary western society: mostly channelled through kinship and step adoptions; but also, if mainly in England and the US, filtered through the public childcare system.

Children not living with both birth parents

A striking feature of family life in the jurisdictions studied is that family breakdown has led to a situation where an increasing number of children are being reared in

3 In 2016, married parents comprised 79.0 per cent of all couples with dependent children in the UK and cohabiting parents 20.7 per cent. See, further, Office for National statistics, 2016.

4 Family breakdown has risen by 8 per cent in the last decade due to the increase in cohabitation. See, further, at: http://marriagefoundation.org.uk/wp-content/uploads/2017/03/MF-paper-Annual-family-breakdown.pdf

households which do not contain both their birth parents. This is the case, for example, in: England, where for the past decade or so, only 68.9 per cent of all children lived with both birth parents;[5] compared with 82 per cent in Germany, 79.5 per cent in France, and 70.7 per cent in the US.[6] It is this cohort of primary carers – who share with a birth parent a home and responsibility for children who are not necessarily genetically linked – that now constitute the largest single source of adoption applicants.

Adoption

Paradoxically, in the midst of the changes fragmenting society, the family and family law, what has not changed is the pressure from childless couples wanting an opportunity to form a traditional nuclear family unit: albeit some prospective adopters are same sex couples; and some adoptees may be adults. In the latter context, it has to be said that the singular, culture specific use of adoption in Japan is such as to suggest that it is very largely outside the definition and reach of international adoption law. Leaving aside that cultural anomaly, all developed western nations have long lists of approved adopters waiting to become parents.[7] For the majority, the probability of realising their aspirations – at least in traditional terms of a third party acquisition of a voluntarily relinquished child – are rapidly fading. A situation not helped by unequivocal judicial rulings, domestically and internationally, declaring that there is no right to adopt.

Sources of adoptable children

Realistically, the options for prospective adopters are becoming very limited. The future of the adoption process is likely to rest on its continued use mainly as a means for sealing the boundaries of a reconfigured family unit and, to a lesser extent, the availability of: young children reluctantly given up for adoption due to parental death or absence; those relinquished by impoverished parents unable to cope, perhaps complicated by lifestyle choices; older ones exiting from the public childcare system; and those acquired as a consequence of private surrogacy arrangements.

Domestic

The dramatic fall in surplus children across almost all of western society has been due in part to the ease and frequency of access to abortion, contraception and

5 www.eif.org.uk/wp-content/uploads/2017/09/CG-IPR_3-1_data-family-breakdown.pdf
6 See, further, the Organisation for Economic Co-operation and Development (OECD) at: www.oecd.org/els/family/database.htm
7 Such is the pressure that in many countries the waiting lists for applicants wishing to register for assessment to be approved as adopters are only open to receive new registrations for a limited number of weeks every year; and many are removed from those lists having been 'timed out' as they grow older and their circumstances change.

divorce, and in part to the disappearance of the social taboo that previously accompanied the role of unmarried mother and its replacement with greater public sympathy and welfare benefits, but also to the inexorable logic of prevailing demographic trends. Consequently, parental relinquishment of a child is now quite rare and third-party adoptions of such children are becoming a thing of the past.

In public family law, an increase in the incidence or detection of child abuse and neglect has led to the development of ever more pervasive interventionist strategies by public childcare agencies. The result has been a steep rise in the number of children entering the public care systems of western society, following a judicial ruling of parental abuse or inadequacy. In response, some jurisdictions have taken the step of equating the grounds for entry to public care with those permitting non-consensual third party adoption; a most significant development for family law as a discipline and one that now divides modern western jurisdictions. The pressure on public childcare systems have forced all jurisdictions to consider which care option – foster home, residential unit or non-consensual adoption – would be most conducive to furthering the welfare interests of traumatised children whose complex social or health care needs generally require care arrangements with ongoing professional and financial support. The few opting for a policy of childcare adoption have had to acknowledge that it provides opportunities for only a small proportion of the childcare population and carries a high risk of breakdown.

The proportion of total annual adoptions made in favour of first parties – step-parents or other kinship adopters – has remained high in all modern developed nations. Adoption is now closely aligned to matrimonial proceedings: the legal functions of the former most often being used as an adjunct to the latter; to assimilate the legal status of either a premarital child or one from a previous marital relationship. Possibly the introduction of such alternatives as guardianship will erode the attraction of adoption as the most authoritative means of securing family boundaries.

Intercountry

As domestic sources ceased it was intercountry adoption that provided the main alternative route for those prospective adopters who could cope with the administrative bureaucracy and the considerable costs involved. Natural disasters and the current ongoing migrant crisis – which has included tens of thousands of unaccompanied children entering Europe – will inevitably require some adopters to provide homes for orphaned and abandoned children. Overall, however, this route is also drying up as the main sending countries develop their own domestic adoption programmes and the constraints of Hague induce caution in the main receiving countries as they search for substitute sources. It would seem that the shame and guilt previously associated with relinquishing single mothers has come to affect relinquishing nations; once economic circumstances change so too does the need to surrender – or be seen to surrender – care responsibility for your children.

Surrogacy

Commercial gestational surrogacy, where the surrogate carries an implanted embryo donated by the commissioning prospective parents, has the advantage of providing the latter not only with a baby but one with whom they have a genetic link. For those who can afford it, surrogacy has already become an attractive alternative to present adoption options; though, where the IVF preliminaries do not allow for a genetic link with the commissioning party or parties, this may well result in an information deficit that will impair the future human rights of the child. International commercial, or 'tourism', surrogacy is now becoming a booming if poorly regulated industry in parts of Asia and eastern Europe, and is an established service in some states in the US. In the near future, surrogacy may be coupled with genetic editing, or the added value of sculpting an embryo to eliminate possible genetic deficiencies,[8] bringing with it the prospect of 'designer babies'.

Permanency

For a child, adoption in the common law carried with it the promise of 'a new family for life'. This was its distinctive feature and one that accurately summarised the legal effect of third party adoptions; which, until divorce became commonplace, was almost the only type of common law adoption. It clearly did not necessarily have that effect in other legal traditions. As has been seen, however, it is also no longer necessarily the case within the common law: kinship and step-adoptions, where the family is not 'new' as child and adopter/s are linked in a familial or genetic sense, have for some years accounted for nearly half of all annual adoptions; while 'openness' and contact orders have permitted many if not most adoptees to retain relationships with members of their 'old' family. Moreover, sadly for many adoptees their new family proves not to be one for 'life' as adoption is not impervious to the stresses that cause family breakdown.

Adoption disruption/dissolution

Traditionally regarded in a common law context as almost immutable, the ties that bind adoptee and adopters have demonstrated an alarming vulnerability in recent years. Although statistical collation makes for difficulties in establishing rates of breakdown (usually focusing on either childcare adoption or intercountry adoptions, seldom on kinship or step-parent rates, almost never on aggregate rates and can fail to distinguish between placement and post-adoption order breakdown) it has been estimated that in England in 2014 the rate of breakdown was approximately 3 per cent,[9] which is likely to be an underestimate, while in the US it is

8 See, for example, the recent experimentation with Crispr-Cas9 a gene-editing tool that enables sections of the DNA sequence in a human embryo to be removed, added to or altered.

9 Selwyn, J. et al., 'Beyond the Adoption Order: challenges, intervention, disruption', Hadley Centre for Adoption Studies, Bristol University, 2014.

probably not less than 10 per cent.[10] As contemporary adoption takes on more of the features known to be associated with a risk of breakdown – older children, those with health or social care needs, those part of a sibling group, etc. – so the rate of breakdown will undoubtedly continue to rise.

The family, human rights and adoption

Adoption may be becoming redundant. The adoption process was legislatively devised to legitimate family units created by law, ensure their legal status corresponded to those established by nature, within the marital framework considered by Church and State to be essential for a stable and moral society. That context has largely disappeared.

Alternative forms of permanency

Given the current trends in the use of adoption, together with the rising rate of adoption breakdown and its catastrophic consequences for the child (links being severed with families of origin and of adoption) as for the adopters, there is a strong argument for no longer viewing it as the gold standard permanency option – at least not in its traditional common law form.

Blending private and public family law

Adoption, in both common law and civil law, was conceived and has mainly served as the most archetypal of all private family orders. In some of the former jurisdictions, however, it now functions largely as a public order and may well continue to grow further in that direction in response to political pressure to use it as the preferred child protection option and as its private family law remit is displaced by special guardianship. In its public role it has shed all traces of 'exclusiveness' and cannot be considered 'absolute' as ongoing State financial and professional support services are now normal and contact with birth family members is often more a requirement than a matter of choice. Even where it continues its customary private law role, the traditional characteristics are becoming compromised by accompanying contact orders, by 'openness' and by information rights. Its previous draconian effects have been ameliorated by the statutory introduction of possible qualifications which is indicative of a more generalised and international movement to the same effect in family law. Arguably, the growing salience of functionality in the common law use of adoption is nudging it towards convergence with the civil law model: perhaps it too will develop a split-level form of definition.

Contemporary changes in the family, society and family law – recognised and addressed by equality, non-discrimination and human rights provisions – are shrinking the scope for absolutism, secrecy and vetoes. It may be that laws designed to protect the integrity and inviolability of the marital family, to facilitate

10 www.childwelfare.gov/pubPDFs/s_disrup.pdf

the artificial creation of such a unit, and to provide a means for denying origins have a limited future. In keeping with contemporary changes, it could in future become more appropriate to use a customised package of private and public family law orders – long-term foster care, special guardianship, respite care, contact and parental responsibility, etc. – which would offer flexibility rather than the exclusive permanence of adoption. The latter might be reserved mostly for the third party adoption of infants for which it was initially intended.

Human rights implications for adoption parties

Currently the application of human rights is generally having a reductionist effect on complex social phenomenon. This would seem to be the case in family law, as evident in relation to the above-mentioned withdrawal from family status concerns to a focus on the welfare of children, and is currently most obvious as regards matters of sexuality and gender: such disaggregating can of course be very positive, bringing niche issues hitherto obscured into the limelight, but it also increases social fragmentation. Some of the consequences for adoption and human rights have become very apparent, and have been addressed in the caselaw previously cited. Others, however, are only beginning to emerge and many must remain speculative. For the parties to an adoption, the following may be seen as potentially among the more significant as regards the intersection of adoption law and human rights

The right to family life

The parameters of this right, as worded in Article 8 of the ECHR, would seem capable of being expanded in many different directions. While a line has been drawn to exclude any right to adopt or to be adopted, there remains room to explore further: the rights of the birth family, particularly in the light of the right to protection for mother and child under Article 25(2) of the UDHR; the interface between the child protection grounds for State intervention in the family and State sanctioning of non-consensual adoption; and the right of others such as members of the LGBT community to found a family under Article 12 of the ECHR. Arguably, those who have developed pre-adoption familial ties with a child (e.g. grandparents, cousins, foster parents), would be entitled to have that 'family life' relationship protected in a post-adoption context. The rights of the very many children in certain countries who remain in residential care facilities, instead of being offered family based placements in foster care, could also be examined while bearing in mind the non-discrimination requirement in Article 2 of the UDHR.

Rights of the child

The deficit in recognition and enforcement of the rights of a child, guaranteed by Articles 13 and 14 of UNCROC, is considerable if difficult to quantify. It must have a bearing upon the verification needed to establish that ICA is the best long-term interests of a particular child; that all alternative options for retaining him or her within the community, language and culture of their birth have been explored and, with good reason, ruled out. It at least requires that the consent of an older child be sought in decisions affecting his or her interests, including if and by whom they are to be adopted and as regards their post-adoption contact with birth family, grandparents and friends. It must imply a right to legal representation equal to that enjoyed by other parties in adoption proceedings. It probably extends to a prohibition on physical chastisement and, depending on age, a right to choose: gender and sex orientation; and many aspects of daily life such as friends, clothes, lifestyle, educational subjects and to attend or reject religious worship; as these must constitute aspects of their right to dignity and respect. It may well have implications for a child sibling's attachment to an adoptee. In all probability, this right has the capacity to be realised much more broadly and assertively than it is at present.

Identity and cultural affiliation

The right to personal identity and cultural affiliation have been repeatedly emphasised in international law. However, as noted earlier, a necessary precondition for the right to acquire an authentic individual identity is an entitlement to access origins information, an entitlement which may well be blocked by the right of a birth parent to anonymity. This clash of rights is as longstanding as the law of adoption, but recent judicial rulings indicate that it is becoming amenable to a 'proportionality' test: in the absence of any statutory endorsement of a parental right to veto the disclosure of identifying information, the courts are increasingly prepared to examine and balance the respective rights and to favour adoptee access unless there is evidence of likely and significant harm to the birth parent. This trend would seem set to become more firmly established.

The right to be recognised as belonging to and representative of a particular culture, and to be treated in a non-discriminatory fashion relative to all other cultures, is now underwritten by a number of international instruments. The present migratory surge of people from tribal and ethnic backgrounds, predominantly Muslim, into Europe and the US has brought a sharp awareness of the significance of cultural identity and the potential for culture clashes to be socially destabilising. It is probable that this factor will become more apparent in future adoption proceedings as greater attention is paid to cultural compatibility between adopters, adoptee and birth family.

Index

For Product Safety Concerns and Information please contact our EU
representative GPSR@taylorandfrancis.com
Taylor & Francis Verlag GmbH, Kaufingerstraße 24, 80331 München, Germany

www.ingramcontent.com/pod-product-compliance
Ingram Content Group UK Ltd.
Pitfield, Milton Keynes, MK11 3LW, UK
UKHW022008180926
475701UK00003B/261
9780367893651